The Collected Courses of the Academy of European Law
Series Editors: Professor Philip Alston and Professor Gráinne de Búrca,
European University Institute, Florence
Assistant Editor: Anny Bremner, *European University
Institute, Florence*

VOLUME X/2
Human Rights, Intervention, and the Use of Force

The Collected Courses of the Academy of European Law
Edited by Professor Philip Alston and Professor Gráinne de Búrca
Assistant Editor: Anny Bremner

This series brings together the Collected Courses of the
Academy of European Law in Florence. The Academy's mission is
to produce sholarly analyses which are at the cutting edge of the two
fields in which it works: European Union law and human rights law.
A 'general course' is given each year in each field, by a
distinguished scholar and/or practitioner, who either examines the
field as a whole through a partcular thematic, conceptual, or
philosophical lens, or who looks at a particular theme in the context
of the overall body of law in the field. The academy also publishes
each year a volume of collected essays with a specific theme in each
of the two fields.

Human Rights, Intervention, and the Use of Force

Edited by
PHILIP ALSTON
and
EUAN MACDONALD

OXFORD
UNIVERSITY PRESS

OXFORD
UNIVERSITY PRESS

Great Clarendon Street, Oxford OX2 6DP

Oxford University Press is a department of the University of Oxford.
It furthers the University's objective of excellence in research, scholarship,
and education by publishing worldwide in

Oxford New York

Auckland Cape Town Dar es Salaam Hong Kong Karachi
Kuala Lumpur Madrid Melbourne Mexico City Nairobi
New Delhi Shanghai Taipei Toronto

With offices in

Argentina Austria Brazil Chile Czech Republic France Greece
Guatemala Hungary Italy Japan Poland Portugal Singapore
South Korea Switzerland Thailand Turkey Ukraine Vietnam

Oxford is a registered trade mark of Oxford University Press
in the UK and in certain other countries

Published in the United States
by Oxford University Press Inc., New York

British Library Cataloguing in Publication Data

Data available

Library of Congress Cataloging in Publication Data
Human rights, intervention and the use of force / Philip Alston and Euan
Macdonald (eds).
  p. cm.
Includes index.
ISBN 978–0–19–955271–9 — ISBN 978–0–19–955272–6
1. Human rights. 2. Intervention (International law) 3. War
(International law) 4. Humanitarian intervention. I. Alston,
Philip. II. Macdonald, Euan, 1965–
  K3240.H863 2008
  341.4′8—dc22   2008023434

Typeset by Newgen Imaging Systems (P) Ltd, Chennai, India
Printed in Great Britain
on acid-free paper by
Biddles Ltd, King's Lynn

ISBN 978–0–19–955271–9 (hbk)
ISBN 978–0–19–955272–6 (pbk)

1 3 5 7 9 10 8 6 4 2

Contents

Contents

List of Abbreviations

ACHR	American Convention on Human Rights
AFDI	Annuaire Français de Droit International
AJIL	American Journal of International Law
Arch Phil Dr	Archives de Philosophie du Droit
BYBIL	British Year Book of International Law
CSCE	Conference on Security and Cooperation in Europe
CYIL	Canadian Yearbook of International Law
ECHR	European Convention for the Protection of Human Rights and Fundamental Freedoms
ECOSOC	Economic and Social Council (United Nations)
ECOWAS	Economic Community of West African States
ECtHR	European Court of Human Rights
EJIL	European Journal of International Law
FRY	Federal Republic of Yugoslavia
GYIL	German Yearbook of International Law
HRLJ	Human Rights Law Journal
IAComHR	Inter-American Commission on Human Rights
IACtHR	Inter-American Court of Human Rights
ICC	International Criminal Court
ICCPR	International Covenant on Civil and Political Rights
ICESCR	International Covenant on Economic, Social and Cultural Rights
ICFM	Islamic Conference of Foreign Ministers
ICIS	Interparliamentary Commonwealth of Independent States
ICISS	International Commission on Intervention and State Sovereignty
ICJ	International Court of Justice
ICLQ	International and Comparative Law Quarterly
ICRC	International Committee of the Red Cross
ICTY	International Criminal Tribunal for the Former Yugoslavia
IHL	International humanitarian law
IILJ	International Law and Justice
ILC	International Law Commission
ILM	International Legal Materials
ILO	International Labour Organization
IRRC	Independent Regulatory Review Commission
JCP	Juris Classeur Periodique
JDI	Journal du Droit International
KLA	Kosovo Liberation Army
LGDJ	Librairie Générale de Droit et de Jurisprudence
LTLSP	Long-Term Legal Strategy Project
MLR	Modern Law Review

MONUL	UN Observation Mission to Liberia
NATO	North Atlantic Treaty Organization
NGO	non-governmental organization
NYIL	Netherlands Yearbook of International Law
OAS	Organization of American States
OAU	Organization of African Unity
OSCE	Organization for Security and Cooperation in Europe
PCIJ	Permanent Court of International Justice
PUF	Presses Universitaires de France
R2P	Responsibility to protect
RBDI	Revue Belge de Droit International
RCDIP	Revue de Droit International Privé
RDILC	Revue de Droit International et de Législation Comparée
RGDIP	Revue Générale de Droit International Public
Riv. Dir. Int	Jura: Rivista Internazionale di Diritto Romano e Antico
RUDH	Revue Universelle des Droits de l'Homme
SFDI	Société Française pour le Doit International
UDHR	Universal Declaration of Human Rights
UNAMID	United Nations–African Union Mission in Darfur
UNCIO	United Nations Conference on International Organization
UNGA	United Nations General Assembly
UNMIK	UN Mission in Kosovo

List of Contributors

Philip Alston is John Norton Pomeroy Professor at New York University Law School and Chair of the New York University Center for Human Rights and Global Justice. Since 2004 he has been UN Special Rapporteur on extrajudicial, summary or arbitrary executions.

José E Alvarez is Hamilton Fish Professor of International Law and Diplomacy and Director of the Center on Global Legal Problems, at Columbia University Law School. He is also President of the American Society of International Law.

Nathaniel Berman teaches public international law, European Union law, international trade law, and human rights at Brooklyn Law School. He previously taught at Northeastern University School of Law.

Richard B Bilder is Foley & Lardner-Bascom Emeritus Professor of Law at the University of Wisconsin-Madison. He previously served as an attorney in the Office of the Legal Adviser at the US Department of State.

Nehal Bhuta is Assistant Professor of Law at the University of Toronto. He has previously worked with the International Justice Program of Human Rights Watch and as a consultant with the International Center for Transitional Justice in New York.

Olivier Corten has a doctorate in law, is Professor at the Université Libre de Bruxelles, and is Co-Director of its Centre de droit international et de sociologie appliquée au droit international. He is also Editor of the *Revue Belge de Droit International*.

Euan MacDonald has a Doctorate from the European University Institute in Florence and is currently a Research Officer on the Global Administrative Law project of New York University's Institute for International Law and Justice. He was previously a Visiting Fellow on the Programme for the Study of International Organizations at the Graduate Institute for International Studies in Geneva.

Anthea Roberts is an Associate at Debevoise and Plimpton in London where she is a member of the firm's International Dispute Resolution Group. She has worked on a variety of public international law and alien tort claim cases and as counsel in several international arbitrations.

Hélène Ruiz Fabri is Professor of International Law at the University of Paris I—Panthéon Sorbonne, and Director of the Paris Institute of Comparative Studies. Since 2006 she has been the President of the European Society of International Law.

1

Sovereignty, Human Rights, Security: Armed Intervention and the Foundational Problems of International Law

Euan MacDonald and Philip Alston

1. Introduction: Three Foundational Problems

The story is, by now, a familiar one. Distilled down to its very essentials, it begins with the Treaty of Westphalia in 1648 as the institution of the basic international legal order that we still study and practice today; it then skips quickly on, often with little or nothing in between, to the world wars of the twentieth century, and in particular to the major global institution-building projects, the ill-fated League of Nations and the (to date) significantly more resilient United Nations. The latter provides the next two moments of regime-shaping import: the near-categorical outlawing of the use of force (which had been developing for some time previously), and the Universal Declaration of Human Rights. These high ambitions, perverted and distorted for decades by the realities of Cold War relations, were finally able to flourish free from cynical misappropriation following the collapse of the USSR and its client Communist regimes in 1989; the international rule of law was at last to become reality and liberal democracy was enthusiastically proposed as the end to which all means should be directed. All of this, however, changed in 2001; since the terrorist attacks on the World Trade Center and the Pentagon in September of that year, we have been living in a radically different world, in which the sovereignty of Westphalia and the human rights of the Universal Declaration compete, often unsuccessfully, with issues of national security as sources of both international legitimacy *and* legality.

Of course, this basic narrative can be nuanced in a variety of ways, and international lawyers pursuing widely differing personal projects will have very different ideas as to the details that should be added to flesh out the story of the development of the international legal order. Nonetheless, and even if few would subscribe entirely to the truncated version of events as outlined above, it is difficult to escape a sense that these dates, 1648, 1945/48, 1989, 2001, provide a basic structure to our understanding of how the bases of authority of contemporary international law came into being. Indeed, it is often tempting to view them in terms of basic and essentially mutually exclusive paradigm shifts, from sovereignty through human rights (at first thwarted by realpolitik, then allowed to flourish), to the national security agenda that has dominated, and attempted to assert itself ever more even on the legal plane, since 9/11.

But the temptation to essentialize the evolution of the international legal regime in this way must be resisted, for both empirical and conceptual reasons. Empirically, the great acceleration in the rate of change reflected in the chronology is noteworthy, suggesting that the recent past may well have been accorded an exaggerated importance within the history of the development of the international legal order. This impression is confirmed by closer analysis of the rhetoric and practice of international law in the relevant periods: Hélène Ruiz Fabri's contribution to this volume indicates clearly, for example, the extent to which national security concerns were prevalent long before 2001,[1] while Olivier Corten notes that, while human rights undoubtedly achieved more vocal support from states during the period from 1989 to 2001, they were very often accompanied by simultaneous affirmations of the continuing importance of respect for the sovereign equality and inviolability of each individual state.[2] It should be clear, then, that while the above dates are undoubtedly of real significance, any attempt to characterize them as points of radical discontinuity between mutually exclusive paradigms of international legal order is empirically unconvincing.

The received wisdom is also reductionist on a conceptual level. While there can be no doubt that the imperatives of sovereignty, human rights, and national security will often pull in very different directions, the relations between these three different notions are considerably more subtle than those of simple opposition. Rather, their interaction may at times be contradictory, at others tense, and at others even complementary. For example, it is not difficult to view sovereignty and human rights as basically contradictory within the international legal framework. The former insists upon the exclusive subjecthood of states, whereas the latter provides rights to individuals; the former insists upon the territorial inviolability of its subjects, while the under the latter all 'peoples' have a right to self-determination; and, perhaps most strikingly, the former insists that international law simply does not speak to the internal affairs of a state, and how it conducts its relations with its own nationals, while the latter aims at establishing international legal norms limiting precisely that freedom of action. These tensions and outright oppositions, however, far from exhaust the interaction between the two concepts; indeed, many have argued that they have begun to develop in a manner that is fundamentally complementary.

---

[1] Hélène Ruiz Fabri, 'Human Rights and State Sovereignty: Have the Boundaries been Significantly Redrawn?', Chapter 2 below.
[2] Olivier Corten, 'Human Rights and Collective Security: Is there an Emerging Right of Humanitarian Intervention?', Chapter 3 below.

By far the clearest example of this latter type of interaction is to be found in the debates surrounding the international legal attitude towards the notion of popular sovereignty, and in particular in the idea that a 'human right' to democratic governance has emerged, or is emerging, in international law.[3] The contours of this debate have been well documented and there is no need to rehearse them here.[4] It is worth noting, however, that the academic espousal of an international human right to democracy has lessened significantly since 2001,[5] and continuing difficulties in building an effective Iraqi political system since the invasion of 2003, as well as the Bush administration's embrace of repressive regimes that are viewed as essential allies in the 'war on terror', have brought the end of its more aggressive variants. Nonetheless there is a degree of agreement between proponents and critics alike that international law is no longer entirely blind to the manner in which a government achieves power within a state. In other words, government must be based upon the consent of the governed, even if the means of manifesting that consent need not be recognizably democratic.[6] This move alone is enough to render the relationship between sovereignty and human rights in international law considerably more ambivalent than many classical analyses might suggest.

The affinity between sovereignty and national security is much more readily evident; indeed, the latter can be viewed, in many respects, as being a simple expansion of the former. The two have, of course, co-existed to a degree in international law for some time: traditionally, national security concerns would have been viewed as falling largely within the internal affairs of the state to which

---

[3] See, eg Thomas Franck, 'The Emerging Right to Democratic Governance', 86 AJIL (1992) 46; Thomas Franck, 'Democracy as a Human Right', in Henkin and Hargrove (eds) Human Rights: An Agenda for the Next Century (1994) 73; Gregory Fox, 'The Right to Political Participation in International Law' 17 Yale Journal of International Law (1992) 539.

[4] See generally Gregory Fox and Brad Roth (eds), *Governance and International Law* (2000); Susan Marks, *The Riddle of All Constitutions* (2000).

[5] For an analysis predicting that the events of 9/11 might dampen enthusiasm for the right to democratic governance, see Euan MacDonald, 'International Law, Democratic Governance and September the 11th', 9 German Law Journal (2002). Former British Prime Minister Tony Blair insisted that the elections in Afghanistan and Iraq must be viewed as a crucially important victory for US and UK foreign policy, implying that similar efforts should continue: 'Iraqi and Afghan Muslims have said it clearly: democracy is as much our right as it is yours. In embracing it, they are showing that they also want a society in which people of different cultures and faiths can live together in peace. This struggle is our struggle'. See Tony Blair, 'A Battle for Global Values', 86 Foreign Affairs (2007), available online at <http://www.foreignaffairs.org/20070101faessay 86106-p30/tony-blair/a-battle-for-global-values.html>. The rhetoric of the Bush administration, however, has been significantly scaled back; the 2006 National Security Strategy eschewed talk of a 'right' to democratic governance; under the heading of 'promoting effective democracies', it noted instead, in Part II.C, that '[b]ecause democracies are the most responsible members of the international system, promoting democracy is the most effective long-term measure for strengthening international stability; reducing regional conflicts; countering terrorism and terror-supporting extremism; and extending peace and prosperity'. The Strategy is available online at <http://www.whitehouse.gov/nsc/nss/2006/nss2006.pdf>.

[6] For this argument from a critic of the proposed right to democratic governance, see Brad Roth, *Governmental Illegitimacy in International Law* (1999).

international law could not speak; and, more recently, many human rights treaties provide that derogations from certain rights may be permitted, either for reasons of national security[7] or under limited circumstances and for a limited time during periods of national emergency.[8] The concepts of national security and national emergency, however, are far from coextensive, and the difference between the two has been exacerbated in recent decades by technological advances, in terms of weapons, transport, and telecommunications, that have seen the scope of the former considerably expanded. These developments have led to an increasing *internationalization* of national security discourse, which is in turn being used to justify an ever more ambitious range of actions and interventions on foreign soil—undermining the claim that they form part of the reserved sphere of 'domestic affairs'.

Often these justifications still take the form of a simple logical extension of classical notions of sovereignty. This seems to be the claim implicit, for example, in much of the rhetoric of the Bush administration on the 'war on terror', be it in terms of the restrictions on individual human rights, or military actions on the territories of other states: that the US is entitled to take whatever steps are necessary to defend itself, its nationals, and its interests from those hostile to it.[9] To simply collapse the current discourse on security into that of sovereignty is, however, a mischaracterization of the role that the latter notion has played in the development of the international legal order, and in particular of the painstakingly crafted, if never unproblematic, distinction between the internal and external aspects of that power.[10]

Under the classical construct, while each state was held to have complete freedom of action within its own boundaries and on matters of purely national interest, this was viewed as translating, in the society of sovereigns at the international level, into the inviolable principles of the territorial integrity and political independence of each. Many actions based upon national security, however, show no sign of prioritizing (or occasionally even recognizing) either these principles or the notion of formal equality on which they are based; indeed, to the contrary,

---

[7] To take, eg only the 1966 International Covenant on Civil and Political Rights (ICCPR), the potential for national security derogations is explicitly provided for in respect of the rights guaranteed in Arts 12 (freedom of movement within a state); 13 (right of review of expulsion decision); 14 (insofar as trials must be public); 19 (freedom of expression); 21 (right of peaceful assembly); and 22 (freedom of association).

[8] To take again the ICCPR, Art 4(2) provides that only Arts 6 (right to life), 7 (freedom from torture), 8 (paras 1 and 2) (freedom from slavery), 11 (non-imprisonment for contractual failures), 15 (no criminal retroactivity), 16 (right to be recognized as a person before the law) and 18 (freedom of thought, conscience and religion) are non-derogable even in times of declared national emergency.

[9] See, eg the US National Security Strategy of 2006, above n 5, which notes in its introduction that 'our approach is idealistic about our national goals, and realistic about the means to achieve them. To follow this path, we must maintain and expand our national strength so we can deal with threats and challenges before they can damage our people or our interests. We must maintain a military without peer—yet our strength is not founded on force of arms alone'.

[10] This distinction is discussed by Ruiz Fabri, n 1 above, p 2.

they remain, in practical terms, the reserve of those states powerful enough on the regional or global level to pursue them with relative impunity without being overly fearful of reprisals from those smaller states who find their own sovereignty thus infringed. In short, then, while in the classical construct external sovereignty was premised upon a basic respect for the equality of all subjects of international law, within the discourse of national security it is the leviathan of internal sovereignty that asserts itself, now on a potentially global scale and with few of the checks and balances developed at the domestic level, and showing little or no respect for those other sovereigns deemed unwilling or unable to protect the interests of the powerful state in question. The current preoccupation with national security as a potential source of justification under international law, signalled by the promotion of new categories such as 'enemy combatant'[11] or 'preventive self-defence',[12] thus represents as much the destruction of classical notions of sovereignty as it does their continuation.

It is the conceptual opposition between national security and human rights that has been brought most dramatically to the fore by the events following the terrorist attacks of September 11 2001. Here the opposition is, in many ways, starkest: as amply demonstrated by the many states that have used security rhetoric to justify some significant derogations from their obligations under international human rights treaties—even to the point at which the potential for a return to certain legalized forms of torture has been openly mooted.[13] Even here, however, it would be too easy to assume that the two concepts are mutually contradictory; they too, like the two other pairings considered above, can be used in ways that are mutually supportive. Consider as an example the differing justifications for restricting the human rights of suspected terrorists adopted by two of the main protagonists on one side of the 'war on terror', the US and the UK: while

[11] The emergence and development of this term has been analysed in some considerable detail in PJ Honigsberg, 'Chasing "Enemy Combatants" and Circumventing International Law: A Licence for Sanctioned Abuse', 12 University of California at Los Angeles Journal of International Law and Foreign Affairs (2007) 1.

[12] Perhaps the strongest early formulation of the 'doctrine' was provided by the 2002 US National Security Strategy, available online at <http://www.whitehouse.gov/nsc/nss.html>, which notes in Part III that, '[w]hile the United States will constantly strive to enlist the support of the international community, we will not hesitate to act alone, if necessary, to exercise our right of self defense by acting preemptively against such terrorists, to prevent them from doing harm against our people and our country'. This has, however met with scant support from scholars and states alike: in terms of the former, see, eg Mary-Ellen O'Connell, 'The Myth of Pre-emptive Self-Defence', *ASIL Task Force on Terrorism Papers* (2002), available online at <http://www.asil.org/taskforce/oconnell.pdf>; and Michael Bothe, 'Terrorism and the Legality of Pre-emptive Force', 14 EJIL (2003) 227–40; while for the latter see the secret advice given by Lord Goldsmith to the UK government on the legality of the 2003 Iraq war, below n 24 and accompanying text; and, for a rare attempt to justify the legality of such action, see Abram Sofaer, 'On the Necessity of Pre-emption', 14 EJIL (2003) 209–26.

[13] Two useful volumes on this debate are Sanford Levinson (ed), *Torture: A Collection* (2004) and Karen Greenberg (ed), *The Torture Debate in America* (2005). For a detailed and powerful rebuttal of pro-torture arguments, see also Jeremy Waldron, 'Torture and Positive Law: Jurisprudence for the White House', 105 Columbia Law Review (2005) 1681–1750.

George Bush made much of the appeal to the sovereign right of self-defence in justifying the very restrictive national security measures adopted, Tony Blair's rhetoric focused to a significant degree on the 'human rights of victims'[14]—that, for example, the government has a duty to protect the right to life of all on its territory, and any limitations on due process rights of suspects must be balanced with that in mind. This example illustrates well the complex ways in which each of the three concepts can interact.

This complexity is further increased upon consideration of another useful, yet problematic distinction well known to international lawyers: that between law and politics. While few if any would suggest that the two can ever be neatly or completely separated,[15] most (including Martti Koskenniemi) still find it an important distinction to retain.[16] In any event, in seeking to justify their actions, states will often make use of an intricate mixture of legal and political rhetoric, differently calibrated to suit different audiences; and each of the three discourses discussed above is itself capable of providing elements of both legal and political authority to any assertion or action. Thus, not only are issues of sovereignty, human rights, and security important factors in determining the international *legality* of any action, they can also be crucial in constructing its international *legitimacy*.[17]

None of this, however, is to doubt the central importance that each of these three discourses has in the contemporary international legal framework. Rather, it is to insist upon the necessary complexity of the manner in which they interact, the inescapable tensions that they introduce into any determination of legality or illegality, and the way that they combine to preclude unproblematic and objectively correct 'solutions' to international legal controversies that implicate them. Achieving a balance among these three factors can be thought of as a foundational challenge for international law. Either in isolation or in interaction with the others, they are usually incapable of providing clear answers, but rather furnish a set of perennial and irreducible challenges to many, even most, attempts to judge the legality of state action in certain fields. They are foundational because the challenges that they pose go to the very heart of some of the most deeply rooted principles of the international legal order.

We note in passing that this characterization is not readily compatible with most notions of so-called 'rights based approaches' to security or development

---

[14] See, eg Tony Blair, 'I don't destroy liberties, I protect them', *The Observer* (26 February 2006), available online at <http://observer.guardian.co.uk/comment/story/0,,1718133,00.html>. See also the exchange between H Porter and Blair in 'Civil Liberties: The Great Debate', *The Observer* (23 April 2006), available online at <http://observer.guardian.co.uk/focus/story/0,,1759344,00.html>.

[15] See generally Martti Koskenniemi, *From Apology to Utopia* (1989); Martti Koskenniemi, 'The Politics of International Law', 1 EJIL (1990) 4.

[16] 'Martti Koskenniemi, Carl Schmitt, Hans Morgenthau, and the Image of Law in International Relations', in Michael Byers (ed), *The Role of Law in International Politics* (2000) 17.

[17] This distinction is central to a number of contributions in this volume, in particular those by Anthea Roberts and Nathaniel Berman.

or whatever, in which human rights alone are said to provide the fundamental normative framework within which all tensions, inconsistencies, and incompatibilities among values ought to be resolved. The proponents of these approaches avoid having to give priority to the other challenges that we have identified by seeking to incorporate them within a comprehensive human rights approach which defines security itself as a human right and sovereignty in terms of a right to self-determination. This is not the place to enter into a detailed questioning of the adequacy or desirability of pushing rights-based approaches this far,[18] but suffice it to note that we do not consider that a human rights framework, properly conceived, is necessarily incompatible with the approach we outline here.

In our view, sovereignty, human rights, and security can constitute the very poles of some of the most intractable dilemmas, or trilemmas, of international law, even as each seeks to use the other for support in its bid to trump all other norms. Nowhere is this more evident than in the relations between each of the foundational challenges and one of the norms at the very apex of the international legal system, the prohibition on the use of force.

2. The Foundational Challenges and the Use of Force

The prohibition on the use of force contained in Article 2(4) of the UN Charter is understood by most to constitute a *jus cogens* principle, a peremptory and non-derogable norm of the international legal system.[19] One of the most striking ways in which the foundational character of the challenges posed by the discourses of sovereignty, human rights, and security is manifested is that each is (or is at least claimed by some to be) capable of founding exceptions to this principle. In terms of sovereignty, the acceptance of this claim is clearest: international law recognizes, both under Article 51 of the UN Charter and customary law more generally, the sovereign right of states to use force in individual or collective self-defence. Considerably more controversial is the proposed human rights exception, which takes the form of a right (or perhaps even a duty) of humanitarian intervention in cases of massive and widespread violations of certain basic rights—and for which NATO's 1999 military bombardment of Serbia remains the most recent, and in many respects paradigmatic, example.

---

[18] For a critique see Philip Alston, 'Ships Passing in the Night: The Current State of the Human Rights and Development Debate seen through the Lens of the Millennium Development Goals', 27 Human Rights Quarterly (2005) 755, at 798–807.

[19] The ICJ has made this clear, noting in its judgment in the *Nicaragua* case that the prohibition on the use of force is 'a conspicuous example of a rule of international law having the character of *jus cogens*', 4 ICJ Reps (1986) at p 100. See also, eg Guennadi Danilenko, 'International Jus Cogens: Issues of Law-Making', 2 EJIL (1991) 42–65, at p 42; and the contributions by Corten and Roberts to this volume.

At the far end of the spectrum lie uses of force putatively justified on the grounds of national or international security: either against a sovereign state where the perceived danger is considerably less imminent and more diffuse than that required to activate the traditional right to self-defence,[20] or against private actors on foreign soil without the consent of the territorial state or authority.[21] That the overwhelming majority of commentators viewed the 2003 Iraq war as illegal, despite assertions of a potentially imminent nuclear threat and of a vaguely-formulated 'right' to preventive self-defence, is testament to the fact that, of all the suggested legal exceptions to the contemporary prohibition on the use of force (outside those granted to the Security Council under Chapter VII of the UN Charter), those based upon a broad notion of national or international security, beyond the right to self-defence, have found the least support, either among states or scholars. The effect of this is that, while broad security concerns are achieving an ever-increasing importance in, for example, justifying the legality of derogations from individual human rights (even, on occasions, from the right to life itself), their role in providing authority for military actions against another state remains, as yet, largely confined to the realm of the political.

Given this, it may seem premature and even rhetorically dangerous to suggest that national security constitutes a foundational challenge for international law on the same level as sovereignty and human rights. Certainly it is plausible that, in so doing, we risk imbuing blatant illegality with a wholly undeserved veneer of legitimacy. However, when powerful states can bypass the institutional mechanisms that protect one of the most cherished norms of the legal system and act as they see fit with relative impunity—disregarding claims both of sovereignty and human rights in the process—then a simple allegation of illegality, while both necessary and desirable, is insufficient. Rather, ways of articulating and addressing the challenge posed by the consistent breach, and the justificatory rhetoric that supports it, must be found. In many ways, then, the characterization as a foundational challenge is intended to alert us to the need to deal with precisely the danger of abuse and distortion of some of the basic norms of the international legal system that security discourse represents, whilst at the same

---

[20] That this is precisely what is intended by the doctrine of preventive self-defence cannot be in any doubt, as the 2002 US National Security Strategy, above n 5, makes quite clear. Part V of the Strategy is entitled 'Prevent Our Enemies from Threatening Us, Our Allies, and Our Friends with Weapons of Mass Destruction', and states that '[w]e must be prepared to stop rogue states and their terrorist clients *before they are able to threaten* or use weapons of mass destruction against the United States and our allies and friends' (emphasis added). This is clearly an explicit attempt to challenge the prohibition on the use of force on the grounds of national security; if the aim is to prevent threats from even arising, then it bears little or no resemblance to the traditional sovereign right of self-defence, seeking as it does to obviate one of its most important limiting factors—the existence or imminent threat of an armed attack. This claim is basically reiterated in the National Security Strategy of March 2006, above n 9.

[21] For a reading of these ideas as a challenge to the international law on the use of force from a national security perspective, see, eg Eyal Benvenisti, 'The US and the Use of Force: Double-edged Hegemony and the Management of Global Emergencies', 15 EJIL (2004) 667–700.

time recognizing the empirical fact of the importance of that discourse in issues of fundamental concern to contemporary international law. We can recognize the challenge posed by security discourse without making the choice to validate all of its claims.

This being said, the principal focus of this volume remains the implications for international law of certain types of military interventions by states; as such, the purported 'security' base will receive relatively little direct analysis here, as, in terms of its capacity to found a legal exception to the prohibition on the use of force, the rejection of its claims such as preventive self-defence is very near-universal. In like manner, the self-defence exception to Article 2(4) is not the subject of detailed examination in these pages, as it is, at a general level, universally accepted by states and scholars alike. Neither traditional self-defence nor its preventive variant, then, presently pose a significant challenge, in the abstract, to the international law on the use of force, for the simple reason that the former is uncontroversially accepted and the latter (fairly) uncontroversially rejected. Instead the focus is, in large degree, on the human rights exception, the doctrine of humanitarian intervention, as that which to date still threatens—or promises—the most in terms of rewriting the international law prohibition on the use of force.

This general point can be illustrated well by reference to the reactions to the three major recent instances of military intervention: Kosovo in 1999, Afghanistan in 2001, and Iraq in 2003. The US bombardment of Afghanistan has created relatively little controversy from an international law perspective, as it seems to have come to be viewed as fairly unproblematically legal: there was an act of terrorism on a sufficient scale to constitute an armed attack against a state, and the terrorist group responsible was sponsored by another state, to which its actions were thus imputable.[22] Likewise, the US and UK-led invasion of Iraq is viewed by most as fairly unproblematically *il*legal. Leaving aside some decidedly tortuous interpretations of Security Council resolutions, the overwhelming majority of commentators and states were in agreement that the decision to go to war in direct opposition to the clear will of a majority of the permanent and non-permanent members of the Council was simply unjustifiable on the basis of any recognizably legal argument.[23] NATO's intervention in Kosovo, on the other

---

[22] On this, see, eg Yoram Dinstein, *War, Aggression and Self-Defence* (4th edn 2005) 236–7: 'The military operations in Afghanistan were a classical State versus State exercise of self-defence'; see also Michael Byers, 'Terrorism, the Use of Force and International Law after 11 September', 51 ICLQ (2002) 401–14. Although Byers does note that, prior to 2001, the claim that terrorist attacks gave rise to a right of self-defence against other states had gained little acceptance, he states that an alteration to the customary legal definition of this exception to the use of force had 'quite clearly occurred' due to the US action in Afghanistan and its international reception, so that '[a]s a result of the legal strategies adopted by the US, coupled with the already contested character of the rule and a heightened concern about terrorism world-wide, the right of self-defense now includes military responses against States which actively support or willingly harbour terrorist groups who have already attacked the responding State.' (Ibid. at 409–10).
[23] There are, of course, some exceptions to this: see, eg WH Taft IV and TF Buchwald, 'Pre-emption, Iraq and International Law', 97 AJIL (2003) 557–63; and John Yoo, 'International

hand, justified (by some at least) on humanitarian grounds, elicited a wide array of different reactions from international lawyers, but very few that viewed it as anything other than a fundamentally *hard case*. Indeed, most positions might be captured by dividing commentators between those for whom it was problematically legal, and those for whom it was equally problematically illegal.[24] Humanitarian intervention thus remains the most pressing legal challenge to the traditional international law on the use of force, and the Kosovo war remains its most striking example. This, then, remains the basic, but by no means only, point of reference for many of the chapters that follow.

These arguments were summed up in the secret advice given to the UK government on the legality of any military action against Iraq by its chief legal advisor, Lord Goldsmith, first leaked in part and then released in full on 28 April 2005.[25] This is a particularly useful document for enabling us to form an idea of the *opinio juris* of at least one major state. He begins by noting three possible bases for the use of force under international law: self-defence, the avoidance of humanitarian catastrophe (in exceptional circumstances), and authorization by the UN Security Council. He rejects out of hand the suggestion that war could be justified, in the case of Iraq, on either of the first two premises. For the first, he notes that the threat facing the state must be, to some degree at least, imminent. And for the second, which he acknowledges as 'controversial' but was 'relied on by the UK in the Kosovo crisis', he states clearly that he knows 'of no reason why it would be an appropriate basis for action in present circumstances'. On the issue of 'preventive self-defence', he notes simply that '[i]f this means more than a right to respond proportionately to an imminent attack (and I understand that the doctrine is intended to carry that connotation) this is not a doctrine which, in my opinion, exists or is recognised in international law'.[26] It is, in this regard, in some

---

Law and the War in Iraq', ibid. at 563–76. Theirs remain, however, very much the minority position on this issue.

[24] See, eg Independent International Commission on Kosovo, *The Kosovo Report*, available online at <http://www.reliefweb.int/library/documents/thekosovoreport.htm>. This ambivalence was, indeed, evident from the very outset: see, eg the editorial comments by Louis Henkin, Ruth Wedgwood, Jonathan Charney, Christine Chinkin, Richard Falk, Thomas Franck, and Michael Reisman, in 93 AJ IL (1999) 824–62. See also, among many others, Michael Reisman, 'Unilateral Action and the Transformations of the World Constitutive Process: The Special Problem of Humanitarian Intervention', 11 EJIL (2000) 3–18; Christine Chinkin, 'The State That Acts Alone: Bully, Good Samaritan or Iconoclast? Multilateralism à la Carte: The Consequences of Unilateral "Pick and Pay" Approaches', 11 EJIL (2000) 31–42; M Hilpold, 'Humanitarian Intervention: Is There a Need for a Legal Reappraisal?', 12 EJIL (2001) 437–637; Martti Koskenniemi, ' "The Lady Doth Protest Too Much": Kosovo, and the Turn to Ethics in International Law', 65 MLR (2002) 159–75; and Christopher Joyner, 'The Kosovo Intervention: Legal Analysis and a More Persuasive Paradigm', 13 EJIL (2002) 597–619.

[25] Available online at <http://www.pm.gov.uk/files/pdf/Iraq%20Resolution%201441.pdf>.

[26] Ibid., paras 2–4. It is worth noting that Lord Goldsmith's qualified advice that military action could be legal if 'there are strong factual grounds' for concluding that Iraq had violated Security Council resolutions by developing weapons of mass destruction, was premised entirely upon the (basically unargued) view that, under these circumstances, the authorization to use force

ways unfortunate that subsequent events in Iraq have illustrated that not only was the presence there of weapons of mass destruction a fiction, but also that the evidence upon which confident assertions of their existence was based was flimsy in the extreme. This has postponed an interesting and important debate over the legality of the use of force without Security Council authorization where a rogue state has, or is acting to acquire, such arms.[27]

The contributions to this volume represent, then, an exploration of the interactions between the foundational challenge of human rights with those of sovereignty and security in the theatre in which these relations are most highly dramatized: that of military intervention by states on territory other than their own. As the foregoing brief introduction has demonstrated, the issues involved are many and varied and defy simple classification or analysis. As such, no claim is made to exhaustiveness of the whole spectrum of possible controversies, or even of all possible perspectives on the specific subject-matter of each chapter; rather, each seeks to highlight and critically examine some of the issues of particular relevance within contemporary international legal discourse, and to propose and defend certain approaches on the basis of these explorations. Despite this lack of comprehensiveness, however, the volume does follow a certain trajectory that attempts to impart an overall structure to the set of analyses that it contains, in order to present to the reader a coherent and detailed, if incomplete, account of the relations between the foundational challenges of international law and the prohibition on the use of force. It is to an outline of that trajectory that we now turn.

3. Sovereignty and Human Rights: The Conceptual/Legal Background

The two chapters immediately following this, by Hélène Ruiz Fabri and Olivier Corten, provide some important background to the interaction between sovereignty and human rights and international law. The first of these presents one reading of the interplay between the two notions at an essentially abstract, conceptual level, examining both traditional approaches and more recent developments in the way in which they are understood in order to discover whether or not the substantive frontiers of each have been 'significantly redrawn' in response

---

contained in Resolution 678 could be 'revived' (ibid., at para 29); as such, it would not, in theory at least, constitute the use of force without Security Council authorization.

[27] For an argument along these lines, see Anne-Marie Slaughter, 'Good Reasons for Going Around the UN', *New York Times*, 18 March 2003. A defence of this kind was also suggested by Sofaer, above n 12, although he does argue that this would mean that the action should 'properly be regarded as part of the "inherent" right of self-defence' (ibid. at p 226). This purported extension of the right to self-defence, although the subject of much scholarly attention, has achieved very little scholarly—or, for that matter, governmental—support.

to prevailing international realities.[28] Ruiz Fabri begins with a brief account of classical conceptualizations of each, insisting on the distinction between internal and external sovereignty in international law (where the latter should be conceived, not as unlimited power, but rather as the unlimited freedom of states to exercise the rights that they have). This, she asserts, is the 'natural' consequence of a society featuring not one but rather a multiplicity of individual sovereigns. Human rights, on the other hand, are fundamentally concerned with the relations between states and their nationals; precisely the area previously thought to have been reserved most emphatically to the freedom of the former. This, she argues, is the basis for the common view that human rights and sovereignty are essentially antithetical, that a gain for one is automatically and inevitably a loss for the other.[29]

From there, she proceeds to map out in some detail the various ways in which this freedom may be limited on the basis of human rights, taking into consideration different theoretical approaches and providing illustrative examples drawn from contemporary legal practice. She suggests a nuanced typology, consisting of various different factors: whether a limitation is desired by a state, or whether it is forced upon it; whether the state in question could, in fact, have resisted the limitation, or whether other factors, in particular economic or political pressure, render the notion of 'choice' in this regard fundamentally illusory; the degree and nature of the constraint imposed; and the compliance mechanisms created in respect of it. This last factor, the issue of 'control', is, she suggests, '[t]he essential aspect regarding the degree of limitation of sovereignty'.[30] As such, a full understanding of the various modalities of enforcement is crucial, ranging from the author and object of the control mechanisms, to the conditions for triggering them, and their nature, scope, and potential effects.

One of the most important aspects of Ruiz Fabri's contribution is that it lays out in detail precisely the complexity and ambivalence of interaction between the foundational challenges of sovereignty and human rights alluded to in the introductory section above. Sovereignty in international law is, she notes, a legal fiction—presented as an absolute and ideal type, but one in which the inevitable and desirable existence of exceptions is, in both theoretical and practical terms, immediately accepted. This ambivalence is also clear in her rejection of the idea that all losses of sovereignty *must* represent gains for human rights, or vice versa. To the contrary, since sovereignty itself remains an important ordering principle of society (with a strong ethical dimension of its own), states are not only the *addressees* of human rights but also often their most effective *guarantors*. In this regard, she notes that the widely recognized attack on state sovereignty, from both above (globalization) and below (nationalism), is unlikely to prove beneficial to levels of human rights

---

[28] Ruiz Fabri, n 1 above, at p 2.
[29] Ibid. p 2.   [30] Ibid. p 2.

protections; particularly in the absence of any alternative means for ensuring their respect.

In this regard, she further notes that the current practice of international human rights law, far from reflecting their oft-proclaimed 'universality' and 'indivisibility', is based instead upon relativism and normative hierarchies, leaving much room for the continuing prerogatives of sovereignty, even as rights discourse, in other fields, is driven by a logic and a rhetoric that can lead to it progressively asserting itself against the wishes of states in a process that she terms 'the conquest of autonomy'. Human rights have thus not—at least, not yet—achieved the status of an 'objective' global *ordre public*, capable of transcending the traditional inter-subjective foundations of the international legal order and imposing a 'true monism' from above on all states and private actors in the international sphere. On this basis, she concludes with a 'hypothesis of shared responsibility',[31] a call for cooperation between states and an international civil society in which each protects the other even as it holds them to account, and in which human rights and sovereignty are understood not as purely antithetical, but rather (or, perhaps better, *also*) as locked in a relation of mutual dependence.

In contrast, the chapter by Olivier Corten (Chapter 3) examines how the conceptual complexities of the relationship between human rights and sovereignty have actually played out in positive international law at the point where they seem to conflict most dramatically: the prohibition on the use of force.[32] Using the tools of classical sources doctrine, and remaining very much within the general formal framework of traditional international law, he considers the issue of whether or not a right to armed humanitarian intervention by one state on the territory of another may be said to have emerged—or be emerging—under contemporary international legal norms. He identifies two basic lines of scholarship in this regard. The first are those who hold only that massive violations of human rights can constitute a threat to international peace and security, enabling the Security Council to take enforcement action under Chapter VII of the UN Charter (which thus entails no breach of the principle of non-intervention). And the second group are those who hold, on the contrary, that the challenge of human rights to state sovereignty is so great as to permit armed force to be used unilaterally wherever a state is guilty of gross abuses of the rights of its nationals.[33]

Given the absence of international agreement on this issue, Corten turns his focus to the possibility that such a right to humanitarian intervention has developed either as an authoritative reinterpretation of the UN Charter, or under customary international law. To this end, he examines both the practice and public pronouncements (as evidence of *opinio juris*) of several states with regard to a number of interventions, widely proclaimed to have been carried out for

---

[31] Ibid. p 2.
[32] Corten, n 2 above.   [33] Ibid. p 2.

humanitarian purposes, beginning with a number of interventions in the early 1990s, such as those in Liberia, Iraqi Kurdistan, Somalia, Rwanda, and Bosnia-Herzegovina, and moving on to a detailed consideration of the Kosovo war in 1999, and finally to relevant events since then.

In each of the early cases, although humanitarian purposes were advanced as the *reasons* for intervention, the *legality* of the action was premised upon quite different grounds: Security Council authorization, either explicit (Somalia, Rwanda, and Bosnia-Herzegovina) or implicit (Iraqi Kurdistan), or on the grounds of collective self-defence (following a request to the Economic Community of West African States (ECOWAS) for intervention from the official Liberian Government, and accusations that rebel fighters were receiving support from foreign states). The issue of alternative grounds of legal justification was rarely if ever raised by any of the intervening states, or indeed by any others who supported their action. Corten argues on these grounds that, far from seeking to oppose or change positive international law, the rhetoric of humanitarianism was in these instances simply employed in application of it. He thus concludes that they cannot be used in support of a unilateral right of intervention, although he does note (as does Ruiz Fabri in Chapter 2) that they provide a powerful illustration of the fact that human rights guarantees mean that international law is no longer blind to the manner in which a state treats its own nationals.[34]

Corten next moves on to a detailed consideration of the use of force by NATO members in Kosovo in 1999, viewed by many as providing evidence of the triumph of human rights over sovereignty in this most important field of international law. Again, his focus is on the official justifications offered by the intervening states for their actions. Here, however, he finds that distinctively legal arguments are difficult to isolate. Rather, NATO members asserted a mixture of political and ethical authority, often bolstered by the use of legally significant terminology and references to Security Council resolutions, but often without providing any autonomous legal basis for the intervention itself. Where such justifications were offered, they tended to focus (with the notable exceptions of the UK and Belgium) not on a right to humanitarian intervention, but rather on Serbia's violation of previous Security Council resolutions. Corten suggests that this recourse to the traditional mechanisms of international law, rather than to a legal, as opposed to an ethical, right to humanitarian intervention, makes it very difficult to identify *opinio juris* as to the emergence of the latter doctrine even in the actions of the vast majority of intervening states.[35] This, of course, applies all the more so to the views of the many states who disapproved of NATO's action.

The chapter concludes with an analysis of potential developments in the field in the period from 1999 to the present day, and finds, once again, very little evidence of any support at all among states for the proposed right to unilateral humanitarian intervention. The majority of states have either condemned the

---

[34] Ibid. p 2.   [35] Ibid. p 2.

doctrine outright, or have limited it to cases in which the Security Council explicitly authorizes action. Very few have come out in favour, and of these most seem to propose that the doctrine should be considered *de lege ferenda*, itself suggesting that no such right currently exists. Corten also notes that the armed actions in Iraq and Afghanistan provide no evidence of increased *opinio juris* favouring humanitarian intervention. Indeed, to the contrary, the fact that the intervening states themselves have eschewed any attempts at such justifications again points to the general lack of acceptance of a human rights-based exception to the prohibition on the use of force. He concludes with a brief analysis of some of the barriers facing any attempt to progressively develop such an exception within the contemporary international legal framework.[36]

Both Ruiz Fabri's conceptual analysis and Corten's more formalist reading of the current state of international law represent important points of departure for consideration of the issues of central importance to this volume. They remain, however, in many ways preliminary. While the former creates the necessary space at the theoretical level for a fuller understanding of the relationship between sovereignty, human rights, and the use of force, it does not speculate on the manner in which these relations have played out, or will play out, in terms of the contemporary global setting. Similarly, while Corten's formalist approach provides a persuasive reading of the relevant issues from a mainstream sensibility, and one especially widely shared by practitioners, it remains firmly within traditional understandings of both sources and subjecthood, and is thus not well situated to reflect on claims that these very understandings are themselves in a process of flux driven, in large degree, by the growing impact of human rights within the international legal framework.

In this regard, one interesting possibility that is not addressed by Corten is whether human rights discourse and practice have succeeded in generating an expanded notion of subjecthood in international law, and what effect this may have on the classical understanding of the right to collective self-defence. In other words, if international law is beginning to recognize not merely states, but also, as Ruiz Fabri insists, peoples and individuals as subjects, could this create some conceptual space *from within the right of self-defence itself* for a justification of unilateral humanitarian intervention? Many domestic legal systems extend their own version of the right to self-defence to also cover the defence of others (with, of course, the same requirements of necessity and proportionality). Might it now be argued that, if international law has begun to recognize individuals or peoples as subjects, then the inherent right of collective self-defence could be activated when a state carries out massive violations of the human rights of its nationals, effectively allowing unilateral intervention on humanitarian grounds? Clearly not as it is formulated by Article 51 of the UN Charter, which is explicitly limited to states. However, the right in question also exists in customary law, and there is

---

[36] Ibid. p 2.

no general requirement that the two be coextensive; indeed, one of the oft-cited benefits of drawing on the latter source is its ability to adapt to fit new situations, and thus to generate law far more quickly than can be achieved through the conclusion or modification of international instruments. In this regard, if the right of collective self-defence under customary law can be defined as applying whenever there is an armed attack against a subject of international law, then the existence of a right to unilateral humanitarian intervention along these lines could perhaps be a plausible suggestion. Anthea Roberts hints at this possibility in her contribution to this volume, when she suggests that international law could benefit from the incorporation of some domestic legal differentiations between forms of *mens rea* and *actus reus* in this field.[37]

4. Broadening the Analysis: Legality, Legitimacy—and Security

The remaining contributions to this volume represent attempts to take a wider perspective on the issues raised by Ruiz Fabri and Corten, seeking to evaluate the implications, from both theoretical and empirical perspectives, of unilateral uses of force (whether premised on sovereignty, human rights, or security) for international law and international society more generally. Chapters 4 and 5, by Richard Bilder and Anthea Roberts respectively, in some respects pick up where Corten left off. The first of these examines the effects of NATO's intervention in Kosovo on a wide range of issues related to international law and politics.[38] The second accepts that Corten's conclusion as to the unlawfulness of the bombardment of Serbia represents the majority view among scholars, but notes that this same majority viewed the action as nonetheless justified on ethical grounds. In light of that paradox, Roberts analyses from within an international legal framework the sustainability of the idea that an action can be 'illegal but legitimate'. Chapter 6, by Nathaniel Berman, considers in more detail the rhetorical construction of legitimacy in attempts to justify contemporary interventions, in terms not merely of instances of the use of force, but also of the steps taken to restore peace and stability in their aftermath. Nehal Bhuta then examines, in Chapter 7, the manner in which traditional categories of legitimate use of force have been undermined by the national security discourse of the global 'war on terror', through the prism of the ever more prevalent practice of targeted assassination of suspected terrorists by states on territory other than their own. Finally, in Chapter 8, José Alvarez subjects the notion of the 'responsibility to protect', which Corten introduces earlier, to critical scrutiny and cautions against its ready

---

[37] Anthea Roberts, 'Can Uses of Force be Illegal but Justified?', Chapter 5 below.
[38] Richard Bilder, 'The Implications of Kosovo for International Human Rights Law', Chapter 4 below.

adoption. Instead he advocates a return to the notion of humanitarian intervention, as appropriately updated and developed.

The contribution by Richard Bilder evaluates the impact of the Kosovo intervention and its aftermath on a number of different areas of international law and relations. It begins by addressing the same issue addressed by Corten in Chapter 3 and, although introducing slightly different perspectives, reaches essentially the same conclusion: that there is little evidence to support the claim that a right to humanitarian intervention exists in, or was introduced to, international law by NATO's bombardment of Serbia. From here, however, the author extends his analysis to its impact on a wide range of other issues of direct relevance to international legal discourse: the laws of war; international criminal law; international political stability; and the role of international civil society. That his concern is largely with something other than the pure legal formality of NATO's actions in this regard is clear, not only from the range of subjects that he addresses, but also from the sources that he uses to justify his claims; he makes substantial use, for example, of contemporaneous newspaper and other media reports, and while, like Corten, he analyses in some detail the official rhetoric of the states involved, he most often does so for purposes other than the strict verification of the existence or otherwise of *opinio juris* on a particular point. Rather, his goal is to highlight in general terms, the perplexing dilemmas that arise at the intersection between the foundational challenges of sovereignty and human rights in terms of the use of force.

The themes of irreducible paradox and dilemma recur in each section of Bilder's analysis. At the most basic level, he notes that, although most were unconvinced, to say the least, of its legality, a combination of the events themselves and the reporting thereof by the media meant that the situation quickly become highly emotionally charged; the finding of formal illegality immediately confronted by the need to *do something* to stop the human rights abuses that were (or were reported to be) taking place. In the context of the right to humanitarian intervention, this dilemma was manifested in the need to avoid a return to Cold War days of the incapacity of the Security Council to deal with urgent crises, but also in the need to avoid undermining the United Nations as the best hope there is for making international human rights guarantees effective. His conclusion in this regard has strong echoes of Ruiz Fabri's warning of the danger of enthusiastically diluting sovereignty in order to enhance human rights protections; in undermining the United Nations, we may be allowing the perfect to become the enemy of the good (however flawed), with potentially disastrous consequences for the very laws that we are seeking to promote.

In terms of the laws of war, Bilder insists that, in relation to humanitarian intervention as well as to self-defence, the *jus in bello* remains strongly linked to the *jus ad bellum*.[39] Thus, even if a right to unilateral humanitarian intervention

---

[39] Ibid. p 139.

were to be accepted, then the subsequent conduct of the war, particularly if it was not necessary to achieving the humanitarian aims and proportional to those aims, could serve to render an intervention illegal *ex post*. In this regard, he questions the escalation of the bombing campaign to include targets of only very indirect military significance, the use of cluster bombs and depleted uranium weapons, and also the decision to protect the lives of NATO pilots (and thus shore up public support for the intervention of NATO member states) by bombing from very high altitude; a practice that resulted in high levels of 'collateral damage', or civilian deaths in ordinary parlance. He also notes that the campaign may well have served to increase, rather than decrease, the practices of ethnic cleansing and other human rights violations, and asks whether, if the form of action taken was unlikely to achieve its ostensible goals, did it thereby lose whatever legal justification it may have had?[40]

With a less overtly legal relevance, Bilder also notes that the manner in which the campaign was carried out served to create high levels of instability, both internally to Serbia and internationally more generally. The vast disparity between the opposing forces, the fact that NATO's planes remained basically invisible throughout the eleven-week bombardment and far beyond the reach of Serbia's defensive capabilities, created for many the impression of a 'bullying' group of rich Western states picking on an essentially defenceless enemy; a claim that has echoes of Richard Falk's likening of the structure of contemporary military interventions to that of torture.[41] One effect of this was to deepen the rifts in an already divided Serbian society. It also increased the anger of those states which had vehemently opposed the action, in particular Russia and China, thus threatening national, regional, and international stability. Thus, we are brought back to more dilemmas: that the unilateral use of force for humanitarian purposes can itself lead to high levels of insecurity, with all of the implications in terms of human rights violations that this invariably involves; and that the use of very high-tech weaponry, ostensibly to protect civilian lives, can itself create perverse yet powerful incentives for weaker states to develop weapons of mass destruction as their only means of protection.

Similar ambivalences emerge in Bilder's analysis of the important role played by the international media in generating, driving, and shaping the public response to the unilateral use of force, and in terms of the potential for humanitarian intervention to increase ethno-national conflict globally. He concludes by recognizing the symbolic importance of Kosovo, as the first time that major powers had asserted a duty to take forceful action on purely humanitarian grounds, noting that international lawyers cannot be content with testing the legality of such action, but must also look to its scope, usefulness, and potential

---

[40] Ibid. p 139.
[41] See Richard Falk, 'The Role of Knowledge in the Cyber-Age of Globalisation', in *Knowledge and Diplomacy* (1999): 'One of the implications of one-sided warfare is that it begets violence that resembles the structure of torture carried out on a large scale'.

consequences—legal or otherwise.[42] In general, this chapter undoubtedly raises more questions than it answers; indeed, it would not be an exaggeration to suggest that, in an important sense, it raises questions that *have* no answers, but that nonetheless need to be identified and confronted if international law is to have any legal or ethical significance.

The theme of irreducible dilemma is central also to Anthea Roberts' contribution to this volume. In contrast to Bilder, however, she focuses on only one, albeit fundamental, example: what states should do when the law forbids following a course of action that morality dictates.[43] This, she asserts, is reflected in the reaction of the majority of Western scholars to the Kosovo intervention: that it was illegal but justified. She begins by noting, with Corten and Bilder, the state of international law on the use of force, at the time of the Kosovo intervention at least: that it was only permitted either in self-defence or on the basis of explicit Security Council authorization. She immediately recognizes, however, that this finding alone cannot be a sufficient conclusion with which to confront the central issue posed by humanitarian intervention: namely, how to act when a state is brutally violating the human rights of its nationals on a massive scale, and the Security Council is unwilling, or unable, to authorize force. In the main, she proceeds by way of an analysis of the work of two of the major mainstream proponents of the 'illegal but justified' approach to certain types of armed intervention, Bruno Simma and Thomas Franck (also, however, drawing frequently on the work of other scholars in this field). Simma proposed that humanitarian intervention of the sort witnessed in Kosovo should be understood as an extra-legal exception to law itself, while Franck argued that the doctrine can be best assimilated into the international legal framework by transposing to that level the domestic law concept of mitigation.

Roberts begins with an analysis of the rhetoric of these claims: the manner in which those seeking to defend a variant of the 'illegal but justified' approach frame their arguments in order to make them appear more palatable, and less threatening to the international legal order. For example, she notes in this regard that the tendency to describe such interventions as 'technically' or 'formally' illegal does not do justice to the violation of law that they represent (it is unlikely that the prohibition on the use of force is a mere technicality or formality in international law) and that the frequent references to the 'paralysis' of the Security Council, evoking the stalemates of the Cold War era, are thoroughly question-begging, in that they already contain the judgment that it has not acted when it should have—precisely the point on which much debate on this issue is centred. She insists also that great care should be taken when importing the vocabulary and conceptual tools of national law to the international legal framework, given the important institutional differences between the two—in particular that in

---

[42] Bilder, n 38 above, p 16.
[43] Roberts, n 37 above, p 16.

the latter, unlike the former, the subjects of law themselves are also its legislators, interpreters, and enforcers.[44]

A significant part of the chapter is devoted to a critical analysis of Franck's claim that humanitarian intervention should be dealt with by reference to the doctrine of mitigation; that is, that the violation of the prohibition on the use of force should be recognized, and that the humanitarian considerations should come into play only in terms of deciding upon the appropriate punishment. There are two main elements to her critique.[45] The first is a more 'formal' argument that the institutional mechanisms that underpin the notion of mitigation in the domestic legal setting are simply not present at the international level. Chief among these is a court or similar body with compulsory jurisdiction and the power to make authoritative declarations of illegality while recognizing that the ethics of the particular case mean that a much reduced sanction is appropriate. Where such authoritative declarations are not normally forthcoming when the Security Council is split on an issue, and sanctions even less so, persistent breaches will likely undermine even the most fundamental of norms. This risk is increased further by the fact that, unlike in domestic law, persistent breach of an international norm can, under certain circumstances, itself lead to the emergence of a new norm. The second, more 'substantive', criticism notes that the 'mitigation' approach does not accurately represent the nature of the claim being advanced. While in domestic law mitigation is used to moderate the consequences of illegal action, and not to justify or excuse the action itself, humanitarian intervention on the other hand is premised upon a moral *duty* to act. Do those seeking to defend NATO's action in Kosovo really wish to construct it as ethically analogous to the case, for example, of a group adrift at sea killing and eating one of their party in order to save the rest from hunger?[46]

Roberts argues that the driving force behind the 'illegal but justified' approach boils down to policy considerations, and in particular the desire to minimize the precedential implications of the Kosovo intervention, and the potential for abuse that this might create. However, she warns that the effect of this is to turn away from a formal understanding of legality towards substantive ethical notions of legitimacy—and that the latter imply, in a world in which substantive notions of the good are deeply contested, a significant potential for abuse of their own. In particular, in attempting to recognize 'illegal but justified' actions as an extra-legal exception to law in general—and thus avoiding the need to lay down criteria for when it might be activated—there is a real possibility that such a rhetoric may be used to justify actions that go far beyond the realm of 'humanitarianism'. She notes, in this regard, that some scholars had argued that, if weapons of mass

---

[44] Ibid. p 16.
[45] Ibid. p 16.
[46] This was the situation in *R v Dudley and Stephens* (1884) LR 14 QBD 273, a case that Franck makes central to his analysis.

destruction had been found in Iraq, then Kosovo could well have been invoked as a general precedent in support of the legitimacy, if not the legality, of the 2003 invasion.[47]

Roberts concludes with a rejection of the idea, implied in many versions of the 'illegal but justified' approach, that formal law and substantive morality exist as opposite poles of an irreconcilable dichotomy. Conceiving of the debate in this way, she insists, impoverishes both our understanding of the issues involved and our capacity to respond effectively to them. Instead of understanding legality as a neutral, binary choice (which ignores the important ethical significance of formalism) and opposing this to legitimacy *qua* substantive morality (which ignores the ease with which appeals to the latter can simply disguise much more cynical motives), she suggests that we incorporate notions of legitimacy more robustly within our understanding of legality itself, in order that the latter no longer is conceived as an either/or dichotomy, but rather as existing on a spectrum, from clearly legal actions at one extreme to clearly illegal at the other, with a full range of possibilities in between. In short, while acknowledging that such a move itself is far from unproblematic, she argues that we should view legality as a matter of degree, with legitimacy playing an important role in determining where on the spectrum a particular action should be placed.

Roberts concludes by problematizing the idea that formal law and substantive morality exist as opposite poles of an irreconcilable dichotomy. For her, conceiving of the debate in this way impoverishes our understanding of the issues involved and our capacity to respond effectively to them. She suggests three different ways in which the relation can be understood: (i) appeals to legitimacy can be used to avoid legal obligation altogether, which carries the obvious risk that the politically powerful actors will determine when intervention is 'legitimate' according to their own standards and interests; (ii) legitimacy can be used to supplement formal legality, maintaining the integrity of 'black and white' prohibitions while introducing 'shades of gray' through recourse to the spectrum of legitimacy; and (iii) legitimacy can be used as a tool to critique existing law, and suggest directions for its progressive development. She concludes by suggesting that either we should understand legality itself as a matter of degree, or that—as most states already seem to do—the prohibition on the use of force should be viewed not as absolute, but rather as graduated according to the gravity of the violation. In any event, she argues, keeping 'legitimacy' as an extra-legal category has led to a reluctance to furnish criteria for precisely determining what constitutes legitimate action in the context of unilateral humanitarian intervention; and that this, almost paradoxically, might actually increase its precedential effect—exactly the opposite result than that hoped for by many of the proponents of the 'illegal but justified' approach.

---

[47] Roberts, n 37 above, p 16.

While Roberts seeks to integrate the challenges posed by the law/legitimacy dilemma into a variegated notion of legality itself, the chapter by Nathaniel Berman takes a quite different, in many ways almost opposite, approach to the interaction between these two concepts. He focuses not on the effect of the 'turn to legitimacy' on certain understandings of international norms, but rather on the manner in which the contradictions internal to international legal discourse are themselves central to its broader attempt to persuade its relevant publics that the interventions it allows, the institutions and mechanisms that it establishes, are not merely formally legal but also, substantively, legitimate. In short, Berman's contribution examines the rhetorical construction of international law's legitimacy in cases of armed intervention and their aftermath.[48]

He begins by challenging the view, noted at the outset to this chapter, that the period between 1989 and 2001 represented something of a 'golden age' of a genuinely unified international community, and of legitimate intervention carried out in its name. Berman speaks of the 'long post-Cold War decade',[49] an evocative term, encapsulating nicely not simply the length of time involved, but also, perhaps, a sense of the exaggerated importance attributed to this period in many narratives of international law's development. He suggests that nostalgia for that time is both historically naïve and philosophically undesirable. In terms of the former, he notes, as do Ruiz Fabri and Corten in their contributions, that the conflicting pulls of the foundational challenges for the international legal system were evident throughout the 1990s, as the inaction in Srebrenica and Rwanda, and action in Kosovo, readily demonstrate. More importantly, in terms of the latter, he contends that attempts to portray the dialectic of power and principle as synthesized within and through the law of a genuinely unified international community, mischaracterize both the reasons for the continued existence of ideological difference, and the manner in which the legitimacy of the international legal system is constructed and reconstructed in its application to particular contexts and controversies.

Berman suggests a distinction between two types of law's legitimacy (corresponding to two major challenges to that legitimacy that have resurfaced at various points and in various guises in recent history): *status* and *coherence*. The former concerns the identity of the system as a whole, and is manifested both in attempts to justify that system and to reject it in its entirety, as characterizations of the international legal order as 'cosmopolitan' or 'imperialist' illustrate.[50] The latter, on the other hand, is concerned with issues internal to the system under consideration, either alleging or denying that the heterogeneous elements with which it has been constructed have been arranged in a manner that is ineffective, irrational, or immoral. Berman notes that when these two types are manifested in terms of critique, they will most often appear with new claims to putative legitimacy of status or coherence: the former in terms of a new identity,

---

[48] Nathaniel Berman, 'Intervention in a "Divided World": Axes of Legitimacy', Chapter 6 below.
[49] Ibid. p 215.   [50] Ibid. p 215.

and driving philosophy, for the system as a whole, and the latter with a call for a *different* coherence between the different elements within it (or perhaps even with a rejection of the attempt to achieve coherence between all the elements, instead privileging one to the complete exclusion of the other, which Berman refers to as legitimacy through *defiance*). He contextualizes this abstract account by reference to various different challenges to international law, and in particular those posed by US unilateralism first in Kosovo and then Iraq, and Islamic fundamentalism.

Central to Berman's chapter is the claim that international law derives its broader legitimacy not from the supposed unity of the international community, but rather from its ability to marshal contradictory ideas within itself, and to con-figure and reconfigure them in particular contexts and for particular audiences. International law's legitimacy thus rests, in large degree, in its ability to be most things to most people, as the exigencies of the situation demands. It is not, then, the pure transcendence of ideological difference that is in question, but rather the ability, however messy, to accommodate different ideological standpoints, in dif-ferent measure at different times, that accounts for international law's resilience; not as a system with a fixed, determinate identity, but rather as a 'work-in-process', constantly redefining itself and its goals as its seeks to respond to, and engage in, the concrete situations that confront it.[51] The various dilemmas created in inter-national law and institutions by the foundational challenges, in isolation or inter-action, are not here viewed as something that must be solved or overcome. Rather, their very existence is portrayed as the greatest strength of the international legal order, even as they represent its Achilles heel. Berman illustrates this through an examination of the rhetorical construction of the legitimacy of the UN Mission in Kosovo (UNMIK) following the 1999 bombardment.

Another example of this impossibility of establishing any pure or perpetual legitimacy for interventions under international law is found in what Berman refers to as the continuous and inescapable 'haunting' of contemporary inter-national solutions to particular crises by the spectres of international law's largely discredited colonial past.[52] Intervention in the name of human rights is often marked by the same narrative structure as, for example, the 'civilising missions' of the colonial era;[53] and, again using the example of the UNMIK, Berman illustrates how these shadows reappear again and again, through use of imper-ial vocabulary such as protectorate, proconsul, or trusteeship. Again, however, the author sees in this not, as many have before him, merely the grounds for a critique of the current international legal solutions to local crises. Rather he recasts it as a potential positive, refusing any objective or secure status to legit-imacy claims and thus ensuring that it remains always a work in progress, fluid and adaptable. Progress, Berman suggests, is not to be achieved through the final,

---

[51] Ibid. p 215
[52] Ibid. p 215.
[53] On this point, see also, eg Anne Orford, *Reading Humanitarian Intervention* (2003).

perfect, impossible integration of power and principle at the global level, but rather through constantly 'goading' those who exercise public power internationally with their similarity to those who did so previously in a manner now widely regarded as thoroughly immoral. The task for those in power is to persuade their relevant publics that they are substantively different from their predecessors, both in terms of the status and coherence of their actions.

Chapter 7, by Nehal Bhuta, is the one that has the strongest focus on the ever-increasing role of national security concerns on the use of force in international law, although both the contributions by Roberts and Berman, on the 'illegal but justified' approach and the rhetorical construction of legitimacy respectively, can also be viewed as of direct relevance in this regard. Bhuta's chapter examines the international legal implications of the global 'war on terror' pursued by the US following the attacks of September 2001 through one particular lens, of ever increasing importance in contemporary international legal discourse: the use of military force in order to carry out targeted killings of suspected terrorists on territory other than that of the acting state—a practice already carried out by the Israelis for decades, and much more recently by the US in strikes against suspected Al Qaeda members.[54]

His starting point is that international law currently recognizes two different regimes for the authorization and regulation for the use of force: international human rights and international humanitarian law. These, however, function on the basis of certain fundamental conceptual distinctions, such as war/peace, combatant/civilian, enemy/criminal, which in turn are premised upon a particular model of conventional warfare. Bhuta begins by noting that, like the partisan of the nineteenth century and the guerrilla of the twentieth, the figure of the international terrorist cannot be made to fit neatly or unproblematically into any of these categories; and that this has serious consequences for international law's ability to respond to certain ever more common uses (and abuses) of force by states on the territory of others. The terrorist, for example, like the partisan before him, is unlikely to openly bear arms, wear distinctive insignia, or obey the laws of war, or any of the other requirements laid down by the Geneva Conventions for the recognition of combatants. In general, humanitarian law seeks to protect 'regular' combatants, while, for the terrorist, it is his very irregularity that constitutes his strongest weapon. However, when terrorists have proven themselves capable of planning and carrying out attacks of the level witnessed in 2001, the very high level of protection afforded by human rights law may well hamstring states in carrying out the justifiable, indeed necessary, measures to ensure national security. The effect of this is that attempts to apply either regime to the exclusion of the other bring with them a set of unpalatable risks; almost as unpalatable as attempts, such as those in evidence in Guantanamo Bay and elsewhere,

---

[54] Nehal Bhuta, 'States of Exception: Regulating Targeted Killing in a "Global Civil War"', Chapter 7 below.

to place those suspected of such attacks beyond the pale of either human rights or humanitarian law. Bhuta's contribution is, in large degree, a detailed examination of those risks.

His first step is an analysis of the different ways in which the relationship between human rights and humanitarian law has been understood in contemporary international legal discourse. He identifies three broad trends, which he terms the 'cumulative', 'interpretive complementarity', and 'incompatibility' approaches, respectively. The first holds that both regimes have a common *telos* in protecting the rights of individuals, such that, in the event of a conflict between the two, whichever provides the highest level of protection in this regard should be adopted. The third holds the opposite conclusion: that human rights and humanitarian law apply to clearly distinct categories of action, and that what is regulated by one cannot be so by the other. In this model, of course, wherever there is an 'armed conflict', the provisions of humanitarian law apply. The second approach, that of 'interpretive complementarity', which is also the most commonly held amongst international legal scholars, provides something of a middle way between the other two, and suggests that *both* regimes might apply simultaneously to the same set of facts, and that their interaction serves either to 'humanize' *jus in bello*, or to give content to vague human rights provisions, such as the right to life, in the exceptional circumstances of armed conflict.[55]

He then moves on to a consideration of these three approaches in the light of the findings of the International Court of Justice (ICJ) in the *Nuclear Weapons* and *Legal Consequences of the Wall* advisory opinions,[56] which held that humanitarian law should be viewed as applying as *lex specialis* to human rights in circumstances of armed conflict. This has been used to support the contention that, in such circumstances, the two regimes are fundamentally complementary. Bhuta, however, problematizes this suggestion, noting that the *lex specialis* doctrine itself is crucially vague, and can in fact be used to support any one of the three approaches to the interaction between human rights and humanitarian law that he distinguishes. His point is not to critique the interpretive complementarity approach itself, but rather to insist that it in no way follows in any logical or conceptually necessary manner from the interaction between the two regimes: instead, it represents a policy choice, and should be clearly articulated—and defended—as such.

From here, Bhuta moves on to a detailed analysis of the conceptual grammar of both human rights and humanitarian law in relation to targeted killing, and outlines the manner in which the figure of the international terrorist, and the rhetoric of a global 'war on terror', subverts the basic distinctions upon which each doctrine rests. Any action of this sort will be judged on a very different basis

---

[55] Ibid. p 243.
[56] 'Threat or Use of Nuclear Weapons Advisory Opinion' [1996] ICJ Reps 226; 'Legal Consequences of the Construction of a Wall in the Occupied Palestinian Territory' (ICJ, 9 July 2004), 43 ILM 1009 (2004).

depending on whether it is viewed in terms of a 'military' or 'law enforcement' model. The former allows the killing of targets if necessary and proportionate to a particular military goal, while the latter views all individuals, regardless of their activity, as having certain basic and non-derogable rights, including, perhaps most importantly, the right to life—the violation of which demands a much higher standard of justification than under the military model. The 'war on terror', however, destabilizes the categories central to each, such as the designation of 'armed conflict' and 'combatant' upon which the military model is based, or the assumption of peace-time 'normality' presumed by the law enforcement regime. Both, if applied in isolation, create very real risks of both under- and over-inclusion. If very narrow definitions of certain key terms are followed (such as 'direct participation in hostilities' for the military model, or 'imminence and necessity' for that of law enforcement), then international law's ability to respond effectively to the threat posed by international terrorism may well be unacceptably diminished. But if (as seems more likely) more expansive understandings of these terms are allowed, the space created for discretionary judgement risks rendering law itself incapable of directing, or constraining, state action.

Neither framework, then, can alone deal adequately with the challenges posed by the imperatives of national security when confronted with the problem of international terrorism; and the law itself gives no clear indication as to which is to be preferred in any given situation within this field. In a manner that strongly echoes Berman's arguments in the preceding chapter, Bhuta concludes with a call to leave behind doctrinal and conceptual analyses of the two legal regimes for authorizing and regulating the use of force in favour of a contextual, 'functionalist' approach, which, while acknowledging the similarities between the 'war on terror' and other, more conventional forms of warfare—and the claim that some elements of humanitarian law should thus be applied—nonetheless seeks to overcome the potential for abuse inherent in the discretionary space this opens up for states through a reaffirmation of values central to human rights discourse including transparency, due process, and, perhaps most importantly, real and effective limitations on any categorical right to kill.[57] Such a formulation is itself, of course, not without risks; the task, then, is a perpetual calling to account of power, to ensure that these risks are not outweighed by those of either human rights or humanitarian law applied in isolation in this context.

In the final chapter in the volume, José Alvarez critically scrutinizes the concept of the responsibility to protect (known as R2P).[58] The concept is of particular salience to the issues dealt with in this volume, not only because some scholars have been enthusiastic about its potential,[59] but because United Nations bodies

---

[57] Ibid. p 43.

[58] José Alvarez, 'The Schizophrenias of R2P', Chapter 8 below.

[59] See, eg Christopher C Joyner, '"The Responsibility to Protect": Humanitarian Concern and the Lawfulness of Armed Intervention', 47 Va. J. Int'l L. (2007) 693 ('Marshalling the political will to implement the responsibility to protect as a functional legal norm promises to make con-

have begun to invoke it in various different contexts. Two examples will suffice for present purposes, both of which relate to Sudan. In March 2007 a 'High-Level Mission' appointed by the UN Human Rights Council decided to frame its analysis and recommendations in terms of R2P. By way of legal analysis it offered the explanation that the concept had been recognized in the outcome of the World Social Summit and that 'The Sudan joined in the adoption of the World Summit Outcome, explicitly accepting its responsibility to protect and pledging to act in accordance with it'.[60] After a lengthy factual analysis, albeit one not based on an on-site visit—permission for which had been refused by the government—the Mission concluded that the Sudanese government had 'manifestly failed to protect the population of Darfur from large-scale international crimes, and has itself orchestrated and participated in these crimes. As such, the solemn obligation of the international community to exercise its responsibility to protect has become evident and urgent.'[61] The Mission did not, however, spell out what particular R2P-specific consequences could be identified from that failure.

Several months later, in adopting a resolution authorizing the deployment of a 26,000 person United Nations–African Union Mission in Darfur (UNAMID), the UN Security Council authorized the Mission to use force to protect civilians.[62] Although the resolution explicitly recognized the sovereignty of the government of Sudan, it also endorsed an earlier resolution which had specifically reaffirmed the provisions of the World Summit Outcome Document dealing with R2P.[63]

R2P emerged out of attempts in the late 1980s and the 1990s to assert a right or a duty to intervene, put forward by authors such as the current French Foreign Minister, Bernard Kouchner, appointed the French Foreign Minister in 2007, and his adviser Mario Bettati and others.[64] The specific formulation of the 'responsibility to protect' was initially put forward by a group of experts, sponsored by the government of Canada, in a Report of the International Commission on Intervention and State Sovereignty.[65] Its key entry point into the debate about reconciling the challenges of sovereignty and respect for human rights was its assertion that the notion of sovereignty should be interpreted as implying

---

siderable progress toward attaining that lofty but clearly necessary goal in twenty-first century international relations.' Ibid. at 723.). For a more sceptical perspective see C Stahn, 'Responsibility to Protect: Political Rhetoric or Emerging Legal Norm?', 101AJIL (2007) 99 (He argues that while R2P 'may gradually replace the doctrine of humanitarian intervention', many of its propositions 'remain uncertain from a normative point of view or lack support'. He concludes that R2P presently remains more a 'political catchword' than a legal norm. Id. at 120.)

[60] Report of the High-Level Mission on the situation of human rights in Darfur pursuant to Human Rights Council decision S-4/101, UN Doc A/HRC/4/80 (2007), para 20.

[61] Ibid., para 76.

[62] Security Council Res 1769 (31 July 2007), para 15(a)(ii).

[63] Security Council Res 1674 (28 April 2006).

[64] M Bettati and B Kouchner (eds), *Le devoir d'ingérence* (1987); and Mario Bettati, *Le droit d'ingérence: mutation de l'ordre international* (1996).

[65] Report of the International Commission on Intervention and State Sovereignty, *The Responsibility to Protect* (2001).

responsibility, a responsibility which was then directly linked to the need to protect the human rights of the citizenry over whom sovereignty was claimed. When a government was unable or unwilling to ensure such protection, the responsibility would then fall to the international community.

Alvarez traces the subsequent endorsement of the concept by various international forums and its evolution through the process of invocation and interpretation by a wide range of actors. Indeed, it is the fact that the concept is capable of appealing to groups with widely divergent interests and constituencies that most troubles him. He undertakes a survey of the different ends towards which the concept has been invoked and concludes that many of them are both inconsistent with one another and not compatible with the original intentions of the concept's authors. He is especially critical on four fronts: (i) the way in which the notion of sovereignty has been redefined for the purposes of overcoming qualms about intervention in specific circumstances; (ii) the expansion of the understanding of what constitutes protection; (iii) the potentially very broad meaning given to the notion of security in this context; and (iv) the purported invocation of legal responsibility on the part of the United Nations and other international organizations in cases in which the responsibility to protect is not respected. Alvarez does not seek to resolve the conundrum of how best to reconcile the foundational challenges of sovereignty and human rights but instead suggests that the more traditional rubric of humanitarian intervention is likely to provide a more fertile and welcoming terrain for such efforts. He thus rejects the promise of R2P as a way out of the dilemma and instead counsels us to return and seek the relevant answers within the debates which are the central focus of the earlier contributions.

5. Conclusion: Armed Intervention and the Ethics of International Law

Although often criticized for an impenetrable writing style, the French philosopher Michel Foucault responded, with perfect clarity, to the charge that his writings committed him to an unrelenting apathy in terms of how to act ethically when confronted with power: '[m]y point is not that everything is bad, but that everything is dangerous, which is not exactly the same as bad. If everything is dangerous, then we always have something to do... [T]he ethico-political choice we have to make every day is to determine which is the main danger.'[66] While the ways in which the various issues that arise in the following chapters interact are too many and complex to detail here, one point that emerges clearly from all is that this statement applies, a fortiori, to the relations between what we have characterized

---

[66] Michel Foucault, 'On the Genealogy of Ethics: An Overview of a Work in Progress', in Paul Rabinow (ed), *Michel Foucault: Essential Works of Foucault 1954–1984:* vol 1: *Ethics* (1997) 253–80, at p 256.

as foundational challenges for international law in terms of the use of force. Each of these presents, both in isolation and in interaction with the others, a set of irreducible and perennial dilemmas that render impossible any one pure, correct, and unproblematic solution to such international legal controversies.

As the various contributions to this volume make clear over the course of the following pages, these dilemmas are generated both within and between the foundational challenges. The contradictions inherent in the notion of sovereignty are, for example, by now well known; as are the often competing imperatives of various fundamental human rights, however strongly and frequently their 'interdependence and indivisibility' is proclaimed. Equally clear is the manner in which the challenges can conflict *inter se*: indeed, sovereignty and human rights are often crudely conceived of as essentially antithetical to each other. And, as suggested at the outset of this chapter, the increasing focus on national security can, in international legal terms at least, be viewed as in many ways antithetical to both. Just as it is reductionist to allow these conflicts to exhaust the relationship between the foundational challenges, however, so it is too easy to lapse into largely unreflective normative judgements of each. In particular, the temptation to view a valorization of human rights as always 'progressive', always representing a basic ethical gain, and, conversely, arguments which favour sovereignty or security concerns as being essentially regressive or reactionary, should be resisted; for it ignores the often powerful ethical dimension to the latter two concepts, while turning a blind eye to potentially problematic aspects of the first, especially when human rights discourse is misappropriated for strategic or other reasons. This is a danger of which Alvarez in particular warns in his contribution below.

As many of the following chapters illustrate, these dilemmas can be properly characterized as irreducible insofar as there is no way of completely transcending them, of disposing of them to the satisfaction of all in every situation. This does not mean, however, that international law is either impossible or futile; only that certain concepts of both legality and legitimacy, premised upon the discovery of the 'right answer' to any controversy, must themselves be jettisoned. It is for this reason that Corten's formalist analysis, for example, resulting in a resounding 'no' to the question of whether a right to humanitarian intervention has emerged into positive international law, represents an important, but only ever preliminary, response to the interaction between the foundational challenges of sovereignty and human rights in terms of the use of force, if, as seems likely given the currently prevailing state of international relations, such arguments will be used again in order to justify unilateral military intervention with relative impunity, limiting evaluation of the legality of such action to formalistic appraisals of the 'state of the art', risks condemning international legal norms to utter irrelevance on this most important of issues. If international law is unable to respond to challenges to principles at the very apex of the system, its credibility in all other fields will be seriously, perhaps irrevocably, damaged.

This risk, of course, must be balanced against its opposite: that allowing powerful states to reform norms as and when they see fit will condemn the law just as surely to irrelevance. That there is no abstract and universal solution to this dilemma of 'normativity' and 'concreteness' is by now well known; however, as Berman insists in his contribution to this volume, far from destroying the international legal project, it is precisely through configuring and reconfiguring these conflicting imperatives in response to concrete situations that we are able to engage ethically with it. Rather than affording us demonstrably correct means of disposing of controversies, then, international law provides us with a set of resources for confronting precisely what is difficult and controversial about them, and in this way enables us to furnish responses that are always provisional, and never more than more or less legitimate, but nonetheless relatively effective. Formalism, in this regard, remains a vitally important element of the international lawyer's toolbox; his commitment to it, however, unlike that of his domestic counterpart, remains a conditional and ethical, rather than a professional one.[67]

It is also in this regard that we must reconsider the notion that armed intervention can be illegal but ethically justifiable. As noted above, the argument put by Anthea Roberts that this combination is unsustainable is rooted in the viewpoint of international law itself,[68] although since international norms can be reformed *if* persistent breach is met with acquiescence, the unsustainability involved seems hypothetical rather than categorical. It is worth considering, however, whether this conclusion must also follow in ethical terms. There are two possibilities in this regard, both of which view law and ethics as essentially coextensive. The first, a classical natural law position, would hold that any positive law that conflicts with a tenet of an objective, substantive ethics is null and void *ab initio*. Any action taken pursuant to such an ethics is thus, by definition, automatically legal. The second, in a sense opposite, view would be that the manner in which legal systems generate norms results in the production of positive laws that are themselves necessarily ethical in all circumstances. Both of these positions have some adherents. In terms of the former, we might think, for example, of Fernando Tesón's approach to humanitarian intervention based upon a Kantian categorical imperative.[69] Philip Allott, on the other hand, seems to come close at points in his book *Eunomia* to endorsing the latter claim, in terms of ideal theory at least.[70] But these 'purists' are a rare breed, and the vast majority of scholars reject either of these extremes. The idea that an action can be illegal but legitimate,

---

[67] This is one way to read Koskenniemi's recent 'return' to formalism; see, eg Koskenniemi, above n 16; see also Koskenniemi, *The Gentle Civilizer of Nations* (2002). This argument is developed in more detail in Euan MacDonald, *International Law and Ethics after the Critical Challenge* (forthcoming 2008).

[68] At p 179 above.

[69] Fernando Tesón, *Humanitarian Intervention: An Inquiry into Law and Morality* (3rd edn 2005).

[70] Philip Allott, *Eunomia: New Order for a New World* (2nd edn 2004), eg at para 11.27. For a detailed critique of *Eunomia* along these lines, see Euan MacDonald, 'The Rhetoric of Eunomia',

however, is a *sine qua non* of any other theory of ethics and their interaction with law.

This point has been made by David Kennedy, in highlighting the manner in which an unreflective and absolute commitment to formalism can blind international lawyers to important ethical issues; issues that, for the reasons outlined above, they can scarcely afford to avoid confronting. He suggests that the debates surrounding the Iraq war in 2003 showed how the rhetoric of formalism could be used to cloak a 'flight from responsibility', particularly in terms of the importance attached to the existence or otherwise of Security Council authorization: 'The whole discussion—"if only the UN decides to do it, then it is fine"—puts to one side the questions of whether it is a good idea or not, who will suffer by it, how long it will take, and what actually will be the consequences for political life in the Middle East afterwards'.[71] The point here is emphatically not to suggest that Security Council authorization is or should be of no import, particularly to international lawyers. Rather it is that its role in justifying armed intervention is only one element (albeit a hugely important one) of the debate that must take place surrounding this most important of decisions. The peculiarities of the international legal system, its low level of institutionalization, its blurred distinction between law and politics, and its mechanisms for enabling persistent breach to become new law, mean that it is a debate with which international lawyers cannot, or at least should not, avoid engaging.

International lawyers are thus compelled (or condemned) to pursue an analysis of the irreducible dilemmas posed by the foundational challenges of sovereignty, human rights, and security, not merely in terms of the formal doctrine of their discipline, but also of the manner in which they can be configured in order to achieve (more or less) persuasive legitimacy as to both its methods and results. The collected papers in this volume represent an attempt to face up to these dilemmas in all of their complexity, and to suggest ways in which they can be confronted productively both in the abstract and in the concrete circumstances of particular cases. The challenges that they pose are perennial; the solutions they suggest provisional and contestable. As each contribution makes clear, however, in terms of the interaction of the foundational challenges with regard to the use of force, there is no universal, risk-free panacea. *Everything* is dangerous; that's what keeps things interesting.

Institute for International Law and Justice Working Paper: History and Theory of International Law Series (NYU Institute of International Law and Justice, 2007).

[71] David Kennedy, 'Contestation of the Outcomes and Procedures of the Existing Legal Regime', 16 Leiden Journal of International Law (2003) 915–17. See his comments following the presentation of this paper, on p 926.

2

Human Rights and State Sovereignty: Have the Boundaries been Significantly Redrawn?

Hélène Ruiz Fabri*

'It is no longer acceptable to see governments flouting their citizens' rights under the pretext of sovereignty'.[1] These words, invoking a putative evolution in international law, were offered in the context of the Kosovo war by the then UN Secretary General Kofi Annan. He further viewed the Pinochet affair as illustrative of this evolution, and, proclaiming the 'triumph of human rights over sovereignty', added that:

the human being is at the centre of everything. The concept of national sovereignty was itself conceived in order to protect the individual: this, and not the inverse, is the *raison d'être* of the state. This, however, does not mean that national sovereignty is no longer relevant. Time will be needed to reconcile sovereignty and individual rights.[2]

That considerations of this sort were, however, raised only at a very late stage—if at all—in the context of other important events, such as the Russian offensive in Chechnya, illustrates well that the reconciliation envisaged by Annan here remains to be achieved.

Nonetheless, these statements contain many elements of direct relevance to us here, underlining not only the continuing topicality of the issues discussed in the present volume, but also the numerous contradictions and tensions contained therein—in particular in the idea that human rights and sovereignty can pull in both complementary and in different, even opposing, directions at the same time. The potential opposition becomes clear when, for example, we acknowledge that sovereignty can serve as a pretext for a lack of respect for human rights; the

---

* This chapter was translated from the French version by Euan MacDonald; thanks are due to Damien Lecarpentier for his invaluable assistance in that process.

[1] Quoted in Afsane Bassir, 'L'UCK pose un problème et l'OTAN doit rétablir rapidement l'ordre public', *Le Monde*, 19 June 1999, p 1.

[2] Ibid.

complementarity when we recognize that sovereignty was originally conceived of in order to protect the individual. We might further note, in this regard, that Annan's statements above gloss over some important nuances: those deriving, for example, from a more historical perspective (in the sense that what he envisages is part of an evolutionary process—a process, moreover, that need not inevitably result in some triumphant synthesis); and also the crucial distinction between that which *is* and that which *ought to be*. His claims are political in nature, containing a strongly subjective element that itself presents a challenge to the legal framework as traditionally understood. As a result, the boundaries of this framework must now be relocated.

Sovereignty

Sovereignty is the characteristic feature, the constitutive attribute of a very specific entity: the state. It is what distinguishes that from other territorial entities—to the extent that to talk of sovereignty is, in reality, to talk of the state. The traditional approach to sovereignty distinguishes between the meaning of the term in the domestic and in the international legal settings. In the former, it designates a supreme power or authority, often presented as absolute or unlimited—which is at least conceivably possible. It is, at any rate, a total and general power, implying the subordination of all individuals and groups encompassed within the state in question.

From the standpoint of international law, however, sovereignty refers not to unlimited power, but to the fact of not being subject to any higher authority, or to any obligation to which the sovereign has not consented. This definition does not, in itself, entail any substantive commitments. It is the legal translation of the political notion of independence (and thus contains the same ambiguities), and should be understood not as a power, but as a freedom:[3] the freedom of the state to exercise as it sees fit the powers at its disposal. This, however, does not necessarily imply that these powers are either unlimited or beyond all possible limitation. In effect, it is important not to confuse sovereignty with the various powers that the status of statehood implies, even if the former term is often used to describe those powers.[4] Talk of limiting sovereignty is thus concerned with placing limits on state freedom.

This proposition is more or less straightforward, given that international sovereignty is not conceived of as a singular or exclusive phenomenon, but rather in terms of a plurality of units existing within a community of equals. As with liberty, then, it can be said that the sovereignty of each finds its limit in that of others; an idea that has been expressed in the term 'reversibility of sovereignty',[5]

---

[3] Combacau, 'Pas une puissance, une liberté: la souveraineté internationale de l'Etat' *Pouvoirs*, n 67, *La souveraineté* (1993) 47–58.

[4] Powers that are thus qualified as 'sovereign'.

[5] See Virally, 'Panorama du droit international contemporain', *Rec. des Cours de l'Académie de droit international* (1983), vol V, tome 183, pp 13–381, esp. pp 76–84.

or in the concept of reciprocity. This becomes even more significant upon consideration of the direct corollary of sovereignty: the principle of equality. That these two notions are complementary is often viewed as self-evident: equality is implicit within, or presupposed by, sovereignty, at least according to the logic of international order (contrary to that of the domestic legal setting, a logic of subordination, in which the two are mutually exclusive). This being said, explicit discussion of this relation can serve to shed light on the concept of sovereignty itself: it signifies parity, the 'non-interchangeability of sovereigns',[6] and thus the prohibition on one state taking decisions for another. Each state has the right to decide for itself. 'Thus, the greatest paradox of international society is that it is founded upon a principle that, far from enabling integration within a single system, reinforces independence, autonomy, the pursuit of individual interests; that is, a principle that constructs a fundamentally individualistic and heterogeneous order.'[7] This corresponds well to the image of international society as characterized by a decentralized, heterarchical structure. However, even if sovereignty is not in itself a power, it has major implications for state powers, as can be seen from the following five supplementary observations.

(a) Even if we accept that the initial freedom (and thus sovereignty) of a state might be total, from the moment that it undertakes international commitments, it limits that freedom. Moreover, the fact that it may have to account for the manner in which it carries out these obligations does not call the idea of sovereignty itself into question. The internationalization of a question or a field creates a limitation on the sovereignty of states, as we shall see below in relation to human rights.

By contrast, any external attempt to get involved in a particular question or field with regard to which a state has intended to reserve its freedom (or sovereignty) will be viewed as interference in the internal affairs of the state concerned. The principle of non-interference in domestic affairs is one of the most strongly affirmed in international law, in classical doctrine at least. It is reflected, for example, in Article 2(7) of the UN Charter,[8] or in the explanations provided by the International Court of Justice (ICJ) in *Nicaragua v the United States* as to the general customary character and the content of the rule:

…in view of the generally accepted formulations, the principle forbids all States or groups of States to intervene directly or indirectly in internal or external affairs of other States. A prohibited intervention must accordingly be one bearing on matters in which each State is permitted, by the principle of State sovereignty, to decide freely. One of these is the choice of a political, economic, social and cultural system, and the formulation of

---

[6] Lejbowicz, *Philosophie du droit international—L'impossible capture de l'humanité*, Paris, PUF (1999) 24.

[7] Ibid.

[8] Guillaume, 'Commentaire de l'article 2 §7', in Cot and Pellet (eds), *La Charte des Nations Unies—Commentaire article par article* (3rd edn, Paris: Economica, 2005) pp 485–507.

foreign policy. Intervention is wrongful when it uses methods of coercion in regard to such choices, which must remain free ones.[9]

Nevertheless, from the perspective of international law, there exist no affairs that are necessarily internal by nature (which is not, of course, necessarily the position taken by domestic law).[10] There does, however, remain the question of whether there is a limit to the possible extent of internationalization, in the sense that, beyond a certain level of commitment, sovereignty could no longer be said to exist (even if the content of this minimum core is not necessarily well defined). This is a question to which we shall return, precisely because the international-ization of human rights seeks to counter one of the basic principles of classical international law, according to which states have the absolute right to determine the fate of their own nationals. In this regard, the state was traditionally viewed as a watertight cell, protected from outside enquiry (with the exception of the early recognition of a 'right of observation' for foreign states in respect of their own nationals, based on the ideas of a 'minimum standard of humanity' and that the state of residence owed a duty of protection to such individuals).

(b) The preceding considerations were based upon the hypothesis of an inter-national law constructed from voluntarist premises. This certainly seems to cor-respond well to the idea of sovereignty implied by an international law created purely intersubjectively, between the subjects of that law—the states—them-selves.[11] This, however, represents only one particular understanding of the rela-tionship between states and law: the self-limitation thesis, which, influenced by certain Hegelian ideas, was most notably set out in the work of Jellenek, and which still has some adherents today. This is not, however, the only way to con-ceive of law, and a number of other perspectives have sought to maintain that, as international legal norms are formulated, certain 'extra-legal' values impose themselves on states. Moreover, there are many practical objections to the prop-osition that the state's freedom to choose its own obligations is unlimited, in particular concerning those drawn from what might be summarized under the general heading of 'interdependence-based constraints'.[12] This brings us on to the third remark.

(c) Sovereignty is marked by the same ambiguity as is the notion of independ-ence, of which it is but the legal version. In this regard, the fictive nature of the

---

[9] *Case concerning Military and Paramilitary Activities in and Against Nicaragua*, ICJ Reps (1986) p 108, para 205.

[10] This explains, eg the questions of constitutionality that may be raised against restrictions on sovereignty arising from integration treaties, such as those of the European Community. See Grewe and Ruiz Fabri, *Droits constitutionnels européens* (Paris: PUF, 1995) at pp 126–33; see also, by the same authors, 'La situation respective du droit international et du droit communautaire dans le droit constitutionnel des États', in 'Droit international et droit communautaire. Perspectives actuelles', *Colloque SFDI deBordeaux* (Paris: Pedone, 2000) at pp 251–82.

[11] Combacau, 'Le droit international, bric-à-brac ou système?', 31 Arch. Phil. Dr. (986) pp 85–105.

[12] Virally, above n 5, p 77.

concept is sometimes stressed, in that it holds as established something that does not in fact exist: its definition does not correspond to the prevailing reality, in which inequalities of power, relations of domination and subordination, and practices of clientelism are widespread. Of course, law has frequent recourse to such fictions, and this one is largely functional in nature. Sovereignty is a model: as with any model, it is presented as absolute, only to immediately produce or recognize exceptions. This is all the easier as there exists no rigid legal framework or a priori definition, which leaves ample space for state strategies that are at once pragmatic and selective. It is, however, important to note that, even if the legal definition of sovereignty does not postulate an a priori and authoritatively identified content to that concept, classical doctrine nevertheless opted to include certain substantive elements in its definition thereof. Thus we generally recognize that, as the ICJ noted in the above-mentioned *Nicaragua* case, sovereignty implies the right to freely choose the political regime and internal organization of the state, to choose its economic system and to control its natural resources, and to govern the status of goods and people on its territory (at least in relation to its own nationals).

(d) Sovereignty has been affected by certain developments, such as the rise in power of human rights (an approximate formulation that will suffice for the moment), or what is sometimes conveniently referred to as 'globalization'. There exists currently an entire current of thought that questions the permanence of the state, even if it has found more support among political scientists[13] or economists[14] than lawyers. The point is generally to stress the growing impotence of states, their openness to a number of movements that challenge their control over their territory or population, and their increasing vulnerability. In any event, it is important to determine whether the differences introduced by these developments are of degree or of kind, and to seek to uncover their legal implications.[15]

(e) Though we earlier distinguished fairly clearly between the domestic and the international sense of sovereignty, this clearly does not mean there is no link between them at all. On the contrary, it is important to take into consideration the effect that an evolution in the understanding of one sense might affect that of the other, particularly as this distinction was traditionally associated with what

---

[13] See, eg B Badie, *Un monde sans souveraineté—Les Etats entre ruse et responsabilité*, (Paris: Fayard, 1999) p 306.

[14] For the basic issue, see Arnaud, *Entre modernité et mondialisation—Leçons d'histoire de la philosophie du droit et de l'Etat* (2nd edn Paris: LGDJ, 2004) ch 4; Arnaud, 'De la régulation par le droit à l'heure de la globalisation', 35 *Droit et société* (1997) 11–35; M Delmas-Marty, *Trois défis pour un droit mondial* (Paris: Seuil, 1998) p 205. See also Ruiz Fabri, 'Immatériel, territorialité et Etat', 43 Arch. Phil. Dr. (1999) pp 187–212; 'Mondialisation et gouvernance', Problèmes économiques (1999) no 2.611–2.612 (numéro spécial); O Dollfus, *La mondialisation* (3rd edn Paris: Presses de Sciences Po, 2007) Chapter 6; Moreau Defarges, *La mondialisation* (6th edn Paris: PUF, 2005); Latouche, *Les dangers du marché planétaire*, (Paris: Presses de Sciences Po, 1998) p 132.

[15] S Sur, 'L'Etat entre l'éclatement et la mondialisation', RBDI (1997) pp 5–20.

has sometimes been referred to as the 'two-spheres theory':[16] an internal sphere regulated by domestic law, and an external sphere governed by international law (which in turn leads on to the issues of the separation of the legal orders and of dualism). According to certain viewpoints, however, 'the introduction of the protection of human rights within the international legal order implies the negation of the two-sphere theory upon which classical international law was constructed'.[17]

Human Rights

Human rights, both historically and substantively, are primarily concerned with the relations between individuals and authority.[18] If we accept the definition of these rights as 'the prerogatives, governed by rules, that the person (physical or legal) holds in his relations with other persons (physical or legal) or with the Government',[19] then the development of human rights protection implies a limitation on state power. This limitation can be brought in at the domestic level; indeed, the first major human rights texts were domestic legal instruments, such as, of course, the *Déclaration des droits de l'homme et du citoyen* of 26 August 1789, immediately preceded by the American Declaration of Independence of 4 July 1776. These texts had in common their claims to the universality of, and their appeal to a rational foundation for, the rights that they guaranteed to individuals, which the public authorities had to respect. It is from this moment on—if we disregard the British case, which was in some senses even earlier—that the slow conquest of the Rule of Law began, in Europe and North America in any event. An important trend in this regard was the drafting of written constitutions, which both made concrete and guaranteed the limitation of power through individual rights, complemented by the doctrine of separation of powers within the internal constitutional structure of the state.

However, events such as the failure of European liberal constitutions in the inter-war period led to the search for guarantees at a supposedly superior level, and thus a turn towards international order. The internationalization of human rights, which had begun in certain sectors before the Second World War,[20] but which mostly developed afterwards, came in response to the will to create a law

---

[16] Virally, 'Droits de l'homme et théorie générale du droit', *Mélanges Cassin*, (Paris: Pedone, 1969) tome 4, 323–30.

[17] F Sudre, *Droit européen et international des droits de l'homme* (8th edn Paris: PUF, 2006) p 45.

[18] Vedel, 'Les droits de l'homme: quels droits, quel homme?', *Mélanges René-Jean Dupuy*, (Paris: Pedone 1991) pp 349–62.

[19] J Mourgeon, *Les droits de l'homme* (8th edn Paris: PUF, 2003) p 10.

[20] The international protection of human rights began with humanitarian law, that is human rights in conflict situations (circumstantial protection), and then developed through various categories of individuals (such as the worker, with the establishment of the ILO), or members of minorities (after the First World War in Europe). It is only after the Second World War that a globalized and general human rights movement began to emerge.

external to, and independent from, power.[21] The individual, as an object of law, thus began his slow journey towards appropriation of the status of international legal *subject*.[22] It is as a result of this process of internationalization that the human rights/state sovereignty issue has emerged.

The Human Rights–State Sovereignty Issue

It is necessary to revise the classical notion of sovereignty, still defined as the fact of not being subject to any higher authority, by attributing to it a certain substance—at the core of which is the state's absolute right to determine the fate of its own nationals. This right is protected and guaranteed by the principle of non-interference in internal affairs, which goes hand in hand with the free choice of political and economic system. The internationalization of human rights has, however, changed the sphere of application of this principle, and, with it, what we might term the 'substantive boundaries' of what has been referred to here as the 'external' element of sovereignty. This evolution is a priori compatible with the idea of sovereignty outlined above, in which the substance of the concept is not abstractly determined from a legal point of view. At the same time, moreover, it has been desired, and encouraged, by certain states, most notably by those who have themselves accepted limitations on power at the domestic level—legal limitations on the state, founded upon the need to protect fundamental individual rights.

It is, moreover, during the same period that what might be termed the 'substantive dimension' of the rule of law began to emerge: it was no longer sufficient to guarantee that the state was subject to the law through the establishment of a hierarchy of laws with the constitution at the top; instead, the state was compelled to respect certain norms expressing values that were no longer to be violated. There is a certain coherence in the manner in which the states in question have sought an internationalization of their domestic situation, which would provide supplementary, or perhaps even additional, guarantees, and to secure their extension to all states. The difficulty, however, lies in ascertaining the extent to which this development can be pushed; for, even in those states that have actively desired, even provoked, such an internationalization of human rights protections, an inevitable tension is created. Driven by the conviction that the state is not 'sufficient' to guarantee respect for human rights—indeed, that it can even compromise such respect—it can clearly serve to call sovereignty itself into question, as is sometimes expressed in the provocative claim that 'human rights represent the subversion of the state'.

---

[21] See P Wachsmann, *Les droits de l'homme* (4th edn, Paris: Dalloz, 2003) p 3.

[22] Sperduti, 'L'individu et le droit international', *Rec. des Cours de l'Académie de droit international* (1983), vol II, tome 90, 733–849; Dupuy, 'L'individu et le droit international', 32 Arch. Phil. Dr. (1987) 119–33.

If we begin with a simplistic understanding of sovereignty, based upon classical definitions, we first come up against a straightforward opposition between that concept and human rights: the idea that the international protection of human rights necessarily implies a limitation of sovereignty. It is true that adopting such a perspective has proved a relatively fruitful way in which to approach the issue: in doing so, we can in effect describe almost the entire development of international human rights law, and grasp the extent to which this has led to the limitation of sovereignty as classically understood. It is above all in this context that the question to be addressed in this chapter, of whether the 'boundaries of sovereignty have been significantly redrawn', is raised. In any event, we must conclude here that the substantive boundaries have been altered, and in many different ways.

The issues are, however, somewhat more complicated than this approach suggests. First of all, even if, as indicated above, the legal definition of sovereignty need not necessarily contain those elements attributed to in the classical approach, it must nevertheless be determined whether, when tested against human rights, some sort of minimum and/or determinate content is implied. Even if the question can be framed in this manner, however, we can immediately see that it remains locked in an apparently paradoxical dynamic—illustrated, for example, by the fact that, by odd historical coincidence, human rights protection has developed at the same time as the number of states has multiplied. It is at this point that the uncertainties and ambiguities begin. Must we accept the hypothesis of a continuing evolution towards the 'objectification' of human rights—towards the recognition, over and above a subjective dimension already indicative of a relatively advanced level of protection, of an objective dimension that would allow us to speak of a general law of humanity, or to approximate the kind of *ius cosmopoliticum* desired by Kant?[23] This would represent a radical break from international law as it is still largely understood today, characterized by an intersubjectivity which turns it into the 'law of sovereignty'. Or might we rather simply conclude that there are certain specific features of international human rights law that sovereignty recognizes—something of a false concession on the part of the latter, as that recognition is also a means of isolating and limiting the potentially subversive force of the tension introduced into classical international legal doctrine by human rights?

The hypothesis of international protection of human rights as a source of an 'international public order', which has acquired an objective dimension and thus moved beyond the classical intersubjective approach derived from sovereignty (or, more precisely, from the juxtaposition of a plurality of competing sovereigns), presupposes, however, a degree of harmonization far beyond that which has been achieved. It must also confront the existence of other, competing trends. In order

---

[23] Habermas, *L'intégration républicaine—essais de théorie politique* (Paris: Fayard, 1998) p 164; N Bobbio, *L'Etat et la démocratie internationale* (Brussels: Editions Complexe, 1998) p 151.

to demonstrate this, it is sufficient merely to consider the widespread banalization of violence and of human rights abuses: only massive violations seem capable today of provoking responses from, and producing effects within, the international legal order. Accordingly, we must consider two further factors in order to be able to locate sovereignty in relation to human rights in the contemporary world.

First, the relativism that characterizes the protection of human rights must be taken into account. This is a direct consequence of the counter-trend towards preservation of traditional sovereign rights. It can be deployed in a variety of different ways, drawing selectively from the plethora of sites and sources of legal significance in relation to the interpretation and protection of human rights, and can readily facilitate strategies of protectionism and/or evasion. Ultimately, it corresponds to an internationalization that remains above all 'inter-statal' in character; that is, to human rights protection at once directed against and guaranteed by the state—which provides little or no protection against the instrumental use of that discourse by the state in order to pursue its own interests.

Secondly, and relatedly, not all limitations on sovereignty are necessarily favourable to human rights; and neither does every affirmation of one represent a threat to the other. Put otherwise, not every advance in terms of human rights protection presupposes an opposite and equal retreat of sovereignty. Human rights are a discourse addressed to power: not only in terms of a demand for respect, but also of protection. Moreover, to question the ordering principle that sovereignty represents seems to require, in the final instance, a determination of what to establish in its place. Sovereignty is, after all, currently faced with a number of fundamental challenges, conveniently grouped together under the rubric of 'globalization': the resulting dilution of power does not automatically correspond to improvements in the level of actual human rights protections, particularly where it is not accompanied by the creation of instruments or other means capable of contributing to the development of a genuine 'law of humanity'.

The overall impression that emerges from the foregoing considerations is that *precisely because* human rights require a limitation of power—and of the concept of sovereignty upon which that power is based— it would be counter-productive to overly weaken the state. Instead, what is needed is consideration of a particular *type* of state—one that approaches the model of the rule of law in its structures and practices. Doing so provides us with a way of taking into account this permanent and inherent ambivalence, this realization that human rights discourse cannot afford to treat the state as nothing more than an oppressive structure to be opposed wherever possible. To the postulation of a simple correlation between the expansion of human rights and the limitation of sovereignty must be added, then, an understanding of the equivocal and ambivalent forces at work in terms of the development of the former and the future of the latter.

1. The Simple Correlation: Expansion of Human Rights and Limitation of Sovereignty

This correlation is without doubt one of the most dramatic aspects of the question at issue here: clearly, what are generally presented as decisive advances in human rights protection normally go hand in hand with limitations on sovereignty. This issue is related to that which underlies the foundations of international law as a whole, reflected in the preoccupation in classical theory with whether limitations on sovereignty were ultimately autonomous or heteronymous. The self-limitation approach, defended by the voluntarists and expounded most notably by Jellinek,[24] holds that the state is bound only by rules to which it has consented: the sovereign understood as free even to limit that freedom.

There exist, however, serious doubts concerning the effectiveness of obligations thus construed—as being vulnerable to relations of power and domination, or simply to the unilateral will of the state, rendering it difficult to ensure the independent authority of law. Such concerns lay behind the proposal of alternative conceptions, such as those of the naturalists or of authors like George Scelle, for whom state sovereignty was limited by extra-legal values, both common to humanity and necessary for effective legal order.[25] This general debate is particularly relevant in the context of human rights, precisely because here we are not simply dealing with supplementary legal norms, but with a discourse of putatively transcendental values. Moreover, outwith the theoretical controversies, there has been a clear historical evolution: while classical positivism, which has its roots in the nineteenth century, understood itself to be indifferent to the content of law, the dominant approach today claims no such neutrality, instead viewing such positions as themselves deeply situated and subjective.

This is why it is necessary to inquire into how limitations on sovereignty function in the context of human rights. The types of limitation to which sovereignty can be subject in the name of human rights are many and varied, particularly if we distinguish between those that are either desired or accepted, and those that are involuntary or beyond its capacity to resist. The degree of limitation is equally variable, according to whether a particular competence is removed entirely or merely conditioned, the type of legal instrument employed, and the existence or otherwise of international mechanisms to monitor and control fulfilment of obligations.

These two aspects—of type and degree—obviously interact. A limitation might go against the wishes of the state in question but remain fairly weak in degree, and thus remain tolerable even where it provokes protest. It is, however,

---

[24] See A Truyol y Serra, *Histoire du droit international public*, (Economica, 1995) 118.
[25] See, eg G Scelle, *Cours de Droit international public* (Paris: Montchrestien, 1948) 4–24.

also possible that certain limitations will, as a result of their degree alone, be necessarily undesired by those subject to them.

A. Types of Limitations: The Formal Question

If, then, the intuitive conviction exists that effective protection of human rights requires limitations on state sovereignty, it is still necessary to ascertain precisely what these limitations consist of. According to the Permanent Court of International Justice (PCIJ), limitations on the independence of states cannot be presumed; in other words, they must be explicit.[26] Does this mean that they must be desired by the state in question, thus remaining compatible with the idea of sovereignty that informed the 'auto-limitation' thesis? This was the position taken by the Court in the case referred to here. In reality, however, the issues are more complex than this suggests; and any attempt to resolve them requires a prior choice of which approach to adopt.

The choice is between an extensive and a restrictive approach to sovereignty: the former allowing involuntary limitations and the latter excluding them. The latter would understand only involuntary limitations as genuine infringements of sovereignty, viewing the free choice to undertake binding obligations as an exercise of that sovereignty itself. Nevertheless, it seems easier to operationalize the former approach, particularly when we realize that, although the distinction between limitations that are accepted or not is the most obvious, it is necessary to distinguish between two further types: those that a state can choose not to engage in, and those that it views itself as powerless to resist or refuse. This latter consideration, which I will term here the element of 'irrecusability', is evidently not legal in nature, but enables us to move beyond the formalism of analyses based purely on the will of states.

Voluntary Limitations

In the *SS Wimbledon* case, the PCIJ clearly endorsed the conclusion that entering into a treaty obligation cannot be viewed as a surrender of state sovereignty. To be sure, it recognized that an international instrument might mean 'a restriction upon the exercise of the sovereign rights of the State, in the sense that it requires them to be exercised in a certain way. But the right to enter into international engagements is an attribute of State sovereignty.'[27] Thus, each time that a state undertakes an obligation in terms of human rights protection, it is in fact exercising its sovereignty. It is worth noting that the number of instruments relating to the protection of human rights has multiplied, particularly during the last 50 or so years. There is no need here to provide an exhaustive account of these; a brief glance is sufficient to tell us that most states have made a range of undertakings

---

[26] *Lotus*, 1927 PCIJ Series A, Nos 10, 18.
[27] 1923 PCIJ Series A, Nos 1, 25.

in this area, and thus find themselves locked into a fairly dense normative network, including instruments of regional and/or global reach, pertaining to certain categories of individuals, certain specific sectors, or, indeed, to everybody, everywhere.

(a) From a historical perspective, the oldest texts are the humanitarian law conventions, the elaboration of which began in the nineteenth century (even if, before this, we might note the existence of a customary norm of a 'minimum standard of humanity').[28] The first Geneva Convention, signed on 22 August 1864, was then followed by a series of others, developed in response to changes in the nature of warfare. The aim was to protect human rights in times of war; that is, in certain special circumstances. That which is called 'humanitarian law' today has acquired a quasi-universal status, the relevant conventions having been ratified by a very large proportion of the world's states.

It was, however, only after the First World War, and in particular after the Second World War, that the international protection of human rights began to take off. In 1918, the Treaty of Versailles introduced two important innovations in this regard, albeit limited in scope to certain categories of individuals. The first was to establish a system of protection of minorities: a protection of the human rights of members of a particular group in order to ensure both non-discrimination and respect for difference. This system, however, after a period of vacuum and great upheaval in Europe, disappeared to be replaced by a new set of instruments that inscribed the protections it offered within a global framework. The second innovation introduced at Versailles was the establishment of the International Labour Organization, again tasked with the protection of a particular category of individual: the worker.[29] It was empowered to negotiate and draft conventions, which nevertheless then required the consent of each individual state, with the provisions only binding between parties.

It was only after the Second World War that the idea of general and more global human rights protections appeared, and that 'the whole international community affirmed the whole body of human rights'.[30] The UN Charter contains traces of this in its preamble and in a number of its provisions, in particular those dealing with the mandate of the General Assembly and of the Economic and Social Council. However, the emblematic text is, of course, the Universal Declaration of Human Rights (UDHR), proclaimed on 10 December 1948. Certainly, formally speaking this was only a resolution of the General Assembly, and as such did not constitute a source of obligations for states; nevertheless, it is widely accepted that the principles it sets forth have now attained the status

---

[28] See generally Hans-Peter Gasser, 'A Measure of Humanity in Internal Disturbances and Tensions: Proposal for a Code of Conduct', 262 International Review of the Red Cross (1988) 38.

[29] Laviec, 'La protection des droits économiques et sociaux de l'homme par l'Organisation internationale du Travail', RUDH (1991) 61–9.

[30] Mourgeon, above n 19 p 75 ['*l'ensemble de la Société internationale affirme l'ensemble des droits de l'homme*'].

of customary law.[31] Moreover, it began the process that would lead to the elaboration of the International Covenants of 16 December 1966 (one on civil and political rights, which also came with an Optional Protocol, and the other on economic, social, and cultural rights). Together, these three instruments became known as the International Bill of Human Rights, to which approximately two thirds of UN Member States are parties. Alongside these fundamental texts, a number of conventions have been adopted on particular issues at the universal level, including on the prevention and punishment of the crime of genocide (in 1948); the suppression of the traffic in persons and of the exploitation of the prostitution of others (in 1949); the abolition of slavery (in 1953 and 1956); the elimination of apartheid (1973); the elimination of all forms of discrimination against women (1979); the struggle against torture and other inhuman or degrading treatment or punishment (1984); the rights of the child (1989); and the creation of the International Criminal Court (ICC) (1998).[32] This list is far from exhaustive, and moreover includes only those instruments that create binding legal obligations; the field is, however, replete with other resolutions, declarations and other texts, important even if only in terms of laying the framework for progress in both normative and behavioural terms.[33]

(b) To this already dense normative network—the individual components of which do not, however, bind all states—we must add the important developments that have occurred at the regional level (with the exception of Asia), which also favour a general approach to protection. In Europe, these developments came about first of all within the context of the Council of Europe, beginning with the European Convention for the Protection of Human Rights and Fundamental Freedoms (ECHR) of 4 November 1950, supplemented by numerous additional protocols. To this we can add the European Social Charter (1961) and a number of specific instruments such as the European Convention for the Prevention of Torture and Inhuman or Degrading Treatment or Punishment (1987); the European Charter for Regional or Minority Languages (1992); the Framework Convention for the Protection of National Minorities (1995); the European Convention on the Exercise of Children's Rights (1996); and the Convention on Bioethics (1997), amongst others.

To the instruments adopted by the Council of Europe, we can further add the work carried out within the framework of the Conference on Security and Cooperation in Europe (CSCE, which later became the Organization for Security and Cooperation in Europe, OSCE) with the Helsinki Final Act

[31] See P Daillier and A Pellet (Nguyen Quoc Dinh), *Droit international public* (7th edn Paris: LGDJ, 2002) p 646.

[32] The limitations on sovereignty that it entails explain in large degree the intitial difficulties it encountered in attracting ratifications. In France, ratification required an amendment to the Preamble of the Constitution.

[33] Decaux, 'De la promotion à la protection des droits de l'homme—Droit déclaratoire et droit programmatoire', in SFDI, *La protection des droits de l'homme et l'évolution du droit international*, (Paris: Pedone, 1998) 81–119.

(initially a non-binding document), and with the development of its 'human dimension'.[34] We can further add here the work carried out within the context of the European Union: although its treaty provisions were initially limited to codifying (and at the same time 'constitutionalizing') the relevant case law,[35] and proceeded essentially by reference to external instruments such as the ECHR, it has now developed its own Charter of Fundamental Rights; although this text, at time of writing, has not yet entered into force. In America, a similar process has developed under the aegis of the Organization of American States (OAS), beginning with the American Declaration of the Rights and Duties of Man in 1948, followed by the American Convention on Human Rights in 1969. In Africa, the African Charter on Human and People's Rights (1981) was elaborated under the auspices of the Organization of African Unity (OAU). The League of Arab States adopted the Arab Charter on Human Rights in 1994.

This list is far from exhaustive, but it does serve to demonstrate the large number of instruments that exist in the field, and to indicate the cumulative effect that can result from this. Together, they constitute a genuine normative network, and we must acknowledge that any state that has subscribed to a large number of these instruments is thus subject to an important set of obligations (even if certain provisions are redundant, and not all are of the same formally binding character, as we shall see below).

(c) If, until this point, we have focused exclusively on treaties, we should perhaps also recognize the existence of unwritten obligations, which many authors view as beyond doubt.[36] Thus, the ICJ was able to affirm, in its advisory opinion on *Reservations to the Convention on the Prevention and Punishment of the Crime of Genocide*,[37] that 'the principles underlying the Convention are principles which are recognized by civilized nations as binding on States, even without any conventional obligation'. It further added, in the *Barcelona Traction* case,[38] that certain 'basic rights of the human person . . . have entered into the body of general international law'; and also recognized, in its Opinion on *The Legality of the Threat or Use of Nuclear Weapons*, the existence of certain 'intransgressible principles'[39] of humanitarian law.[40] Affirmations of this sort lend credence to the claims of

---

[34] A shorthand phrase to refer to the human rights and humanitarian provisions concluded within the framework of the Helsinki process. See E Decaux and L-A Sicilianos (eds), *La CSCE: dimension humaine et règlement des différends* (Paris: Montchrestien, 1993) 281.

[35] F Sudre, 'La Communauté européenne et les droits fondamentaux après le Traité d'Amsterdam: vers un nouveau système européen de protection des droits de l'homme?', JCP (1998) I, 100.

[36] Flauss, 'La protection des droits de l'homme et les sources du droit international', in S.F.D.I., Colloque de Strasbourg, La protection des droits de l'homme et l'évolution du droit international, Pedone, Paris, 1998, p 13.

[37] Advisory Opinion of 28 May 1951, ICJ Rep (1951) 23.

[38] Judgment of 5 February 1970, ICJ Rep (1970) 32.

[39] Advisory Opinion of 8 July 1996, ICJ Rep (1996) § 79.

[40] See Ruiz Fabri and Sorel, 'Chronique de jurisprudence de la Cour internationale de Justice—année 1996', JDI (1997) 869–83.

numerous scholars as to the declaratory and codifying nature of the UDHR, and to the work of the International Law Commission on the international responsibility of states, to name but a few examples. However, taking unwritten laws into consideration leads us away from the firm and certain terrain of obligations based upon the clear consent of states that we find in the context of treaty law; and it can provide grounds for those who argue in favour of non-voluntary limitations on state sovereignty.

Non-Voluntary Limitations

This category refers to all limitations imposed, whether by coercion or otherwise, on the liberty of states in the name of human rights—the key question being whether and under what circumstances the objective of rights protection can render such limitations legal under international law.

(a) We might thus consider from this perspective any sanctions imposed for violations of human rights: the classical problem of countermeasures. For example, can a state or group of states unilaterally decree an embargo against another, such as the Ugandan embargo imposed by the US in 1978? More recent examples of the same phenomenon include the regional embargo against Burundi in the years following the Rwandan genocide, and the oil embargo imposed upon the Federal Republic of Yugoslavia by NATO in 1999, before the latter began its 'direct intervention'. This is a thorny issue, as it is necessary to determine whether countermeasures based upon the claim that a certain type of illegal act has been committed (for example a violation of human rights) are themselves legal even though the states concerned claim no violation of 'their' rights.[41] When such a measure is adopted by a state or group of states, the logic of reciprocity does not suggest that the aim of 'human rights protection' can alone render legal actions that would otherwise be impermissible. Such actions are always suspect, and 'caution is required whenever a universal right to take unilateral counter measures is invoked'[42]—even where this 'right' is exercised collectively and in the name of human rights. Certainly, the ICJ referred, following its enumeration of the obligations *erga omnes* in the *Barcelona Traction* case, to 'rights of protection' corresponding to the fundamental rights of the human person that have 'entered into the body of general international law', or are 'conferred by international instruments of a universal or quasi-universal character';[43] but 'it would be rash, on the basis of this dictum alone, to include in these "rights of protection" a capacity for states only indirectly wronged to take counter-measures'.[44] The uncertainties, even doubts, over the right to act in such circumstances thus remain strong. What, then, can be said in terms of more direct forms of intervention?

---

[41] On this point, see D Alland, *Justice privée et ordre juridique international—Etude théorique des contre-mesures en droit international public* (Paris: Pedone, 1994) at p 503.

[42] Ibid. p 360.

[43] *Barcelona Traction* judgment above, n 38.

[44] Alland, above n 41 at p 364.

(b) The central issue within the context of non-voluntary limitations on sovereignty is, of course, that of interference in the 'internal affairs' of a state—particularly in the form of coercive action. The key question here is whether such action
acquires specific characteristics when its objective is the protection of human
rights; a debate nourished by the movement from a 'right of intervention' to a
duty to provide 'humanitarian assistance'.[45] The putative existence of an obligation, and not merely a power, to intervene clearly impacts profoundly on the issue
in question.

The theme of humanitarian intervention has been much discussed in the course
of the last decade. At the very least, the existence of a right to provide assistance
finds support in statements of the ICJ, according to which 'the provision of strictly
humanitarian aid to persons or forces in another country ... cannot be regarded
as unlawful intervention', on the condition that it is non-discriminatory.[46] This
potential right, however, suffers from the imperialist connotations that have historically (and justly) been attached to those actions conveniently referred to as
interventions 'for the sake of humanity', and which weigh heavily on any decision
to intervene taken unilaterally by a state or group of states.[47] The Vietnamese
intervention in Cambodia in 1979 raised questions of this sort: was it to be
regarded as legal simply because it had made the world a better place? The issue is
rendered even more complex by the fact that the general—and related—question
of the use of force also arises. This explains why an institutional response has been
sought, in the form of an organization charged with policing the use of force: the
United Nations.

The General Assembly has, of course, often considered the issue of humanitarian intervention. And even if its resolutions do not have a formally binding character, states might nonetheless be tempted to draw from them a capacity to act.
In any event, these resolutions normally characterize themselves as respecting the
sovereignty of the state targeted by the intervention.[48] Thus, Resolution 43/131
of 8 December 1988 declares itself 'mindful of the importance of humanitarian
assistance' even as it reaffirms 'the sovereignty of states and their primary role'[49]
in providing such assistance on their own territories. A similar formulation is

[45] See, eg Pellet, 'Droit d'ingérence ou devoir d'assistance humanitaire', 758–9 *Problèmes
politiques et sociaux* (1995) 133. This movement has gained in momentum considerably since the
2005 World Summit, in which states endorsed the idea of a 'responsibility to protect': see Alex J
Bellamy, 'Whither the Responsibility to Protect? Humanitarian Intervention and the 2005 World
Summit', 20 Ethics and International Affairs (2006) 143–69.
[46] *Nicaragua* judgment above n 9, at pp 125–6.
[47] Sorel, 'Le devoir d'ingérence: longue histoire et ambiguïté constante', 3 Relations internationales et stratégiques (1991) 95–108.
[48] Eisemann, 'Devoir d'ingérence et non-intervention: de la nécessité de remettre quelques pendules à l'heure', 3 Relations internationales et stratégiques (1991) 67–75.
[49] GA Res. 43/131 (1988), 'Humanitarian assistance to victims of natural disasters and similar
emergency situations', Art 2. See also Bettati, 'Souveraineté et assistance humanitaire: réflexion
sur la portée et les limites de la résolution 43/131 de l'Assemblée générale de l'ONU', *Mélanges
René-Jean Dupuy*, 38–42.

used in Resolution 45/100 of 14 December 1990.[50] Both, however, are limited in scope, as they deal only with cases of natural catastrophe or comparable emergencies; not with situations in which the humanitarian necessity is linked to human rights violations, to that which might termed 'political catastrophes'. The latter situations were quite deliberately excluded—which is hardly surprising. What we can draw from the wealth of discussions on the existence of a duty of humanitarian assistance—including those falling under the 'Annan Doctrine', which promoted an obligation to intervene when confronted with massive human rights violations—is that such assistance may only be imposed upon a state under certain precise conditions, in particular the use of Chapter VII powers by the Security Council. It is only in such circumstances that humanitarian intervention, itself limited to cases involving massive violations of human rights, is envisaged; if human security is at all considered, it is thus only insofar as this exists in a tight and symbiotic relationship with that of states.

This practice is heavily influenced by the fact that the competence of the Security Council—although very broad indeed, and all the more so because it retains the discretionary power to define the character of any given situation—is not in itself unlimited. There must exist a threat to or a breach of international peace and/or security. We know that the Security Council has already accepted that massive violations of human rights can fall under this description—and this is in no way an abusive extension of the Preamble to the Charter, which clearly links peace and human rights, making the latter a precondition of the former. Nevertheless, this linkage is mentioned nowhere in the actual definition of the Council's powers. These powers must thus be interpreted according to a contextual approach, even a principle of effectiveness, if we are to account for the manner in which practice has evolved. In other words, a dynamic view must be taken of the Security Council's capacity to respond to situations as they arise. In fact, the Council has already authorized interventions on this basis: in Iraq, with Resolution 668 of 5 April 1991 (although it is worth noting that, even if it did compel Iraqi cooperation, this was limited to 'insisting' that Iraq allow access to persons in need of assistance); in Somalia, with Resolution 794 of 3 December 1992; and again in East Timor in 1999. Of these, the Somalian case is particularly interesting, in that there the Security Council based its action upon the collapse of the Somali state (which thus lacked capacity to request or accept an intervention) and upon the needs of the Somali people, whereas in other cases a (more or less constrained) consent on the part of the state in question could be relied upon. Nevertheless, the example of Bosnia, followed by that of Kosovo, demonstrates that humanitarian assistance can become the principal objective of collective intervention, the justification both for the resort to force and the adoption of coercive measures such as embargoes. It can even prove to be one stage in

---

a process of acquiring independence, and thus sovereignty—as the examples of Kosovo and East Timor illustrate.

(c) The manner in which the Security Council has used its powers raises the issue, alongside that of intervention, of the creation of tribunals that can compete with states in the exercise of their functions, without these functions having been consented to. The clearest example remains the establishment of the international criminal tribunals for ex-Yugoslavia and for Rwanda, which are not only competent to pass judgment on a wide range of crimes committed on the territories of the respective states, but also, in exercising this function, are given primacy over national courts.

Formulated in this manner, the question remains ambiguous: everything depends upon the proximity required between consent and relevant action. It can always be claimed—and this is the magic of the 'institutional filter'—that by joining the United Nations, all states have accepted that this type of decision can be taken. From this perspective, there remain only a few extreme cases, such as the (academic) hypothesis of the invocation of the Security Council's Chapter VII against states that are not members of the UN, or—more importantly—situations such as the use of force by NATO Member States in Kosovo in 1999. In any event, even if we embrace an extremely broad notion of 'consent', we arrive here at the supplementary criterion referred to above: that of *irrecusability*.

The Element of Irrecusability

The distinction between voluntary and involuntary limitations find its own limit in what I have here termed as the 'element of irrecusability'. This can arise in a number of different ways, such as situations in which states are powerless to refuse; in which normative consequences are unforeseeable; or in which new limitations are generated or developed through a process of normative evolution.

(a) First, even limitations to which states have formally consented can be characterized as irrecusable, most often for economic reasons. This is the case, for example, in human rights conditionality clauses in aid agreements, which in reality the receiving state is powerless to resist even if their formal consent is required. Certainly, such consent is real, and conditionality clauses are not illegal as they are linked to the granting of a benefit and not to the fulfilment of an obligation. Nevertheless, everything depends here on the degree to which the receiving state *needs* the benefit in question. Conditionality clauses are widely used, and a large number of them include human rights elements: the European Union, for example, has developed a policy in this regard, reflected in its frequent insertion of clauses relating to democratic governance and respect for human rights in the Association Agreements that it concludes with non-Member States. One of the clearest examples of this practice is to be found in the mid-term revision of the Lome IV Convention of 1989, which contained a provision mandating the suspension of cooperation in the event of grave violations of human rights, which was further strengthened in the Lome V Convention by the inclusion of an obligation to participate in the fight against corruption. Similar practices can also be identified in the policies of the IMF and the World Bank,[51] for example in the 'good governance' programme of the latter.

Another example, albeit in a slightly different sense (in which, although the aim remains the same, we are no longer operating within the context of treaty provisions or of essentially economic necessity), is provided by the attempt of many EU Member States to make the recognition of the new states emerging from the break-up of Yugoslavia conditional upon the fulfilment of certain conditions, amongst which both a commitment to respect human rights, and to ratify the relevant international treaties in this regard, figured prominently. This was the aim behind the 'Guidelines on the Recognition of New States in Eastern Europe and in the Soviet Union' of 16 December 1991,[52] with the Yugoslavia Arbitration Commission then examining each of the emerging states in order to ascertain whether these conditions had been met.[53] Again in this sense, we might consider also the attempts to promote a doctrine of 'automatic accession' to international human rights treaties in the event of state dissolution, which emerged notably during the break-up of the Soviet Union and Yugoslavia, and the separation of Czechoslovakia.[54] A solution of this sort would imbue the international human rights regime with something very similar to an 'objective' element.

(b) This brings us on to a different aspect of the issue under consideration here: the political irrecusability of human rights discourse, which leads states to undertake obligations that they may find distasteful. This often arises in the context of the need to offer guarantees and make concessions in any given negotiating process; we might, for example, read the Chinese ratification of the International Covenant on Economic, Social and Cultural Rights (ICESCR) in March 2001 in these terms. This conclusion must, however, remain ambiguous, as the Chinese decision could equally be analysed in terms of an instrumentalization or a functionalization, perhaps even a strategic misuse, of human rights discourse—a point to which I will return below.

Another ambiguity results from the play of the notion of irrecusability itself. For example, the manner in which the concept of a 'duty of humanitarian intervention' functions means that such intervention is imposed both on the target state and on the state or states carrying it out. The latter can thus find themselves bound by pre-existing commitments in situations that were never originally envisaged. When the UK ratified the 1984 Torture Convention, it

---

[51] Sorel, 'Les aspects juridiques de la conditionnalité du FMI', EJIL (1996) 42–66.

[52] The text of the guidelines is available as an annex to Danilo Türk, 'Recognition of States: A Comment', 4 EJIL (1993) 72. See also Charpentier, 'Les déclarations des Douze sur la reconnaissance des nouveaux Etats', RGDIP (1992) 343–56.

[53] Pellet, 'Notes sur la Commission d'arbitrage de la Conférence européenne pour la paix en Yougoslavie', AFDI (1991) 329–48.

[54] Flauss, above n 36 at p 33.

did not suspect that this would lead directly to the obligations that it faced in the *Pinochet* affair; however, in this case its vulnerability to the demands of human rights discourse—a vulnerability resulting from its own nature as a state governed by the rule of law—meant that it was forced to exercise jurisdiction in a manner that it would undoubtedly have preferred to avoid. More generally, it is not uncommon for diplomatic actions to be driven by a state's need to ensure coherence between at least its words and perhaps also its deeds, on the one hand, and the values that it proclaims as its own, or the commitments that it has undertaken, on the other—even if the resulting 'coherence' is far from systematic.[55] The French attitude towards the creation of the ICC provides a clear example of this.

(c) Irrecusability can also result from unforeseeability: for example, the unforeseeability of the manner in which the international regimes for the protection of human rights will develop. Many such developments were not necessarily envisaged or foreseen—or were perhaps actively rejected—by those involved in the initial negotiations that established the regimes in question. Such regimes can acquire a certain degree of autonomy from the will of their creators. This might be termed the irrecusability of the progressive development of human rights. In this regard, many States Parties to the ECHR had not contemplated (and in some cases, would have expressly excluded had they done so) that certain questions would later be brought within the scope of the Convention and its system of protection. One example of this can be found in the application of Article 6 (dealing with the right to a fair trial) to a number of constitutional disputes.[56] In a similar sense, we might consider the 'human dimension' contained in the Helsinki Final Act, without doubt undesired by many signatories insofar as the Act itself was initially conceived of as an instrument of East–West détente, intended to reinforce certain principles such as the inviolability of frontiers, and not as a declaration of human rights.[57] Lastly in this regard, we might also consider the diffusion of human rights into areas in which we would not have expected to find them expressed so fully, if at all. Thus, we have witnessed a real surge in the use of human rights discourse in cases brought before the ICJ, in, for example, the *Nuclear Weapons*[58] and *Special Rapporteur*[59] Opinions, and in the *Breard* judgment.[60] Even if, in these cases, questions of human rights were not at the core

---

[55] See the chapter entitled 'droits de l'homme entre ruse et raison' in Badie, above n 13, at pp 259–85.

[56] See, eg the judgment of the ECtHR in *Ruiz-Mateos c Espagne*, Série A, no 100; see also Ruiz Fabri, 'Egalité des armes et procès équitable dans la jurisprudence de la Cour européenne des droits de l'homme', in *Egalité et équité* (Paris: Economica, 1999) 47–64.

[57] E Decaux et L-A Sicilianos, above n 34.

[58] *Nuclear Weapons* Opinion, above n 39; see also Ruiz Fabri and Sorel, (above n 40).

[59] Advisory Opinion on the *Difference Relating to Immunity from Legal Process of a Special Rapporteur of the Commission on Human Rights*, Order of 10 August 1998, ICJ Reps (1998) 423.

[60] Case concerning the Vienna Convention on Consular Relations (*Paraguay v United States of America*), Order of 9 April 1998 on Request for the Indication of Provisional Measures, ICJ Reps

of judicial deliberations, the possibility of developing them further in this context has clearly arisen.

B. Degrees of Limitation: The Substantive Question

As we have seen, there are a number of different ways in which sovereignty can be limited; however, the question remains of the *scope* of the limitations thus effected. The level of legal constraint that can be brought to bear against a state— whether it has consented or not—can in practice be extremely variable; and it will be weaker or stronger as a direct function of the degree of control that can be exercised over a state's fulfilment of its obligations. The relative strength of control mechanisms is, moreover, itself related to the degree of autonomy enjoyed by the bodies charged with their operation.

The Degree of Constraint

Here, we can distinguish between constraints that are legal in nature (those deriving from legal instruments) and those that are 'material' (such as coercive actions). The latter type is, of course, particularly strong, and raises again the question of intervention and the structural bias that this implies. In effect, the issues involved here focus on emergency responses to massive violations of humanitarian standards, whereas the international human rights protection regime deals instead above all with the proclamation, and ultimately the guarantee, of human rights in 'normal' situations, in which violations are conceived of as sporadic, individual occurrences. However, in examining the weight of the burden of obligation placed upon states, it is above all legal constraints that are of interest to us here. Certainly, one factor in this will be the formal legal status of the instruments or norms in question; others, however, might relate to the normative density of their content, and even to the nature of the obligation incumbent on the state.

(a) The legal force of the instruments and norms proclaiming human rights thus provides us with our first standard: are they 'hard' or 'soft' law in a *formal* sense? States, and, generally speaking, judges, do draw a distinction between that which is legally binding and that which is not. Thus, direct reliance upon the UDHR is thus often held to be inadmissible by national courts. An analysis founded upon this distinction alone will thus reduce considerably the number of instruments held to be relevant; although consideration of the degree of control exercised over the fulfilment of these obligations may further nuance any conclusions reached.

(b) The normative density of the rights inscribed in international instruments presents us with our second standard: are they 'hard' or 'soft' law in a *substantive*

(1998) 248; see also Ruiz Fabri and Sorel, 'Chronique de jurisprudence de la CIJ—année 1998', JDI 3 (1999) 861–8.

sense? This question can be broken down into a number of different elements. First, it is worth noting that formally non-binding instruments are often more 'daring' and far-reaching in the rights they proclaim, as a comparison between the UDHR and the two subsequent Covenants—which are much more cautious in their formulations—amply illustrates. This cannot be explained by reference to the time difference—between 1948 and 1966—alone; rather, it suggests a direct relation between the formal status of an instrument and its substantive content. States tend to favour restrictive formulations when they know in advance that they will be legally bound by the instrument they are negotiating; thus, the boldness of 1948 finds its echo in the prudence of 1966.[61] Moreover, it is clear that the formulation of ostensibly the same right can vary from one instrument to the next, depending on the choices made by the negotiators, and that different hierarchies or priorities can be constructed between different rights.

Thus, the promotion and above all the protection of civil and political rights is stronger than for their economic, social, and cultural counterparts, even if we can currently observe—for reasons to which I will return below—the latter beginning to 'take off'.[62] It is worth noting, moreover, that even if the Universal Declaration (which can be viewed as the point of origin of contemporary human rights discourse) unifies all these rights in a single document, the subsequent, formally binding, instruments disaggregate them—both on the universal level, with the two 1966 Covenants, and on the regional level, as evidenced by disassociation between the ECHR of 1950 and the European Social Charter of 1961. Very often, instruments dealing with economic and social rights are vaguer and less binding in their formulations than are those concerned with civil and political rights. This is generally explained by the fact that the former would imply an economic cost, whereas the latter require nothing other than abstention from action on the part of the state.

It is in this context that distinctions between different 'generations' of rights, or between negative and positive rights, have been proposed. These distinctions, however, have limits—not only conceptual, but also and above all, practical. Closer investigation quickly confirms that these categories are not always adequate, for a variety of different reasons: certain rights refer neither to a precise object nor to a specific domain (such as, for example, the rights of free association and protest); not all economic rights are positive rights; and a number of civil and political rights contain economic elements, such that their effective guarantee will necessarily imply an economic cost to the state. Thus, the right to a fair trial can have economic implications for the state; for example, where it is obliged to provide free translation services to foreigners brought before its courts in order

[61] This point becomes even more clear upon consideration of the time required to garner sufficient ratifications for the 1966 Covenants to enter into force—more than ten years for each of them.

[62] Cançado Trindade, 'La question de la protection internationale des droits économiques, sociaux et culturels. Evolution et tendances actuelles', RGDIP (1990) 913–46.

to ensure that they fully understand the process. Nevertheless, the distinction between positive and negative rights is drawn formally, often quite deliberately, in order to define and limit the content of the rights in question. This leads on to two basic questions: first, do international human rights contain genuine 'personal' rights, enabling individuals to act in certain ways or to make certain demands? And secondly, what is the nature of the obligations placed on states by international human rights law?

(c) The level of legal constraint can also vary according to whether the instrument in question is directly applicable or not. This issue speaks to the degree of mediation by the state between the international norm and its applicability in domestic courts. The direct applicability of its provisions is often indicated in the text of an instrument itself: this is the case, for example, of the ECHR under Article 1, whereas the European Social Charter was based upon a different model. In any event, this question ultimately remains dependent upon domestic laws, in particular on whether the instrument in question has been incorporated into national law in dualist systems.

(d) Lastly, the level of legal constraint varies according to the extent to which the powers of the state in question have been affected, and in the nature of the obligations incumbent upon it. We can distinguish, for example, between transfers of powers, 'pooling' or sharing of powers, limits on the exercise of retained powers, and so on. In most cases, the goal is to condition the exercise of sovereign power in order that human rights are respected, perhaps after having obliged the state to bring its national legislation into line with an international instrument, as required, for example, by the ECHR on accession. It can, however, go further than this, and, in this regard, without doubt one of the most fertile concepts in international human rights law is that of the 'positive obligation': the duty on states to take positive measures to ensure the effective enjoyment of the rights proclaimed. Such obligations can impose changes to domestic law: as where, for example, the requirement to provide effective remedies for violations obliges states to make human rights justiciable in national courts (which, after all, is, or at least should be, the natural forum for questions of this sort). They can also, however, be used to confer an element of 'horizontal' applicability on the rights concerned; in such cases, it is no longer sufficient for the state itself to respect human rights, but rather it must undertake to take the measures necessary (in terms of a 'due diligence' requirement) to ensure that the rights in question are respected in relations between individuals, who are thus protected under human rights law against the actions of third parties. The positive measures contemplated can either be normative or more practical in nature. In such cases, the normative density of the rights in question can be considered relatively high, as illustrated by European human rights law. However, the question remains of punishment in cases in which they are violated.

While the requirement to provide for such punishment is normally incumbent on states, at least where the instruments concerned do not content themselves

with merely proclaiming rights and nothing more, it is worth noting the existence of overlapping jurisdictions in some cases, with, for example, the possibility
of recourse to the idea of 'universal jurisdiction'. Closer examination, however,
reveals that this tool is used with caution;[63] and that, moreover, it is most often
limited to particularly serious or extreme cases of violations. In terms of human
rights, it is essentially limited to the domains of humanitarian law, crimes against
humanity and torture;[64] thus to the most serious violations, the repression of
which can be considered a matter of general interest. The *Pinochet* affair provides
an illustration of this point, although whether this is an isolated case or indicative
of a more general evolution in international law remains contentious;[65] moreover,
it has given rise to accusations of judicial activism. There is also, however, the creation of the international criminal tribunals to be considered here, based upon a
different idea of universal jurisdiction; the key question here is whether the tribunal in question is in a position of primacy (as with the ad hoc Tribunals), complementarity (as with the ICC) or subsidiarity with regard to national courts.

As the preceding considerations make clear, the degree of legal constraint
imposed upon states does not depend entirely on the manner in which the rights
concerned are formulated. It further depends on whether or not the proclaimed
rights are accompanied by effective guarantees, and is thus closely linked to the
degree of control that can be brought to bear on states to ensure that they respect
their commitments. It is to this issue that I now turn.

The Degree of Control

The crucial aspect in terms of evaluating the degree of any limitation on sovereignty is without doubt that of control. This issue is not limited to the field of
human rights, but concerns international law in its entirety. Some authors have
even talked of a 'new sovereignty' to designate the growth in control mechanisms
designed to ensure respect for international commitments.[66] The existence or
otherwise of such mechanisms is indicative of the degree of constraint that the
system was intended to impose. This has both institutional and substantive elements: it is necessary to consider not only the author of the control but also its
object, its triggering mechanisms, its scope, and its effects. There are thus multiple and interacting criteria for assessment. On this basis, it appears plausible
to conclude that not only is there a diverse range and increasing number of control mechanisms (as testified, for example, by the creation of both a UN High

---

[63] See Guillaume, 'La compétence universelle—Formes anciennes et nouvelles', *Mélanges
Levasseur* (Paris: Litec, 1992) 23–36.

[64] See generally Chanet, 'La Convention des Nations Unies contre la torture et autres peines ou
traitements cruels, inhumains ou dégradants', AFDI (1984) 625–36.

[65] Cosnard, 'Quelques observations sur les décisions de la Chambre des Lords du 25 novembre
1998 et du 24 mars 1999 dans l'affaire Pinochet', RGDIP (1999) 309–28.

[66] A Chayes and A Handler Chayes, *The New Sovereignty—Compliance with International
Regulatory Agreements* (Cambridge MA: Harvard University Press, 1995) at p 417.

Commissioner and a European Commissioner for Human Rights), but that such mechanisms exist more often than not. This fact, of course, sets human rights apart from many other fields of international law; however, these mechanisms remain for the most part fairly limited. This situation is, however, progressively developing; moreover, alongside the formal control mechanisms expressly created by the instruments in question, there exist also techniques of spontaneous, 'informal' control, exercised in particular by certain private actors such as NGOs (for example through 'naming and shaming' practices). Through the exercise of such 'empirical' control, NGOs in effect enter into a dialogue with other states and international organizations, which use their work as leverage in their efforts to ensure the domestic protection of human rights. Some commentators even regard such action by private actors as the most effective means of achieving this goal. At a minimum, it can prove embarrassing—if not actually constraining—for the states it targets, particularly where it becomes the subject of sustained media attention.

(a) The existence of control mechanisms can help bridge the gap between the proclamation of human rights and their effective guarantee in practice, the latter being generally viewed as essential if they are to be considered positive law. They can also serve to undermine the importance of the distinction between formally binding and non-binding instruments, when the former lack control mechanisms that the latter have—a practice that is becoming increasingly common today. This in turn translates into a wide variety of different mechanisms, any analysis of which must take full account of the following considerations:

- The *author* of the control. The basic principle involved clearly calls for the intervention of a third party, but of what kind? Is it an inter-statal organization (made up of state representatives, as is the recently established UN Human Rights Council)? Or perhaps a body that, if not supranational, is at least composed of individuals independent of states (such as the Human Rights Committee)? Is it a judicial tribunal (such as the European or Inter-American Courts of Human Rights) or not? Of course, judicial protection is generally viewed as providing the most powerful guarantees; and it is certainly true that, when effected by a supranational tribunal, it also presents the greatest challenge to sovereignty (although it is worth noting that often, even in such tribunals, not all traces of politics or diplomacy have been wiped out—consider, for example, the systematic presence of a national judge in cases before the European Court of Human Rights (ECtHR), even if his role is not to represent his state). In more general terms, the central issue is that of the independence of the control mechanism vis-à-vis the states. In practice, this independence can also flow from the creation of a chain of delegation. Even if, for example, the Human Rights Council is an intergovernmental body, it can nonetheless create panels of experts that are themselves independent.

- The *object* of control is equally important. First, much depends on whether the oversight performed by the control mechanism is limited to a single instrument, or perhaps even a single provision or a precise theme. A number of conventions concluded under the auspices of the UN—relating, for example, to racial discrimination, torture, and the rights of the child—establish committees composed of independent individuals to monitor the application of their provisions. Moreover, it is important to ascertain whether the object of control is a general state practice or certain specific facts; whether it relates to individual violations or more general situations; and whether it is to be monitored on the basis of complaints or reports. Generally speaking, complaint-based control can be considered to offer a higher degree of guarantee than can oversight based on reports, with the qualification that here too other factors may serve to undermine and even reverse this.

- The *conditions* for triggering the control mechanism must also be taken into consideration. Can it, for example, act on its own initiative on the basis of information transmitted to it? Do individuals claiming to have suffered human rights violations have standing to bring claims? In terms of report-based control, it is necessary to further distinguish between obligations to supply periodic reports, and situations in which special reports may be demanded—a power granted, for example, to both the UN General Assembly and to the UN's Economic and Social Council (ECOSOC), and also, in emergency situations in which human rights protections in a State Party to the International Covenant on Civil and Political Rights (ICCPR) are seriously compromised, to the Human Rights Committee.

Other possibilities that must be taken into consideration include thematic procedures, in which an oversight body (such as the Human Rights Council) establishes a working group composed of independent experts or appoints a special rapporteur charged with investigating and reporting on a particular issue. The capacity for the oversight body to act on its own initiative is therefore important. Complaint-based control procedures, where they exist, are generally open to states, who nevertheless display a strong tendency to avoid using them wherever possible (whether at the international or regional level); however, the real crux of the issue lies in the extent to which such procedures are open to private parties, in particular to victims of (alleged) human rights violations. This can range from the admission of individual claims or complaints to limiting jurisdiction to collective petitions or claims. The key question here is whether the control mechanism in question forms an integral part of the human rights instrument it belongs to (meaning that the rights proclaimed therein automatically benefit from certain guarantees, as is now the case with the ECHR), or whether rather the operation of the mechanism requires the additional, explicit consent of the state, as found in provisions allowing states to accept the compulsory jurisdiction of the oversight body. This latter approach was followed until 1998 in the ECHR, and still structures the complaint-based oversight of the ICCPR (with its Optional Protocol) and the European Social Charter (which, similarly, has an Additional Protocol).[67] In this regard, the system established within the framework of the ICC is particularly well-developed, with its use of independent prosecutors. The negotiating history of the ICC Statute suggests a real concern to establish safeguards limiting the power of these prosecutors, but nonetheless an important step has been taken in this regard. In any event, the example of the ICC remains something of an exceptional case, given the scope of its jurisdiction and powers.

- The *means* of control are also important. Does the control mechanism have the power to conduct independent investigations? Can it demand from states and other actors the information that it feels that it requires? In terms of report-based oversight, it is necessary to consider the degree of accuracy of the information that the control mechanism succeeds in obtaining. In this regard, the Human Rights Committee has elaborated a set of 'general directives', obliging states to provide detailed and accurate studies; and it retains the power to request supplementary information should it so desire. The general trend appears to be toward the development of fairly precise questionnaires, which facilitate the submission of clear and adequate information. Even if states fulfil these requirements—which is far from universally the case—they are relatively limited in nature, and can as a consequence limit both the scope and effect of the control thus exercised. Nevertheless, report-based oversight is by far the most widespread control mechanism used; the possibility of conducting international investigations into particular cases of human rights violations remains the exception. The Human Rights Council does possess the latter power, but the effectiveness of its work depends largely on the goodwill of the state concerned. Indeed, perhaps the only genuinely effective instance of this control mechanism is to be found in the Committee established by the European Convention for the Prevention of Torture, which has the power to investigate relatively freely within state parties, including in traditionally restricted areas such as prisons or police stations. There is, moreover, a need to adopt a preventive approach, which is more active than reactive. It is this mindset that led, for example, to the establishment of some of the monitoring procedures established within the Council of Europe since the early 1990s.

- The *scope and effects* of the control mechanism also constitute an important variable. It is necessary to consider what the outcomes of the oversight process are (for example recommendations or decisions), and what the

---

[67] See F Sudre, 'Le protocole additionnel à la Charte sociale européenne prévoyant un système de réclamations collectives', RGDIP (1996) 714–39.

consequences of these might be, in particular the possibility of imposing sanctions. The only examples of (binding) decisions that can be found are where there is a legal oversight mechanism, in the context of complaint-based control procedures. However, the results of other procedures cannot simply be dismissed as completely 'non-binding'; there is not here a simple dichotomy, but rather a graduated scale between the two extremes. For example, the Optional Protocol regulating the complaint-based control conducted by the Human Rights Committee only authorizes that body to make its views known to the state party in question. Nevertheless, the Committee has pushed these limitations as far as possible, taking the view that, in ratifying both the Covenant and the Protocol, the state has recognized that its findings have legal consequences, and that it should adopt the measures that the situation calls for—measures that the Committee is not shy in identifying and proposing. Moreover, it has established a procedure for monitoring the adoption of these measures and publicizing the results, even though, legally speaking, the measures suggested by the Committee are nothing more than proposals. However, in the majority of other cases, the output of the control mechanism is essentially limited to recommendations. It is also important to consider the level of publicity given to both the oversight procedure and its results, and whether the process is confidential or not.

On the basis of these different criteria, we can extract a number of general observations regarding the degree of control exercised. The most complete and constraining forms of control, in that they result in binding decisions and perhaps even in the possibility of reparation, are those based upon judicial processes. They are also the least common, existing only in the European and American regional contexts. To this we might soon be able to add the African region, as there now exists the African Court of Human and People's Rights, although it has only just begun to operate;[68] and its jurisdiction does not, generally speaking, extend to economic and social rights, even if this distinction tends to become blurred as case law develops.[69]

Moreover, we can also bring in, in this context, the possibility of private individuals triggering the control mechanisms. A number of international treaties establish mechanisms that resemble conciliation rather than judicial processes, in which the individual concerned can seek moral satisfaction through an effective and official recognition of the violation suffered. This is the model adopted in, for example, the Optional Protocol to the ICCPR, the Convention on the Elimination of Racial Discrimination, the Convention Against Torture, and International Labour Organization (ILO) Convention 87 on Freedom of

---

[68] See Mubiala, 'La Cour africaine des droits de l'homme et des peuples: mimétisme institutionnel ou avancée judiciaire?', RGDIP (1998) 765–80.

[69] See, eg C Russo, 'La justiciabilité des droits économiques et sociaux', Rec. des Cours de l'Acad. Dr. Euro. (1994) III, book 2, 207–35.

Association. Certainly, in all of these cases, the state concerned is called upon to provide an explanation to an international body outwith its own boundaries of the manner in which it treated an individual on its territory; and it is called upon to do so at the request of a private actor, which clearly represents a real, qualitative leap with regard to the classical conception of sovereignty. It is important to recall, however, that numerous restrictions remain in place, in particular the ubiquitous requirement that the individual in question has sought relief at the national level, and in doing so has exhausted domestic remedies. There must thus be persistent failings, in terms of human rights standards, in the functioning of the state apparatus.

Report-based control procedures, whether political or 'administrative' (that is, conducted by an independent body), are by far the most widespread. Their basic goal generally is to provide an analysis of the human rights situation in the state in question, and on this basis to educate gradually both the state itself, which will become accustomed to the monitoring process, and those individuals involved in human rights protection and advocacy, who know best the situation on the ground and can thus fine-tune their strategies. In legal terms, the results of these processes only impose weak constraints on states, and leave ample room for reaffirmations of the traditional concept of sovereignty (through, for example, formally consenting to and cooperating with the control mechanism).

The vulnerability of many of these reporting mechanisms to the influence of political considerations has been repeatedly stressed. This situation has, however, been evolving in a slow and, although contested, nonetheless effective manner, as illustrated by the example of the ICESCR. Here, the system intended to guarantee implementation of the rights contained in the Covenant essentially consisted of the submission of reports by states on measures adopted and progress made to ECOSOC, which could then send them on to the Commission on Human Rights for further study and possibly the formulation of recommendations. In effect, however, ECOSOC superseded this procedure by creating a committee of independent experts (the Committee on Economic, Social and Cultural Rights) charged with the task of analysing and debating the reports submitted by states.[70] This indicated a desire to free at least some aspects of the oversight procedure from the relatively politicized treatment it would otherwise receive, in which it often comes to form part of broader bargaining processes. This is not an isolated example, meaning that, above and beyond the nature of the control mechanism

---

[70] Efforts are currently afoot to enhance the legal status of the Committee on Economic, Social and Cultural Rights with a view to placing it on a par with all other UN treaty monitoring bodies whose existence is established, and ensured, by explicit treaty provisions. See Human Rights Council Res. 4/7 (2007) on the 'Rectification of the legal status of the Committee on Economic, Social and Cultural Rights'. See also 'Rectification of the legal status of the Committee on Economic, Social and Cultural Rights: report of the Committee', UN Doc. A/HRC/6/20 (2007); and 'Report of the Office of the United Nations High Commissioner for Human Rights on the rectification of the legal status of the Committee on Economic, Social and Cultural Rights', UN Doc. A/HRC/6/21 (2007).

we are studying, we must also take into consideration the use to which its work is put, and—perhaps above all—the degree of autonomy that it has managed to appropriate through various different methods of extending its sphere of influence. The autonomy thus gained supplements that which the subject-matter tends to acquire of its own accord.

The Appropriation of Autonomy

This tendency—by no means inevitable—to appropriate increasing degrees of autonomy results from the play of various different factors. We can observe a progressive enrichment of many control mechanisms, both in terms of organizational structure and of the substantive field with which they are concerned, which very often takes them well beyond the intentions of those that initially established the mechanism in question. Developments of this sort are undoubtedly facilitated by the particularities, indeed the fundamental logic, of human rights discourse, which seem to tend towards objectification.

(a) This 'emancipation' of control mechanisms can be observed in a number of different extra- or para-conventional developments, which we might group together as 'organizational accretions', 'procedural accretions', and 'substantive accretions'.

The United Nations provides us with one fairly typical example of the first type of innovation. At its first meeting in 1946, ECOSOC, acting under Article 68 of the UN Charter, established the Commission on Human Rights. It was to be composed of state delegates, and charged with the elaboration of human rights instruments. Very quickly, however, it began to receive complaints from individuals and information from NGOs regarding alleged human rights violations. Initially, it was reluctant either to examine these claims or to refuse to receive them; however, after the adoption of the Covenants in 1966, it decided to place on its order of business each year an item on 'questions of human rights violations'. This initiative was approved by ECOSOC in 1967, thus authorizing the Commission to examine evidence of flagrant violations of human rights, and to study situations that revealed a consistent pattern of such violations. Later, the Commission developed a number of new control initiatives. These undoubtedly bore the imprint of political considerations, and were extremely flexible but they also enjoyed a certain degree of independence, as the consent of states was not required for them to function. Chief among these initiatives were the formation of groups of experts and the appointment of special rapporteurs, all of whom were able to carry out their work relatively removed from political contingencies.[71] The concrete consequences of such investigations were, in effect, limited to the possibility of generating negative publicity.

---

[71] O de Frouville, *Les procédures thématiques: une contribution efficace des Nations Unies à la protection des droits de l'homme* (Paris: Pedone, 1996) at p 139.

Perhaps most important here, however, was the dynamic that developed within the context of these thematic procedures. The achievements of the Working Group on Arbitrary Detention are considered particularly remarkable in this regard.[72] These were extra-conventional procedures in which different strategies were used to bypass sovereignty through recourse to more informal processes, which allowed for the circumvention of the traditional, cumbersome channels of inter-state negotiation. The fact that states can be greatly disturbed by such developments is illustrated well by the ICJ's Opinion in the *Special Rapporteur* case, in which it strongly reaffirmed the immunity from prosecution enjoyed by special rapporteurs in the performance of their duties, in order to counter the convoluted techniques employed by the state in question to hamper an investigation into the independence of its judicial system.[73] Thus we can clearly see how an accumulation of non-binding elements can give rise to constraints that, if not in themselves 'legal', are none the less genuine.

The same trend can be observed in terms of procedural accretions. The practice, noted above, of the Human Rights Committee provides an illustration of this: in, for example, its use of General Directives to structure the reports that states are required to submit; in its view that states are obliged to implement its recommendations; and in its establishment of a follow-up mechanism to monitor this implementation. In the context, then, of its internal functioning alone, this control mechanism has developed a number of procedures that have served to increase the existing burden of obligation on states, and which can even, through the play of different interconnected norms, contribute to the creation of entirely new obligations.

Lastly, there are what might be termed 'substantive' accretions. By this, I am referring to certain tendencies that favour the increasing independence of human rights protection systems; or, to be more precise, to the fact that the material scope of the protection afforded can come to exceed by far that envisaged by those who originally established the system. Two examples drawn from the European context can illustrate this process. The first is the technique of 'de-partitioning' introduced by the ECtHR in its judgment in the *Airey* case. Based upon the idea that the rights proclaimed in the ECHR must also be effectively guaranteed, it concluded that:

[w]hilst the Convention sets forth what are essentially civil and political rights, many of them have implications of a social or economic nature. The Court therefore considers...that the mere fact that an interpretation of the Convention may extend into the sphere of social and economic rights should not be a decisive factor against such an interpretation; there is no water-tight division separating that sphere from the field covered by the Convention.[74]

---

[72] E Decaux (ed), *L'ONU face à la détention arbitraire—bilan de six années de fonctionnement du Groupe de travail sur la détention arbitraire* (Paris: Du CEDIN, 1999) at p 133.

[73] Advisory Opinion on *Difference Relating to Immunity from Legal Process of a Special Rapporteur of the Commission on Human Rights*, Advisory Opinion of 29 April 1999, ICJ Reps (1999).

[74] *Airey v Irlande*, judgment of 9 October 1979, series A no 32, § 26.

Also illustrative of this general trend are those cases in which the Court favours an extensive, progressive interpretation of rights, expanding them to include elements not originally envisaged. Here we might consider, for example, the finding that a failure to furnish sufficient information pertaining to neighbouring environmental hazards can constitute a violation of the right to privacy—an extremely indirect way of extending the scope of the Convention to include environmental considerations, despite the fact that no right to a healthy environment was intended.[75] The same tendency can also be identified in the use of 'autonomous concepts', of which the case law of the ECtHR again provides the most advanced examples. This technique has enabled the Court not only to free itself from reference to national legal systems,[76] but also to exert relatively strong pressure on those systems, leading to the introduction of concepts and techniques of control that did not necessarily exist beforehand. The examples of the autonomous concept of the 'criminal charge' or the use of the 'doctrine of appearances' in evaluating the impartiality of domestic tribunals illustrate well that these techniques can result in genuine encroachment upon the independence of states: the former obliging them to introduce an adversarial element to a number of procedures that the ECtHR viewed as relating to criminal law in nature (even although they were not categorized as such under domestic law); and the latter requiring that certain particularities of judicial procedure, developed in the historical context of individual legal systems, be changed (for example, challenging the presence of the public prosecutor during judicial deliberations).

This appropriation of the autonomy to rule on conceptual issues becomes all the more important when we realize that there can be something of a 'contamination effect' between different protection regimes. Interactions of this sort are of real importance, particularly through the use of interpretative techniques that tend to further reinforce a normative convergence on rights discourse already substantially in existence.[77] This 'conceptual autonomy' is, moreover, itself made possible—as are all of the other accretions outlined above—by the particular logic and structure of human rights, even as it reinforces them.

(b) Human rights instruments have a specific character which is linked to the fundamental logic underpinning these rights, and which contributes to their independence. It seems generally accepted that 'human rights have an "objective nature" which sets aside mechanisms based on the notion of reciprocity or on

---

[75] See Dejeant-Pons, 'Le droit de l'homme à l'environnement et la Convention européenne des droits de l'homme', *Mélanges M-A Eissen* (Brussels: Bruylant, 1995) 79; F Sudre, 'Les aléas de la notion de "vie privée" dans la jurisprudence de la Cour européenne des droits de l'homme', *Mélanges LE Pettiti*, (Brussels: Bruylant, 1998) 689–705.

[76] Sudre, 'Le recours aux "notions autonomes"', in F Sudre (ed), *L'interprétation de la Convention européenne des droits de l'homme* (Brussels: Bruylant, 1998) 93–131; E Kastanas, *Unité et diversité: notions autonomes et marge d'appréciation des États dans la jurisprudence de la Cour européenne des droits de l'homme* (Brussels: Bruylant, 1996) at p 480.

[77] Conforti, 'L'interaction des normes internationales relatives à la protection des droits de l'homme', in SFDI, above n 10 at pp 121–6.

the play of counter-measures',[78] even though reciprocity is the 'normal' operating principle of international law. First, 'provisions relating to the protection of the human person are neither terminated nor suspended as a consequence of a breach'[79] of the instrument in which they are contained. This rule was codified in Article 60(5) of the 1969 Vienna Convention on the Law of Treaties, and the ICJ confirmed that it constituted a 'general principle of law' in its *South West Africa* Advisory Opinion.[80] In other words, human rights-related instruments escape the intersubjective logic of the non-performance exception. Secondly, human rights are connected to the notions of *jus cogens* and international crimes. They are 'all, in turn, implicated in all concepts that aim, in terms of *lex lata* or *de lege ferenda*, to strengthen the protection of certain obligations. Respect for, if not human rights in general then at least certain among them constitutes without any doubt a principle of *jus cogens*.'[81] Moreover, Article 19 of the first part of the ILC's project on state responsibility, adopted in 1976, affirmed that 'a serious breach on a widespread scale of an international obligation of essential importance for safeguarding the human being, such as those prohibiting slavery, genocide and apartheid' should be considered as an 'international crime' of the state.

We also speak, in relation to human rights, of certain fundamental duties that can be considered as obligations *erga omnes*.[82] This is based in particular on the dictum of the ICJ in the *Barcelona Traction* case, according to which '[s]uch obligations derive, for example, in contemporary international law, from the outlawing of acts of aggression, and of genocide, as also from the principles and rules concerning the basic rights of the human person, including protection from slavery and racial discrimination'.[83] In a similar way, the notion of an 'international public order' of which human rights form an important part is often relied upon: certain European institutions have, for example, had recourse to this idea, holding that the ECHR had established a 'public order', or that it represented a 'constitutional instrument of European public order'.[84]

Does this mean that human rights have acquired an 'objective' dimension in international law, in a manner similar to that which has occurred in certain domestic contexts? This would mean moving beyond a purely subjective understanding, according to which fundamental rights are viewed as 'personal' rights whose sole aim is the protection of the individual, and thus abandoning a

---

[78] Alland, above n 41 at p 267.

[79] Ibid. p 268.

[80] Advisory Opinion on the *Legal Consequences for States of the Continued Presence of South Africa in Namibia (South West Africa) notwithstanding Security Council Resolution 276 (1970)* of 21 June 1971, ICJ Reps (1971) 55, §122.

[81] Alland, above n 41 at p 274.

[82] Carrillo Salcedo, 'Souveraineté des Etats et droits de l'homme en droit international contemporain', *Mélanges Wiarda* (Cologne: Carl Heymanns Verlag, 1988) 91–5.

[83] *Barcelona Traction* judgment, above n 38 §34.

[84] ECtHR, *Loizidou c Turquie*, judgment of 23 March 1995, A.310, §75. See also F Sudre, 'Existe-t-il un ordre public européen?', in P Tavernier (ed), *Quelle Europe pour les droits de l'homme?* (Brussels: Bruylant, 1996) 39–80.

concept of these personal rights as 'a creation of the state, the consecration and the operationalisation of which depends entirely upon the goodwill of public institutions'.[85] In its place, an approach that imparts to human rights a degree of protection and that seeks 'to imprint human rights, understood as social values, upon the state—which is no longer perceived as the author, but rather the servant, of the rights in question'.[86] An evolution of this sort is inscribed within the transition to the rule of law in the domestic context, which presupposes not only a hierarchy of norms but also a unified legal order 'dominated by the basic core that fundamental rights represent'.[87]

The different concepts of international law mentioned above are undoubtedly related. This becomes apparent first through the appropriation of international subjecthood by individuals and private actors in general, and through the increasingly important role of non-governmental actors in these processes. The very fact that such actors can play a role favours the development of systems that reflect their involvement—which itself requires the prior existence of formal possibilities for action. This dynamic is reflected in the oft-made argument that, where there is no action, there is no law. The converse of this is also true: the existence of action is itself makes previously existing rights concrete, laying the basis for their objectification. We can further observe this objectification in the fact that states have undertaken international obligations vis-à-vis all individuals under their jurisdiction, and not merely other states' parties. The term 'objective obligation' as used here is, then, distinct from that which informs the concept of 'objective regimes' in international law. Yet there remain genuine doubts over the capacity of these concepts to adequately reflect and respond to the practical context in which international human rights law operates. It seems difficult to speak of an 'objective global dimension' capable of turning instruments relating to human rights into general rules of universal application; any analysis of the issues involved is simply confronted by too many contradictions to allow such a conclusion.

It is also far from clear that notions such as *jus cogens* or international crime are entirely appropriate: for example, in concentrating on those obligations considered the most important, they both presuppose and impose a selection, and thus a hierarchy, between different obligations—an idea that seems to run counter to the putative universality of human rights. Of course, many human rights instruments themselves contain distinctions between the rights that must be guaranteed in all circumstances and those that are susceptible to derogation, which provides a corresponding limit on the potential scope of any eventual objectification. Moreover, this distinction does not, in general, speak to the issue of whether or not states can enter reservations to the commitments that they

---

[85] Grewe and Ruiz Fabri, above n 10 at p 170.
[86] Ibid. p 176.
[87] Ibid.

undertake—an issue that illustrates the gap between the 'verticality' presupposed by objectification and the 'horizontality' of international obligations understood as intersubjective commitments. Ultimately, it must be acknowledged that the most demanding procedures are established in relation to the gravest of human rights violations; and the clearest affirmations of binding, imperative norms are to be found in the context of armed conflicts. The key point here is whether these situations must be treated as exceptions, or whether they rather express a legal position capable of generalization.

Therefore, however important the development of international human rights law might have been, it does not yet appear adequate to confirm the hypothesis outlined earlier in this paper: that of the international protection of human rights as a source of an 'international public order', which has acquired an objective dimension and thus moved beyond the classical intersubjective approach derived from sovereignty (or from the juxtaposition of a plurality of competing sovereigns). While it remains evident that the basic function of human rights is the protection of the individual's sphere of liberty from unwanted encroachment by public authorities (which places the emphasis on their subjective dimension), it is less clear whether the progressive systematization of these rights can impart to them an 'objective dimension' that would place all states under a general obligation to develop, encourage, and guarantee respect for human rights. This is not to say, however, that there is no evidence at all of the emergence of the latter. The concept of 'positive obligations'—which is an important first step in this regard—is, of course, no stranger to international human rights law. A concern with the goals underlying those rights is also becoming increasingly pronounced—as illustrated, for example, by the recent resurgence in interest in the notion of the 'just war'. The idea of 'public order' has itself entered into the lexicon of international law, even if many of those working in the field doubt its effectiveness. We could even recall here the statements made by Kofi Annan, quoted in part at the beginning of this article, in which he encouraged NATO to move quickly to re-establish public order following the Kosovo crisis. Indeed, if these examples and others like them told the whole story, we could view Annan's claim of an evolution in international law as entirely vindicated; this, however, is not the case.

2. Ambivalent Tendencies: The Evolution of Sovereignty and the 'Becoming' of Human Rights

Although the idea of an objectification of human rights presupposes a degree of harmonization that is, as yet, far from realized (even if such a state of affairs is not, in itself, inconceivable), this does not mean that no elements of objectification exist. There are two basic obstacles to any attempt to reduce the human rights/sovereignty question to a linear, 'zero-sum' question of expansion/limitation. First, the evolution of human rights is not necessarily one of continuous development.

Rather, it is often relativism that prevails; a relativism that not only accommodates but can even support the preservation of certain elements of sovereignty.

This relativism can manifest itself in a number of different ways, and can become even more attractive when we consider a second point: that not all limitations on sovereignty are necessarily favourable to the protection of human rights. As noted at the outset, sovereignty is currently facing a number of challenges, including those conveniently grouped together under the rubric of 'globalization', and the resulting dilution of power does not automatically result in improved human rights protection, particularly where it is not accompanied by other positive measures designed to advance this goal. Even if the notion of a genuine 'law of humanity', replacing the law of sovereignty, seems to fit well with the idea of globalization, its realization is by no means automatic or inevitable, and poses the problem of the place and role envisaged for the state in the new order. In effect, these two ambivalences—that the preservation of sovereignty is not necessarily incompatible with human rights, and that the dilution of sovereignty is not necessarily favourable to those rights—themselves merely reflect the fundamental ambivalence in the nature of the state itself, between its 'power function' and its 'protection function',[88] and demonstrate that the protection of human rights has not yet superseded the nation state. In what follows, this dual question of compatibility and negation will be explored.

A. Human Rights and the Preservation of Sovereignty

As Kofi Annan noted, it will undoubtedly take time to reconcile sovereignty and human rights; at least, however, we can deduce from this that the two are not in principle irreconcilable. From a theoretical perspective, the definition of sovereignty as a freedom to act contains absolutely no indication or direction on the powers to be retained and the manner in which they should be exercised, at least once it is accepted either that the conditioning of power does not necessarily equal the negation of sovereignty, or that the substantive boundaries of that concept as traditionally understood have been significantly altered. From a more practical, or positive, perspective, it should be noted that the legal instruments and mechanisms of human rights protection leave states with plenty of room for manoeuvre. This can be treated as a manifestation of the relativism referred to immediately above, but also as resulting from the fact that human rights can, as a consequence of their legitimacy-enhancing properties, become instruments of legal policy, and of international relations more generally.

We might, therefore, note, on the one hand, the manner in which sovereignty seeks to accommodate human rights and preserve itself in relation to them, and, on the other, the ways in which it can actively instrumentalize those rights in its efforts at self-preservation. This way of presenting things may seem provocative.

---

[88] M Chemillier-Gendreau, *Humanité et souverainetés* (Paris: La Découverte, 1995) at p 329.

Certainly, it deals with only one aspect of the issue at hand, but it can draw support from a relatively large number of different arguments. In any event, it has its roots in the empirical observation that it is not the sovereignty of those states that in general respect human rights, that 'suffers' the most. Lastly, it takes account of the fact that 'being fundamentally state-centric, the international law can only bring about a profound change in the situation of human rights through the intervention of states themselves, and thus through the efficacy that they choose confer on, or withhold from, the rules that they create, or at least to which they appear to adhere'.[89]

Preservation through Relativism

(a) It is well known that, despite their claims to universality, contemporary human rights are far from universal, and the normative field that they seek to constitute still contains numerous lacunae. Of course, the Vienna Declaration issued at the UN World Conference on Human Rights in 1993 affirmed that '[a]ll human rights are universal, indivisible and interdependent and interrelated'; however, 'the confrontations that characterised the drafting process ... demonstrated that the fact that universalism prevailed over all particularisms in this Declaration does not mean that all states are genuinely convinced by that proposition'.[90] Moreover, the temptation—not always unfounded—to denounce such instruments as manifestations of an excessively Western-centric approach is always present.

Secondly, human rights-related instruments are far from binding on all states. If the vast majority of states are parties to the Geneva Conventions on humanitarian law, the Convention on the Rights of the Child, and the Convention on the Elimination of Discrimination Against Women, this figure drops to less than two thirds of states in the context of the 1966 Covenants, despite the fact that it was precisely these texts that were intended as 'global' proclamations. Two thirds is, of course, already a significant amount, and it has been pointed out both that relatively few universal conventions suffer from a serious lack of ratifications (essentially only the 1985 Convention Against Apartheid in Sport; the Conventions of 1954 and 1961 relating to the issue of stateless persons; the 1965 Convention on Consent to, and Minimum Age for, Marriage; and the 1990 Convention on the Protection of the Rights of Migrant Workers), and that the general tendency has been towards relatively large-scale ratifications of not only UN instruments,[91] but also those elaborated at the regional level (other than in, for example, Asia, where such instruments tend not to exist). This process can, however, take a long time: the period of latency between the adoption of a human rights treaty and

---

[89] Mourgeon, above n 19 at p 113.
[90] Wachsmann, above n 21 at p 49.
[91] Flauss, above n 36 at p 16; see also Dhommeaux, 'De l'universalité du droit international des droits de l'homme: du pactum ferendum au pactum latium', AFDI (1989) 399–423.

its entry into force can be somewhere in the region of—and can even on occasions exceed—ten years, as illustrated nicely by the example of the 1966 UN Covenants. Moreover, a state is only bound from the date of its own individual acceptance of the instrument in question, as demonstrated by the *Pinochet* case: here, only those claims relating to the period subsequent to the UK's ratification of the 1984 Convention Against Torture were admitted.

Other factors operate to increase the role of relativism in the preservation of sovereignty still further. It is necessary, for example, to recall that a number of powerful states have not ratified a number of important instruments. Of course, China relatively recently ratified the ICESCR, but this cannot hide that fact that it remains unbound by a number of other treaties, as do Indonesia, India, and Pakistan, amongst others. This means—and it is important to count in terms of individuals, not simply states—that more than one third of the world's population remains outside the scope of much human rights protection. The rights of individuals might also fall outside the scope of protection mechanisms through the potentially incomplete nature of state undertakings: the fact that a state has consented to be bound by an international agreement need not in and of itself tell us much about the scope of protection offered, given that, in most circumstances, it retains the right to adjust the level of its commitment.

The use of reservations is rarely expressly prohibited by international human rights instruments; only a very few specific conventions contain such a provision.[92] The classic argument often advanced in favour of this practice— that it is preferable to encourage a large number of states to ratify, even if this undermines the integrity of its normative content[93]—has been partially validated by the observation that, in the field of human rights at least, a number of states have progressively distanced themselves from the reservations that they entered at time of ratification. In fact, a majority of conventions explicitly allow for reservations to be entered, sometimes providing also the general framework for doing so. As a result, their use is not uncommon; and a large number thereof are 'substantive' in nature, that is, pertaining to the rights guaranteed themselves. (The possibility that another state could object to reservations of this kind, although open in theory, in practice often proves to be profoundly limited in both substance and scope.) It is well known, for example, that the reservations entered by the US to the ICCPR are both numerous and important. On those rare occasions that they exist, mechanisms for overseeing the acceptability of reservations appear relatively loose: even in the context of the ECtHR, for example, such control is largely limited to a formal evaluation of the precision with which the reservation in question has been formulated.[94] Nevertheless,

---

[92] Cohen-Jonathan, 'Les réserves dans les traités relatifs aux droits de l'homme', RGDIP (1996) 915–49.

[93] P-H Imbert, *Les réserves aux traités multilatéraux* (Paris: Pedone, 1979).

[94] Sudre, above n 17 at p 122; see also Cohen-Jonathan, 'Les réserves à la CEDH (à propos de l'arrêt Belilos du 29 avril 1988)', RGDIP (1989) 273.

the jurisprudence of these control mechanisms has tended towards the creation of a specific regime for the evaluation of reservations to human rights treaties, which includes perhaps most importantly a rejection of the more general principle that a state that has entered a reservation judged to be incompatible with the object and purpose of the treaty is, as a consequence, not bound by any of the provisions of the treaty in question.

The state retains the possibility to withdraw from systems of human rights protection, as illustrated by the Peruvian withdrawal from the Inter-American Convention on Human Rights in July 1999,[95] and by the Greek denunciation of the ECHR in 1969. It might be objected that in these cases, the capacity to withdraw had been explicitly recognized beforehand; such denunciation clauses are not, however, particularly rare, and in any event the claim that any convention silent on this issue should be understood as having precluded the possibility of withdrawal remains controversial. It thus seems clear that the legal *acquis* developed, even in the context of the most sophisticated systems, cannot be viewed as irrevocable in principle (although we must also recall here the possibility that, even upon withdrawal, a state remains bound by customary norms).

Lastly, the principle of reciprocity is not totally excluded from the field of human rights. For example, certain protection mechanisms can be accepted 'on condition of reciprocity', as is the case for the legal proceedings established in the European and American regional contexts, or the competence of the Human Rights Committee in the context of the interstate communications procedure.

(b) Moreover, the universalistic pretensions of human rights discourse run up against the fact that even those rights considered to be theoretically of equal import in practice are often afforded profoundly unequal levels of protection. In other words, where the overriding principle should be that of the inherent equality of all rights, stemming from their interdependence and indivisibility, we find in reality selectiveness and hierarchy. This can be observed from three different perspectives, the first of which is that of the categorization of rights. Even if it is easy to denounce the artificiality—or at least the limits—of distinguishing between civil and political rights on one hand, and economic and social rights on the other, the fact remains that this distinction produces some real consequences (which in turn reveal the purposes behind its use): the use of different legal instruments, and the establishment of varying degrees of protection, the choice of which appears to be made largely as a function of the perceived 'costs' of the rights in question to states.

The second perspective concerns the establishment of a hierarchy between rights within the legal instrument that contains them itself. Most distinguish between non-derogable rights, which are rights that states must respect at all times and in all places, and ordinary rights, susceptible to restriction and/or

---

[95] Cassel, 'Peru Withdraws from the Court: Will the Inter-American Human Rights System Meet the Challenge?', 20 HRLJ (1999)167–75.

derogation under certain circumstances. The former are limited in number, consisting essentially of rights relating to bodily integrity and to the non-retroactivity of criminal law. Only they impose absolute obligations upon states. The third perspective is that of the rights-holders themselves, a category that is becoming increasingly diverse. This means in turn that the state must adjudicate on human rights issues pertaining not only to the relations between individuals and itself, but also between groups and other collective entities.

(c) Generally speaking, the effective enjoyment of rights remains largely at the mercy of individual states. Protection mechanisms operate first and foremost at the domestic level; those international mechanisms that do exist are generally regarded as supplementary in this regard, as illustrated by the requirement of exhaustion of domestic remedies before an individual claim can be pursued at the international level. A real objectification of human rights of the kind discussed above would require the establishment of a genuinely monist legal system in which the state would become entirely 'transparent', with respect for individual interests guaranteed by an effective, 'supra-state', global law. States, however, remain the masters of the domestic effect of international instruments. In its most extreme form, this power can manifest itself as a refusal to incorporate the instrument in question into national law at all, which in effect removes all possibility of relying upon it before domestic courts. This was the approach adopted, for example, by the UK in relation to the ECHR until its incorporation in the 1998 Human Rights Act—even though, in this case, the possibility remained of recourse to the ECtHR in cases of alleged violation.

Even without such extreme resistance on the part of states, however, domestic effects of human rights treaties remain largely dependent upon the particular constitutional law framework of each state, which might reject, or accept only partially, the primacy of the international instrument in question. Even the legal techniques through which human rights are effected are not 'neutral', often heavily marked by the values and concerns of the 'host' legal order. The realm of private international law provides us with a good example of this, where the relative efficacy of different legal techniques for operationalizing fundamental rights deriving from an international instrument is considered, in cases in which the applicability of a foreign law that allegedly violates those rights is at issue. Recourse to the doctrine of direct effect in such cases directly poses the problem of sovereignty (both of the state whose judge is called upon to decide, and of that whose law has been challenged), when refusing to apply a foreign law on the basis of an international norm.[96] This solution, somewhat radical in that it empowers a national judge to evaluate the compatibility of foreign laws with international norms even where he has no such jurisdiction over his own domestic laws, tends not to find widespread support. Instead, the general preference seems to be the classical technique of resort to notions of public order based on fundamental

---

[96] Hammje, 'Droits fondamentaux et ordre public', RCDIP (1997) 1–31.

rights; a technique in which the notion of public order is inevitably mediated by the domestic legal context invoking it, with all of the particularities—and thus relativism—to which this gives rise.

Even if, above and beyond this specific example, an international instrument contains a provision expressly stating that it is to have direct effect, its application may well give rise to problems of interpretation—which will in turn almost certainly undermine the uniformity of protection afforded, given that a general standardization of the relevant concepts is a long way from being realized. In any event, most provisions resulting from international negotiations remain relatively vague and general; and even those examples of international control mechanisms that do exist cover only a tiny percentage of cases when compared to the daily business of implementing rights at the domestic level. Lastly, the implementation of rights presupposes an element of contextual adjustment—and this, in turn, creates numerous possibilities for generating limitations on, or particular interpretations of, the rights in question. This last dimension is, in fact, envisaged by the protection systems themselves since, as noted above, most rights guaranteed by most international instruments can, under certain circumstances, be subject to restrictions and/or derogations. The possibilities for restrictions are linked to the idea of protection of the public order—broadly understood—and to the idea that this aim can justify state interference in the exercise of certain rights. Everything then depends upon the degree of precision with which such interference is framed. The simple existence of a requirement to precisely frame the need for any restrictions, in terms specific to each right in question, undoubtedly places limitations on state action. However, the reliance, in the context of international control mechanisms, on notions such as the 'national margin of appreciation'[97] indicates the recognition and acceptance of a certain degree of pluralism, and therefore also of relativism. Derogation clauses generally refer to states that find themselves in exceptional circumstances that can render necessary exceptional laws imposing severe restrictions on, or even total suspensions of, the rights in question—even though, paradoxically, these periods tend to be those in which basic rights are most threatened. In this context, sovereignty continues to 'triumph' over human rights, even to the extent that effective control procedures seem unlikely—the ECHR providing a solitary exception in this regard.

Even without the need to have recourse to such mechanisms, however, many states take advantage of the lack of 'fit' between the international and domestic legal orders in order to circumvent human rights protections. That such practices can produce perverse effects is illustrated well by the example of the Declaration on the Right and Responsibility of Individuals, adopted by UN General Assembly

---

[97] P Mahoney et al., 'The Doctrine of the Margin of Appreciation under the European Convention on Human Rights: Its Legitimacy in Theory and Application in Practice', 19 HRLJ (1998), 31–6; see also Kastanas, above n 76.

resolution on 9 December 1998,[98] even though here we are dealing with a non-binding instrument. This text, on the 'protection of protectors', was above all aimed at supporting and encouraging the work of human rights advocates. Its adoption, however, provided the opportunity for a number of states to openly claim the uniqueness and particularity of their own situation, presenting a discourse intended to legitimize the increasingly common practice of developing national security or anti-terrorist laws that are often used, in practice, to repress the work of human rights advocates and protectors. Each state thus makes claims regarding the particular exigencies of its own domestic legal order, interpreting for its own benefit the idea that certain circumstances can justify the restriction or suspension of rights.

(d) This issue of the differing articulation of human rights standards between different sites of legal authority has another, if slightly less significant, aspect, resulting from the multiplication and variation of such sites to which reference can be made in passing judgment. This can, of course, create problems of both coordination and coherence, either where the body or regime in question ignores human rights entirely, or instead adopts its own approach thereto. Certainly, complete indifference to human rights standards is becoming increasingly difficult today, in particular because the logic that drives them cuts across traditional substantive and organizational boundaries. This is, for example, one of the concerns often raised in connection with the World Trade Organization.

In fact, the majority of these sites of legal authority appear concerned to generate their own sets of norms in this regard, hence the proliferation of different rights-related texts and mechanisms. States, when implicated in various different instances of such sites (even as they themselves constitute one) are thus the point at which various different protection systems intersect—which carries an obvious risk of generating incoherence and even contradiction. Nonetheless, this is a relatively rare occurrence; as we have seen, the dominant trend appears to be towards encouraging the convergence of diverse instruments.[99] Nevertheless, we might recall here the conflict between European Community law and that of the ILO on the issue of women working at night, which ultimately led many European states to withdraw from ILO Convention No 89.[100] States, it should be recalled, retain extensive powers of decision, and can thus choose to privilege one site of legal authority over another. This can, of course, lead to increased human rights protections; however, it is equally clear that states can, to a certain degree, either choose the standard of protection to which they are bound or at least exert a considerable amount of influence over that standard. On the other hand, we might also recall that, when the integration of the Eastern bloc countries into the

---

[98] UNGA Declaration on the Right and Responsibility of Individuals, Groups and Organs of Society to Promote and Protect Universally Recognized Human Rights and Fundamental Freedoms, A/53/144.

[99] See Flauss, above n 36 at p 19; Conforti, above n 77 at pp 121–6.

[100] Pursuant to an ECJ judgment of 25 July 1991, C-345/89, *Rec.* I 4062.

Council of Europe and the ECHR regime in the early 1990s created fears that the standard of human rights protection would be lowered, this in turn was a significant factor, if not the only cause, in the drive to develop a more robust protection regime within the European Community itself. This emerged perhaps most notably with the project of drafting the Charter of Fundamental Rights—even if that document, in the final instance, could not but bear a strong substantive resemblance to the ECHR.

All of these factors summarized here under the general heading of 'relativism' provide states with much room for manoeuvre in determining and enforcing the appropriate levels of human rights protection. This, combined with the non-legal but nonetheless very significant factor of 'interstate tolerance' means that strong state reactions to human rights abuses are limited to either the most serious cases (in which the notion of 'grave and massive violations' remains the central point of reference) or to the most opportune ones, in terms of their own interests—for human rights discourse is also very susceptible to strategic instrumentalization in service of state interests.

Preservation through Instrumentalization

The assertion that human rights can be so instrumentalized is, of course, fairly banal; this, however, does not mean that it should not be made—particularly as it represents one facet of the idea that states will not act contrary to their own interests. It is not sufficient in this regard to note, as we did above, that states can choose the commitments that they undertake, and even the terms under which they undertake them; nor that they may be subject to outside intervention in the name of human rights. It is also important to understand that, even though they have become *instruments* of international relations, human rights do not as a result inevitably represent genuine *objectives* in that field—even if such instrumentalization is not necessarily antithetical to an increased level of protection, but can on the contrary work in its favour. Beyond the fact that human rights can function as a means of protecting the state—and even promoting a particular type of state—they are almost never the direct and exclusive basis for international action, nor even the principal one. They are merely one diplomatic strategy amongst others, one legal policy among others. And if we continue to assert that human rights represent the subversion of state power, it is crucial to recall that this subversion only exists insofar as it is driven by other states.

(a) Certainly, the existence of a normative apparatus for the protection of human rights imposes a number of constraints on states. Some scholars even speak of an 'obliged rhetoric', and from this perspective, the gains in terms of human rights are very significant. In this sense, the *Pinochet* case illustrated that states—or at least Western democracies—have had to integrate into their political and legal discourse certain demands of justice that simply were not present in traditional diplomacy. Similar considerations were in play in the process leading to the Convention establishing the ICC. The same states were unable to avoid endorsing—even formally—the Annan Doctrine, formulated at a UN General Assembly meeting in October 1999, which called for recognition of an obligation on the UN to intervene in cases of massive human rights violations.[101] Many other examples can be given of this trend. However, this particular rhetoric that a commitment to human rights imposes also has a functional component. On one hand, it plays a justificatory role, in that it is capable of imparting legitimacy to action, and is thus systematically invoked in all instances of intervention. On the other hand, the same considerations can also lead to the imposition of a counter-discourse: that of a 'sovereigntist rhetoric', generally viewed as nationalist and conservative.

Two main themes remain current in this regard: first, that of 'reconversion' or 'recovery', based ultimately on the same appeal to legitimacy, with the proclamation of a specific doctrine of human rights as occurred, for example, in Marxist theory and in many of those approaches that integrate human rights and duties (which often even subordinated the former to the latter). This is only ever a practical translation of the fact that it is often in the interest of states to anticipate the types of rights-claims that will be made upon them. States are, of course, the primary addressees of such claims; however, in responding to those claims, they also perform the function of organizing rights—an organization that provides both 'the framework for, and an obstacle to' their effective guarantee.[102] This is all the more true in situations involving a multiplication of both claims and addressees, which places the state in a position to arbitrate between them.

The second theme is that of the denunciation of the desire to interfere (of judicial interference in, for example, the *Pinochet* case, or of the discourse of humanitarian intervention as imperialist), reflected also in the idea that we have today passed beyond the time of intervention to that of 'cooperation'. This counter-discourse is all the easier to deploy given that the principle of non-interference itself retains a powerful legitimacy, particularly in crisis situations in which arguments based upon nationalism or ideas of solidarity against external forces are very effective. International action remains essentially understood in terms of the question of intervention, located within the classic interstate paradigm despite many important changes and developments, for example the increasing role afforded to actors such as NGOs (who often appear as little more than the 'secular' branch of certain states). Moreover, it remains conspicuously selective in its application.

(b) This selectivity can be observed at a number of different levels, confirming that while states often use human rights as a means to denounce others, they rarely use them as grounds for concrete action; they do not intervene unless they are obliged to do so (as they are in an increasing number of cases) or it is in their

---

[101] Annan, 'Deux concepts de la souveraineté', *Le Monde* (22 September 1999).
[102] Mourgeon, above n 19 at p 65.

own interests to do so.[103] The existence of even relatively sophisticated mechanisms for the protection of human rights is thus insufficient; they must also be actively used. Interstate complaints, for example within the framework of the ECHR, are extremely rare, despite the fact that this regime is often offered as a model for others. Similarly, while it is true that the European Community developed a policy of using human rights conditionality in its foreign policy, in practice the mechanisms thus established are rarely set in motion. The same point can also be observed in the field of humanitarian intervention, in which the denunciation of inconsistency of action has become commonplace, and it which it appears that certain states are 'untouchable'. This illustrates well the obstacles facing any attempt to objectify human rights, which must confront the prevailing realities of vast disparities in power; we might cite the example of the Russian offensive in Chechnya in this regard. This creates the impression of different categorizations of states as, on the one hand, 'respectable' or 'virtuous' (and here the accession to certain legal regimes can function as a sort of 'certificate of respectability', even where the fulfilment by the state in question of the demands normally required by the regime is hardly verified, as notably illustrated by the accession of Russia to the Council of Europe despite a number of lively objections),[104] and, on the other, those that are less so—those cast out from international society, as, for example, was Burma at the ILO over the issue of forced labour. It remains undeniable that 'human rights are instruments of policies that seek to advance objectives other than the protection of the dignity of individuals. These objectives might be to destabilize a regime, to protect markets or to further the cause of world peace, but the ultimate goal is rarely the protection of human rights.'[105] As a result, human rights can even be 'forgotten' if necessary, for example, as illustrated by the years of international neglect for the populations of Iraq and Bosnia-Herzegovina.

Conversely, however, human rights can also function as a kind of all-purpose justification for attacks on the sovereignty of others. They can thus be used in support of national laws with putatively extra-territorial effect. For example, among the justifications for the American Helms-Burton Law (enacted to enable the US to impose sanctions on practically anyone trading with Cuba) is the explicit objective of restoring democracy and ensuring respect for human rights in that country.[106] In all cases, as already noted, the point is to ground intervention upon some powerful legitimating principles in an international society that has proved 'incapable of fashioning the states whose multiplication it has tolerated'.[107] It is

---

[103] Badie, above n 13.

[104] Parliamentary Assembly of the Council of Europe, 'Report on the conformity of the legal order of the Russian Federation with Council of Europe standards', Doc. AS/Bur/Russia (1994); HRLJ (1994) 249–300.

[105] Imbert, 'L'utilisation des droits de l'homme dans les relations internationales', in SFDI, above n 10, at p 283. For a similar perspective, see Sudre above n 17, at p 48.

[106] Stern, 'Vers la mondialisation juridique? Les lois Helms-Burton et D'Amato-Kennedy', RGDIP (1996) 979–1003.

[107] Sur, 'L'Etat entre l'éclatement et la mondialisation', RBDI (1997) 9.

important, then, to recall that the development of numerous mechanisms for the protection of human rights at the international level is driven by the failure of the domestic legal order to fulfil this function: this is not a challenge to the state itself (after all, those that more effectively guarantee human rights and accept international obligations in that regard are not somehow 'less sovereign' than others), but rather to ensure the promotion of a certain *model* of state (a sort of political education). In this sense, human rights are an instrument for configuring a particular type of state.

(c) This ambition of creating identically-structured states is not, however, an ideological project, as demonstrated by the fact that it is often eclipsed by other considerations; rather, the point is above all to guarantee stability. The discovery that states have an interest in effectively protecting some or all human rights in order to guarantee their own stability is not entirely new. Indeed, this consideration was the driving force behind the elaboration of minority rights after the First World War: it was to preserve the then recently redefined state frameworks, to protect them from separatist claims, that this particular legal tool was developed. Moreover, the contemporary renewal of minority rights has largely been driven by the same considerations: it cannot simply be understood as motivated by an interest in preserving the identity of groups that are still, essentially if not legally, identified by the threat that they might pose to the state. The scope of this realist calculation today exceeds by far the question of minorities: a more general correlation is widely recognized between the stability of the state and a respect for human rights. To be sure, since the drafting of the UN Charter, peace and international security have been linked to human rights protection; this, however, above all represents the utopian element of international law.[108] It cannot be considered to have crystallized into a genuine ordering principle of international law when all concrete action that actually results from it remains confined to the relatively limited sphere of humanitarian intervention, and thus to situations of massive human rights violations.

Other (perhaps complementary) points of view have exhibited a growing awareness that the maintenance of democratic regimes that respect human rights is ultimately less expensive that the alternatives, be it in terms of security, politics, economics, or influence more generally. This can also be seen at the institutional level, for example in the policies of organizations such as the IMF and the World Bank, and finds further expression in modern concepts such as good governance and sustainable development, and in the foreign policies of certain states. As has been very frequently observed, even the most democratic of states were not particularly discerning in the company they kept internationally, often not hesitating to support downright dictatorial regimes if they thought it could provide them with some additional guarantees of stability. Nevertheless, a number

---

[108] Sur, 'Système juridique international et utopie', 32 Archives de Philosophie du Droit (1987) 35–54; A Lejbowicz, above n 6 at pp 275–309.

of recent experiences have nuanced—if not actually undermined—this perspective, demonstrating that neither dictators nor dictatorships age particularly well, and that the short-term gains in terms of stability might well be more than offset by the costs resulting from the brutal destabilization that often accompanies the end of such regimes. In any event, this represents only one variable among many others: and, even if the demands of democratization and respect for human rights are often expressed in a very clear manner in situations of state or governmental upheaval—and in particular in actions aimed at the restoration of the state—they are rarely maintained in a sustained and vigorous fashion. Any objectification of human rights—even if we admit that it exists—remains extremely limited, and the consequences that flow from it must still pass through the classical interstate channels, as illustrated by the examples of Kosovo and East Timor at the end of the last century.

Nevertheless, there are a number of other forces at work that often lead to doubts that it is states that are fully in control of international issues and relations—but even if this is so, it is not necessarily a trend favourable to increased human rights protections.

B. Human Rights and the Dilution of Sovereignty

The notion that sovereignty has been somehow 'diluted' is without doubt exaggerated. It refers to a number of different phenomena, perhaps most importantly international integration but also transnationalization, in which a number of new actors play prominent roles, competing with the state and seeking to evade its influence. These actors might be public bodies such as the institutions of integration processes, or they might be private entities like multinational corporations. In general terms, a number of private entities—including individuals—now lay claim to international subjecthood. These developments can have contrasting, either negative or positive effects on the protection of human rights. The risks lie in allowing the competing actors to undermine the state without the concurrent establishment of alternative mechanisms of human rights protection. The positive effects lie in the creation of what political scientists refer to as a genuinely international public sphere of which human rights are foundational principles, translating, from a legal perspective, into a shared obligation to protect them.

The risks of competition without alternatives

The legal protection of human rights begins with states, and its establishment at the international level depends upon intergovernmental processes. As noted above, human rights are above all a discourse addressed to power—and thus to the state, from the moment that it centralizes power (and with it assumes a monopoly on the legitimate use of force)—in order not only that such power is not used to abuse individual rights, but also that it serves to actively guarantee them.

All legal mechanisms for the protection of human rights have been conceived of within this basic paradigm; we might, however, question their efficacy when confronted by a decline in sovereignty itself. No social organization can operate without answering the question of 'who does what?', which leads on directly to the issue of the identity of those who will exercise the competences and functions that have been taken out of state hands.

(a) This issue becomes particularly acute when we recognize that any decline in sovereignty is not necessarily synonymous with an increase in the level of protection of human rights. It is one thing to 'lift the veil' of the state; quite another to make it disappear entirely. The idea of a direct correlation between a decline in sovereignty and an increase in human rights protection presupposes that the state is always and only an oppressive structure for private individuals—a position that, as the foregoing has demonstrated, simply cannot be maintained. To be sure, the historical function of human rights was first and foremost the protection of the individual vis-à-vis the state; however, the idea that public power should be harnessed in service of human rights has also come to form part of legal and political doctrine (made concrete in the notion of the rule of law). The ultimate objective in this regard is to condition the exercise of such power in order that it acts positively to protect rights from any infringements they may suffer from other sources. It is further necessary either that the state has both the capacity and the means to impose this protection (which, of course, depends upon the competition to which it is subject, and the changes it is forced to undergo) or that alternative mechanisms of protection emerge. And, a fortiori, any possible appropriation by human rights discourse of an 'objective dimension'—which would itself presuppose a general obligation to develop rights protections—must confront the issue of who apart from the state, might, as things actually stand, be capable of performing that function?

(b) It has been generally observed that the state is today subject to the play of two different sets of tensions. The first is a consequence of 'globalization', leading to what has been referred to as a 'trivialization of the state'.[109] The second results from the multiplication of minority and nationalist movements that have plunged a number of states into a process of 'convulsive decomposition'[110]—a process that human rights can, moreover, function to support, through recognizing the legitimacy of certain aspirations, and developing plural allegiances (to minority groups, to churches, etc.) that compete with the loyalty traditionally owed to the state. This second source of tensions usually does not seem to undermine sovereignty itself, in that the majority of movements involved do not seek to challenge 'the state' as an abstract model, but rather with the actual state frameworks currently in existence, of which they seek only the redefinition. The basic model is thus reconfirmed,

---

[109] B Badie and M-C Smouts (eds), *L'international sans territoire* (Paris: L'Harmattan, 1996) p 422 ['*banalisation de l'Etat*'].

[110] S Sur, 'The State between Fragmentation and Globalization', 8 EJIL (1997) 421, at p 424.

and, with it, sovereignty. Nevertheless, the undermining of the nation-state and the weaknesses that result are hardly themselves favourable to human rights; rather, they are most often accompanied by the trivialization of both violence and violations. Moreover, the two different sets of tensions are not entirely unrelated to each other; quite the contrary, in fact. In effect, the further the state retreats and the more it gives the impression that it is no longer in control, the greater its vulnerability to contestation. With globalization, a number of actors free themselves from the state, and compete with it for power; which in turn raises the issue of the protection of human rights in the new sites constituted by those actors—the issue being whether the sovereignty, even if not defined by any precise substantive content but rather as a freedom, has meaning only if linked to a certain quantity of power. Does the state still have this power, or has it lost control with the 'erosion or abandonment of certain accepted methods of regulation',[111] and the increasing trend towards the 'privatization of norms'?[112]

The state is first of all subject to competition from other 'public' actors, within the framework of 'a progressive realization of international federalism',[113] in which it is but one site among others. This leads to the relativization of all the functions that it discharges, including the protection of human rights. In this regard, the paradigmatic case is that provided by the European Community. This is the most developed example, in that it involves a regional integration organization to which Member States have transferred significant powers—to the point that, since the 1960s, the issue of the protection of the human rights of the nationals of these states within the context of the exercise of the powers transferred has been raised. The problem appeared first in a concrete sense in Germany, where it gave rise to some 'protectionist' behaviour with the objective of protecting human rights: the German Constitutional Court decided to exercise control over Community acts for as long as they were not convinced that Community law offered, in terms of fundamental rights, guarantees at least equivalent to those provided for in German law.[114] This example demonstrated first of all that sovereignty can serve to fortify human rights protection. It also illustrated that such an integration project, in which states have consented to important limitations on, and thus competition in, the exercise of their powers, can be profoundly deficient in terms of human rights protection, offering lesser guarantees than those of national systems.

It can certainly be objected that European states are characterized by highly developed internal protection systems; and that, amongst these, the most

---

[111] Ibid. p 429.

[112] Delmas-Marty, *Trois défis pour un droit mondial*, above n 14.

[113] Sur, above n 108 at p 424.

[114] On this, see the 1974 German Constitutional Court decision in the *Solange I* case (*Internationale Handelsgesellschaft v Einfuhr und Vorratsstelle für Getreide und Futtermittel* BVerfGE 37, 271; English translation at [1974] 2 CMLR 540C). See also Grewe and Ruiz Fabri, *Droits constitutionnels européens*, above n 10 at pp 126–33.

demanding are to be found in those countries in which sovereignty has played an important role historically. This illustrates well the idea that there may be certain trends that states are powerless to resist—the element of irrecusability—which limit their capacity to protect human rights in the manner and to the extent that they desire. This is, however, as far as the European Community example can be taken as paradigmatic, precisely because of the recognition in that context that integration could only be successfully achieved through seeking to establish a 'community governed by the rule of law' (a significant term). However, both the recognition of the need for, and the establishment of, such a Community arrived late when compared with the trend towards economic liberalization. Moreover, it contained a number of gaps, as the example, cited above, of the rights of women working at night demonstrates.

At this point, we might also consider the example of the WTO, important precisely because of the protests and contestation to which it gives rise—involving, amongst other things, implications in terms of respect for human rights. In this context, it is easy to demonstrate how the protection of these rights can suffer as a result of a loss of state control over important processes. One almost caricatured example is provided by the protection of intellectual property. The economic justification for this regime has been repeatedly stressed; however, it also has the effect of permitting economic operators who hold patents for retroviral drugs to oppose (sometimes with the support of their national state) the diffusion of low-cost medicines to those suffering from the AIDS virus—even where such a programme has been instigated by a national government itself. This basically puts effective care beyond the reach of huge numbers of sufferers from developing countries, for whom any possible enjoyment of civil and political rights—if they exist and however sophisticated they might be—can offer only the scantest of consolations. The objection might be raised that this intellectual property regime was itself desired by states—the very same states that elsewhere elaborated the admirable human rights conventions. Such reasoning is, however, insufficient. Another factor must be taken into consideration: the competition of increasingly powerful private—particularly economic—actors, operating according to a logic that scarcely resembles that which underpins human rights. As is well known, these actors are in a position to both develop strategies of evasion or escape from the national laws they consider overly burdensome, and to lobby heavily for legislation favourable to their interests, for example, legislation intended to attract foreign investment.

The foregoing illustrates why globalization gives rise to contrasting narratives. If some scholars talk of a 'superclan', enabling individuals to rediscover or to find other forms of solidarity (which might appear a priori favourable to human rights, but which in reality is not necessarily so—alternative structures to the state may be oppressive or illiberal), the lively protest movements that have existed for some time now are testament to the fears to which this gives rise. This is one way of bringing to the forefront the issue of interdependence.

(c) The recognition of this interdependence is illustrated nicely by Resolution 1999/59 of the Commission on Human Rights, devoted, significantly, to 'Globalization and its impact on the full enjoyment of all human rights'. This resolution noted in particular that:

... globalization affects all countries differently and makes them more susceptible to external developments, positive and negative, including in the field of human rights ... [and that it] is not merely an economic process but also has social, political, environmental, cultural and legal dimensions which have an impact on the full enjoyment of all human rights.[115]

This was echoed by the statement issued by the G8 following its summit from 18–20 June 1999, in which it affirmed its desire to promote 'the social dimension of economic globalization'—which illustrates well that this is not something that will follow automatically or inevitably. And, even if in this process the central point of reference remains the state, as a result of widespread interdependence the idea of *shared responsibility* has taken root.

The Idea of Shared Responsibility

As a counterpoint to, or indeed in correlation with, the movements referred to above, we can observe the development—or perhaps the recurrence—of certain normative themes, such as those of ethics or responsibility; and, at the same time, a recognition of the need both to retain the state and to adopt a global, coordinated approach to the protection of human rights.

(a) Human rights, and human concerns more generally, are in search of a genuinely international public space. The retreat of sovereignty does not necessarily create such a space; however, from certain perspectives at least, it is being constructed, driven by the weight of public opinion, and the various different roles developed by NGOs, 'horizontal' and transnational organizations that deal with transnational or communal issues with significant implications for human rights. This international space has not been entrusted entirely to states, but rather accommodates these other actors who are now capable of acting effectively. To be sure, the public opinion referred to above as playing an important role remains essentially limited to that in developed and democratic states. Moreover, it is only sporadically manifested, often linked to media exposure (and in particular to the diffusion of powerful images), and is thus readily susceptible to manipulation. An essentially emotional, 'compassionate' approach has thus developed: it is significant, in this regard, that it is in this era that the notion of 'orphaned conflict' has emerged in order to designate humanitarian disasters that failed to elicit an international response. This sometimes gives the impression that we are still stuck within the same logic as that which informed the actions of the bourgeois ladies of the industrial revolution, donating small amounts of the profits made by

---

[115] Commission on Human Rights Res. 1999/59, Preamble paras 5–6.

their husbands to 'charitable works'. The current approach is, however, at least a small improvement on this, in particular due to the impact that public opinion can have in a globalized system in which information can travel quickly and in great quantities. The ethical demands that it expresses have provided a significant impetus in the trends towards self-regulation among private economic actors, in particular where the issue has been the regulation of humanitarian concerns, broadly conceived. Thus, the commitments publicly (always publicly!) undertaken to, for example, end the use of child labour or to eradicate certain working conditions can always be linked back, more or less directly, either to a desire for self-promotion ('ethics' and 'fairness' are good selling points) or to the threat of a boycott. Such practices, however, remain relatively isolated; and, even if they do show that everyone has a role to play, the fact remains that this international public space is still structured for, and unified by, states.

Human rights are, in effect, structurally dependent upon the existence of an authority capable of guaranteeing them; and, in the absence of any 'horizontal effect' of these rules (which would represent one further step on the path to their objectification), the subjects of the obligations both to respect and protect them are states. This was expressed by the Commission on Human Rights, in the Resolution quoted above, when it recognized 'that, while globalization, by its impact on, inter alia, the role of the State, may affect human rights, the promotion and protection of all human rights is first and foremost the responsibility of the State'.[116] This is linked to the fact that, however large the numbers of private actors who now act for the protection of human rights might be, their role is more to mobilize the state rather than to genuinely compete with it; we might talk more accurately of a proliferation of warning mechanisms—mechanisms that we can nonetheless expect the state to protect.[117] Ultimately, only the state (or states) can, in the final instance, impose these communal 'rules of the game'—rules that would lead to an assumption of responsibility by each actor in a context of generalized interdependence. We might note, in this regard, the attempt to encourage the assumption of responsibility in the UK in legislation imposing on major investors, such as pension funds, an obligation to disclose their investment criteria—which could force them to take other factors, beyond pure economic profit, into consideration. The same example, however, suggests that this type of behaviour is unlikely to generalize itself of its own accord; rather, the intervention of the state is required. This essential role of the state is, in general, very well understood by public opinion: the whole thrust of the protests over the WTO, expressed with such hostility at its Seattle Conference in 1999, has been to express the conviction that it is incumbent upon *states* to ensure that non-commercial concerns are taken into consideration—as only they are capable of

---

[116] Ibid., Art 1.
[117] See generally the UNGA Declaration on the Right and Responsibility of Individuals, above n 98.

doing so. This is also the logic driving the introduction of laws and institutions to help in the fight against corruption. It is the administration of interdependence; an administration that cannot be anything other than communal.

(b) 'Beyond this enduring need for the state, however, there is also a need for a global and coordinated approach; not only to the different aspects, human or otherwise, of globalization, but also to the relations between different human rights themselves.' In this regard, it is significant that the field has focused on social rights, despite the fact that they had until very recently been constantly undermined, at least in terms of legal protection, and notwithstanding the frequent affirmations of the universality and indivisibility of human rights. This rise in importance is not, however, surprising; rather, it reveals the recognition of the need for coherence if we are not to create fertile ground in which human rights catastrophes will flourish. It is no coincidence that this discourse has gained in strength in the aftermath of a number of major crises, in particular in South East Asia, and that it grows weaker as the crises are themselves forgotten. The rise in importance of social rights is not, moreover, entirely innocent, in that it is not driven solely by an appreciation of the merits of sharing the benefits of prosperity. It is also a discourse that renders vulnerable those actors, such as multinational companies, emerging in competition with states and seeking to emancipate themselves from states, just as states themselves proved vulnerable to the discourse of political rights. In more general terms, the dependency of human rights on economic factors is becoming more and more evident—and it is on this terrain that sovereignty, *qua* liberty, is more and more powerfully called into question.

We are thus brought back to the basic opposition between real (for example property) rights and formal rights, and to the question of the basic, indispensable prerequisites for rendering rights effective. In this regard, the impression remains that sovereignty has undergone a process of evolution without becoming somehow fundamentally different in kind; that it must be rethought, rather than replaced. Such an approach to sovereignty need no longer imply 'the presumption of innocence from which [states] benefit in that which was considered their state of nature'[118]—both because the use of force has now generally speaking been outlawed, and because the establishment of a positive law regime for punishing crimes against humanity implies recognition of the fact that individuals can act on behalf of the state even where the latter cannot be directly brought to trial for the results of these actions. Without doubt, this would leave us with the possibility of reacting only to the worst forms of human rights abuses; but might we not also allow ourselves to dream as to the proximity of what Kant envisaged, a time in which:

The peoples of the earth have thus entered in varying degrees into a universal community, and it has developed to the point where a violation of rights in *one* part of the

---

[118] Habermas, above n 23 at p 177 ['la présomption d'innocence dont (les Etats) bénéficiaient dans ce qui était considéré comme leur état de nature'].

world is felt *everywhere*. The idea of a cosmopolitan right is therefore not fantastic and overstrained; it as a necessary complement to the unwritten code of political and international right, transforming it into a universal right of humanity. Only under this condition can we flatter ourselves that we are continually advancing towards a perpetual peace.[119]

---

[119] Immanuel Kant, 'Perpetual Peace' (1795), in HS Reiss (ed), *Kant: Political Writings* (Cambridge: Cambridge University Press, 1991) pp 107–108.

3

Human Rights and Collective Security: Is There an Emerging Right of Humanitarian Intervention?

*Olivier Corten**

The existence of links between international security and the protection of individual rights has been widely recognized for some years now.[1] It is generally accepted today that the maintenance of peace presupposes a certain respect for individual rights, and, conversely, that severe violations of fundamental rights may create a situation threatening international peace and security within the meaning of Chapter VII of the UN Charter.[2]

On the basis of this finding, two trends have developed in legal scholarship. The first considers that the link between maintaining the peace and protecting human rights does not call into question the cardinal principle of the sovereignty of states.[3] By exercising their sovereignty to commit themselves to respect and guarantee certain fundamental rights, states have accepted that these rights go beyond their national competence and have accordingly waived the invocation of

* I particularly wish to thank Barbara Delcourt and Pierre Klein for their observations and suggestions, which have helped to improve this text.

[1] See, eg UN Secretary General, 'Agenda for Peace', S/24111 (1992) at 40; Declaration by the President of the Security Council, S/23500 (1992) in 96 *Revue Générale de Droit International Public* (1992) 256 and the note from the President of the Security Council in which the Council 'looks favourably on the observations contained in the Agenda for peace regarding humanitarian assistance and its relationships with the restoration of peace, maintenance of peace and consolidation of peace... In certain particular cases there may be a close link between critical needs for humanitarian assistance and threats to international peace and security', S/25344 (1993) 1.

[2] See, eg JM Sorel, 'L'élargissement de la notion de menace contre la paix' in Société française du droit international (ed), *Le chapitre VII de la Charte des Nations Unies* (1995) 3 and Y Kerbat, *La référence au chapitre VII de la Charte des Nations Unies dans les résolutions à caractère humanitaire du Conseil de sécurité* (1995).

[3] See, eg O Corten and P Klein, *Droit d'ingérence ou obligation de réaction?* (1996); O Paye, *Sauve qui veut? Le droit international face aux crises humanitaires* (1996); PM Eisemann, 'Devoir d'ingérence et non-intervention: de la nécessité de remettre quelques pendules à l'heure', 3 *Relations internationales et stratégiques* (1991) 67. For a view of this doctrinal controversy see A Pellet (ed), *Droit d'ingérence ou devoir d'assistance humanitaire?* (1995).

the principle of non-intervention in connection with them. On this view, every UN Member State has also accepted that the Security Council should, in conformity with the Charter, take measures to maintain international peace and security. Should the Security Council find that severe violations of human rights constitute a threat justifying the adoption of coercive measures, as expressly indicated by Article 2(7) of the Charter there is no breach of the principle of non-intervention.

A second line of scholarship, on the contrary, interprets the strengthening of rules protecting human rights as a challenge to the principle of the sovereignty of states.[4] In this context the emergence of a 'right of humanitarian intervention' has been noted, understood as consecrating the progress made in recent years in the human rights area. The idea is far from being revolutionary,[5] but has become topical again with the war waged by NATO member states in Kosovo, essentially in the name of 'humanitarianism'.[6] The 'right of intervention' was, according to some people, genuinely consecrated in that context, auguring the advent of a new era for the international legal system.[7]

This study seeks to choose between these two lines of scholarship in the light of recent developments in the concept and practice of the right of humanitarian intervention.[8]

Delimiting the focus of the study requires consideration of a more exact definition of the 'right of humanitarian intervention'.[9] 'Right' means here a legal title by definition incompatible with the traditional rules of international law, and in particular with the concept of sovereignty. 'Intervention' is used to mean an offensive military action that goes well beyond not only coercive measures that may be taken in the economic sphere but also non-offensive military operations

---

[4] See, eg RJ Dupuy, 'L'assistance humanitaire comme droit de l'homme contre la souveraineté des Etats' in F Kalshoven (ed), *Assisting the Victims of Armed Conflicts and Other Disasters* (1989) 27; M Bettati, *Le droit d'ingérence : mutation de l'ordre international* (1996).

[5] See, eg G Rolin-Jacquemyns, 'Note sur la théorie du droit d'intervention', 8 RDILC (1876) 673; A Rougier, 'La théorie de l'intervention d'humanité', 14 Revue Générale de Droit International Public (1910) 468.

[6] See the discussion in Part 2 below.

[7] See, eg the statements by the French President, 15 *Documents d'Actualité Internationale*, (1999) 575.

[8] Emphasis will be placed, within the scope of this article, on state practice, and not on the extensive commentary on this topic. The author will only point, aside from certain references contained in the article itself, to the following contributions: FK Abiew, *The Evolution of the Doctrine and Practice of Humanitarian Intervention* (1998); JF Halzgrefe and R Keohan (eds), *Humanitarian Intervention: Ethical, Legal and Political Dilemma* (2003); SD Murphy, *Humanitarian Intervention: The United Nations in an Evolving World Order* (1996); O Ramsbotham and T Woodhouse, *Humanitarian Intervention in Contemporary Conflict: A Reconceptualization* (1996); F Teson, *Humanitarian Intervention. An Inquiry Into Law and Morality* (1997).

[9] French-speaking scholars frequently use the expression 'droit' or 'devoir d'ingérence [duty to intervene]' (see, eg M Bettati and B Kouchner (eds), *Le devoir d'ingérence* (1987)), which for the purposes of this study we shall treat as being a right of intervention as defined below.

such as monitoring a ceasefire or helping local police forces to maintain order.[10] 'Humanitarian' is used to indicate an official justification directed at satisfying the most basic needs of a civilian population. The 'humanitarian' part need not be exclusive, but must be an essential aspect of the justification put forward by those intervening. The criterion thus refers to the justificatory discourse rather than the true reasons for military action, with the gap between these two giving rise to highly interesting debates;[11] these will, however, be avoided as far as possible below, as being ill-suited to resolving the question raised here.

The object of this study will in fact be to determine whether international law is evolving in the direction of recognizing a right of humanitarian intervention thus defined. Emphasis will be placed in this connection on the will of the states, with the question being whether, and if so how far, their will testifies to a shift in traditional rules oriented towards sovereignty. We are thus taking a resolutely positivist and voluntarist viewpoint, aimed at establishing a judgment of fact (does the right of intervention exist?), without directly speaking in terms of value judgments (should there be a right of intervention?). From this viewpoint one must start by noting that the response may be differentiated according to different groups of states, so that at first sight there can in principle be nothing against a right of intervention existing in certain legal relations (among states that have accepted its establishment) but not in others (in particular where one of the two parties to the legal relation has not accepted the 'right of intervention').[12] The outcome is that in theory the emergence of a right of humanitarian intervention would have to be studied for each of the states concerned. We shall, however, endeavour to provide an overview by taking examples drawn from the positions of a range of states, while of course not claiming to be exhaustive.[13]

As mentioned above, the analysis will essentially be based on a survey of recent practice in relation to humanitarian interventions. The relevant texts indeed reflect a traditional conception of the issues.[14] The UN Charter, based on the sovereignty

---

[10] Accordingly, we shall in principle not deal with 'peace-keeping operations' in the classical sense; in this connection see O Corten and P Klein, 'Action humanitaire et Chapitre VII: la redéfinition du mandat et des moyens d'action des Forces des Nations Unies', 39 *Annuaire Français de Droit International* (1993) 105.

[11] See, eg Bedjaoui, 'La portée incertaine du concept nouveau de "devoir d'ingérence" dans un monde troublé: quelques interrogations' in Actes du colloque organisé par l'Académie royale du Maroc, *Le droit d'ingérence est-il une nouvelle législation du colonialisme?* (1991) 232; JM Sorel, 'Le devoir d'ingérence: longue histoire et ambiguïté constante', 3 *Relations internationales et stratégiques* (1991) 95 and more recently, B Kingsbury, 'Sovereignty and Inequality', 9 EJIL (1998) 599.

[12] On this subject see *Case of military and paramilitary activities in Nicaragua and against it*, ICJ Rep. (1986) 97 *et seq.* at 183 *et seq.*

[13] Let us, finally, note that voluntarist positivism is in no way incompatible with a critical attitude that may develop once the agreement of states is established, in particular on the question of the functions or ideological role of such concepts as sovereignty or 'right of humanitarian intervention'. Some openings in this direction will be made towards the end of this study.

[14] For developments concerning the whole range of these issues, reference may be made to Corten and Klein, above n 3 as well as to RB Lillitch (ed), *Humanitarian Intervention and the*

of states, has not been revised in the sense of granting states a right of intervention. Similarly, non-treaty acts, in particular resolutions of the General Assembly, have announced the advent of a 'new international humanitarian order', but with strict respect for state sovereignty.[15] Accordingly, only practice can be taken into account, and only to the extent that it may show the existence of an agreement liable either to constitute authentic interpretation of a treaty (specifically, the UN Charter), or to demonstrate the existence of a new customary rule.[16]

Only recent practice will be considered from this viewpoint.[17] Older precedents such as Vietnam's intervention in Cambodia or India's in Bangladesh have already given rise to many interpretations which have not, taken together, fundamentally called into question the traditional principle of non-interference.[18] This is probably why the International Court of Justice (ICJ) has twice very clearly confirmed the classical legal regime.[19]

The period starting with the Gulf War has by contrast witnessed what many regard as a paradigm shift in international relations, with the logic of the Cold War having to make way for the advent of a 'new world order', allegedly based on international law in general and human rights in particular.[20] In this context several 'humanitarian' interventions took place in the 1990s, and it will be these on which the analysis in Part 1 will focus. Given its importance, the Kosovo war will be covered separately in Part 2. Finally, in Part 3 the post-Kosovo period will be studied.

1. 'Humanitarian Interventions' Prior to the Kosovo war

Since 1990, several military operations have been carried out in the territory of foreign states on the basis of humanitarian justifications. One might, in particular, mention the cases of Liberia (intervention in August 1990), Iraqi Kurdistan (*Provide*

United Nations (1973); I Brownlie, 'Humanitarian Intervention' in JN Moore (ed), *Law and Civil War in the Modern World* (1974) 217; F Teson, *Humanitarian Intervention. An Inquiry into Law and Morality* (1988) and M Akehurst, 'Humanitarian Intervention' in H Bull (ed), *Intervention in World Politics* (1984) 107.

[15] See GA Res. 43/131 (1988), 45/100 (1990), 45/101 (1990) and 45/102 (1990).

[16] See Art 31(3)(b) of the Vienna Convention on the law of treaties, and the *Military and Paramilitary Activities in Nicaragua and against it*, ICJ Rep. (1986) 98 at 186, and MH Mendelson, 'The Nicaragua Case and Customary International Law' in *The Non-Use of Force in International Law* (1989) 85–99; see also G de Lacharrière, 'La réglementation du recours à la force: les mots et les choses', in Centre National des Lettres (ed), *Mélanges offerts à Charles Chaumont* (1974) 346–62.

[17] The critical date is set at 1990, for reasons set out below.

[18] See an analysis of these precedents in Corten and Klein, above n 3 no. 126 *et seq.* and CH Thuan, 'De l'intervention humanitaire au droit d'ingérence' in CH Thuan and A Fenet, *Mutations internationales et évolution des normes* (1994) 94 *et seq.*

[19] *Strait of Corfu* case, ICJ Rep. (1949) 35; *Military and Paramilitary Activities in Nicaragua and against it* case, ICJ Rep. (1986) 134–5 at 268.

[20] See, eg G Bush, 'State of the Union Message, 29 January 1991', 6 *Documents d'Actualité Internationale* (15 March 1991) and the other statements made, commented on in P Herman, 'Le monde selon Bush: genèse d'un nouvel ordre mondial' in Association droit de gens, *A la recherche du nouvel ordre mondial, Tome I, Le droit international à l'épreuve* (1993) 7 *et seq.*

Comfort operation, April 1991), Somalia (*Restore Hope* operation, December 1992), Rwanda (Operation *Turquoise*, July 1994) and Bosnia-Herzegovina (Operation *Resolute Force*, August 1995).[21] In each of these cases the need was to intervene offensively in an internal conflict that had degenerated to the point of engendering a dramatic humanitarian situation for a major part of the civil population.[22] Does this practice testify to the emergence of a new 'right of humanitarian intervention'? The answer to this question must be given in the light of the official position taken by the states concerned, in the first rank of which one may locate the intervening powers. On this basis, two categories of precedents can be distinguished on the basis of the decisive legal criterion constituted by explicit authorization through a Security Council Resolution.[23] The first covers cases where the intervening powers base their action on this sort of explicit authorization, and the second covers those where there was no such authorization.

A. Precedents Where the Intervening Powers Based their Actions on Explicit Authorizations from the Security Council

The military interventions that took place in Somalia,[24] Rwanda[25] and Bosnia-Herzegovina[26] were all based on explicit authorization previously formulated in UN Security Council Resolutions. These three precedents will accordingly be analyzed in the first section. The cases of Haiti[27] and Zaire,[28] which also gave rise to explicit authorizations to intervene militarily in an internal situation, will not, however, be dealt with here. This is partly because these authorizations were not followed by offensive military action: in the case of Haiti the military deployment came in a cooperative framework; in the case of Zaire, the authorization was quite simply not followed up. On the other hand, it is not obvious that the Haitian precedent can be regarded as a case of 'humanitarian' intervention, to the extent that the official justification referred rather to restoring a legitimate government overthrown by a *coup d'état*.[29]

---

[21] These cases are cited by Antonio Cassese to show an evolution in positive international law; see A Cassese, 'Ex iniuria ius oritur : Are We Moving towards International Legitimation of Forcible Humanitarian Countermeasures in the World Community?', 10 EJIL (1999) 26; see also C Greenwood, 'Is There a Right of Humanitarian Intervention?', *The World Today* (February 1993) 34.

[22] In connection with these conflicts see the articles in LF Damrosch (ed), *Enforcing Restraint. Collective Intervention in Internal Conflicts* (1993).

[23] We shall start from the classical viewpoint that international law only exceptionally admits the use of force, in principle in cases of self-defence or Security Council authorization; eg I Brownlie, *International Law and the Use of Force by States* (1968).

[24] For the factual aspects see *Keesings* (1992) 39225.

[25] For the factual aspects see *Keesings* (1994) 40038.

[26] For the factual aspects see *Keesings* (1995) 40631.

[27] cf. Res. SC 940 (1994).   [28] cf. Res. SC 1080 (1996).

[29] O Corten, 'La résolution 940 du Conseil de sécurité autorisant une intervention militaire en Haïti: l'émergence d'un principe de légitimité démocratique en droit international?', 6 EJIL (1995) 116.

For each of the precedents considered, we shall start by detailing the official justifications put forward by the intervening powers, and in a second stage seek to draw the consequences in terms of the evolution of positive international law.

Official justifications: explicit authorization from the Security Council

The military interventions in Somalia, Rwanda, and Bosnia-Herzegovina were justified in various ways, depending on the audience concerned. It is thus very hard to identify a single official justification valid for all states and in all circumstances. We shall therefore confine ourselves to some general features that should be refined in terms of the specific aspects of each of the situations mentioned. From this angle we may begin by stating that the essentially humanitarian objective of each of the operations was emphasized. In more specifically legal terms, the argument was based on Security Council Resolutions containing explicit authorization.

One must indeed insist on the specific features of these three precedents, which all gave rise to resolutions regarded at the time as innovatory, whereby the Security Council authorized military intervention in internal conflicts with a view to pursuing objectives of a humanitarian nature.

As regards Somalia, we shall cite Resolution 794 of 3 December 1992 by which the Council:

10. Acting after Chapter VII of the Charter of the United Nations, authorizes the Secretary-General and Member States cooperating to implement the offer referred to in paragraph 8 above to use all necessary means to establish as soon as possible a secure environment for humanitarian relief operations in Somalia.[30]

In the case of Rwanda, the Council, in Resolution 929 of 22 June 1994:

3. Acting under Chapter VII of the Charter of the United Nations, authorizes the Member States cooperating with the Secretary-General to conduct the operation referred to in paragraph 2 above using all necessary means to achieve the humanitarian objectives set out in subparagraphs 4 (a) and (b) of resolution 925 (1994).

The case of Bosnia-Herzegovina is more complex since it involved the adoption of several similar Resolutions, among them: Resolution 770 of 13 August 1992, whereby the Council:

2. Calls upon States to take nationally or through regional agencies or arrangements all measures necessary to facilitate in coordination with the United Nations the delivery by relevant United Nations humanitarian organizations and others of humanitarian assistance to Sarajevo and wherever needed in other parts of Bosnia and Herzegovina.

SC Res. 836 of 3 June 1993, whereby the Council:

Acting under Chapter VII of the Charter of the United Nations, [...]

---

[30] See also SC Res. 814 (1993), at 5.

9. Authorizes UNPROFOR [United Nations Protection Force], in addition to the mandate defined in Resolutions 770 (1992) of 13 August 1992 and 776 (1992), in carrying out the mandate defined in paragraph 5 above, acting in self-defence, to take the necessary measures, including the use of force, in reply to bombardments against the safe areas by any of the parties or to armed incursion into them or in the event of any deliberate obstruction in or around those areas to the freedom of movement of UNPROFOR or of protected humanitarian convoys;

10. Decides that, notwithstanding paragraph 1 of resolution 816 (1993), Member States, acting nationally or through regional organizations or arrangements, may take, under the authority of the Security Council and subject to close coordination with the Secretary-General and UNPROFOR, all necessary measures, through the use of air power, in and around the safe areas in the Republic of Bosnia and Herzegovina, to support UNPROFOR in the performance of its mandate set out in paragraphs 5 and 9 above.[31]

The military operations in these three countries took place on the basis of these texts. Where those intervening felt the need to justify themselves in legal terms, they clearly invoked the title constituted by the extracts just mentioned.

As regards Somalia, one might cite as particularly characteristic the speech to the House of Commons by Douglas Hogg, Minister of State, during a debate on the role of the UN in British policy:

I think the powers under the Charter are perfectly adequate. Although the United Nations is prohibited in intervening in the internal affairs of Member States, Article 2.7 of the Charter speaks of matters which are 'essentially' internal affairs, and humanitarian matters are, of course, now matters of international concern. The prohibition of interference by the United Nations in internal affairs has also an important exemption: if you take action under Chapter VII, the prohibition does not apply. But to take action under Chapter VII, as is presently being considered by the Council, does require a determination that the situation or the dispute is a threat to international peace and security. In the case of Somalia the Council has already reached that determination some months ago when it imposed an arms embargo because the lack of stability in the country was, of course, a threat to its neighbours, as was the refugee situation.[32]

The operation carried out by the French army in Rwanda was justified on the basis of similar legal arguments. The Prime Minister at the time put it fairly clearly to the National Assembly:

[This is a] humanitarian operation intended to save threatened populations [, and it is subject to a] number of conditions or specific principles governing this humanitarian intervention.

First principle: France will act only with a mandate from the UN Security Council. The Government considered that action of this type, responding to a humanitarian duty, ought despite its urgency to be authorized by the international community.[33]

---

[31] One might also mention SC Res. 816 (1993) at 4, SC Res. 844 (1993), SC Res. 871 (1993), and SC Res. 1031 (1995).

[32] Reproduced in 63 BYBIL (1992) 823.

[33] Reproduced in 40 *Annuaire Français de Droit International* (1994) 1032; see E Spiry, 'Interventions humanitaires et interventions d'humanité : la pratique française face au droit international', 102 *Revue Générale de Droit International Public* (1998) 429–30.

The NATO bombings of Serb forces in Bosnia-Herzegovina from 1994 to
September 1995 were again supported by the Security Council Resolutions cited
above. On 9 August 1993 the North Atlantic Council approved the possibility of
air strikes, confirming that:

NATO's actions take place under the authority of the United Nations Security Council,
within the framework of the relevant UNSC resolutions, including UN Security Council
resolutions 770, 776 and 836, and in support of UNPROFOR as it carries out its overall
mandate.[34]

Despite the diversity of the situations involved, it will be noted that the statement of the humanitarian objective is accompanied by the mention of a clear
legal basis constituted by one or more explicit authorizations previously given
by the Security Council.[35] As the declarations cited well reflect, the moral
concerns are deployed in a legal framework constituted by principles everyone
agrees to reaffirm as relevant. One might of course cite other discourses that
do not take up this legal justification. But the fundamental thing to point out
at this stage is that where a legal argument is raised it refers to a UN Security
Council Resolution.

Confirmation and re-actualization of existing international law

In the light of these considerations, it is at least disputable that the military operations in Somalia, Rwanda, or Bosnia-Herzegovina precedents testify to the emergence of a right of humanitarian intervention. Where humanitarian concerns are
invoked this is not in opposition to, but in application of, positive international
law in existence.[36] No state has on those occasions claimed that unilateral military action to alleviate human suffering was authorized by a right of intervention.[37] The extracts reproduced above, especially the speech by the French Prime
Minister, are particularly persuasive in this regard. Legally, the action is based on
Chapter VII of the UN Charter, which authorizes the Council to adopt military
measures which member states may be empowered to implement. There is no
breach here of the traditional principle of non-interference which, pursuant to
Article 2(7) of the Charter, 'in no way detracts from application of the coercive

---

[34] Text in 19 *Documents d'Actualité Internationale* (1993) 420–21; see also the decisions
taken by the Council authorizing recourse to the NATO air strike force to support the action
of UNPROFOR, specifically at Sarajevo, of 9 February 1994; text in 6 *Documents d'Actualité
Internationale* (1994) 118, and the Declaration on the situation in former Yugoslavia by the North
Atlantic Council, of 30 May 1995; text in: 14 *Documents d'Actualité Internationale* (1995) 426.

[35] This does not mean that none of these military actions raises problems of interpretation,
especially as regards NATO actions in Yugoslavia; see R Higgins, 'Some Thoughts on the Evolving
Relationship Between the Security Council and NATO' in Boutros Boutros-Ghali, *Amicorum
Discipulorumque Liber* (1998) 523 *et seq.*

[36] See, eg Spiry, above n 33, 432.

[37] See the discussions in the run-up to adoption of pertinent resolutions; S/PV 3106 (res. 770),
S/PV 3145 (res. 794), S/PV 3228 (res. 836) and S/PV 3392 (res. 929).

measures provided for in Chapter VII'. By ratifying or adhering to the UN Charter each state agrees not to invoke internal affairs in such a case.[38]

It is true that it is also necessary for the Security Council to have itself acted in the strictest respect for the conditions of procedure and of substance required for any military action. As to the procedure, it is fairly easy to verify compliance with it, since it amounts essentially to a positive vote by nine members of the Council, with no vote against by any of the five permanent members. One may at most note that China's abstention was not, despite the letter of Article 27(3) of the Charter, regarded by anyone as an obstacle, which only confirms an extensive interpretation already authorized by the International Court of Justice.[39] As to the conditions of substance, the Charter requires first the finding of the existence of an act of aggression, of a breach of peace or of a threat to international peace and security. This is in fact why the Resolutions cited contain references to Chapter VII. That there was a threat to peace in Somalia, Rwanda, or Bosnia-Herzegovina could, moreover, scarcely be doubted. This characterization is based inter alia on the gravity of the humanitarian situation, combined with other factors such as the severe loss of authority by the governments concerned (Somalia, Bosnia-Herzegovina).[40] It will be noted in any case that a restrictive interpretation limiting the applicability of Chapter VII to armed threats by one state against another, or a fortiori to combat between armies of different states, is contradicted by these precedents, to which one could, moreover, add many others.[41] Finally, traditional international law is also reinforced since all the Resolutions are, in accordance with the Charter, officially aimed at restoring peace and stability in each of the situations referred to.[42] The humanitarian considerations seem quite subordinate to the pursuit of these objectives, and do not as such seem to confer any legal title whatsoever upon the intervening powers.[43]

While they do not testify to the renewed questioning of the principles of sovereignty or non-interference, these precedents do nonetheless make some clarifications as to their interpretation. To that extent it is clear that they do show some evolution in international law. In particular, they decisively condemn the abusive interpretations aimed at ruling out humanitarian action on the pretext that events remained confined within the frontiers of a state.

However, and this is no less interesting to emphasize, this first category of precedents also discards certain arguments that might be used in favour of unilateral

---

[38] O Corten and P Klein, 'L'autorisation de recourir à la force à des fins humanitaires: droit d'ingérence ou retour aux sources?', 4 EJIL (1993) 506.

[39] *Namibia* case, ICJ Rep. (1971) 22.

[40] Corten and Klein, above n 38, 511 *et seq.*

[41] Confining ourselves to authorizations for recourse to force, we shall recall the precedents of Haïti and Zaire (see SC Res. 940 (1994) et 1080 (1996)).

[42] VCM Diaz Barrado, 'L'emploi de la force autorisé par le Conseil de sécurité et les motifs humanitaires in MJ Domestici-Met (ed), *Aide humanitaire internationale: un consensus conflictuel?* (1996) 297 *et seq.*

[43] T Christakis, *L'ONU, le chapitre VII et la crise yougoslave* (1996) 162.

humanitarian intervention. One might think, first, of the reasoning that the absence of effective control by a government over its territory amounts to the disappearance of the state and hence of its sovereignty, implicitly authorizing any foreign power to intervene without running the risk of breaching international law.[44] Precedents such as Somalia, Bosnia-Herzegovina, and in a different context Albania,[45] are incompatible with this reasoning. In all these situations no one felt empowered to intervene on the pretext that the state no longer existed. In the case of Somalia, the Secretary General, quite to the contrary, considered a few days before adoption of Resolution 794 that:

> There is not at present in Somalia any government able to demand and authorize such recourse to force. It would accordingly be necessary for the Security Council to find, in conformity with Article 39 of the Charter, the existence of a threat to peace... and to decide the measures to take in order to maintain international peace and security.[46]

The only legal consequence of the loss of authority of a government is thus to create a threat to peace such as to enable the Security Council to respond. One cannot deduce, *a contrario*, any general empowerment that would enable third states to intervene militarily on the territory concerned.[47]

There is one other clarification leading to the restriction of the possibilities of unilateral armed action which concerns not the situation before intervention but the details of the latter. Whereas in the case of the Gulf War, the authorization given to states 'to use all necessary means' to pursue the objectives stated in the Resolution was not accompanied by any monitoring procedure,[48] procedures of this type were legally instituted and actually followed in the cases of Somalia, Rwanda, and then Bosnia-Herzegovina.[49] Without going into details of the measures of control provided for in each of these cases—to which one could, moreover, add many others—this practice shows the concern of UN member states to retain some control over actions undertaken within the framework of what must remain collective security. In other words, these precedents rule out

---

[44] See J Charpentier, 'Le phénomène étatique à travers les grandes mutations politiques contemporaines' in SFDI (eds), *L'Etat souverain à l'aube du XXIème siècle* (1994) 24; JM Sorel, 'La Somalie et les Nations Unies', 38 *Annuaire Français de Droit International* (1992), 72, 75, and 78 and Spiry, above n 33, 418.

[45] The development of civil war and the resulting state of anarchy in Albania in 1997 induced Italy not to intervene unilaterally but to request and obtain authorization from the Security Council to that end; see SC Res. 1101 (1997) and 1114 (1997).

[46] Letter of 29 November 1992, cited in Corten and Klein, above n 38, 519–20.

[47] At any rate, nothing allows one to assert that in such a case the state has legally ceased to exist or that the people of the state concerned has otherwise lost all its rights, including that of political independence in relation to any external power; ibid. 520–21 and Paye, above n 3, 150 *et seq*.

[48] See the criticisms by Y Le Bouthillier and M Morin, 'Réflexions sur la validité des opérations entreprises contre l'Iraq en regard de la Charte des Nations Unies et du droit canadien', 29 CYIL (1991) 142.

[49] See Corten and Klein, above n 38, 527 and Domestici-Met, above n 42, 71; JD Mouton, 'La crise rwandaise de 1994 et les Nations Unies', 40 *Annuaire Français de Droit International* (1994) 220 *et seq*.

the possibility of invoking a sort of 'blank cheque' from the Security Council for conducting actions without any form of collaboration with the UN.[50]

Ultimately, this first category of precedents shows that if a right of intervention exists, it is within the limits set by the UN Charter, in particular Chapter VII. This at any rate seems to be the opinion of most states, foremost among them the intervening powers themselves. Be it in Somalia, Rwanda, or Bosnia-Herzegovina, the legal justification has essentially consisted in linking the humanitarian situation to a threat to peace, which in turn justifies authorization of the recourse to force given by the Security Council to states it has then undertaken to monitor. Whether in this or that specific case the action actually respected the terms of the Resolution is a question not dealt with in the context of this paper. The intention is not to rule upon the legality of any specific military action but to seek to draw from the practice of states their position regarding the existing law. This is also the method adopted in considering a second category of precedents, where armed action for humanitarian ends could not be based on explicit prior authorizations from the UN Security Council.

B. Precedents Where the Intervening Powers Were Unable to Base their Actions on Explicit Authorization from the Security Council

Two military interventions for humanitarian ends will be analysed. These are the operations that took place in Liberia in August 1990 and in Iraq in April 1991.[51] Cases such as the Russian intervention in Georgia[52] or in Tajikistan,[53] or again of certain member states of the Community of West African States in Sierra Leone[54] are not considered since they are not based in any substantial way on objectives of a humanitarian nature.[55] The sending of foreign military forces to the Central African Republic[56] and Guinea-Bissau[57] do not, for their part, meet the definition of 'intervention' in the sense defined in the introduction, given that both cases involved non-offensive actions accepted by the protagonists in

---

[50] See, eg S/PV. 3106.

[51] These two precedents are occasionally cited as examples of humanitarian interventions; see P Daillier and A Pellet, Nguyen Quoc Dinh, *Droit international public* (1999) 973, n 597.

[52] See, eg SC Res. 858 (1993), SC Res. 896 (1994), SC Res. 934 (1994), SC Res. 937 (1994), SC Res. 971 (1995), SC Res. 993 (1995), SC Res. 1036 (1996), SC Res. 1065 (1996), SC Res. 1096 (1997), SC Res. 1124 (1997).

[53] See, eg SC Res. 968 (1994), SC Res. 999 (1995), SC Res. 1061 (1996), SC Res. 1099 (1997), SC Res. 1138 (1997), and SC Res. 1167 (1998).

[54] See, eg the final Communiqué of the OASU in Conakry on 26 June 1997; text in 14 *Documents d'Actualité Internationale* (1997) no 304. As to the Security Council's action, see SC Res. 1132 (1997).

[55] For the factual context of these various crises, see JM Balencie and A de La Grange, *Mondes rebelles. Acteurs, conflits et violences politiques* (1999).

[56] See SC Res. 1125 (1997), 1136 (1997), 1152 (1998), 1155 (1998), 1159 (1998).

[57] See *Keesing's* (1999) 42826 and the Secretary General's Report submitted pursuant to Security Council Resolution 1216 (1998) relating to the situation in Guinea-Bissau, S/1999/294 (1999), at 11.

the internal conflict. For similar reasons, the case of East Timor will not be dealt with here. We would further note that, by contrast with these latter examples, the operations in Iraq and Liberia have been adduced by legal scholars to suggest the emergence of a right of humanitarian intervention.[58]

The argument, however, supposes that one could show that this practice is accompanied by an *opinio juris* attesting to a radical redefinition of the principle of non-interference and its corollary, that of state sovereignty. To test this hypothesis, we shall once again start from the official justifications supplied by the intervening powers, before seeking to deduce from these more general assertions as to the state of positive international law in this area.

The official justifications: classical legal arguments

The official justifications relating to the operations in Liberia and then Iraq are obviously very different, not just from a reading of the declarations made by the political leaders concerned, but also in view of the very significant factual and legal differences between these interventions. We shall take each of them up in turn, in order to provide a detailed understanding of the arguments put forward by the intervening powers. At this stage we shall refrain from criticizing or assessing the legal relevance of these arguments, the objective being only to identify the opinion of the states concerned.

Intervention of ECOWAS in Liberia

During 1989 an armed rebellion took shape in Liberia aimed at overthrowing President Doe, who had come to power following a *coup d'état* some nine years earlier.[59] In the first months of 1990, several hundred thousand Liberians embarked on an exodus, their destination being mainly the neighbouring countries.[60] In July the rebel forces, themselves divided into two dissident groups, approached the capital and threatened the government in place. According to the international press each of the forces involved was guilty of considerable extortion against civilians, resulting in many victims and bringing an increase in the flow of refugees and displaced persons.[61] On 24 August, after vain attempts at mediation to bring about a ceasefire among all the belligerents, troops of the Economic Community of West African States (ECOWAS), totalling four thousand men from Nigeria, Ghana, Gambia, Guinea, and Sierra Leone, entered Liberian territory.[62] After violent fighting, which tore the country apart for several months,

---

[58] B Kouchner, *Le malheur des autres* (1991) 229–30; see also 260, 265–6, 271; Greenwood, above n 21, 37.

[59] D Wippman, 'Enforcing the Peace: ECOWAS and the Liberian Civil War' in Damrosch, above n 22, 157.

[60] *Keesing's* (1990) 37174.

[61] *Keesing's* (1990) 37601.

[62] *Keesing's* (1990) 37644 and 37908.

a first ceasefire was concluded on 28 November.[63] Severe tension, however, continued for several years, with ECOWAS troops leaving the country only in January 1998.[64]

The intervening powers advanced several types of arguments to justify their operation.[65] In general terms, in August 1990, an ECOWAS communiqué put forward the objective of 'stopping the senseless killing of innocent civilians, nationals and foreigners, and to help the Liberian people to restore their democratic institutions'.[66] It will, however, be noted that these objectives are accompanied by a justification based on fairly classical legal arguments, namely consent by the state and legitimate collective defence. In a letter of 14 July 1990, addressed to the ECOWAS bodies, the President in office of Liberia indicated in fact that:

It would seem most expedient at this time to introduce an ECOWAS Peace-keeping Force into Liberia to forestall increasing terror and tension and to assure a peaceful transitional environment.[67]

A few days later the press reported that President Doe had accepted an ECOWAS peace proposal comprising a ceasefire, deployment of a peace-keeping force and the immediate formation of a government of national unity.[68] The rebel forces led by Charles Taylor, for their part, rejected any foreign intervention, which could only delay or prevent the fall of the government.[69] It was thus only on the basis of the appeal from the government in place that the troops of Nigeria, Ghana, Gambia, Guinea, and Sierra Leone disembarked in force at Monrovia a few weeks later. We are undeniably in a classical legal framework, which in certain circumstances allows foreign military intervention in a civil war through agreement with the authorities of the state concerned.[70]

---

[63] See *Keesing's* (1990) 37766.

[64] *Keesing's* (1998) 41992. Subsequent events, which were marked by a deterioration of the situation followed by a new military operation in 2003, will not be taken into consideration here.

[65] See the arguments set out in E Kwaka, 'Internal Conflicts in Africa: Is there a Right of Humanitarian Action?', 2 *African Yearbook of International Law* (1994) 24–5; E Kannyo, 'Civil Strife and Humanitarian Intervention in Africa: A Preliminary Assessment', 4 *African Yearbook of International Law* (1996) 60 and in C Ero, 'ECOWAS and the Subregional Peacekeeping in Liberia', Journal of Humanitarian Assistance (1995) (<http://jha.ac/?s=ECOWAS+and+the+Sub regional+Peacekeeping+in+Liberia>).

[66] Cited in Greenwood, above n 21, 37. The same terms can be found in the letter from the Nigerian Delegation to the UN Secretary General; S/21485, 10 August 1990, and the final Communiqué of the First Session of the Community's standing mediation Committee, Banjul, ECW/HSG/SMC/1/5/rev. 1, cited in F Meledje Djedjro, 'La guerre civile au Libéria et la question de l'ingérence dans les affaires intérieures des Etats', 26 *Revue Belge de Droit International* (1993) 411–12.

[67] Letter addressed by President Samuel K Doe to the Chairman and Members of the Ministerial Meeting of ECOWAS Standing Mediation Committee, 14 July 1990, Document 39 in Marc Weller (ed), *Regional Peace-keeping and International Enforcement: The Liberian Crisis* (1994) 61.

[68] *Keesing's* (1990) 37602.

[69] Wippman, above n 59, 167.

[70] See, eg *Case of military and paramilitary activities in Nicaragua and against it*, ICJ Rep. (1986) § 246.

This is most particularly the case where the state is the victim of armed aggression by one or more other states, including through military support of rebel forces.[71] In the case in point the Liberian government accused the Ivory Coast, Burkina Faso, and Libya of participating, more or less directly, in the military actions pursued by Charles Taylor's troops.[72] These accusations were relayed by the international press.[73] Burkina Faso, moreover, according to several African sources, publicly acknowledged its support of the Liberian rebels.[74] The legal title of the ECOWAS states is, in this context, a classic case of legitimate collective defence, with the state suffering aggression calling for the aid of allied states to eliminate the aggression of which it is a victim.

It should be noted in this connection that in the case of ECOWAS a special institutional framework was invoked to justify the operation. A *Protocol on Mutual Assistance on Defence*, adopted in Freetown on 29 May 1981, provided that 'any armed threat or aggression directed against fellow members shall constitute a threat or aggression against the entire Community', specifically mentioning the case of 'internal armed conflict within any member state engineered and supported from the outside...likely to endanger the peace and security in the region'. In such a case ECOWAS can initiate collective intervention in the territory concerned on condition that the government concerned so requests. This protocol, ratified by Liberia among others, was explicitly invoked as the basis for the intervention, as the possibility for peace-keeping forces to act in self-defence when attacked on the ground was similarly invoked.[75] These are again fairly classical arguments, referring to regional defence and security mechanisms organizing and institutionalizing the right of legitimate collective defence.[76]

Operation *Provide Comfort* in Iraqi Kurdistan

At the very moment that Iraq suffered severe military defeat in the Gulf War, an uprising broke out in both the North and the South of the country.[77] Saddam Hussein's military troops, however, reacted fairly quickly and managed

---

[71] The lawfulness of foreign intervention in an internal conflict that has not stemmed from prior aggression from a foreign State is by contrast controversial; see DJ Harris, *Cases and Materials on International Law*, (1979) 673 *et seq.*

[72] See the President's message of 24 December 1989, reported in *Keesing's*, 1990, p 37174. See also E Kannyo, above n 65, 61.

[73] *Keesing's* (1990) 37601.

[74] F Meledje Djedjro, above n 66, 401.

[75] Ero, above n 65. See the speech by the representative of the Ivory Coast in the discussions leading up to adoption of Resolution 788 of 19 November 1992, PV. 3138, p 27, and the one by the representative of Nigeria (ibid. p 47).

[76] The revised ECOWAS Treaty of 24 July 1993 contains an Art 58 constituting a new appropriate legal framework (<http://www.ecowas.int>).

[77] A Daems, 'L'absence de base juridique de l'opération *Provide Comfort* et la pratique belge en matière d'intervention armée "à but humanitaire"', 25 *Revue Belge de Droit International* (1992) 264.

to re-conquer the portions of territory that had fallen into rebel hands.[78] This campaign was accompanied by brutal repression that led to the exodus of several hundred thousand refugees. The Iraqi Shi'ites took refuge in Iran, while the Kurds were prevented from entering Turkish territory by that country's authorities. The UN Security Council adopted Resolution 688 on 5 April 1991, condemning the repression of the civilian population, the consequences of which were to create a genuine threat to international peace.[79] In the face of the resulting humanitarian disaster, negotiations began between Baghdad and representatives of the UN Secretary General. Just as these negotiations were on the verge of succeeding,[80] French, British, American, Dutch, Italian, Spanish, and Australian troops entered Iraqi Kurdistan, officially to constitute safe havens to encourage the return of those blocked in the mountains which form the frontier with Turkey.

Operation *Provide Comfort* was justified essentially by moral considerations, particularly vis-à-vis Western public opinion. The intervening powers and their allies insisted on the humanitarian disaster and the imperative to put an end to it.[81] Where the top political leaders found themselves in the position of supplying legal arguments, however, it will be noted that they were far from systematic in invoking the existence of a right of humanitarian intervention authorizing unilateral military action, decided upon and carried out without Security Council authorization. Despite the profound ambiguity of some of the declarations made at the time, one must rather conclude that the legal arguments referred to a sort of implicit authorization contained in Security Council Resolution 688.

By way of example one might first cite extracts from a British memorandum of 2 December 1992 on the growing role of the UN and its implications for British foreign policy:

The principle of provision of relief by the UN in areas of internal conflict is well established. The UN is increasingly acting upon that principle. We support both the principle of such intervention in cases of extreme humanitarian need, and the relief operations of this type in which the UN is involved [. . .] We have demonstrated our support for such UN operations by financial assistance and, in the case of military operations by our provision of British troops for protection duties (for example: Iraq, former Yugoslavia);[82]

We believe that international intervention *without* the invitation of the government of the country concerned can be justified in cases of extreme humanitarian need. This is why we were prepared to commit British forces to Operation Haven, mounted by the

---

[78] *Keesing's* (1991) 38126 and C Rousseau, 'Chronique des faits internationaux', 95 Revue Générale de Droit International Public (1991) 738.

[79] The link between the repression, the refugee flows and the threat to peace was fairly clearly brought out in the discussions leading up to adoption of the Resolution (see S/PV. 2982).

[80] According to some sources Iraq gave its agreement to the establishment of United Nations reception centres for Kurdish civilians on 16 April 1991, ie the eve of the armed intervention (*Keesing's* (1991) 38128 and 37 *Annuaire Français de Droit International* (1991) 1057)).

[81] Spiry, above n 33, 424.

[82] Reproduced in 63 BYBIL (1992) 825–6.

Coalition in response to the refugee crisis involving the Iraqi Kurds. The deployment of these forces was entirely consistent with the objectives of SCR 688.[83]

A second example in this connection can be found in a letter from the Dutch ministers of Defence and Foreign Affairs sent to the Dutch Parliament to explain the Netherlands' participation in the operation:

[…] the Government underlines the fact that this is a strictly humanitarian action, in the course of which all military security actions are purely concerned with the execution of the humanitarian task. Furthermore, the Government is of the opinion that an adequate judicial basis for this action is provided by Security Council Resolution 688, and particularly by that which is stated under operative paragraph 1, wherein the consequences of the oppression of the Iraqi civilian population are described as a threat to international peace and security in the region. Both the Twelve and the United States Government also take this position […].[84]

One might, finally, mention the declaration by the then French President, namely that 'the UN Security Council on 5 April 1991 adopted Resolution 688, on the basis of which the biggest humanitarian operation in history is at present being organized in favour of the Iraqi Kurds and Shi'ites'.[85]

    While these declarations are far from being unambiguous, they indubitably show a concern to base the reference to humanitarian objectives on an extensive interpretation of a resolution previously adopted by the Security Council. In this respect the case of Liberia is very different, since the Security Council (in that case) had never adopted any resolution before the interventions started.

    In conclusion, the precedents of Liberia and Iraqi Kurdistan show, over and above their specific features, a number of common points. The humanitarian justifications are in fact in both cases based on legal argumentation of a technical nature referring to the two major classical arguments capable in positive international law of justifying recourse to force. In the first case it was essentially self-defence that was invoked. In the second, it was the authorization given, even if only implicitly, by the UN Security Council.

A possible evolution of existing international law, within defined limits

What consequences are to be drawn from this finding in terms of the evolution of positive international law? Clearly an answer is hard to provide since we would have to rely on only two precedents, and on which no court has pronounced. It should, moreover, be recalled that in accordance with the methodology, we have chosen to follow the question that could be given different answers for different states in international society, and there is nothing at first sight to prevent one thinking that some might have a much more restrictive position than others. We

---

[83] Ibid. 826–7; see also the other declarations 824 and 825.

[84] Reproduced in 23 NYIL (1992) 362.

[85] Cited in M Bettati, 'Un droit d'ingérence?', 95 *Revue Générale de Droit International Public* (1991) 644, n 5.

shall start by interpreting the position taken individually by the different states, before considering the behaviour of the UN and the consequences that might be drawn therefrom.

The positions of different states

A first observation is called for in view of the position taken by the intervening states, as set forth above. The concern to refer to traditional legal rules is particularly significant as it points to their reluctance to assume the inclusion in international law of a right of humanitarian intervention that would fundamentally call into question the principles of sovereignty and non-interference. It thus seems a priori difficult to deduce from these precedents the emergence of a fundamentally innovative right that would relegate these principles to second place in the name of humanitarianism.[86]

It is true that the legal argumentation that was developed in both the Liberian and the Iraqi cases is debatable. As regards Liberia one might dispute that the outside support given to the rebels could be characterized not just as a resort to force but as genuine aggression, a notion implying inter alia a degree of severity[87] that was far from being clearly present in the case in point. Some have therefore challenged the lawfulness of the intervention, considering that it amounted purely and simply to an external interference in an internal conflict, which had in any case been authorized without respect for the special procedures laid down by ECOWAS.[88] Concerning the Iraqi precedent, the existence of implicit authorization in Resolution 688 is at least debatable.[89] Apart from the absence of any ground in any provision whatsoever in the text of the Resolution, this interpretation is hard to reconcile with the discussions leading up to its adoption, which show that authorization of recourse to force had never been contemplated.[90]

The point here is not, however, to rule upon the legality of these interventions, by rejecting the legal arguments on which they are based.[91] The fact that the

---

[86] In this sense see Paye, above n 3.

[87] See the definition of aggression accepted by consensus (GA Res. 3314 (1974)), esp. Art 2.

[88] Meledje Djedjro, above n 66, 410 ff; Kannyo, above n 65, 61.

[89] See in this sense, P Malanczuk, 'The Kurdish Crisis and Allied Intervention in the Aftermath of the Second Gulf War', 2 EJIL (1991) 129; O Schachter, 'United Nations Law in the Gulf Conflict', 84 AJ IL (1991) 469; M Shaw, *International Law* (1997) 875; T Franck, 'The Security Council and "Threats to the peace": Some Remarks on Recent Developments' in Académie de droit international de la Haye (ed), *Le développement du rôle du Conseil de sécurité* (1993) 102–103; C. Carpentier, 'La résolution 688 (1991) du Conseil de sécurité : quel devoir d'ingérence?', 23 Etudes internationales (1992) 279 *et seq.*; A Daems, above n 77; O Paye, above n 3,142 *et seq.*

[90] See S/PV. 2982, esp. p 58.

[91] Some scholars consider that Resolution 688 constitutes an adequate legal base for the intervention; see, eg M Bettati, 'Ingérence humanitaire et démocratisation du droit international', 1 *Le Trimestre du monde* (1992) 34; 'Droit d'ingérence ou droit d'assistance?', 2 *Le Trimestre du monde* (1993) 13; 'Les résolutions de l'ONU relatives au principe de libre accès aux victimes' in MJ Domestici-Met (ed), above n 42, 269; TG Weiss and KM Campbell, 'Military Humanitarianism', 33 *Survival* (1991) 451; PM Dupuy, 'Droit humanitaire et maintien de la paix: harmonie ou

official justifications are undoubtedly awkward to maintain reveals all the more the concern of the states in question to keep within existing law, even where it provides only very fragile grounds.

The same conclusion can be extended if we examine the position of other states that did not intervene but supported the intervention. One might for instance cite in this connection the Belgian Foreign Minister, answering a question from an MP on the position of his country, which was at the time chairing the Security Council, regarding the intervention in Iraq by the Coalition:

A legal basis must first be found. If it does not exist it must be created. To do so, consensus is necessary. If I am not mistaken, Article 3 of the Geneva Convention drawn up in 1949 already contained legal elements in this connection. But this article does not mention the means available to the international community to impose this humanitarian inter-ference in certain countries...We must, alas, find that the reactions of certain countries (like China or the USSR) are fairly negative...Accordingly, we find it more appropriate to give an extensive interpretation to an existing text. I have in mind paragraph 5 of Resolution 688, which provides that the Secretary-General can use all means....[92]

We find the same reasoning as developed by the intervening powers: the humani-tarian nature of the operation is not enough, implying that a legal basis 'must be found'. One is accordingly led to pursue the 'extensive interpretation' of trad-itional features rather than to invoke some innovative legal principle.

In these circumstances neither can one deduce, from the relative silence of states that are not involved in the operations concerned, an *opinio juris* in favour of the emergence of a right of humanitarian intervention.[93] To be able to make this conclusion, one would in fact have to overcome two obstacles that appear decisive in the case of the Liberian and Iraqi precedents.

First, one would have to show that silence indicates tacit acceptance moti-vated by legal considerations rather than political or moral ones. This condi-tion is particularly important in the case of humanitarian interventions, which may, according to the circumstances, be approved in ethical terms without this necessarily implying a particular legal position. If, when it comes to interpret-ing silence, everything depends on the specific circumstances,[94] we must, with Malcolm Shaw, note that:

It is not inconceivable that in some situations the international community might refrain from adopting a condemnatory stand where large numbers of lives have been saved in

---

contradiction?' in R Ben Achour and S Laghmani (eds), *Les nouveaux aspects du droit international* (1994) 94; S Marcus-Helmons, 'Le droit d'intervention, un corollaire des droits de l'homme', 12 *Revue trimestrielle des droits de l'homme* (1992) 479.

[92] Cited in A Daems, 'L'absence de base juridique...', 25 *Revue Belge de Droit International* (1992) 266.

[93] Certain states nonetheless protested, at least in the case of Liberia; see Meledje Djedjro, above n 66, 412 ff. See also Wippman, above n 59, 175.

[94] *Préah Vihéar Temple* case, ICJ Rep. (1962) 27 ff; IC MacGibbon, 'The Scope of Acquiescence in International Law', 25 BYBIL (1954) 170.

circumstances of gross oppression by a state of its citizens due to an outside intervention. This does not, of course, mean that it constitutes a legitimate principle of international law.[95]

Second, even assuming that the silence of states ought to be interpreted in legal terms, it would be hard not to regard the approval as directly linked to the legal arguments of the intervening states, which, as we have just seen, refer not to an innovative principle but to a particular interpretation of existing legal rules.

UN Activity

Consideration of the activity undertaken by the UN in respect of the two situations confirms these elements of evaluation.

In the case of Kurdistan, the competent bodies generally preferred to abstain from any condemnation or approval. Only the then Secretary General stated that while the intervention could be understood from a moral viewpoint it was hard to defend in legal terms.[96] Otherwise, it should be noted that UN civilian and police forces went to the area shortly after Operation *Provide Comfort*, but on the basis of and according to the details laid down in the agreement previously negotiated with the Iraqi authorities,[97] conduct that is hard to interpret as legal approval for the operation.

Regarding Liberia, the UN played a much more active role.[98] Initially it explicitly approved the part played by ECOWAS in the conflict and it imposed an arms embargo intended to bring the Liberian rebels around to respecting the principles defended by the regional organization. After several declarations had been made,[99] a first Resolution (788) was adopted on 19 November 1992 whereby the Council:

Determining that the deterioration of the situation in Liberia constitutes a threat to international peace and security, particularly in West Africa as a whole,

Recalling the provisions of Chapter VIII of the Charter of the United Nations, [...]

Welcoming the continued commitment of the Economic Community of West African States (ECOWAS) to and the efforts towards a peaceful resolution of the Liberian conflict,

Further welcoming the endorsement and support by the Organization of African Unity of these efforts, [...]

---

[95] Shaw, *International Law*, (3rd edn) (1991) 725; see however the different formulation in 4th edn (1997) 803.

[96] See the statement by Javier Pérez de Cuéllar in the press at the time; *De Standaard* (11 April 1991), and R Zacklin, 'Le droit applicable aux forces d'intervention sous les auspices de l'ONU' in Société française pour le droit international (eds), above n 2, 195.

[97] Text in 30 ILM (1991) 860–62.

[98] See BG Ramcharan, 'Cooperation Between the UN and Regional/Sub-regional Organizations in Internal Conflicts: the Case of Liberia', 4 *African Yearbook of International Law* (1996) 3 *et seq.*

[99] See the declarations by the President of the Security Council of 22 January 1991 (S/22133) and of 7 May 1992 (S/23886).

Taking into account the request made by the Permanent Representative of Benin on behalf of ECOWAS (S/24735),

Taking also into account the letter of the Foreign Minister of Liberia endorsing the request made by the Permanent Representative of Benin on behalf of ECOWAS (S/24825), [...]

4. Condemns the continuing armed attacks against the peace-keeping forces of ECOWAS in Liberia by one of the parties to the conflict; [...]

8. Decides, under Chapter VII of the Charter of the United Nations, that all States shall, for the purposes of establishing peace and stability in Liberia, immediately implement a general and complete embargo on all deliveries of weapons and military equipment to Liberia until the Security Council decides otherwise.

The Security Council then consistently congratulated ECOWAS or the Organization of African Unity (OAU) on their support for the peace process,[100] condemned the attacks to which ECOWAS forces were subject,[101] and even encouraged the African states to supply additional military contingents or else 'financial, logistical and other types of assistance'.[102] It was in a context of close collaboration that it decided to send the UN Observation Mission to Liberia (MONUL), security of which was entrusted to ECOWAS contingents.[103]

How is the UN's conduct to be interpreted against the yardstick of the legal criteria typically laid down for establishing the *opinio juris* of states? Undeniably, the Security Council approved the ECOWAS action in the conflict.[104] However, it is hard to deduce from this approval some sort of support for a form of 'right of humanitarian intervention'. The Council does not insist on the commencement of military action but rather concentrates on the period during which the ECOWAS presence was formally accepted by the parties to the conflict; it does not even mention the humanitarian objectives, strangely underplayed or even ignored in the texts cited; it dwells almost exclusively on the maintenance and restoration of peace, referring to the classic provisions of the UN Charter. Second, even if one were to consider that the UN Member States had through these resolutions given a form of legal approval, the presentation of the operation as relating to a sort of peace-keeping mission is significant.[105] What seems to be approved is action taken at the request of and with the reiterated consent of the government in place, not a foreign offensive operation against a sovereign state.[106] If one follows the logic of their discourse, the UN Member States apparently ratify a posteriori only

---

[100] See esp. SC Res. 813 (1993) at 2 and 3; SC Res. 856 (1993) at 6; SC Res. 866 (1993) at 7; SC Res. 911 (1994) at 8; SC Res. 972 (1995) at 11.

[101] See esp. SC Res. 1041 (1996) at 4; SC Res 1083 (1996) at 7.

[102] See esp. SC Res. SC 1014 (1995) at 6 and 11; SC Res 1083 (1996) at 11.

[103] See esp. Res. SC 866 (1993) and the debates leading up to its adoption (S/PV. 3138, p. 47); SC Res. 1001 (1995) at 11; SC Res. 1020 (1995) at 12, SC Res. 1041 (1996); SC Res. 1059 (1996) at 14.

[104] Wippman, above n 59, 174.

[105] This was, moreover, the way the operation was presented in the letter sent to the Security Council by the permanent representative of Nigeria; see S/21485 (10 August 1990).

[106] Wippman, above n 59, 176 *et seq.*, esp. 180.

non-coercive action, as being action accepted by the government in place, meaning that Chapter VIII of the Charter, which prescribes prior Security Council authorization only for coercive actions, has not been infringed.[107] Once again we find ourselves facing interpretations of classical legal rules, even if these interpretations can be challenged.[108] But that would constitute another discussion, which we shall not go into here.

Ultimately, all the precedents raised lead to the same single conclusion. It is indisputably difficult to interpret them as testifying to the emergence of a right of humanitarian intervention that would overthrow traditional principles of sovereignty of states and non-interference in their domestic affairs. Neither the intervening states nor other states, individually or in the UN, clearly issued an *opinio juris* that would point in this direction.

This clearly does not mean that positive international law did not evolve on these occasions. In the cases of Somalia, Rwanda, and Bosnia-Herzegovina, UN members confirmed the possibility for the Security Council to act to put an end to humanitarian situations threatening international peace and security, while specifying the scope and limits of such action. The cases of Liberia and Iraqi Kurdistan are certainly more complex, and would deserve nuanced approaches taking into account, in detail, of the legal position of each of the states. One might, for example, claim that the Western states invoking Resolution 688 considered that henceforth armed action could be authorized implicitly by the Security Council, implying a considerable modification of classical international law. To be erected into a general rule, however, it would have to be shown that this position transcends the specific case of Kurdistan, with any state whatsoever being henceforth empowered to act militarily on the territory of another merely because the Security Council has designated a situation 'a threat to peace' and invoked Chapter VII of the Charter. It is doubtful whether this position has truly been adopted by any state, and it is significant to note that in the context of other crises, the need for explicit authorization has been regarded as legally essential.[109] As to the Liberian precedent, it undoubtedly testifies to a liberal interpretation of Chapter VIII of the Charter, to the extent that military action such as that taken by ECOWAS was regarded as non-coercive, and consequently did not require prior authorization from the Security Council under Article 53. Other

---

[107] See the debates leading up to the adoption of SC Res. 788 (1992), S/PV. 3138, especially the presentation of the position by the ECOWAS representative, pp 3–12, and the speech by the Liberian representative, pp 12–20.

[108] Simply reading the Security Council resolutions gives a poor account of the events on the ground, that often attest to the offensive nature of the ECOWAS forces; see, eg *Keesing's* (1990) 37699, 37766 and (1992) 39131.

[109] See, eg the precedent of Albania, n 44 above, or of the Central African Republic, n 55 above. See in particular what was said by the French representative, who very clearly reaffirmed the principle of the primacy of the Security Council and absolute respect for the provisions of the Charter (SC, S/PV.3808, (6 August 1997) 6–7). See also Olivier Corten and François Dubuisson, 'L'hypothèse d'une règle émergente fondant une intervention militaire sur une "autorisation implicite" du Conseil de sécurité', 105 *Revue Générale de Droit International Public* (2000) 873.

precedents, such as those of Georgia or Tajikistan may, moreover, be interpreted in the same sense.[110]

In any case, it can be noted that, on the basis of the foregoing analyses, it is difficult to argue that a right of humanitarian intervention has emerged in opposition to the traditional framework. The need now is to tackle the specific case of the Kosovo war in order to determine whether it is capable of furnishing new arguments in this respect.

2. The Precedent of Kosovo

The military intervention by NATO member states on 24 March 1999 has been regarded by some as pointing to a genuine paradigm shift at the level not just of international relations but also of international law itself. It has been written in this connection that 'interference to protect human rights, and then humanitarian interference, seems definitively to have gained the upper hand over state sovereignty'.[111]

We shall not speak here as to the political and ethical aspects underlying these assertions, nor go specifically into the disputes over the sincerity of NATO's humanitarian motivations—by comparing the Kosovo crisis with (other) similar ones.[112] Rather, the analysis will once again focus on the legal problem of the emergence of a new customary rule. In a similar way to our consideration of the other precedents, the point will be to start from the official justifications put forward by the intervening powers and then to deduce more general lessons regarding a possible evolution of positive international law.

A. The Ambiguity of the Official Legal Justifications for Intervention

The war waged for nearly three months on Yugoslav territory undeniably meets the definition of 'humanitarian intervention' given earlier. It was an offensive action officially motivated by humanitarian considerations. A reading of the relevant documents, however, reveals some ambiguity. In general terms it will be noted that the legal aspect of the reasoning is often hard to distinguish from the political or moral aspect. However, where on some occasions a more specifically legal argument is put forward, there seems to be reference to an argument of a technical nature relating to the interpretation of the resolutions previously adopted by the Security Council regarding Kosovo.

---

[110] See the relevant Security Council Resolutions cited above, nn 51 and 52.

[111] M Torrelli, 'Chronique des faits internationaux', 103 *Revue Générale de Droit International Public* (1999), 488.

[112] On this point see F Cerutti, 'Crisi del Kosovo ed intervento NATO: questioni etiche', 3 *Quaderni Forum* (1998-XII) 33, as well as, more stealthily, E Vigliar, 'La crisi dei Balcani nell'odierno ordine europeo ed internazionale', *La Comunità Internazionale* (1999-LIV), 26.

A legal argument hard to distinguish from moral and political considerations

The arguments put forward by the most senior officials responsible for the intervention, to justify its commencement, seem to have been fairly diverse, as shown by this statement made on 23 March 1999 by the Secretary General of NATO:

We are taking action following the Federal Republic of Yugoslavia Government's refusal of the International Community's demands :

- Acceptance of the interim political settlement which has been negotiated at Rambouillet.
- Full observance of limits on the Serb Army and Special Police Forces agreed on 25 October.
- Ending of excessive and disproportionate use of force in Kosovo.

As we warned on the 30 January, failure to meet these demands would lead NATO to take whatever measures were necessary to avert a humanitarian catastrophe.

NATO has fully supported all relevant UN Security Council resolutions, the efforts of the OSCE and those of the Contact Group.

We deeply regret that these efforts did not succeed, due entirely to the intransigence of the FRY [Federal Republic of Yugoslavia] Government.

This military action is intended to support the political aims of the International Community.[113]

This text puts forward at least four distinct grounds for intervening: refusal by Yugoslavia to sign the Rambouillet plan, its breach of the October 1998 agreement, its disproportionate recourse to force in Kosovo, and the risk of humanitarian catastrophe. These grounds are, however, presented with no form of legal basis other than a vague allusion to the Security Council's actions. The stress is more on the political side, especially the 'political aims of the international community'.[114]

On other occasions a justification of an ethical nature was advanced. Thus on 24 March Javier Solana declared that 'we must put an end to the violence and to the humanitarian disaster now sweeping Kosovo. For us, that is a moral duty',[115] with President Clinton stating the same day that 'putting an end to this tragedy is a moral imperative, and of great importance to the national interest of the United States'.[116] Similarly, when the French President on several occasions stated that it

---

[113] Statement of 23 March 1999; English text in Marc Weller (ed), *The Crisis in Kosovo 1989–1999*, (1999), 495; French version in 9 *Documents d'Actualité Internationale* (1 May 1999) 341.

[114] See also the Washington Declaration on Kosovo, 23–24 April 1999, French version in 11 *Documents d'Actualité Internationale* (1 June 1999) 421.

[115] NATO press release, 24 March 1999, (1999) 41.

[116] Speech on 24 March; English text in Weller, above n 113, 498; French version in 9 *Documents d'Actualité Internationale* (1 May 1999) 342.

had to do with a 'war for right',[117] he is evidently referring more to a natural right with a strong ethical dimension than to positive international law.[118]

The difficulty of identifying an autonomous legal argument returns[119] if we consider what the representatives of the intervening states said in the debates at the Security Council on 24 March 1999, the very day military operations started. Several of them wrapped up what they said in considerations about which it is sometimes unclear whether they are of a political, moral or legal nature:

The NATO action was justified and necessary to stop the violence and prevent an even greater humanitarian disaster;[120]

NATO's objectives were to avert a humanitarian crisis [...]. They could not simply stand by while innocents were murdered, an entire population was displaced, villages were burned and looted, and a population was denied its basic rights merely because the people concerned did not belong to the 'right' ethnic group;[121]

as stated by the Secretary-General, diplomacy had failed, but there were times when the use of force might be legitimate in the pursuit of peace;[122]

over recent weeks, the world had witnessed [...] a heightening of tension and confrontation, and an amassing of powerful offensive means by the Yugoslav army. That had inspired fear in a community of two million people. What was at stake today was peace, peace in Europe, and also human rights;[123]

we have taken this action with regret, in order to save lives [...]. The action being taken was legal. It was justified as an exceptional measure to prevent an overwhelming humanitarian catastrophe.[124]

Here we find very general assertions that might possibly be interpreted as attesting to the emergence of a right of humanitarian intervention. In order to assess its scope one would further have to note that they are accompanied by specific legal references, in particular to resolutions previously adopted by the Security Council.

The technical argument about interpreting Security Council resolutions

Whether in these same debates or elsewhere, the intervening powers had occasion to make their arguments in somewhat more detailed, specifically legal, terms. According to the French representative on the Security Council:

The Security Council [...] had indicated in its relevant resolutions that it was acting under Chapter VII of the UN Charter. It had affirmed in resolution 1199 and 1203

---

[117] See, eg his television address on 6 April 1999, reproduced in 10 *Documents d'Actualité Internationale* (15 May 1999) 383.

[118] See also Tony Blair's statement on 22 April 1999, cited in *Keesing's* (1999) 42901.

[119] In this sense, see M Torrelli, 'Chronique des faits internationaux', 103 *Revue Générale de Droit International Public* (1999) 487.

[120] UN Press Release SC/6657 (1999), US Representative, at 3–4.

[121] Ibid., Representative of Canada, at 4.

[122] Ibid., Representative of the Netherlands, at 7.

[123] Ibid., Representative of France, at 7.

[124] Ibid., Representative of the United Kingdom, at 9.

that the deterioration of the Kosovo situation threatened regional peace and security. He said that through resolution 1199, the Council had demanded of the Belgrade authorities an immediate end to the hostilities and the maintenance of a ceasefire, as well as immediate measures to avert imminent catastrophe [...]. The Council had demanded that existing agreements be applied promptly and in their entirety by the FRY. Those included commitments and obligations of a precise nature, yet those were not respected by Belgrade, despite every effort to prompt it to do so. Thus, those efforts had been exhausted.[125]

The argument can accordingly be summarized in three stages. First, the Security Council adopted the resolutions in the context of Chapter VII of the Charter. Second, Yugoslavia broke these resolutions. Third, and consequently, the NATO member states are entitled to act, even militarily, to put an end to these violations.

This line of argument can be found emanating from almost all the intervening powers.[126] It was defended at the Security Council on 24 March,[127] but also two days later when a draft resolution condemning the intervention was rejected.[128] It can be found again before the International Court of Justice in connection with certain pleadings following the request for a restraining order submitted by Yugoslavia on 25 April.[129] One can note its relatively technical nature, appealing to classical legal mechanisms: interpretation of Security Council resolutions and the UN Charter, and the implicit reference to the theory of countermeasures or reprisals, since the military intervention was officially aimed at getting the state in question to cease its prior violation of international obligations.[130]

The ethical appeals for humanitarian intervention, along with the predominantly political considerations relating to the risks of destabilization of the region, are thus based on a legal argument with fairly classical references. What we have a priori is a fairly similar notion to that raised in Operation *Provide Comfort*, in relation to which we saw how moral justifications of a humanitarian type and legal grounds referring to Resolution 688, previously adopted by the Security Council, were structured. The point now is to determine whether it may be considered that this precedent has brought a substantial change to the state of positive international law.

---

[125] Ibid., at 7. See also the speech by the French Prime Minister during the debates in the National Assembly on 26 March 1999, Compte-rendu analytique officiel, Sess. ord. 1998–1999, 79ème jour, 203ème s.

[126] See, eg the Declaration of 8 April by the Council of the European Union, taken up again in the Declaration of 10 May 1999, 13 *Documents d'Actualité Internationale* (1 July 1999) 526.

[127] See the declaration by the representatives of the United States (at 3–4), of Canada (at 4), and of the United Kingdom (at 9).

[128] UN Press Release SC/1036 (26 March 1999).

[129] See the pleadings by Belgium (11 May 1999, CR 99/15, p 15). It is true that Belgium has invoked a parallel right of unilateral humanitarian intervention.

[130] See the discussion of this hypothesis by A Cassese, above n 21.

B. A Relative, Limited Evolution of Existing International Law

As when considering the other precedents, we shall below seek to ascertain the justifications supplied by the intervening powers and the responses they led to, so as to draw conclusions about any evolution in existing international law.

In general terms, given that the concept here is similar to that in Operation *Provide Comfort*, it should not be surprising if the consequences were also similar. It is hard to maintain that traditional legal principles have been fundamentally called into question, when even the intervening powers continue to refer to them, in rather peculiar fashion to be sure, but in any case without challenging in principle the rule of non-interference as stated in particular in the UN Charter.[131] However, it will be noted that, in contrast to the Iraqi precedent, Kosovo gave rise to numerous reactions, positive and negative, as well as to fairly sustained activity by several UN organs. These reactions will be detailed, bearing in mind that once again the conclusions to be drawn might be different according to the states for which one seeks to derive an *opinio juris*. In this context we shall distinguish the states that supported the intervention from those that did not, with a special place reserved for the response of UN organs to the commencement and continuation of the intervention.

The position of states that supported the intervention

The legal argumentation of the intervening states has already been detailed. In fact, only Belgium, on one occasion, and the United Kingdom, made reference to a right of humanitarian intervention.[132] The other states did not. We would insist here on the fact that, as in the Iraqi case, this legal argumentation is based on an extensive interpretation, admittedly sometimes hard to uphold, of the classical legal rules.[133] The fact that these are nonetheless still referred to, instead of invoking some innovative right, is accordingly all the more meaningful as a pointer to a concern to preserve the traditional legal framework.

How does the reasoning of the NATO states raise problems that make all the more noteworthy the sense of having to justify themselves in relation to existing law?

This reasoning is based on one indisputable premise: the existence at the time of the intervention of three Security Council resolutions on the Kosovo situation. The proposed conclusion, however, is hardly orthodox: the right of UN Member States to secure respect for these resolutions by force. The source of this right can hardly be found in the Charter itself, which contains no empowerment in this sense. On the contrary, Article 53 provides that any coercive action carried out by

---

[131] It is significant from this viewpoint to read all the debates that took place at the UN Security Council (see references below).

[132] C Gray, *International Law and the Use of Force* (2000), at 37–42.

[133] See, eg the nuanced critique by B Simma, 'NATO, the UN and the Use of Force: Legal Aspects', 10 EJIL (1999) 1.

a regional organization requires prior authorization from the Security Council,[134] and it seems problematic to claim that this authorization could be implicit where military measures are involved.[135] In any case, it is hard to find in the case in point any authorization, explicit or implicit, in the resolutions cited. At no point can an empowerment be found for the states to use 'all means necessary' to bring violations to an end or meet certain objectives, on the model of what has been noted in the cases of Somalia, Rwanda, and Bosnia-Herzegovina.[136] The mere description of a threat to peace can scarcely be regarded in itself as constituting an authorization, since this would amount to considering that any reference to Chapter VII would entail a right of armed response by all states to any breach of a resolution, without any form of evaluation or monitoring by the Council itself. This whole construction also runs counter to the traditional rules of international responsibility, which rule out the possibility of unilateral armed reprisals, whatever the gravity of the initial violation.[137]

Political figures[138] have sometimes invoked paragraph 16 of Resolution 1199 of 23 September 1998 whereby the Council:

Decides, should the concrete measures demanded in this resolution and resolution 1160 (1998) not be taken, to consider further action and additional measures to maintain or restore peace and stability in the region.

It is in any case hard to understand how a provision that gives the Security Council competence to assess the advisability of additional measures could amount to the empowerment of states to act unilaterally, without obtaining any form of endorsement from the Council.[139] The Council, moreover, stated that it was still considering the matter,[140] and a few days later adopted Resolution 1203 welcoming conclusion of the ceasefire agreements and the beginnings of normalization of the situation on the ground.[141]

The legal reasoning further clashes with the position of Russia and China, which, at the time of adoption of the resolutions concerned, indicated fairly

---

[134] See also Art 1(d) of the 'Declaration on the Enhancement of Cooperation between the United Nations and Regional Arrangements or Agencies in the Maintenance of Peace', GA Res. 49/57, Annex.

[135] G Ress, 'Article 53' in B Simma (ed), *The Charter of the United Nations. A Commentary* (1994) 733, and Higgins, above n 35, 522; T Farer, 'A Paradigm of Legitimate Intervention' in Damrosch, above n 22, 318.

[136] See above, and the resolutions cited.

[137] See in particular GA Res. 2625 (XXV) cited above, and Art 50 of part two of the International Law Commission's draft on the responsibility of States.

[138] See, eg what was said by Jean-Bernard Raimond, French parliamentarian, in the debates at the French National Assembly on 26 March 1999, Compte-rendu analytique officiel, Sess. ord. 1998–1999, 79ème jour, 203ème s.

[139] In this sense, see M Kohen, 'L'emploi de la force et la crise du Kosovo: vers un nouveau désordre international', 33 *Revue Belge de Droit International* (1999) 122. It is true that Belgium has invoked a parallel right of unilateral humanitarian intervention.

[140] SC Res. 1199 (1998) at 17.

[141] SC Res. 1203 (1998) at 1.

clearly that these texts contained no empowerment for recourse to force. When Resolution 1199 was adopted, the Russian representative stated that 'it is only by peaceful means that the Kosovo situation can be settled',[142] while China abstained because it considered that reference to Chapter VII was abusive.[143] The discussions surrounding adoption of Resolution 1203 are clearer still. Russia insisted that 'the draft resolution provides a mechanism for informing the Council, which will monitor the course of the procedures for applying the peace measures through the Secretary-General', adding that it hoped that 'the decisions to place NATO forces on alert will be lifted', and finally abstained from voting.[144] As for China, it explicitly condemned 'the decision taken without Security Council authorization by a regional organization to interfere in the domestic affairs of the Federal Republic of Yugoslavia, creating a dangerous precedent of challenge to the authority of the Security Council'.[145] The Chinese representative stated in this context the reasons for abstention:

China is not in principle opposed to a technical resolution in the Kosovo question, but is opposed to exercise of pressure on the FRY that amounts to interference in its domestic affairs. It has noted that the resolution contains no authorization to use force or threat to use force in the FRY.[146]

What these two representatives of states with the veto had to say clearly indicates that the resolutions were adopted only because they contained no explicit or implicit authorization to use force, something in any case not disputed by the United States or France, speaking later.[147] The argument by the intervening powers invoking such authorization a few weeks later is therefore extremely difficult to uphold.[148]

Finally, let us mention one last difficulty specific to the argument developed in order to justify intervention, which has more to do with the 'spirit' of the resolutions, supposedly able to legitimize the intervention. This difficulty is based on the fact that only Yugoslavia is allegedly responsible for breaches of the Security Council resolutions, which would justify massive military action directed against it alone. But this fact is in itself disputable. Reading of the Security Council resolutions demonstrates consistent condemnation of the extortions committed by the Albanian nationalists.[149] Moreover, the reports supplied to the Security

---

[142] Press Release SC /974 (23 September 1998) 9.

[143] Ibid.

[144] Press Release SC /981 (24 October 1998) 14.

[145] Ibid., at 15.

[146] Ibid.

[147] Ibid., at 15, 16.

[148] In this sense, M Spinedi, 'Uso della forza da parte della NATO in Jugoslavia e diritto internazionale', 3 *Quaderni Forum* (1998–XII) 27.

[149] SC Res. 1199 (1998), para 9; SC Res. 1203 (1998), para 9; see also the presidential declaration of 19 January 1999 whereby the Council, while condemning the Racak massacre, 'also gives a forceful warning to the "Kosovo Liberation Army" against acts that contribute to heighten tensions' (S/PRST/1999/2).

Council by the Secretary General furnish arguments in this direction. Not only are extortions and violations of humanitarian law attributed not just to Serbian and Yugoslav forces but also to Albanian separatist forces, but these forces are also fairly clearly blamed as being at the root of the failure of the ceasefire secured in mid-October 1998.[150] To cite a particularly significant extract, the Secretary General stated on 12 November 1998 that he was 'deeply concerned at reports that Kosovo Albanian paramilitary units had taken over positions evacuated by the government forces and were continually launching attacks against the security forces and civilians'.[151] A month later he stated that:

Following the agreement of 12 October between President Slobodan Milosevic and US Special Envoy Richard Holdbrooke, the Kosovo paramilitary units took advantage of the interruption in fighting to take back control of many villages in Kosovo and of some areas close to urban centres and major highways. These actions merely provoked the Serbian authorities, which stated that if the verification mission could not control these units the Government would.[152]

As for the Organization for Security and Cooperation in Europe (OSCE) observers, they summarized the position as follows in late January 1999:

One can see a cycle of confrontation that can generally be described as follows, with possible variants in the sequence of events: the Kosovo Liberation Army (KLA) attacks vehicles, buildings and members of the Serbian police (special Interior Ministry police); the authorities of the Federal Republic of Yugoslavia react disproportionately to the attacks, often by ordering the Serb police to cordon off the area and carry out mopping-up operations, with the assistance of the Yugoslav army, sometimes using heavy weapons; the result is a population exodus and a political polarization of the victims of the violence, whatever their ethnic origin, as well as a resumption of KLA activity in other areas.[153]

These texts show that the information forwarded to the Security Council to verify respect for its own resolutions suggested a qualified verdict apportioning responsibility for the breaches on *both* parties to the conflict.[154] It is therefore not obvious that the 'spirit' of the resolution dictates that intervention be directed exclusively against the Yugoslav side.

The legal argument of the intervening countries is thus supported by an interpretation of the legal rules, and also of the facts, that undeniably raises

---

[150] See the agreements between Yugoslavia and the OSCE on the one hand and NATO on the other; S/1998/978 and S/1998/1991.

[151] S/1998/1068, at 48.

[152] S/1998/1221 (24 December 1998) at 13; see also the annexed report by the OSCE mission, esp. at 6.

[153] Report annexed to Secretary General's report, S/1999/99 (1999).

[154] We refer in the same sense to the *Monthly Report on the situation in Kosovo drawn up pursuant to Resolutions 1160, 1199 and 1203*, annexed to the letter of 20 March 1999 addressed to the Secretary General by the President of the OSCE (S/1999/315). See also the *Report on the human rights situation in former Yugoslavia* of 17 October 1997 (GA/A/52/490, p 44, para 178) and the *Report on the human rights situation in Kosovo* of 30 October 1998 (A/53/563, paras 8 and 11).

considerable problems. The point here is not to speak decisively to the lawfulness or not of starting the war, as have several authors who condemned it as contrary to the UN Charter.[155] Important for our argument here is to insist on the obstinate will to refer to relatively classical legal arguments, even if such argumentation were doubtful, rather than to assume a reference to some new 'right of humanitarian intervention'.[156]

It should be added that this 'right of intervention' was not really claimed in the ensuing weeks, even when the occasion lent itself. In general terms we can in fact note a constant concern by many intervening states to restore UN authority,[157] and bring their action back under its auspices, which is as we know what led to the adoption of Resolutions 1239 (1999) and 1244 (1999), to which we shall return. Moreover, at a gathering commemorating the fiftieth anniversary of NATO a debate was held on the assertion of a new doctrine assuming the possibility of military intervention without Security Council authorization.[158] Without knowing precisely whether the dispute was of a political or legal nature, we would point out that the text finally adopted could not be more classical on this particular point, since it reads:

We acknowledge the principal responsibility of the United Nations Security Council in maintaining international peace and security, as affirmed in the Treaty of Washington.[159]

Let us recall that the Treaty clearly recognizes the authority of the UN Security Council,[160] whose 'principal responsibility' is contained in Article 24 of the Charter. The Preamble and Article 1 of the Treaty of Washington, moreover, reaffirm in general terms the obligation to respect the UN Charter.[161]

Finally, the intervening states evinced an *opinio juris* that is hard to interpret as re-questioning the fundamental principle of non-interference and sovereignty as contained in the UN Charter. This conclusion would certainly need qualification

---

[155] See the criticisms by Simma, above n 133, 11; Cassese, above n 21, 24; Spinedi, above n 148, 23 *et seq.*; M Kohen, 'L'emploi de la force et la crise du Kosovo: vers un nouveau désordre international', above n 139; N Ronzitti, 'aerei contro la Repubblica federale di Iugoslavia e Carta delle Nazioni Unite', *Riv.Dir.Int.* (1999—LXXXII), 476; Daniel Thürer, 'Die NATO-Einsätze in Kosovo und das Völkerrecht', *Neue Zürcher Zeitung*, 3/4 Avril 1999 and Christian Tomuschat, 'Völkerrechtliche Aspekte des Kosovo-Konflikts', *Die Friedens-Warte*, (1999), 33–7.

[156] See Simma, above n 133, 22.

[157] See, eg President Chirac's statements, reproduced in 14 *Documents d'Actualité Internationale* (15 July 1999) 572.

[158] This doctrine was first implicitly enshrined in the resolution adopted in November 1998 by the NATO Assembly, asking governments to state that the self-defence contained in Art 51 of the Charter, 'must include defence of common interests and values, including when the latter are threatened by humanitarian catastrophes, crimes against humanity, and war crimes' (NATO Doc. AR 295 SA (1998), cited in Simma, above n 133, 16).

[159] Washington Summit communiqué, 24 April 1999, para 38; reproduced in French in 10 *Documents d'Actualité Internationale* (1 June 1999) 420.

[160] See Art 7 of the Treaty.

[161] See Art 1 of the Treaty and its Preamble.

regarding some of the states,[162] with the United States, for instance, adopting an indubitably more interventionist position,[163] although they finally agreed to reiterate their commitment to respect for Security Council authority by accepting the text cited. It is in any case significant to note that, invited to plead before the International Court of Justice, the ten NATO member states did not base their argument on the emergence of a 'right of humanitarian intervention'. They all preferred to plead exclusively that the Court was not competent and that the conservatory measures requested were inappropriate, with the only legal arguments on the merits relating, with one exception,[164] to pre-existing Security Council resolutions, in accordance with the pattern set out above.

States not supporting the intervention

Many states refused to support the intervention, for various reasons which will not be detailed here. We shall seek to pick out elements from the various reactions to facilitate the establishment of an *opinio juris* that might be attributed to them.

A first category of states frankly condemned the intervention, invoking essentially classical legal arguments. We have already mentioned the reticence of Russia and China before the operation. It will accordingly be understood that these states vigorously condemned its commencement, considering that it was contrary to the most elementary rules of international law in existence.[165] These states are far from isolated in this attitude. India, for instance, violently denounced the intervention during the Security Council debate on 24 March:

The crisis could only be resolved through consultation and dialogue, and not through military action. The attacks clearly violated Article 53 of the United Nations Charter. No country, group or arrangement could take arbitrary and unilateral military action against others. That would mean a return to anarchy.[166]

The representatives of Namibia,[167] Gabon,[168] and to a lesser extent Argentina,[169] took similar lines. In the debates held a few days later in the Council one could add

---

[162] See Tony Blair's ambiguous statements in a speech in Chicago on 22 April 1999; *Keesing's* (1999) 42901; and by contrast the legalistic discourse of Prime Minister Lionel Jospin when opening the session of the General Assembly on 20 September 1999 (UN Press Release, GA/908).

[163] See the document giving a speech by an American Secretary of State cited by Simma, n 133 above, 15. This interventionist position is reflected in other precedents which, while they cannot be called 'humanitarian intervention', also reflect a tendency to consider that military operations are permissible to secure respect for Security Council resolutions without its explicit authorization. The case of the air strikes against Iraq is certainly significant in this respect; see President Clinton's statements reproduced in SD Murphy, 'Contemporary Practice of the United States relating to International Law', 93 AJIL (1999) 477.

[164] The pleadings by the counsel for Belgium, who as well as referring to Security Council resolutions mentioned the existence of a right of humanitarian intervention (CR 99/15 (11 May 1999) 15–16 and CR/26 (13 May 1999) 9).

[165] SC/1035 (24 March 1999) 3 and 10.

[166] Ibid., 12–13, Press Release SC/6657.

[167] Ibid., at 8.   [168] Ibid.   [169] Ibid., at 8–9.

to these the speeches by the representatives of Belarus,[170] Ukraine,[171] Cuba,[172] and, of course, Yugoslavia itself.[173]

In a collective context one could mention a decision of the Interparliamentary Assembly of CIS member states of 30 April 1999 (Armenia, Belarus, Kazakhstan, Kyrgyzstan, Moldova, Russia, Tajikistan, Ukraine) condemning the military intervention and asking Yugoslavia to resolve the Kosovo conflict peacefully.[174]

In another context, the majority of Latin American states (Argentina, Brazil, Chile, Peru, Venezuela, Bolivia, Columbia, Paraguay, Ecuador, Uruguay, Panama, Costa Rica, Mexico) adopted, within the 'Rio Group', a communiqué, dated 25 March, stating:

> The member countries of the Rio Group stated their concern at the commencement of air attacks on Serb targets by the North Atlantic Treaty Organization (NATO) and in particular at the fact that no paths to peaceful solution in conformity with international law to the dispute between the various parties involved in the Kosovo conflict had been found.... Additionally, the Rio Group complained that there had been recourse to force in this Balkan region without observing the provisions of Articles 53 (para 1) and 54 of the UN Charter....[175]

Several of these states, such as Brazil[176] and Costa Rica,[177] moreover, indicated very clear reservations concerning NATO's action at the Security Council itself. The press also noted criticisms made by several other states, such as South Africa, Libya, Iran and Iraq, based particularly on respect for international law.[178]

The position of the Non-Aligned Movement, which in itself forms the majority of member states in the UN, should also be referred to. According to an important declaration adopted on 9 April 1999:

> The Non-Aligned Movement, reaffirming the Movement's commitment to the sovereignty, territorial integrity, and political independence of all states, and reaffirming the Non-Aligned Movement's principles and the sanctity of the United Nations Charter, is deeply alarmed at the worsening crisis in Kosovo, Federal Republic of Yugoslavia and the Balkan region.

---

[170] SC/1036 (26 March 1999) 9–10 and SC /1050 (14 May 1999) 11.

[171] SC/1050 (14 May 1999) 10–11.

[172] SC/1036 (26 March 1999) 10.

[173] Ibid., at 9.

[174] Annex to the letter of 21 April 1999 addressed to the Secretary General by the Russian representative at the UN, A/53/920; S/1999/461.

[175] GRIO/SPT-99/10; forwarded to the Security Council by the permanent representative of Mexico by a letter of 26 March 1999, A/53/884-S/1999/347.

[176] See SC /981 at 13.

[177] Ibid., 11.

[178] *Le Monde* (3 April 1999). The position of certain States is, however, not always easy to establish. In certain cases (such as the Czech Republic), the head of State and the government adopted radically different positions, with the former approving and the latter condemning the intervention (*Le Monde* (31 March 1999) 4).

The Non-Aligned Movement reaffirms that the primary responsibility for the maintenance of international peace and security rests with the United Nations Security Council.

The Non-Aligned Movement is deeply concerned by the deteriorating humanitarian situation in Kosovo, and other parts of the Federal Republic of Yugoslavia, and the displacement, both internal and to neighbouring countries, of vast numbers of the Kosovo civilian population. In this regard, the Non-Aligned Movement urges the Secretary General to intensify the role of the United Nations in alleviating the suffering of the displaced persons and refugees who are fleeing Kosovo, and to investigate all abuses of human rights.

The Non-Aligned Movement calls for an immediate cessation of all hostilities, and the swift and safe return of all refugees and displaced persons.

The Non-Aligned Movement firmly believes that the urgent resumption of diplomatic efforts, under the auspices of the United Nations and the relevant Security Council resolutions 1199 and 1203, constitutes the only basis for a peaceful, just and equitable solution to the conflict.[179]

It is clear from the text that the majority of states are far from accepting a unilateral right to humanitarian intervention. On the contrary, the role of the Security Council is underlined and the call for an immediate end to hostilities in the midst of the conflict can hardly be interpreted as anything else but disapproval for the war.

These examples, which might perhaps be extended with a little further research, show that for many states—in particular in the Third World—any idea of a 'right of humanitarian intervention', departing from the precepts of the UN Charter, is unacceptable.

Nor can one interpret the silence maintained by other states as a sign of favouring such a right. For the same reasons as those set out in connection with other precedents, one would in fact have to show that this attitude corresponded to a desire for legal change, something extremely hard to demonstrate. In general, such silence can be explained by political reasons (for instance the fear of denouncing the great Western powers), or ethical reasons (refusing to condemn something one regards as morally legitimate), without it being possible to draw any decisive consequences in legal terms. In this connection, even tacit support for intervening powers ought logically to be linked with the legal arguments advanced by those powers, which, as we have noted, cannot by any means be reduced to the promotion of a right of intervention.

We thus arrive at the conclusion that it is extremely hard to demonstrate the existence of an *opinio juris* that tends to alter the existing legal position, even among the intervening states.[180] One might, however, ask whether the positions taken by several UN organs testify to an evolution in international law.

---

[179] Statement by the NAM on the situation in Kosovo, Federal Republic of Yugoslavia, 9 April 1999, <http://www.nam.gov.za/media/990409kos.htm>.

[180] Except perhaps for the Vatican, which seems to have condemned the intervention while nonetheless proclaiming the possibility of a right of interference.

The position of UN organs

We know that the Security Council refused to condemn the NATO intervention on 26 March 1999, and a few weeks later adopted a resolution indirectly consecrating its effects.[181] Can this conduct be seen as a sort of ratification of the operation, with the consequence that some humanitarian interventions might find a legal basis in acceptance not beforehand, but a posteriori? This claim can hardly be justified.

Regarding rejection of the draft resolution presented jointly by Russia and India, it should first be recalled that this cannot, as such, constitute approval within the meaning of UN institutional law: since no resolution was adopted, there is no legal act that can have any effect. The argument further meets with an obstacle of a logical nature: if the rejection of condemnation amounted to approval, rejection of approval would normally have to amount to condemnation. Since the Council did not do either, it would in fact simultaneously have done both! More seriously, one might perhaps consider that certain states individually issued significant opinions on that occasion pointing in the direction of a right of intervention. A consideration of the debates, however, shows that once again it was political and ethical arguments that determined the votes, with several states pointing out, for instance, that the Russo-Indian draft did not even mention the responsibility of Yugoslavia for the breaches of individual rights committed in Kosovo.[182] For some of these states—of which at least one, moreover, condemned the intervention—it is extremely hard to draw the conclusion of their genuine approval.[183] For those that manifestly approve the operation we fall back on the same reasoning as detailed above: accepting intervention in no way amounts to accepting a right of intervention that would substantially alter the traditional legal rules.[184]

The adoption on 13 April 1999 of a Resolution on Human Rights in Kosovo by the Human Rights Commission of the UN General Assembly[185] leads *mutatis mutandis* to the same conclusions. While the repression is vigorously condemned, military intervention by the NATO member states is neither legitimized nor condemned. Once again it is extremely difficult to deduce from the adoption of this text an *opinio juris* in favour of a right of intervention.

---

[181] We shall not, however, take into account the Declaration by the President of the Security Council dated 14 May 1999 regarding the bombing of the Chinese Embassy in Belgrade; Press Release SC/1048 (14 May 1999).

[182] UN Press Release, SC/1036 (26 March 1999) 3.

[183] This is Argentina, a member of the 'Rio Group' that explicitly condemned the intervention, which nonetheless refused to support the draft resolution (ibid. at 7).

[184] A reading of the explanations of votes by such States as Canada (at 4) or the United States (at 5) shows this.

[185] GA Res. 1999/2; text in 12 *Documents d'Actualité Internationale* (15 June 1999) 456–7; see also GA Res. 1999/18 on the human rights situation in the FRY, Croatia and Bosnia-Herzegovina of 23 April 1999, text in 12 *Documents d'Actualité Internationale* (15 June 1999) 460–64.

As for the adoption by the Security Council of Resolutions 1239 and 1244, it can hardly provide support for arguments in either direction,[186] since these texts carefully refrain from legitimizing the intervention, or a fortiori any right of humanitarian intervention. Officially, Resolution 1244 is based not on the war waged by NATO, but on acceptance by the Yugoslav authorities of a political agreement. It even contains a reaffirmation of the 'principal responsibility of the Security Council for the maintenance of international peace and security', and a condemnation of 'all the acts of violence against the population of Kosovo', 'whoever the culprits may be',[187] which might theoretically be interpreted as applying equally to the massive bombings of that part of Yugoslavia! Consideration of the debates leading up to the adoption of this resolution shows that division on the advisability of the intervention persisted[188] and that the emergence of a right of humanitarian intervention, to be regarded as henceforth replacing the traditional principles of the Charter, is not invoked any more than it was previously.[189] On the contrary, the French representative even stated that

those among us who wished to recall the primacy, laid down in the Charter, of the Security Council in the maintenance of international peace and security have found satisfaction.[190]

As for the representative of Argentina, he insisted on conciliating promotion of individual rights and respect for the UN Charter in the area of international security, considering that the resolution

also confirms the central, irreplaceable role of the UN, in particular the Security Council and the Secretary-General. The resolution, finally, conveys an interpretation of the United Nations Charter that reflects the growing importance of human rights.[191]

The conduct of the Security Council and its member states thus in no way attests to the emergence of a right that would run counter to traditional legal rules. On the contrary, it confirms the tendency, considered earlier in cases such as Somalia, to interpret these rules with an insistence on the need for improved respect for individual rights.

---

[186] We shall have little to say on Resolution 1239, adopted on 14 May 1999, other than that it contains no approval of the intervention, shown by the fact that one of the States that co-authored the draft resolutely condemned NATO action elsewhere (see the statements by the representative of Namibia; SC/1050, 14 May 1999, pp 5–6). Nor shall we analyze the presidential Declaration of 14 May 1999 whereby the Council expresses its profound consternation and great preoccupation at the bombing of the Embassy of the People's Republic of China', but without either condemning—or approving—the armed action as a whole (Press Release, SC/1048 (14 May 1999)).

[187] See the first and 3rd recitals in the resolution.

[188] See the critical declarations by the representatives of Russia (SC/1058 (10 June 1999) 13), China (at 14), and Brazil (at 18).

[189] See, eg the statements by the US Delegate; SC/1058 (10 June 1999) 17.

[190] SC/1058 (10 June 1999) 15; see also the statement by the Canadian representative (16).

[191] Ibid., at 19.

The stance of the UN Secretary General can also be understood from this perspective. On 24 March Kofi Annan declared:

It is indeed tragic that diplomacy has failed, but there are times when the use of force may be legitimate in the pursuit of peace. In helping maintain international peace and security, Chapter VIII of the United Nations Charter assigns an important role to regional organizations. But as Secretary-General I have many times pointed out, not just in relation to Kosovo, that under the Charter the Security Council has primary responsibility for maintaining international peace and security—and this is explicitly acknowledged in the North Atlantic Treaty. Therefore the Council should be involved in any decision to resort to the use of force.[192]

The text shows approval of the operation on a personal basis by Kofi Annan, but also his concern to maintain the existing legal rules, with the objective of reconciling the rigour of the law and generosity towards humanitarian objectives.[193]

Finally, let us note that the refusal by the UN's main judicial body to accept the request for interlocutory measures presented by Yugoslavia, which asked for a stoppage of the air strikes by ten of the NATO member states,[194] evidently can not be understood as in any way ratifying a right of humanitarian intervention. The Court justified its refusal exclusively with considerations of a technical nature, relating to the question of its competence. Additionally, it took care to recall the traditional legal rules in its recitals:

The Court declares itself profoundly concerned with the use of force in Yugoslavia, which under the present circumstances raises very serious issues of international law [. . .].

The Court deems it necessary to emphasize that all parties before it must act in conformity with their obligations under the United Nations Charter and other rules of international law, including humanitarian law [. . .].

Whether or not States accept the jurisdiction of the Court, they remain in any event responsible for acts attributable to them that violate international law, including humanitarian law [and that] any disputes relating to the legality of such acts are required to be resolved by peaceful means, the choice of which, pursuant to Article 33 of the Charter, is left to the parties.

In this context, the parties should take care not to aggravate or extend the dispute [and that] when such a dispute gives rise to a threat to the peace, breach of the peace or act of

---

[192] Press Release SG/SM/6938 (24 March 1999).

[193] See in this connection the speeches given by Kofi Annan at the University of Michigan on 3 May 1999 (Press Release SG/T/2177) and on the occasion of the Centenary of the first Hague Peace Conference on 18 May 1999 (Press Release SG/SM/6997), and the press conference following the high-level meeting on the Balkans crisis on 14 May 1999, 13 *Documents d'Actualité Internationale* (1 July 1999) 529. See also *Keesing's* (1999) 42848 and *Le Monde* (22 September 1999), 20. We would finally note Kofi Annan's speech in opening the General Assembly session on 20 September 1999 (UN Press Release, GA/908).

[194] See the introductory petitions in the action lodged with the Clerk of the Court on 29 April 1999.

aggression, the Security Council has special responsibilities under Chapter VII of the Charter.[195]

Once again we would at the present moment seem to be far from questioning the traditional principles of the UN Charter, which authorize armed action for humanitarian objectives only through Security Council resolution.

Finally, what the International Court of Justice had to say in 1986, in condemnation of intervention officially justified by defence of individual rights, retains its full relevance. For the Court noted that even if many states in practice engaged in interventions, they 'have not justified their conduct by reference to a new right of intervention or a new exception to the principle of its prohibition'.[196] It went on to note that '[...] the United States has, on a legal plane, justified its intervention expressly and solely by reference to the 'classic rules involved [...]'.[197] This *dictum* could, with the appropriate adjustments, be applied to all the precedents detailed above, from Iraqi Kurdistan to Yugoslav Kosovo.

3. After the Kosovo War

In the final part of this analysis, we will attempt to demonstrate that the right of humanitarian intervention is far being accepted, after the end of the war in Kosovo. On the contrary, there have been repeated condemnations of it from the end of 1999, in particular within the UN. These persistent misgivings can be explained further by a number of factors which cast doubt, in the long term, on the acceptance of such right of humanitarian intervention by all, or even a significant majority, of states.

A. Repeated Condemnations of the 'Right of Humanitarian Intervention'

The Kosovo precedent has undeniably provoked certain doubts both among commentators and within states. While almost no one has defended the legality of this intervention, many have referred to it as a legitimate, albeit illegal, war.[198]

---

[195] Orders of 2 June 1999, *Yugoslavia v Germany* at 16, 18, 35, 36 and 37; *Yugoslavia v Belgium* at 17, 19, 48, 49 and 50; *Yugoslavia v Canada* at 16, 18, 44, 45 and 46; *Yugoslavia v United States* at 16, 18, 31, 32 and 33; *Yugoslavia v Italy* at 16, 18, 36, 37 and 38; *Yugoslavia v Spain* paras 16, 18, 37, 38 and 39; *Yugoslavia v France* at 16, 18, 36, 37, and 38; *Yugoslavia v Netherlands* at 17, 19, 48, 49 and 50; *Yugoslavia v Portugal* at 16, 18, 47, 48, and 49; *Yugoslavia v United Kingdom* at 16, 18, 40, 41, and 42.

[196] *Case of the military and paramilitary activities in Nicaragua and against it*, ICJ Rep. (1986) at 207.

[197] Ibid. at 208.

[198] See Independent International Commission on Kosovo, *The Kosovo Report*, <http://www.reliefweb.int/library/documents/thekosovoreport.htm>. According to the final terms of this report:

Far from opening up a new area of humanitarian intervention, the Kosovo experience seems, to this Commission at least, to teach a valuable lesson of scepticism and caution. Sometimes, and

These doubts lead us to reflect on the need for international law to evolve towards a greater acceptance of the idea of a right of humanitarian intervention. Positions adopted in this context will be further addressed below. We shall conclude that no opposition to the UN Charter's rules may be found, whether in the framework of UN debates, in related international forums, or in situations (such as Afghanistan and Iraq) in which arguments pointing to a right of humanitarian intervention could have been made.

Condemnations of the right of humanitarian intervention in the framework of the UN

At the opening of the Assembly General's session following the war against Yugoslavia, the UN Secretary General placed the question of the right of humanitarian intervention at the centre of the debate. According to Kofi Annan, this precedent raised the need to think about redefining relations between sovereignty and human rights, with a view to making the rule of non-interference more flexible.[199] The debates that followed showed that states refused to question the necessity of obtaining an authorization from the Security Council to mount a military operation, whether based on humanitarian reasons or not.

Given these debates, we can put states into four categories. A first group of states firmly condemned the idea of the right of humanitarian intervention, on the grounds that it was contrary to the UN Charter. States in this group belong to very different geographic regions, though most of them are Third World countries. They included: Algeria, Barbados, Belarus, China, Cyprus, Colombia, Costa Rica, Cuba, Egypt, Ecuador, India, Indonesia, Iraq, Jordan, Libya, Laos, Malaysia, Mexico, Mongolia, Namibia, North Korea, Norway, Peru, the Philippines, Qatar, Russia, South Africa, Syria, Venezuela, and Vietnam. Two examples of such positions illustrate the concerns. The Norwegian representative

feared that the introduction of such doctrines could be hazardous and lead to an international order founded not on international law but one based on power politics. Might could come to replace right and the security of smaller States could be put at risk.[200]

Similarly, Singapore noted that:

Before the introduction of the United Nations Charter and the concept of sovereignty, the law of the jungle prevailed—the strong preyed on the weak. Implementation of the doctrine of humanitarian intervention would be a reversal to that principle.[201]

Kosovo is such an instance, the use of military force may become necessary to defend human rights. But the grounds for its use in international law urgently need clarification, and the tactics and rules of engagement for its use needs to be improved. Finally, the legitimacy of such use of force will always be controversial, and will remain so, so long as we intervene to protect some people's lives but no others.

[199] See ICIS, *The Responsibility to Protect* (December 2001) at 2.
[200] Press Release, GA/9659 (1999).   [201] Press Release, GA/9627 (1999).

A second group of states, whose views were actually quite close to those in the first group, was composed of states which did not exclude the idea of humanitarian intervention, assuming it was based on a resolution of the Security Council. The representative from Pakistan, for example, argued that:

The international community had strongly reacted to unilateral action by the North Atlantic Treaty Organization (NATO) against the Federal Republic of Yugoslavia without any authorization by the Security Council, he continued. That action had been precipitated by the failure of the Council to agree on a common course of action. The situation had highlighted the urgency of streamlining the work of the Security Council, facilitating effective and unified response to crisis situations based on their merit. A related issue was the efforts by some countries to assign a new role to the regional organizations. They should play a limited role in the prevention of armed conflict, and all their actions should be in consonance with Chapter VIII of the Charter. The Security Council must maintain its neutral and universal character.[202]

The following states concurred in this view: Brazil, Gambia, Iran, Jamaica, Liechtenstein, Mali, Moldova, Sierra Leone, South Korea, and Tunisia, which all insisted on the need to go through the Security Council in order to be able to justify launching military operations.

A third group of states developed a more ambiguous position, criticizing inaction or passivity on the part of the Security Council, without, however, questioning its powers. Spain, for example, stated that 'the right to interfere must be authorized or supported by the Security Council',[203] but added that 'the United Nations could not be paralysed in the face of massive violations of human rights, wherever they might take place' and that 'while the principle of State sovereignty continued to be essential in contemporary international society, it must not be used as a protective shield to trample on human rights with impunity'.[204] Australia, Bolivia, Canada, Macedonia, and Poland all criticized the abusive use of the veto power to paralyze the Security Council, but they did not uphold a right to circumvent the UN in such a situation.

Lastly, there were those rare cases of states which expressly argued in favour of introducing a right of humanitarian intervention in international law. The President of Slovenia, for example, stated that

[a] new chapter of international law must be written, based on contemporary international morality. Norms now are vague and either unknown or deliberately violated. The doctrine for humanitarian intervention must be based on a modern interpretation of the Charter in line with new norms, with an emphasis on protecting human rights.[205]

---

[202] Press Release, GA/PK/165 (2000).
[203] Press Release, GA/9633 (1999).
[204] Press Release, GA/9766 (2000).
[205] Press Release, GA/9753 (2000). See also Press Releases GA/9769 (2000) and GA/9782 (2000).

Lithuania argued that:

When there was evidence of the brutal murder of helpless people, the dilemma before the international community became a moral choice: between the sanctity of human lives and strict international standards [...]. New trends in inter-State relations tended to justify involvement from the outside to stop flagrant violations of human rights. The newly evolving concept of humanitarian intervention was now a real fact: it had taken place in practice, and was likely to be repeated.[206]

Even in both these cases, which seemed to be the only ones,[207] the argument in favour of a right of humanitarian intervention seems to indicate, *a contrario*, that such a right did not yet exist, *de lege lata*. At any rate, and for the great majority of states, the use of force is prohibited except upon the authorization of the Security Council or in the context of legitimate self-defence.

Following the debate in the UN, an International Commission on Intervention and State Sovereignty was created on a Canadian initiative, to study the issue of humanitarian intervention. This Committee, made up of twelve independent members of various nationalities, organized many debates and consultations and delivered its report on 30 September 2001. Its recommendations included the following:

(3) Right Authority

A. There is no better or more appropriate body than the United Nations Security Council to authorize military intervention for human protection purposes. The task is not to find alternatives to the Security Council as a source of authority, but to make the Security Council work better than it has.

B. Security Council authorization should in all cases be sought prior to any military intervention action being carried out. Those calling for an intervention should formally request such authorization, or have the Council raise the matter on its own initiative, or have the Secretary-General raise it under Article 99 of the UN Charter.

C. The Security Council should deal promptly with any request for authority to intervene where there are allegations of large scale loss of human life or ethnic cleansing. It should in this context seek adequate verification of facts or conditions on the ground that might support a military intervention.

D. The Permanent Five members of the Security Council should agree not to apply their veto power, in matters where their vital state interests are not involved, to obstruct the passage of resolutions authorizing military intervention for human protection purposes for which there is otherwise majority support.

E. If the Security Council rejects a proposal or fails to deal with it in a reasonable time, alternative options are:

---

[206] Press Release GA/9637 (1999).

[207] Uruguay adopted an ambiguous position since one of its delegates first seemed to accept humanitarian intervention, without making it a right (Press Release, GA/9783 (2000)), while another argued that a Security Council resolution was necessary (Press Release, GA/9634 (1999)). See also the ambiguous position of Georgia, Press Release, GA/9777 (2000).

I. consideration of the matter by the General Assembly in Emergency Special Session under the 'Uniting for Peace' procedure; and

II. action within area of jurisdiction by regional or sub-regional organizations under Chapter VIII of the Charter, subject to their seeking subsequent authorization from the Security Council.

F. The Security Council should take into account in all its deliberations that, if it fails to discharge its responsibility to protect in conscience-shocking situations crying out for action, concerned states may not rule out other means to meet the gravity and urgency of that situation—and that the stature and credibility of the United Nations may suffer thereby.[208]

The Commission did not conclude that there exists, or that there is a need for, a unilateral right of humanitarian intervention. Such a right is considered only within the UN framework. The proposed reforms, at most, confer a greater role on the General Assembly vis-à-vis the Security Council, but still in a multilateral setting. This report has not, despite its authors' ambitions, been in any way endorsed per se by the Security Council or any other organ of the UN. On the contrary, a number of states have, despite its prudential language, deemed it to be too innovative, as can be seen in declarations adopted in several forums related to but outside the UN framework.

The concept of the responsibility to protect was at the heart of debates on the occasion of the UN's sixtieth anniversary celebrations in 2005. In a report the High-level Group of Experts, established by the Secretary General, affirmed that:

... the Council and the wider international community have come to accept that, under Chapter VII and in pursuit of the emerging norm of a collective international responsibility to protect, it can always authorize military action to redress catastrophic internal wrongs if it is prepared to declare that the situation is a 'threat to international peace and security', not especially difficult when breaches of international law are involved.

We endorse the emerging norm that there is a collective international responsibility to protect, exercisable by the Security Council authorizing military intervention as a last resort, in the event of genocide and other largescale killing, ethnic cleansing or serious violations of international humanitarian law which sovereign Governments have proved powerless or unwilling to prevent.[209]

This statement calls for two remarks. First, it is clearly for the UN Security Council to decide if an intervention should be undertaken. No one could argue that certain states could intervene without such authorization. In reality, the responsibility to protect involves using one of the two traditionally recognized exceptions to the prohibition of the use of force, that of Council authorization, and it does not create a new exception. It cannot then be portrayed as introducing into existing international law some sort of right of unilateral intervention.

---

[208] ICIS, *The Responsibility to Protect* (December 2001) at XII–XIII.
[209] *A More Secure World: Our Shared Responsibility*, Report of the Secretary-General's High-level Panel on Threats, Challenges and Change, United Nations, A/59/565 (2004), para 203.

Second, it is far from evident that we are in the presence of a 'new norm', as the report indicates. In so far as this norm relies on the well established provisions of the Charter—concerning the Security Council's competence in cases of threats to international peace—and also on several precedents which most states have recognized that this competence may be used in certain particularly dramatic cases of humanitarian crises, the novelty seems entirely relative.

The Secretary General has approved this position in his report in response to the work of the High-level Panel. After affirming that 'the task is not to find alternatives to the Security Council as a source of authority',[210] he notes that:

> ...we must embrace the responsibility to protect, and, when necessary, we must act on it. This responsibility lies, first and foremost, with each individual State, whose primary raison d'être and duty is to protect its population. But if national authorities are unable or unwilling to protect their citizens, then the responsibility shifts to the international community to use diplomatic, humanitarian and other methods to help protect the human rights and well-being of civilian populations. When such methods appear insufficient, the Security Council may out of necessity decide to take action under the Charter of the United Nations, including enforcement action, if so required. In this case, as in others, it should follow the principles set out in section III above.[211]

Given that section III reiterates the rules on the use of force as they appear in the Charter, it is clear that the latter part of this statement leaves no doubt as to the rejection of any unilateral initiative taken in response to extreme situations such as those mentioned.

These impressions are confirmed by the 2005 World Summit Outcome adopted by the General Assembly. The section of the Outcome devoted to the use of force makes several references to multilateralism in general and to the powers of the Security Council in particular. There is no trace of any right of intervention for democratic or humanitarian purposes either in the Outcome itself or in the reports that preceded it.

Another section of the Outcome, entitled 'Responsibility to protect populations from genocide, war crimes, ethnic cleansing and crimes against humanity', after having insisted upon the primary responsibility of each state concerned in this regard, indicates that:

> The international community, through the United Nations, also has the responsibility to use appropriate diplomatic, humanitarian and other peaceful means, in accordance with Chapters VI and VIII of the Charter, to help to protect populations from genocide, war crimes, ethnic cleansing and crimes against humanity. In this context, we are prepared to take collective action, in a timely and decisive manner, through the Security Council, in accordance with the Charter, including Chapter VII, on a case-by-case basis and in cooperation with relevant regional organizations as appropriate, should peaceful means

---

[210] *In larger freedom: towards development, security and human rights for all*, Report of the Secretary-General, A/59/2005 (2005), para 126.

[211] Ibid., para 135.

be inadequate and national authorities are manifestly failing to protect their populations from genocide, war crimes, ethnic cleansing and crimes against humanity.[212]

Again, this statement leaves no doubt as to the multilateral character of the implementation of this duty to protect. There is no qualification, exception or ambiguity that would allow for the possibility of any unilateral right of armed intervention, a fact also reflected in the very clear positions adopted in the debates on this subject in the General Assembly. For the Ukranian representative, for example, speaking for the Georgia-Uzbekistan-Ukraine-Azerbaijan-Moldova Group:

... it is important to define and adopt criteria for the legitimate authorization by the Council of the use of force. Situations in which national authorities are unwilling or unable to protect their populations from genocide, ethnic cleansing or crimes against humanity may require effective action by the international community in accordance with international law, including enforcement measures in exceptional circumstances. We believe that such measures can be taken only as a last resort and under the explicit mandate of the Security Council.[213]

Uganda affirmed that 'the prior authorization of the Security Council should be obtained' before any action is taken,[214] San Marino considered that responsibility for such action 'is collective and remains within the purview of the Security Council',[215] while, for Russia, 'such action can only be taken when authorized by the Security Council'.[216] There can thus be no doubt that, as the Representative of Chile emphasized:

It is not a question of recognizing a right of humanitarian intervention or accepting pretexts for aggression, but rather of enunciating an international obligation to be exercised by the Security Council if States are unable to do so in extreme situations.[217]

In addition, it should be noted that, to our knowledge, *no* state has officially taken the opposite position, and affirmed that the responsibility to protect opens up the legal possibility of unilateral military action, that is, action without the authorization of the Security Council.

Finally, and in the same spirit, it must be recalled that in December 2001 the General Assembly had taken note of the Articles on State Responsibility drafted by the International Law Commission over many years of work.[218] In the course of this drafting process, it was proposed to interpret certain circumstances excluding illegality as paving the way to a right of humanitarian intervention. This

---

[212] GA Res. 60/1, 24 October 2005, para 139.

[213] A/59/PV.88, 7 April 2005, p 22.

[214] A/59/PV.88, 7 April 2005, p 8.

[215] A/59/PV.86, 6 April 2005, p 24.

[216] A/59/PV.87, 7 April 2005, p 6.

[217] A/59/PV.86, 6 April 2005, p 20.

[218] I.L.C., 53th sess., A.G., *Doc. 56ème sess., Supp. No 10 (A/56/10).*

was suggested in the case of hardship[219] and the state of necessity. But the final commentary adopted by the International Law Commission clearly sets this interpretation aside. Concerning hardship, it states that persons against whom hardship may be claimed must indeed be under the control of the state in question, which excludes humanitarian intervention.[220] As for the state of necessity, the Commission specified that '[t]he question whether measures of forcible humanitarian intervention, not sanctioned pursuant to Chapters VI or VII of the Charter of the United Nations, may be lawful under modern international law is not covered by article 25'.[221] In his second report, James Crawford had already pointed out that the necessity defence has almost never been invoked in contemporary situations of humanitarian intervention,[222] and then underlined that the issue of humanitarian intervention in foreign territory is not included in the state of necessity.[223]

The Charter's rules may therefore not be circumvented by invoking the general framework of international responsibility. This is confirmed by the general condemnations of the right of humanitarian intervention advanced by the great majority of states in forums related to, but outside the United Nations, to which we now turn.

Condemnations of the right of humanitarian intervention in other forums

On 24 September 1999 an important declaration was adopted by the Foreign Ministers of 132 states in the context of the 'Group of 77':

> The Ministers stressed the need to maintain clear distinctions between humanitarian assistance and other activities of the United Nations. They rejected the so-called right of humanitarian intervention, which has no basis in the UN Charter or in international law. The Ministers stressed the need to follow scrupulously the Guiding Principles of Humanitarian Assistance outlined in the Annex to the General Assembly resolution 46/182.[224]

This declaration was restated almost word for word a few months later at the Havana Summit.[225] The fact that these texts do not explicitly mention the Kosovo precedent is significant: the point here is to express a general legal position transcending particular cases. This position is indisputably free of any ambiguity.[226]

---

[219] A/CN.4/488, United Kingdom.

[220] *Commentary*, Art 24, para 7. See also A/CN.4/498/Add.2, para 272.

[221] *Commentary*, Art 25, para 20.

[222] A/CN.4/498/Add.2, para 279.

[223] Ibid., para 287.

[224] Declaration on the 35th anniversary of the creation of the Group of 77, available at <http://www.g77.org/docDecl1999.html>, paras. 69 and 70.

[225] See 104 *Revue Générale de Droit International Public* (755) at 755 (Havana Summit, 12–14 April 2000).

[226] We would further recall that the annex to GA Res. 46/182 (1991) provides in particular that 'the sovereignty, territorial integrity and national unity of States must be fully respected in accordance with the United Nations Charter' (§ 3).

Most of these states have, within the Non-Aligned Movement, reiterated similar positions. Thus, during the Kuala Lumpur Conference on 24 and 25 February 2003, these 115 states expressed themselves in the following terms:

The Heads of State or Government reiterated the rejection by the Non-Aligned Movement of the so-called 'right' of humanitarian intervention, which has no basis either in United Nations Charter or in international law and requested the Co-ordinating Bureau in New York to continue to be seized with this issue as well as other related matters in accordance with the principled position of the Non-Aligned Movement; they also observed similarities between the new expression 'responsibility to protect' and 'humanitarian intervention' and requested the Co-ordinating Bureau to carefully study and consider the expression 'the responsibility to protect' and its implications on the basis of the principles of non-interference and non-intervention as well as the respect for territorial integrity and national sovereignty of States.[227]

This text echoes previous declarations, such as the one according to which 'humanitarian assistance should be neutral and impartial, be provided at the request of the country concerned, and fully respect its territorial integrity and sovereignty'.[228]

Similarly, the 57 member states of the Organization of the Islamic Conference adopted the following statement on 30 June 2000, following the Kuala Lumpur Conference:

It affirmed its rejection of the so-called right to humanitarian intervention under whatever name or from whatever source, for it has no basis in the Charter of the United Nations or in the provisions of the principles of the general international law.[229]

The Heads of State of these countries presented similar views a few months later in Doha,[230] and again on 27 June 2001 in Bamako.[231]

On the whole, the debates held in the aftermath of the Kosovo war were very instructive. The Secretary General, supported by a few Western countries, insisted on discussing the right of humanitarian intervention within the UN. This initiative prompted the great majority of states to adopt firm positions which categorically rejected any unilateral military action. At the dawn of the third millennium, it has become clear that the proposed doctrine has next to no support, with one or two exceptions. The same dynamic was to be observed again during

---

[227] Final Document of the XIII Conference of Heads of State or Government of the NAM Kuala Lumpur, 24–25 February 2003, <http://www.nam.gov.za/media/030227e.htm>, para 16.

[228] <http://www.nam.gov.za/xiisummit/chap1.htm>, para 63. See also Final Document of the XI Summit, Carthagena, para 13.

[229] Final Communiqué of the 27th session of the Islamic Conference of Foreign Ministers, Kuala Lumpur, Malaysia, <http://www.oic-oci.org/index.asp>, para 79.

[230] Final Communiqué of the 9th session of the Islamic Conference of Heads of States, Doha (Qatar), 12–13 November 2000, UN Doc. A/55/716 (2001), p32, para 88, available at <http://daccessdds.un.org/doc/UNDOC/GEN/NO1/209/45/IMG/NO120945.pdf?OpenElement.

[231] ICFM/28-2001/FC/Final, Final Communiqué of the 28th session of the Islamic Conference of Foreign Ministers, Bamako (Republic of Mali), 25–27 June 2001.

the wars in Afghanistan and Iraq, where the right of humanitarian intervention is far from emerging as a new rule of international law.

The precedents of Afghanistan and Iraq

The United States, in collaboration with certain allies, launched two massive military campaigns in the aftermath of September 11 2001. Operation *'Enduring Freedom'* began on 7 October 2001 in Afghanistan, and led, a few weeks later, to the collapse of the Taliban regime. On 23 March 2003, Saddam Hussein's government was, in turn, the target of Operation *'Iraqi Freedom'*, which brought about a new regime in Iraq. In both cases, as evidenced by the names chosen for these operations, the intervening powers justified their actions by the dictatorial and tyrannical nature of the regimes in place. In this context, a 'right of demo-cratic intervention', or even a 'right of humanitarian intervention', could have emerged as a justification for war.

But this was not the case. The United States, and its allies, preferred to invoke the traditional exceptions to the prohibition on the use of force. In the case of Afghanistan, legitimate self-defence was the official justification.[232] As for Iraq, the authorization given by the Security Council in Resolution 678 (1990) was invoked, through a complex legal argument taking subsequent resolutions into account, namely Resolutions 687 (1991) and 1441 (2002).[233] Neither the United States, nor other states, have dared to invoke, on the legal plane, a right of demo-cratic or humanitarian intervention, despite the fact that, according to these states, there was a situation of serious and massive violations of human rights. This attitude reveals the absence of belief, even on the part of states such as the United Kingdom, in a unilateral right of intervention.

As for other states, one cannot infer a change of position on this point. In the case of Iraq, there are, on the contrary, a number of declarations recalling the principle under which a political regime may not be toppled by force, even if such regime does not adhere to the intervening states' idea of democracy.[234] To take but one example, Malaysia declared before the Security Council that:

The focus in the Council should be on promoting United Nations diplomacy to resolve the problem through effective inspections and weapons destruction, not on legitimizing war against Iraq to affect 'regime change'. Removing the head of State or Government of a sovereign State is illegal and against the Charter, and it must be never be a project that

---

[232] S/2001/946 (2001). See Olivier Corten et François Dubuisson, 'Opération *Libert immuable*: une extension abusive du concept de légitime défense', 110 *Revue Générale de Droit International Public* (2002/1).

[233] S/2003/351 (2003) (United States), S/2003/350 (2003) (United Kingdom), S/2003/352 (2003) (Australia). See Olivier Corten, 'Opération *Iraqi Freedom* : peut-on admettre l'argument de l'autorisation implicite du Conseil de sécurité?', 36 *Revue Belge de Droit International* (2003) 205.

[234] See S/PV.4625 (Resumption 1) (2002), Iran; S/PV.4625 (Resumption 2) (2002), Viet Nam; S/PV.4709 (2003), League of Arab States; S/PV.4709 (Resumption 1) (2003), India and Zimbabwe; S/PV.4714 (2003), Germany; S/PV.4717 (2003), South Africa, League of Arab States and Libya; S/PV.4721 (2003), Russia; S/PV.4726 (2003), Yemen, Libya, Cuba, Iran, Lebanon.

has the endorsement of this Council. The provisions of the Charter on this matter are very clear and unambiguous, as has been underscored by many speakers in this debate.[235]

This not does mean that all military interventions seeking to fulfil democratic or humanitarian objectives are prohibited. As we have seen in the first part of this analysis, it is always possible, political conditions willing, for the Security Council to authorize such action. After the Kosovo war, there are precedents for this option: East Timor and the Ivory Coast. First, on 15 September 1999, the Security Council authorized the member states of a multinational force, with a mission to restore peace and security and facilitate humanitarian aid operations, to 'take any measures necessary to fulfil this mandate'.[236] Next, on 4 February 2003, the Security Council authorized states to take 'any necessary measures' to carry out the same type of mission in the Ivory Coast.[237] In both cases, the (partially) humanitarian operation was unanimously considered legal precisely because it had been authorized by the Security Council and had not been launched and carried out in a unilateral manner. Recent practice therefore confirms the conclusions we had drawn from analyzing the period prior to war against Yugoslavia.

In sum, the practice after 1999, including the intervention in Iraq, shows a clear and categorical refusal to allow a unilateral right of military intervention under international law, other than in the case of legitimate self-defence. The statements of position we have laid out are numerous, varied and concurring. We can only ask ourselves why the quasi-totality of states are so reluctant to admit an idea which, at first sight, seems generous enough, a fact which brings us to the last part of this study.

B. Obstacles to the Early Emergence of a 'Right of Humanitarian Intervention'

One can certainly not rule out the possibility that a concern to assure better protection for individual rights might in the future be reflected in the affirmation of a unilateral right of action going beyond these classical mechanisms. It must, however, be made clear that any such evolution would presuppose the overcoming of a number of obstacles which are by no means negligible, not only in political, but also in legal terms.

Obstacles of a political nature

Seeking to summarize the present situation, one might say that beyond the general trend pictured above, the positions of different states are in fact fairly diverse. Some, like China, stick to an extremely restrictive interpretation, according to

---

[235] S/PV.4625 (Resumption 2) (2002) at 7.
[236] UN SC 1264 (1999), para 3.
[237] UN SC 1464 (2003), para 9.

which even dramatic humanitarian situations in a civil war context cannot be termed a threat to peace within the meaning of Chapter VII of the Charter. Others, like the United States, feel by contrast that there is an evolution towards a considerable flexibility of the classical rules, even though there is no clearly emerging legal doctrine in favour of a right of intervention. The majority of states would seem, over and above the specific question of the legitimacy and lawfulness of the Kosovo war, to be agreed in seeking to reconcile humanitarian concerns and existing legal principles. The current balance of forces thus seems more favourable to certain evolutionary interpretations of these principles rather than to a fundamental questioning of them.

Obstacles of a legal nature

In legal terms it should be stated that any such change would have to meet very strict conditions. Technically, the consecration of a 'right of humanitarian intervention' could only emerge from three equally difficult paths: formal amendment of the UN Charter, authentic interpretation of the Charter, or the establishment of a new customary rule which would supplant the principles of the Charter.

The first path, as we know, presupposes not just a two-thirds majority of the General Assembly but also a two-thirds majority of the organization's members, including all the permanent members of the Security Council. In other words, Articles 108 (amendments) and 109 (revision) of the Charter give China, among others, a veto right.

The second path is more flexible, and has, in particular, been taken with the effect that abstention by one of the permanent members of the Council does not, despite the letter of Article 27(3) of the Charter, amount to a veto.[238] It presupposes, however, in accordance with Article 31(3) of the Vienna Convention on the Law of Treaties, that *all* parties to the treaty have indicated their agreement.[239] In terms of the extent of agreement, therefore, we are faced with even stricter conditions than in the previous case.

The possibility remains of the emergence of a customary rule, which at first sight presents the advantage of being able to take shape among the states that have indicated their agreement, without being imposed on others. The possibility of the emergence of a regional custom, however, encounters considerable difficulties, both practical and theoretical. Practically, the birth of such a custom would potentially have the effect of rendering humanitarian intervention lawful only among states adhering to it. Specifically, one could not invoke such a rule in relation to states such as Yugoslavia, Iraq, Afghanistan, Sudan, and, in short, against all the states that have been past, present or future targets of interventions by the great powers.

---

[238] Berner and Simma, above n 134, 447 *et seq.*

[239] See the commentary on the International Law Commission's final draft submitted to the Vienna Conference, *United Nations Conferences on the law of treaties*, A/CONF.39/11/Add.2, 45 at 15.

In fact the regional custom would have the effect only of justifying interventions by one Western power against another, something that a priori seems unlikely. In theoretical terms, it must further be pointed out that the argument comes up against the fact that the ban on aggression is unanimously regarded as a rule of *jus cogens*,[240] which as we know does not permit derogation by a group of states. In application of the principles laid down in the 1969 Vienna Convention, only the emergence of a new rule of *jus cogens* would accordingly be capable of changing the position.[241] In other words, the consecration of a 'right of humanitarian interference' would presuppose agreement by the 'international community of states as a whole', of a norm that would no longer permit any derogation. Legally, one may even conclude that only this last path is conceivable. Even a formal amendment to the Charter would in fact have to be seen as consecrating the emergence of a new rule of binding law. Given the present position of states on the matter, it may be doubted that this scenario can be realized in the short term.

Obstacles relating to legal policy

There obviously remains the prospect of a moderate evolution—rather than a revolution—of the existing rules. A problem of principle then arises regarding the possibility of making adjustments that constitute a genuine opening in favour of humanitarian actions, without fundamentally calling into question the principles of the Charter. The question is fairly old; it is that of a consistent definition of a right, albeit limited, of humanitarian intervention. Without going into the details of the various definitions proposed,[242] we would stress the dilemma that seems, systematically, to mark them: the criteria proposed are either so flexible as to open the way to abuses incompatible with the existing law, or else so strict as in practice to rule out intervention at all.[243]

The suggestion put forward by Antonio Cassese perfectly illustrates the difficulties of formulating a new rule.[244] According to him, a right of humanitarian intervention might in future be legitimate if six conditions are all met:

1. severe, flagrant violations of individual rights, amounting to a downright crime against humanity;
2. systematic refusal by the state concerned to cooperate with the international organizations, in particular the UN;
3. blockage of the Security Council, able only to condemn or deplore the situation, while calling it a threat to international peace and security;

---

[240] See, eg the qualification made by the ILC 1980, part 2, P 42, para 22 and Hannikainen, *Peremptory Norms (Jus cogens) in International Law* (1989) sp. 323 *et seq.*

[241] See Art 53 of the Vienna Convention on the Law of Treaties.

[242] See the extracts from a British memorandum cited above, devoted *inter alia* to this point, in: 63 BYBIL (1992) 826; see also the official French position established as from 'Operation Turquoise'; 38 *Annuaire Français de Droit International* (1992)1032 *et seq.*

[243] Corten and Klein, above n 3, no 111 *et seq.*, esp. no 116.

[244] Cassese, above n 21, 27.

4. exhaustion of all peaceful and diplomatic channels;
5. organization of armed action by a group of states, not a single hegemonic power, with the support or at least the absence of opposition of a majority of UN member states;
6. limitation of the military intervention to what is strictly necessary to reach the humanitarian objectives.

Assessing these conditions against the case of Kosovo—or more generally all the precedents mentioned in the course of this study—the great difficulty is obviously in applying condition 1, and, especially, conditions 2, 4, 5, and 6. For each of them, no answer is indisputably compelling,[245] and we have briefly mentioned the disputes among states in this regard. The decisive criterion, as in the definition of any rule of international law, would be that which determined who is to have the power to interpret and characterize a situation. It is accordingly the third condition that is decisive, but it is important at this stage to note that we have to assume the hypothesis that we are in the presence of a general rule *pre-existing* the intervention. This means that, *ex hypothesi*, each Security Council member state would be aware that by condemning or deploring grave human rights violations and calling the situation a threat to peace, it would implicitly be authorizing a group of states to intervene, giving up the possibility of assessing in the future the advisability of such an intervention. The problem of the veto is thus in no way avoided by this proposal; it is only shifted to the moment when the facts are to be characterized. In practice, the system might have the effect of multiplying opposition to the adoption of any resolution based on Chapter VII, and accordingly lead to effects contrary to the ones aimed at. We are back at the dilemma mentioned earlier. Either the intervening powers themselves decide that the legitimacy criteria are met, with all the risks of abuse that involves, or a procedure is undertaken at the UN that would ultimately amount to subjecting intervention to a veto right.

There remains one obvious possibility, namely a reform of the voting procedures in the UN. Legalizing the system initiated by the Acheson resolution and extending it to authorization for military action is one possibility, but would require satisfying the strict majority conditions already mentioned.[246] Reforming the composition of the Security Council, including the number of permanent members, is a more credible option, and seems gradually to be taking shape.[247] But in reality, by increasing the number of bearers of the veto right, it risks making even more exacting the conditions required for authorization of recourse to force.

---

[245] This does not seem to be Antonio Cassese's opinion; he fairly quickly concludes that they are met: n 21 above, 28–9.

[246] EK Kaoussi, 'Rôles respectifs du Conseil de sécurité et de l'Assemblée générale dans le traitement des opérations de maintien de la paix' in Académie de droit international de La Haye (eds), above n 89, 435; in relation to the Kosovo war, see Simma, above n 133, 17.

[247] See, eg JP Quenedec, 'A propos de la composition du Conseil de sécurité', 99 *Revue Générale de Droit International Public* (1995) 955 and MC Wood, 'Security Council Working Methods and Procedure: Recent Developments', 45 ICLQ (1996) 150.

Obstacles of a sociological nature

Ultimately, all the difficulties described can be explained perfectly if one is willing to bring the rules governing the recourse to force into accord with the special features of contemporary international society.[248] The nineteenth century had a largely permissive system in which recourse to force was legal as long as the intervening power could base it on a 'legitimate motive'.[249] The humanitarian argument was often used in this context.[250] This regulation corresponded to a society in the course of formation, in which the Western states were extending by violence their hold over the whole of the planet. Once colonization was completed and states were formed everywhere in the world, and following the murderous conflicts that occurred between the great powers at the time, this permissive regime became totally counter-productive.[251] It was accordingly replaced by a prohibitive system, maximally limiting recourse to force and erecting peace and security into fundamental features of international law. This system theoretically ruled out military domination—at any rate between states—but left wide open the possibility of economic domination in the context of the spread of the market economy.[252] From this viewpoint one might consider that the ban on a recourse to force corresponds to what Weber noted as marking the history of Western national territories: the arrival of a liberal capitalist society goes hand in hand with that of a positive law with the primary function of ensuring security and predictability in the market and in society, conditions that require strict regulation of the use of force.[253]

Seen from this perspective, the proposal to introduce a right of humanitarian intervention looks less like progress than a return to the permissive legal system of the nineteenth century, the insecurity of which seems hard to reconcile with the sociological features of contemporary international society. In this connection one has to state that if it were accepted tomorrow, the right of intervention could also be invoked by regional military powers, with largely unpredictable consequences, thereby undermining stability. This may perhaps be what explains the reluctance of states, including the great powers, to embark on a substantial questioning of the principle of non-recourse to force, be it for humanitarian or other ends.

---

[248] O Corten, 'Droit, force et légitimité dans une société internationale en mutation', 37 *Revue interdisciplinaire d'études juridiques* (1996) 71.

[249] See, eg A Verdross, 'Règles générales du droit international de la paix', 5 *Recueil des Cours de l'Académie de Droit International* (1929) 497 and H Wehberg, 'Le problème de la mise de la guerre hors la loi', 4 *Recueil des Cours de l'Académie de Droit International* (1928) 153.

[250] U Beyerlin, 'Humanitarian Intervention' in *Encyclopedia of International Law* (1982) 212; H Gros Espiell, 'Les fondements juridiques du droit à l'assistance humanitaire', in UNESCO, *Colloque international sur le droit à l'assistance humanitaire, actes* (1996) 13.

[251] See C de Visscher, *Théories et réalités du droit international public*, 4ème éd. (1970) 335.

[252] E David, 'Quelques réflexions sur l'égalité économique des Etats', 7 *Revue Belge de Droit International* (1974) 401; A Cassese, 'Return to Westphalia? Considerations on the Gradual Erosion of the Charter System' in A Cassese (ed), *The Current Legal Regulation of the Use of Force* (1986) 508.

[253] Weber, *Sociologie du droit* (1986), 162; Weber, *Economie et Société, Tome I* (1995).

4

The Implications of Kosovo for International Human Rights Law

Richard B Bilder

1. Introduction

The main purpose of this chapter is to reflect on certain aspects of the intervention in Kosovo that occurred in 1999 the aftermath of which continues today. The Kosovo crisis seems a particularly useful springboard for discussion because it so deeply implicates human rights law and illustrates, in a salient and relevant context, some of the perplexing quandaries and dilemmas that even the most well-intentioned human rights efforts can pose.

NATO justified its bombing campaign and other actions primarily on humanitarian considerations, and there is little doubt that public support at the time for NATO's policies was based essentially on broad public acceptance of that justification, bolstered by a deluge of television, newspaper, and other media reports of ethnic cleansing, endless outflows of refugees, and appalling Serb atrocities. To some, NATO's intervention in Kosovo represented a positive sea-change in international law and, indeed, international affairs, whereby, for the first time, a group of nations was willing to take wholly selfless, risky, and forceful action simply to vindicate human rights and prevent and redress terrible atrocities. To others, the Kosovo intervention was a grave 'concern', demonstrating the cynical and hypocritical exploitation or 'hijacking' of human rights ideals by powerful states intent on furthering their own political interests and agendas, and, what is more, it was a tragic instance of clumsy meddling that left death, destruction, and continuing problems and misery in its wake. So, what are some of the implications of the Kosovo crisis for human rights law—and international law more generally—in the following areas:

- The UN and the doctrine of humanitarian intervention
- the laws of war;
- international criminal law;
- international political stability;

- the role of the media and non-governmental organizations (NGOs);
- sovereignty and ethnic conflict; and
- national attitudes towards international human rights efforts.

By the 'Kosovo conflict', I refer to the events that unfolded in Kosovo from NATO's 78-day bombing campaign, the 4 June 1999 'Petersberg' Peace agreement and the UN Security Council resolution authorizing the establishment of a UN force and administrative presence in Kosovo.[1] It is said that, on the margins of certain medieval maps, there appears the warning *hic dragones*—'here be dragons'. We have seen the many achievements and promises of the last 30 years. But Kosovo and other recent developments suggest that there may also be some dragons in the path ahead—problems, dangers, and dilemmas of which we should at least be aware.

Some of the issues in the above list are simply the inevitable result of the still limited capacity and highly political character of the existing international system and institutions.[2] Others involve the hard choices, tradeoffs and compromises we often have to make in structuring and managing our communal affairs and governance arrangements, for example, what many see as the trade-offs between civil and political rights on the one hand and economic rights on the other, or between civil and political rights on the one hand and personal or national security or social or political order, on the other—the so-called 'freedom vs order' problem. But perhaps the most interesting problems spring, paradoxically, from the very power and popular appeal of the human rights idea and, in particular, the claim for this idea that it has a preferred status over all other kinds of social claims, including those of the state and positive law. Professor Ronald Dworkin has well captured this claim in his evocative phrase 'rights as trumps'.[3] Arguably, this concept of rights as trumps undergirds the ideology of human rights and explains its energy and at least partial success.

But it is important to recognize that the human rights idea has revolutionary and potentially destabilizing implications not only as regards the limits of legitimate state authority and the relations of the individual to the state within the national context—its historical origin and function, but as regards the limits of legitimate state authority within the international system as well. This is so,

---

[1] See 'Agreement on the Principles (Peace Plan) to Move Towards a Resolution of the Kosovo Crisis', UN Doc. S/1999/649, agreed to by the Yugoslav Parliament 3 June 1999, reproduced in Security Council Resolution 1244, Annex 2 (10 June 1999), reprinted in 38 ILM 1351 (1999). The unofficial text of the Kosovo Peace Plan was also posted on the *Washington Post* website, as translated from the Serbian by the Associated Press; see <http://www.washingtonpost.com/wp-srv/matl/ddily/june99/plan_text03.htm>. The resolution is UN Security Council Resolution 1244, reprinted in 38 ILM 1451 (1999). The end of the bombing campaign and the peace agreement are extensively covered in the *New York Times*, issues of 4–6 June 1999.

[2] See R Bilder, 'Rethinking Human Rights: Some Basic Questions', [1969] Wisconsin Law Review 171, also published in 2 *Revue de Droits de l'Homme* (Human Rights Journal) (1969) 557.

[3] R Dworkin, *Taking Rights Seriously*, (1978), at xi ('Individual rights are political trumps held by individuals').

because, if human rights are trumps within the international legal order, they can in theory also prevail over potentially inconsistent, though accepted principles of our present international system, such as the notions of sovereignty, the sanctity of treaties, and constraints on the use of force. Indeed, if international human rights are trumps, then the claim by a state that its actions or policies are aimed at protecting such rights can, at least in theory, become an excuse for that state to seek to prevail over other, conflicting international norms. Consequently, the human rights idea may have a potentially dark side, and states, organizations, or individuals may seek to appropriate, exploit, or pervert this potential to their own purposes.

The Kosovo crisis, during which NATO justified its intervention largely on human rights grounds, raised a number of particularly salient problems and issues in this respect in terms of the future directions of international human rights law and policy. The crisis, to begin with, was an enormous humanitarian disaster involving the exodus of 850,000 to one million Kosovars from their homes and, according to reports by the British government, the brutal massacre of 10,000 and possibly many more Kosovars.[4] At the time NATO spokespersons, the media and NGOs reported that the evidence proved overwhelmingly that both the exodus and the alleged orgy of killing were primarily, if not exclusively, the result of a deliberate policy of ethnic cleansing and expulsion perpetrated or orchestrated by the Yugoslav government and military. After weeks of intense bombing, coupled with the threat of a land invasion and the apparently considerable pressure exerted by Russia, and significant concessions by NATO relative to its demands at Rambouillet, Milosevic finally agreed to the terms of the Petersberg agreement. These terms included the return of the Kosovars, the withdrawal of almost all Yugoslav troops from Kosovo, the occupation of Kosovo by a UN-authorized, though essentially NATO force, but also, significantly, the continued recognition of Yugoslavia's sovereignty over Kosovo.

A certain return to normality has been achieved since. The creation of an international administration in Kosovo, United Nations Mission in Kosovo (UNMIK), brought reasonable stability to the province and independence would have been proclaimed in December 2007 had it not been for the promised veto by Russia in the Security Council. The indictment,[5] overthrow, and subsequent handover of the Yugoslav President Slobodan Milosevic to the International

---

[4] For examples of the very extensive reporting of atrocities, see 'Atrocities', *New York Times*, 19 May 1999, at A11, which reports allegations by Scheffer, US Ambassador-at-Large for War Crimes; King, 'British Say 10,000 Kosovars Killed', *Wisconsin State Journal*, 18 June 1999 at 4A; 'The Horrors of Kosovo', *New York Times*, 21 June 1999, at A8; L Dobbs, 'In Belgrade, Kosovo Didn't Happen', *International Herald Tribune*, 25 June 1999, at 1.

[5] *Prosecutor v Milosevic*, No IT-99-37. 'Indictment and Decision on Review of Indictment and Application for Consequential Orders' (24 May 1999), <http://www. washingtonpost.com/ wp-srv/inatl/daily/june99/plantext03.htm>, abstracted in *ASIL International Law in Brief*, vol 2, No 6 (June 1999) at 14. For extensive coverage, see *New York Times*, 28 May 1999, at A1, A10–13 and A26.

Criminal Tribunal for the Former Yugoslavia (ICTY) for crimes against humanity helped to set the region on the path of reform and recovery.

However, the disputes over the facts and their implications continue and are
in a sense made no less intense by these supervening events. Milosevic, for one,
made the challenge of NATO's intervention a central part of his defence before
the ICTY, before his death terminated the proceedings. The disputes relate, for
example, to the cause and the character of the occurrences in Kosovo; the nature
of the Kosovo Liberation Army (KLA) and its activities prior to the beginning of
the bombing, particularly with regard to the KLA's actions against the Yugoslav
military; the police and civilians and how they were influenced by NATO's statements and policies; the respective motivations of the US, NATO and Milosevic;
the wisdom and effect on the situation of NATO's removal of the Organization
for Security and Cooperation in Europe (OSCE) observers; the reasons for the
failure of diplomacy; the morality, legality, and efficacy of NATO's intervention;
whether Milosevic had planned and was undertaking a deliberate policy of massive ethnic cleansing of the Kosovars before the bombing or whether the bombing
precipitated or at least accelerated the killing and expulsion by Yugoslavs of the
Kosovars and the massive exodus of the Kosovars; what actually happened within
Kosovo prior to and after the beginning of the bombing in terms of the scope of
the atrocities and who was primarily responsible—the army and police, paramilitary forces, private criminal gangs, or all of the above; and whether Milosevic
would have accepted the Petersberg terms if they had been offered earlier by
NATO, thus avoiding at least some of the bombing and civilian casualties. More
broadly, there are differences in viewpoint in the world at large and within the US
and the NATO countries as to whether the NATO intervention in Kosovo represented a significant advance in international human rights and the international
order, or a retreat to a more lawless and hegemonic world.

Many people were ambivalent—or even managed to hold inconsistent views—
about the situation, and particularly NATO's bombing campaign, indicating the
genuine moral quandaries, ambiguities, and dilemmas posed. Moreover, the
issue of Kosovo was highly emotional; it was impossible to see, hear, or read about
the refugees and the alleged atrocities without a feeling of anger and outrage and
wanting 'to do something', rather than listening to talk only about abstract questions of law.

Finally, the Kosovo crisis offers a fascinating study of the way we think about
and talk about human rights and related issues and of how people will fight over
words, because words *do*, indeed, have consequences. For example, how should
we characterize the Kosovo situation? Was it an insurgency, a civil war, or a
humanitarian disaster? Were the KLA fighters terrorist separatists or freedom
fighters? What are the analogies we use and the memories we draw on? Is Kosovo
like Vietnam, or does it remind us of the Holocaust? Are the Kosovars like the
Kurds, the Tutsis, the Tibetans, the East Timorese, the Tamils, or the Catholics
in Northern Ireland? Was Milosevic, like the leaders of Guatemala, El Salvador,

or the Republic of Vietnam (all supported by the US), simply fighting an internal insurgency, or was he a Hitler, a Pol Pot, a monster trying to maintain an oppressive totalitarian regime? What are the appropriate words to use about what has happened in Kosovo: genocide, ethnic cleansing, population transfer, or simply collateral damage?

That the rhetoric of humanitarian intervention is here to stay is attested by the fact that it has resurfaced in the most unexpected circumstances in the midst of military strikes aimed at Afghanistan and Iraq purportedly based on self-defence. There is thus all the more reason to examine the Kosovo intervention with a critical eye.

2. Kosovo, the UN, and the Doctrine of Humanitarian Intervention

The first and most salient issue raised by the strikes concerns the legality and appropriateness—particularly under the law of the UN Charter—of NATO's intervention in Kosovo and bombing in Yugoslavia, which it has justified on humanitarian grounds. We have all heard and read many statements by NATO leaders and spokespersons claiming a humanitarian purpose—indeed, a humanitarian necessity—for the bombing. For example, a letter from President Clinton was published in the *New York Times* defending the bombing campaign as, in the words of his title, 'A Just and Necessary War'.[6] British Prime Minister Tony Blair argued in a similar *New York Times* piece that NATO 'must be willing to right wrongs and prosecute just causes'.[7] President Clinton called the bombing a 'moral duty',[8] and he subsequently proposed that Elie Wiesel, the Holocaust survivor and Nobel Laureate, go to Kosovo. Wiesel duly made the trip and pronounced the bombing 'a moral war', adding that 'when evil shows its face..., you must intervene'.[9]

The relevant legal principles are fairly familiar. The UN Charter generally prohibits the threat or use of force against the territorial integrity or political independence of any state, except in self-defence or as authorized by the Security Council under Chapter VII of the Charter. Chapter VIII of the Charter permits regional arrangements to take enforcement action under certain circumstances, but only with the authorization of the Security Council. Other, related principles

---

[6] W Clinton, 'A Just and Necessary War', *New York Times*, 23 May 1999, at A17.

[7] T Blair, 'A Military Alliance and More', *New York Times*, 24 April 1999, at A29. See also T Blair, 'A New Moral Crusade', *Newsweek*, 14 June 1999, at 35: 'We are succeeding in Kosovo because there was a moral cause'.

[8] W Mathis, 'Our bombing a moral duty, Clinton says. "Ethnic cleansing" like the Holocaust, he argues', *Wisconsin State Journal*, 14 May 1999, at 2A.

[9] See D Rohde, 'Wiesel, a Man of Peace, Cites Need to Act', *New York Times*, 2 June 1999, at A12.

of international law, reflected in various treaties and General Assembly resolutions and endorsed by the International Court of Justice (ICJ) in the *Nicaragua* case[10] as binding customary law, prohibit coercive intervention in the internal affairs of another state. There is broad agreement that the prohibition on the unauthorized use of force is at the heart of the Charter and contemporary international law and one of the most significant legal advances in human history.

NATO never sought or obtained Security Council authorization for either its ultimatum, or its subsequent bombing of Yugoslavia, nor did it assert that it was acting in self-defence. Moreover, some of NATO's principal leaders, such as President Clinton or Prime Minister Blair, either ignored or relied on tenuous arguments of international law to justify NATO's actions. Consequently, Yugoslavia claimed that the 19 NATO countries committed aggression and intervened in its internal affairs in clear violation of Charter obligations and international law—a claim that was supported by Russia, China, and some other states.

On 29 April 1999, following up its protests with legal action, Yugoslavia instituted proceedings against the US, the UK, France, Germany, Italy, the Netherlands, Belgium, Canada, Portugal, and Spain, accusing these ten states of bombing Yugoslav territory in violation of their obligation not to use force against another state and asking the Court for relief.[11] In its applications, Yugoslavia maintained that the ten states were committing 'acts by which [they] have violated [their] international obligation[s] not to use force against another state, nor to intervene in [that state's] internal affairs' and 'not to violate [its] sovereignty'; 'the obligation to protect the civilian population and civilian objects in wartime, [and] to protect the environment; the obligation relating to free navigation on international rivers'; the obligation 'regarding the fundamental rights and freedoms'; and the obligations 'not to use prohibited weapons [and] not to deliberately inflict conditions of life calculated to cause the physical destruction of a national group' (that is, genocide). Yugoslavia rested its claims for the Court's jurisdiction on various foundations, including the Genocide Convention, to which all the NATO countries and Yugoslavia are parties and which contains a 'compromissory clause' automatically vesting the Court with jurisdiction over disputes relating to the Convention.

Yugoslavia asked the Court to order the states involved to 'cease immediately [their] acts of force against Yugoslavia' and to refrain from such threats or acts in the future.[12] On 2 June 1999 the Court, by a 12–4 decision and in a very complex judgment, rejected Yugoslavia's request for the indication of such

---

[10] 'Military and Paramilitary Activities in and against Nicaragua' (*Nicaragua v US*), 1986, ICJ 14.

[11] *ICJ Press Communique*, No 99/17, 29 April 1999.

[12] M Simons, 'Yugoslavia Seeks a Legal Order to Halt the NATO Bombing', *New York Times*, 12 May 1999, at A14.

provisional measures.[13] In two of the ten cases (against Spain and the US), the Court held that it manifestly lacked jurisdiction and dismissed these cases, noting that both the US and Spain had filed reservations to that 'compulsory jurisdiction' clause of the Genocide Convention. In the other eight cases, the Court found that it lacked prima facie jurisdiction, but that it remained seized of the case and that a fuller consideration of the question of jurisdiction would take place later. In its reasoning, the Court expressed its deep concern 'with the human tragedy, the loss of life, and the enormous suffering in Kosovo which form the background' of the dispute and 'with the continuing loss of life and human suffering in all parts of Yugoslavia'. It also set out its profound concern with the use of force in Yugoslavia, which 'under the present circumstances... raises very serious issues of international law', and emphasized that 'all parties before it must act in conformity with their obligations under the UN Charter and other rules of international law, including humanitarian law'. The Court stressed, however, that, 'whether or not States accept the jurisdiction of the Court, they remain in any event responsible for acts attributable to them that violate international law, including humanitarian law', and that 'any disputes relating to the legality of such acts are required to be resolved by peaceful means, the choice of which, pursuant to Article 33 of the Charter, is left to the parties'. In this context, 'the parties should take care not to aggravate or extend the dispute'. The Court reaffirmed that 'when such a dispute gives rise to a threat to the peace, breach of the peace or act of aggression, the Security Council has special responsibilities under Chapter VII of the Charter'. The judges from China, Russia, and Sri Lanka, and the Yugoslav-appointed ad hoc judge, dissented from the Court's opinion.

Of course, it is difficult to see of what use Yugoslavia's resort to the World Court could have had in what is now Serbia and Montenegro. Since the US was doing most of the bombing, it is not clear how any provisional order by the Court ordering a stop to the bombing could in any case have affected the situation; presumably, any such order could not have extended to the US or Spain, since they were no longer parties to the case. At any rate, the Court handed down its decision on December 2004, ruling that it did not have jurisdiction over the charges brought against the eight remaining states on the grounds that the former Republic of Yugoslavia's membership in the UN during the critical period of 1992–2000 was 'ambiguous and open to different assessments'.[14] Nevertheless, the mere filing of the case may further discourage US willingness to accept the compulsory

---

[13] The full text of the orders and opinions can be found at <http://www.icj-cij.org/docket/index.php?p1=3&p2=3&k=2e&PHPSESSID=da963f39077575543eb31f21dfc2dcca&case=111&code=ypo&p3=3> and 38 ILM 950 (July 1999). See also *ICJ Press Communique*, 99/33, 2 June 1999. An abstract appears in the American Society of International Law's *International Law in Brief*, vol 2, No 6 (June 1999). See also M Simons, 'Judges at the Hague Refuse to Halt the NATO Bombing', *New York Times*, 3 June 1999, at A14.

[14] 'Legality of Use of Force (Serbia and Montenegro v Belgium), Preliminary Objections, Judgment', ICJ Reports 2004, 279, at para 64 available at <http://www.icj-cij.org/docket/files/105/8440.pdf>.

jurisdiction of the Court and may well affect the views of some of the other NATO allies as well. It is interesting that this case received little coverage in the US press until the Court's ruling dismissing Yugoslavia's complaint against the US was issued. This was also the reaction of the US press as regards Nicaragua's suit against the US in the World Court in the 1980s.

The position of the NATO countries is that NATO's actions were for one reason or another a legitimate exercise of a privilege of humanitarian intervention. The NATO countries have insisted that they were acting not in their own interests, but because they were morally compelled to do so in order to forestall and, if possible, reduce the humanitarian disaster resulting from the deliberate policy of ethnic cleansing and other atrocities perpetrated by Slobodan Milosevic, his government and his military that, they said, represented a genocidal policy recalling that employed during the Holocaust. The *New York Times*, reporting on the hearings before the Court on provisional measures, said that the ten NATO countries, in their replies to the World Court, had all 'mocked Yugoslavia's claim, calling it cynical and absurd' and that the US had called Belgrade's suit 'a feat of hypocrisy and cynicism of Orwellian proportions'.[15]

What is particularly interesting is that the justifications cited by the US and NATO for their actions in Kosovo rest on a reinterpretation of the Charter by these governments and at least some academics, whereby a broad right of humanitarian intervention is permitted. Thus, NATO lawyers might conceivably suggest that Article 2(4) of the Charter bars only 'the threat or use of force against the territorial integrity or political independence of any state, or in any other manner inconsistent with the purposes of the United Nations' and thus does not prohibit humanitarian interventions which are consistent with the human rights purposes of the Charter. Conceivably, they might also argue that, under a reasonable contemporary reading of Chapter VIII of the Charter, a regional organization (and they may claim NATO is one) may exercise such a privilege of humanitarian intervention, at least absent express denial by the Security Council of such authorization; arguably, the collective character of any decision by a regional organization like NATO to intervene in such cases will serve as a guarantee against any reliance on an exceptional doctrine of collective humanitarian intervention so as to further selfish or other than humanitarian aims. (It is noteworthy that, during the Cuban missile crisis, the US argued, inter alia, that the Security Council's silence in the face of the Organization of American States (OAS)-authorized quarantine was in effect 'consent' to the OAS action under Chapter VIII.)[16]

In an article entitled 'The New Interventionism',[17] Professor Michael Glennon, in supporting NATO's actions, claimed that the Charter provisions are simply inadequate to deal with human rights and other challenges such as Kosovo and

    [15] Simons, 'Yugoslavia Seeks a Legal Order' above n 12.
    [16] See, eg L Meeker, 'Defensive Quarantine and the Law', 57 AJIL(1963) 523.
    [17] M Glennon, 'The New Interventionism: The Search for a Just International Law', 78 Foreign Affairs (1999) 2.

need not be respected. He argued that, instead, NATO and other nations committed to international justice should expressly adopt an '*ad hoc*, opportunistic approach'; in his view, openly breaking the law in such cases is much less dangerous to international order than pretending to comply with it. He concludes that

> the new interventionists should not be deterred by fears of destroying some lofty imagined temple of law enshrined in the UN Charter's anti-interventionist proscriptions. . . . If power is used to do justice, law will follow.[18]

And US Secretary of State Albright wrote:

> The crisis in Kosovo should cause a reexamination of the paradigms of the past. As the world has changed, so have the roles of key institutions such as the EU, NATO and the United Nations. And so have American interests. In today's world of deadly and mobile dangers, gross violations of human rights are everyone's business.
>
> As for the use of force, Kosovo tells us only what we should have already known. Yes, in confronting evil and otherwise protecting our interests, force is sometimes required. No, as before Kosovo, it is not wise to formulate assumptions based on any single experience about exactly when and how force should be applied. In coping with future crisis, the accumulated wisdom of the past will have to be weighed against factors unique to that place and time. This is why foreign policy is more art than science, and how chief executives earn their pay.[19]

Clearly this leaves a lot of elbow room for decisions over whether or not to intervene by the world's single remaining superpower.

The apparent position of the US and NATO—at least as reflected in Professor Glennon's and Secretary Albright's statements—raises fundamental and serious legal and policy issues. Professor Glennon's arguments challenge the integrity of the UN Charter and of the core principles of contemporary international law, on both of which international human rights law and the future of our human rights efforts so depend.

The so-called 'doctrine of humanitarian intervention' and, more recently, the argument that there is a broad implied exception to the prohibition of force in Article 2(4) of the Charter with respect to humanitarian intervention have, of course, been around for a long time; indeed, the doctrine goes back at least to Grotius. The case for the doctrine has always been, as now, that 'human rights are trumps', that decent countries cannot stand idly by while human beings in other countries are subjected to atrocities and that, under these circumstances, moral necessity must prevail over any rival claim of law or expediency. The counterargument has been that, even if there may be a few extreme cases in which a claim to moral necessity is genuinely justified, more typically—as in Nazi Germany's seizure of the Sudetanland in Czechoslovakia on the grounds of the alleged

---

[18] Ibid., at 7.
[19] M Albright, 'To Win the Peace...', *Wall Street Journal*, 14 June 1999, at A20.

mistreatment of Sudetan Germans—'humanitarian intervention' has simply been a cover for the pursuit of national power and interests.

While the debate over the years has spawned an extensive and learned literature pro and con, the arguments for humanitarian intervention have generally been rejected. For example, in his 1985 Hague Lectures, Professor Oscar Schachter concluded

governments by and large (and most jurists) would not assert a right to forcible interven-tion to protect the nationals of another country from atrocities in their own country....

...The reluctance of governments to legitimize foreign invasion in the interests of humanitarianism is understandable in the light of past abuses by powerful states. States strong enough to intervene and sufficiently interested in doing so tend to have polit-ical motives. They have a strong temptation to impose a political solution in their own national interest. Most governments are acutely sensitive to this danger and they show no disposition to open up Article 2(4) to a broad exception for humanitarian intervention by means of armed force.[20]

In 1997 an eminent study group of the Carnegie Commission published a report, 'Preventing Deadly Conflict',[21] which addressed the question 'as to when, where and how individual nations, and global and regional organizations, should be willing to apply forceful measures to curb incipient violence and stop potentially much greater destruction of life and property'. The Commission concluded that the first broad principle that should govern any such decision was that:

First, any threat or use of force must be governed by universally accepted principles, as the UN Charter requires. Decisions to use force must not be arbitrary, or operate as the coercive and selectively used weapons of the strong against the weak.[22]

Significantly, during the first meeting of the Commission on UN Human Rights after the NATO bombardments, the then UN Secretary General Kofi Annan acknowledged that using force to protect human rights poses 'fundamental chal-lenges to the UN'.[23]

---

[20] O Schachter, 'International Law in Theory and Practice', 178 *Recueil des Cours* (1985-V) 9, 143–4. See Professor Schachter's excellent and more extensive discussion of these issues in the revised version of his Hague Lectures, published as O Schachter, *International Law in Theory and Practice* (1991), at 117–26, where he notes, inter alia, at 126: 'Even in the absence of such prior approval [by the Security Council], a State or group of States using force to put an end to atroci-ties when the necessity is evident and the humanitarian intention is clear is likely to have its action pardoned. But I believe it is highly undesirable to have a new rule allowing humanitarian interven-tion, for that could provide a pretext for abusive intervention. It would be better to acquiesce in a violation that is considered necessary and desirable in the particular circumstances than to adopt a principle that would open a wide gap in the barrier against unilateral use of force.'

[21] Carnegie Commission on Preventing Deadly Conflict, 'Preventing Deadly Conflict: Executive Summary of the Final Report' (1997), at 15.

[22] Ibid.

[23] The Secretary General made the statement on 7 April 1999, SG/SM/6949-HR/OV/898. Subsequently, in his annual report to the UN membership, the Security General said that enforce-ment action without clear UN approval—as in the case of the NATO intervention in Kosovo—represents a threat to the 'very core of the international security system' founded on the UN

An early April 1999 *New York Times* news analysis of the international legal 'rationale' for NATO's intervention, while indicating the continuing debate and arguments that intervention to halt 'genocide' could be justified, noted that:

A broad spectrum of legal scholars agree that there is currently no simple, straightforward or obvious legal basis for the bombing of Serbian targets to be found in treaties, the United Nations' Charter or binding resolutions or any other written international legal code.

'The traditional view of international law would clearly prohibit what is happening', Professor Abram Chayes of the Harvard Law School said in an interview.[24]

Of course, this does not mean that the international community need stand helplessly by in the face of genocide or some other gross atrocity or humanitarian disaster. It is now clear that the Security Council—acting under its Chapter VII authority, especially as this has been extensively and creatively interpreted and applied in many situations since the Gulf War and, in particular, the Haiti intervention[25]—can respond with the full weight of the UN's collective might in such crises;[26] Article 2(7) of the Charter does not prohibit the UN from intervening in matters within the domestic jurisdiction of a state when the UN is applying enforcement measures under Chapter VII. Of course, any such action would require approval by the Security Council, including the concurrence of the permanent members—ostensibly the reason why NATO, knowing of at least

Charter. See 'Report of the Secretary-General on the Work of the Organization', GAOR, 54th Session, Supplement No. 1 (A/54/1); 'Secretary-General Presents his Annual Report to General Assembly', *UN Press Release*, SG/SM/7136, GA/9596, 20 September 1999; *The Financial Times*, 9 September 1999. See also K Annan, 'Two Concepts of Sovereignty', *The Economist*, 18 September 1999; Kofi Annan's address at Ditchley Park, UK, SG/S/W6613, 26 June 1998, in 'The Quotable Kofi Annan' at <http://www.un.org>.

[24] N Lewis, 'A Word Bolsters Case for Allied Intervention', *New York Times*, 4 April 1999, at 7. But cf. J Bolton, 'Clinton Meets "International Law" in Kosovo', *Wall Street Journal*, 5 April 1999, at A23: 'The real lesson of Kosovo is that "international law" in political and military matters is increasingly exposed as an academic sham'. See also the excellent articles by B Simma, 'NATO, the UN and the Use of Force: Legal Aspects', 10 EJIL (1999) 1 and A Cassese, 'Ex iniuria ius oritur: Are We Moving towards International Legitimation of Forcible Humanitarian Countermeasures in the World Community?', 10 EJIL (1999) 23, both of which, while apparently sharing the opinion that NATO's bombing without UN authorization is illegal, seem to view the bombing somewhat less critically. Thus, Simma considers Kosovo a 'hard case', in which there may have been no choice but to act outside the law, but which should in any event be regarded as exceptional and not as a precedent; Cassesse disagrees with Simma that NATO's breach of the Charter may be regarded as negligible and countenanced as exceptional, but suggests it may be taken as evidence of an emerging doctrine in international law whereby the use of forcible countermeasures is allowed to impede a state from committing large-scale atrocities in its own territory and in circumstances where the Security Council is incapable of responding adequately to the crisis.

[25] See Security Council Resolution, 841 (June 1993), 917 (May 1994) and particularly 940 (July 1994); eg DM Malone, *Decision-Making in the UN Security Council: The Case of Haiti 1990–97* (1998), but see R Falk, 'The Haiti Intervention: A Dangerous World Order Precedent for the United Nations', 36 Harv Int'l LJ (1995) 341.

[26] See, generally, eg S D Murphy, *Humanitarian Intervention: The United Nations in an Evolving World Order* (1996).

the opposition of Russia and China, did not seek such authority for its Kosovo intervention. However, even in the event of a veto by a permanent member, there remains the possibility that the General Assembly could seize itself of the matter under the 'Uniting for Peace' Resolution,[27] which might even be able to authorize at least voluntary collective action.

Thus, a refusal to recognize a unilateral or NATO privilege of humanitarian intervention need not disable the international community's capacity effectively to respond to humanitarian tragedies or encourage a moral 'cop-out'. This means that an assessment of a crisis situation, the decision to respond and the choice of means can still be carried out by a more internationally representative and less self-interested collective body rather than a single state or group. Moreover, this also means that the position can be rejected that only NATO governments have sufficient moral concern and fibre to be outraged by and respond to such crises.

If this analysis is correct, NATO's action represented a serious threat both to the law of the Charter and to international law more broadly. If NATO, under the authority of the doctrine of humanitarian intervention, can decide on its own that Yugoslavia's treatment of its Kosovar minority warrants the NATO bombing of Yugoslavia and the occupation and de facto severance from Yugoslavia of Kosovo, then what is to prevent any country or self-defined regional group from claiming a similar authority? For example, under such a precedent, what is to prevent the Arab League from deciding on its own that Israel's treatment of its Palestinian minority warrants the League's bombing of Israel, or China from deciding that Indonesia's treatment of its Chinese minority warrants China's attacking Indonesia, or Russia from deciding that Turkey's treatment of the Kurds permits Russia to bomb Turkey or that Estonia's treatment of Russians warrants Russia's reoccupation of Estonia, and so on and on? Do we really want a doctrine which will encourage this sort of behaviour? Moreover, if the NATO countries can simply ignore or flout the Charter and international law because they are powerful and no one is in a position to stop them, what then is left of the Charter and international law, and will the NATO countries ever again be able credibly to invoke the Charter against other states? Or, if they seek to do so, will this simply show that, as cynics maintain, there is one law, one Charter, for the weak and another for the strong?

Moreover, clearly honest differences of opinion have emerged as to the genuineness of the alleged motives for NATO's intervention. While NATO claimed— and its public appears generally to accept—that it was acting only from the highest humanitarian motives, Russia, China, some other countries and peoples, and even some NATO citizens, have been more sceptical. They saw NATO's claim of humanitarian motives as simply a pretence, designed to justify the bombing and to sway NATO public opinion in its support. These critics accuse NATO of a variety of more self-serving motives, including, for example, the desire to establish a

---

[27] G A Res. 377 (1950).

NATO sphere of influence in the Balkans and further humiliate and intimidate Russia; NATO's need to justify its continued existence and expansion, thereby assuring security to its bureaucrats and a market for its arms and industries; US and NATO diplomatic blundering and the consequent need to save face; NATO's desire to maintain its credibility after its bluff was called at Rambouillet; the desire of the US and NATO to 'get even' with Milosevic for what they considered his past betrayals and atrocities in Bosnia, which embarrassed US and NATO diplomats; the concern of the US and NATO over the criticism that they had faced for failing to prevent the atrocities in Bosnia and their consequent desire to forestall similar criticism for failing to take action regarding Kosovo; the Pentagon's desire to test its high-technology weapons and establish their value before the US Congress and public, and even Secretary of State Albright's need to save face because of her failed strategy and ultimatum at Rambouillet, in sharp contrast to Ambassador Holbrooke's highly publicized and widely praised success at Dayton; or all of the above. In support of their scepticism about the genuine humanitarian motives of the US and NATO, critics have pointed to what they regard as the US's record of support for governments and groups involved in human right violations in Vietnam, Guatemala, El Salvador, Nicaragua, Indonesia, and elsewhere, to what they regard as suspect US 'humanitarian' rationales for intervention in Vietnam, Grenada, Panama, and Haiti, and to the failure of the US and NATO to do anything about the many equally or even more horrendous violations of human rights in Cambodia, Uganda, Angola, East Timor, Liberia, Sierra Leone, Tibet, and elsewhere, but particularly the genocide in Rwanda, where at least 500,000 people were slaughtered over eight weeks, while the US, Belgium, and other NATO countries simply watched.[28]

Of course, the fact that the US and NATO did not act to prevent or halt previous humanitarian disasters does not mean that they should not have acted in Kosovo. Governments, like people, can learn from their mistakes and 'do better next time'. Moreover, arguably, the world will be a better place if countries do the right thing even occasionally. Still, the critics have raised doubts in people's minds about the sincerity of the West's motives in espousing 'the new interventionism'.

So, we seem to be left with a dilemma. If we say that humanitarian intervention is not permissible absent UN Security Council approval, we may find ourselves in a Cold War-type stalemate, whereby efforts to deal with urgent crises can be stymied by a veto of any of the permanent members of the Security Council. But if we permit the US or a regional organization such as NATO to ignore the UN and act on its own, then we may be undercutting the authority and even the very existence of the UN—an organization crucial to our hopes for international law and human rights—since it seems clear that the veto and other voting provisions

---

[28] For a discussion, see, eg P Gourevich, *We Wish to Inform You that Tomorrow We will be Killed with Our Families: Stories from Rwanda* (1998); G Prunier, *The Rwanda Crisis: History of a Genocide* (1995); J Alvarez, 'Crimes of States/Crimes of Hate: Lessons from Rwanda', 24 Yale J of Int'l L(1999) 365.

are at the heart of the acceptance by the permanent members of Chapter VII of the Charter.

Nonetheless, as the 2004 Report of the Secretary-General's High-level Panel on Threats, Challenges and Change points out,[29] the Charter continues to be our best hope for preserving peace and achieving effective international cooperation and governance. We should therefore think long and hard before we do anything to jeopardize it. In the case of Kosovo, it is clear that Russia and China, two of the world's leading powers, and certainly many other UN members, had grave objections or at least serious reservations about the legality and the appropriateness of the bombing. Rather than being viewed as simply an obstacle to NATO policies, this lack of broad and open support and consensus might have been viewed by NATO governments as an opportunity for them to reconsider whether the NATO policies were the correct ones. After all, the UN membership has been prepared to support—or at least not to veto—humanitarian interventions in situations in which it believes action is warranted, as in the cases of Iraq, Bosnia, Somalia, and Haiti, among others. To deal with future Kosovos, we should develop special understandings and arrangements with respect to Security Council approval, whereby the permanent members will agree under certain conditions not to exercise their veto prerogatives, perhaps to abstain rather than to veto Security Council action, in order to deal with situations of urgent humanitarian crisis as evidenced by a consistent pattern of gross and reliably attested violations of human rights[30] that require immediate action and in which there is widespread support by the general membership for such action. This was the approach advanced by both the Secretary-General's High-level Panel Report and the Report of the International Commission on Intervention and State Sovereignty (ICISS),[31] each of which put forward guidelines for when the UN might invoke its Chapter VII powers and rely on the use of force to combat a humanitarian crisis. In contrast to this, a 'solution' which involves simply ignoring or bypassing Charter obligations seems ill-advised.

Certainly, Kosovo will stand as a precedent for the recognition of the legitimacy of a doctrine of unilateral or regional 'humanitarian intervention'.[32] Nonetheless, as the Kosovo crisis fades from memory, as the doctrine's potential for weakening the Charter becomes more apparent, as public and NGO demands for similar interventions in human rights crises in other parts of the world multiply, and,

---

[29] 'Report of the High-level Panel on Threats, Challenges and Change, A More Secure World: Our Shared Responsibility', 2 December 2004.

[30] This language draws on and slightly modifies the criteria set out in 'Procedure for Dealing with Communications Relating to Violations of Human Rights and Fundamental Freedoms', ECOSOC Resolution 1503 (XLVIII) (1970).

[31] Report of the International Commission on Intervention and State Sovereignty, 'The Responsibility to Protect' (December 2001).

[32] For indications of the limited effectiveness of assertions that particular actions should be regarded as 'exceptional' and 'should not be regarded as a precedent', see, eg Malone, n 25 above, at 85, 146–7.

especially, as the US and NATO become more aware of the doctrine's potential application by other countries with which they do not agree, NATO's enthusiasm for the doctrine may wane. In that case, we may see an artful manoeuvring so that Kosovo becomes accepted as a 'unique situation' and a gradual return to more traditional views about the limits of humanitarian intervention and the Charter proscriptions on the use of force.

3. Kosovo and the Laws of War

Apart from the questions raised by NATO's bombing of Yugoslavia without UN authorization, the *jus ad bellum* of the humanitarian intervention, the Kosovo crisis also evoked issues because of the way NATO conducted the war, the *jus in bello* of the intervention. The two are closely related.

Presumably a humanitarian intervention, even if it is legally and morally justified, should be carried out only in a humanitarian way and solely in pursuit of humanitarian purposes. Both the Secretary-General's High-level Panel Report and the ICISS Report recommend that forces use proportional means such that military action does not exceed what is needed to accomplish the mission. The ICISS Report also calls for the strict adherence to International humanitarian law (IHL). But as the Kosovo bombing campaign progressed, many people became increasingly troubled in this respect. Thus, according to the *New York Times*, as of 6 June 1999, when the bombing campaign ended, NATO had been bombing Yugoslavia for six weeks, had deployed 1,100 airplanes, which had carried out over 33,000 sorties, had hit Yugoslavia with over 14,000 missiles or bombs, including large numbers of cluster bombs and, apparently, bombs containing depleted uranium, and, according to estimates, caused at least $40 billion worth of damage.[33] In its 29 April 1999 submission to the ICJ, Yugoslavia asserted that both military and civilian targets had come under attack during the bombings, causing many casualties (as of late April, 'about 1,000 civilians, including 19 children, were killed and more than 4,500 sustained serious injuries'), enormous damage to schools, hospitals, radio and television stations, cultural monuments and places of worship, and the destruction of a large number of bridges, roads, and railway lines, as well as refining and chemical plants, resulting in serious health and environmental damage. Subsequently, NATO's targets were expanded to include Yugoslavia's electric grid and water supply, civilian factories or enterprises ostensibly having some relation to military efforts or owned by the family or reputed supporters of the Milosevic government, and the personal residences of Milosevic and his family (on the grounds that they were used as

---

[33] *New York Times*, 11 June 1999, at A12, A15. See also *Newsweek*, 21 June 1999, at 44. For some subsequent estimates, see *New York Times*, 29 September 1999, at A10, and 3 October 1999, at wk2.

'command posts'). On various occasions, there were additional reports of 'collateral damage'—to the Chinese embassy, villages, civilian buses, a hospital, a prison, a nursing home, and so forth. NATO now claims it killed at least 5,000 Yugoslav military and wounded 10,000 more, while Yugoslavia says that NATO killed over 1,500 civilians and wounded many more.[34]

NATO, of course, was well aware of the sensitivity of this issue. It seems clear—and this is to NATO's credit—that there was a deliberate effort, at least on the part of the civilian leaders of NATO, to avoid civilian casualties and that the 'smart bomb' technology employed helped avoid more substantial civilian casualties. NATO repeatedly asserted that its war was solely aimed against Yugoslavia's 'evil leadership'—Milosevic—and not the Yugoslav people; that its bombing was directed only at military targets and the 'degrading' of the capacity of the Yugoslav military to carry out ethnic cleansing and commit atrocities against the Kosovars; that civilian casualties were regrettable, but inevitable errors or 'collateral damage', and that, when Kosovars were bombed, this was the result of a Yugoslav policy of using them as 'human shields', which, in itself, is a war crime. But as the bombing continued, there was clearly a deepening rift between the politicians and the military over how the war should be conducted. The NATO politicians counselled restraint, stressing the need to retain public support for the bombing and the potential fragility of that support if civilian casualties and damage increased. The military, however, apparently chafed under this restraint and urged that military forces be allowed to 'do the job': a policy which, it claimed, incidentally, would, by shortening the conflict, ultimately save rather than sacrifice lives.

In an article in *Atlantic Monthly*, an eminent historian quoted the military doctrine succinctly stated by US Air Force General Curtis LeMay, whose B-52 and other bombers killed as many as 800,000 Japanese, injured perhaps a million more and demolished the homes of some eight million Japanese in the carpet and atom bombing of Japanese cities during a period of about five months towards the end of World War II. 'I'll tell you what war is about', LeMay said. 'You've got to kill people and when you've killed enough, they stop fighting!'[35] There are indications that at least some NATO military leaders were moving towards this philosophy.

'We are aware that this will have an impact on civilians, but we are in the midst of a military campaign against Slobodan Milosevic', explained a Pentagon official in justifying the targeting by NATO of electrical transformers. '. . . compare that to the consequences suffered by the civilian population of Kosovo who have been driven from their homes'.[36]

---

[34] See generally Human Rights Watch, *Under Orders: War Crimes in Kosovo* (2001).

[35] See D Kennedy, 'Victory at Sea', *Atlantic Monthly* (1999), at 78.

[36] M Becker, 'NATO Calls Transformers a Key Target in War Plan', *New York Times*, 25 May 1999, at A4; see also, eg *New York Times*, 25 June 1999, at A13, reporting that General Wesley Clark, the NATO Commander, meeting with Albanian residents of Pristmar, 'told the jubilant

'There are, in the end, no humanitarian wars', wrote former Prime Minister Margaret Thatcher in a newspaper article. '... [I]t is the men of evil, not our troops or pilots, that bear the guilt.'[37]

'There are times, and Kosovo is one, when we need to be as ruthless and determined in our choice of means as we have been high-minded in our choice of ends',[38] wrote Michael Ignatieff, a noted commentator on human rights, at the conclusion of an article in *The New York Review*.

Clearly Kosovo—and any humanitarian intervention—poses special dilemmas and challenges for the laws of war. For example:

- If, as NATO claimed, the war was only aimed against Milosevic and his policies and atrocities, what justified the escalation of the bombing against the Yugoslav people and the social infrastructure, including civilian factories, roads, bridges, radio stations, electric grids, and waterworks, with predictable 'collateral damage'? Of course, NATO could argue—as Prime Minister Blair seems to have done—that NATO's purpose was to bomb Yugoslavia until Milosevic decided to yield to its demands or the Yugoslav people forced him to do so to avoid their own destruction, a strategy that NATO claims eventually worked. But is this not using the Yugoslav people and the Yugoslav economy as hostages? How does this square with NATO's ostensibly humanitarian purposes? And what justified NATO's use of cluster bombs and depleted uranium ordinance, both of which posed obvious dangers to civilians, even following the cessation of hostilities? 'Even for the world's only superpower, the ends do not always justify the means', former President Jimmy Carter has written.[39]

- How was the high-level bombing campaign intended to accomplish NATO's purpose of stopping the ethnic cleansing and permitting the return of the Kosovars? While it is true that the bombing inevitably, given the vast disparity of forces, created pressure for Yugoslavia to give up, some commentators argued that the bombing precipitated or at least accelerated the ethnic cleansing and the exodus of the Kosovars and that everyone knew that high-altitude bombing could not, in any event, hope to stop the atrocities. A *New York Times* analysis reported the following comment by Special Envoy Holbrooke after his failed attempt on March 23 to get Milosevic to accept NATO's ultimatum or face the bombing, which began the next day:

> On his way out of the country, Mr. Holbrooke was asked if he feared that NATO's air attack would ignite a humanitarian catastrophe.

Kosovars that he believes the horrors being uncovered provide clear justification for the alliance's 78 days of punishing air raids'.

[37] M Thatcher, 'The West Must Answer Evil with Strength', *Wall Street Journal*, 16 May 1999, at A26, and *Wisconsin State Journal*, 6 June 1999, at A26.

[38] M Ignatieff, 'Human Rights: The Midlife Crisis', *The New York Review*, 20 May 1999, 58, at 62.

[39] J Carter, 'Have We Forgotten the Path to Peace?', *New York Times*, 27 May 1999, at A31.

'That is our greatest fear, by far, by far,' he replied.

Asked what NATO, operating only from the air, could do to prevent such a catastrophe, Mr. Holbrooke went silent and shrugged.[40]

Moreover, some have argued that the bombing, by further fueling ethnic hatreds and causing enormous damage in Kosovo, was likely to increase the problems following the return of the Kosovars and eliminate any hope of eventual reconciliation between Serbs and Kosovars. In view of the difficulties subsequently encountered by UNMIK in encouraging communities to live together, there would seem to be more than a grain of truth in this assertion.[41]

If the bombing was unlikely to accomplish its ostensible purpose, did it thereby lose its rationale and its moral and legal justification?

- If NATO's bombing caused as much or more destruction as it ostensibly prevented among the Kosovars, the Serbs and surrounding countries and peoples, did it thereby lose its moral justification? Must not a 'just war' not only have a 'just' purpose, but also be conducted by 'just' means and have the likelihood of a 'just' and beneficial outcome? Was punishment, retribution, or deterrence a sufficient justification for NATO to continue the bombing and the destruction? What is the legitimate function of humanitarian intervention? If Yugoslavia was prepared to yield to most of the NATO demands and accept the G-8 principles, including repatriation of the Kosovars, but insisted only on a UN rather than a NATO-led protective force, the restriction of NATO forces to Kosovo rather than authorization to enter Serbia as well, and Yugoslavia's nominal retention of sovereignty, all conditions NATO seems ultimately to have agreed to, was NATO's political desire for a total 'victory' so as to 'maintain its credibility', sufficient justification for the continuation of the bombing for so long?

- If it is permissible to bomb strictly 'military' targets and, as NATO seems to have believed, *also* permissible to bomb targets that might conceivably be of even indirect relevance to the military, such as an electric power grid or any road or any bridge (including the bridges over the Danube which are quite remote from Kosovo) and, as NATO also seems to have believed, *also* permissible to bomb targets, including the homes, families and businesses of a leader and his supporters, the destruction of which might conceivably exert pressure on a government to stop alleged human rights violations and permit a humanitarian occupation, is there then *any* conceivable target, including

---

[40] *New York Times*, 6 June 1999, at 12Y. See also, eg 'Back From Belgrade: Congressman Says NATO is Worsening Refugee Crisis', *New York Times*, 23 April 1999, reporting a statement of US Representative Saxton, an eight-term Republican Congressman from New Jersey. 'I know when the ethnic cleansing started,' he said. 'I know when the refugees started to move. It was when we started the bombing.' See also *The Economist*, 8 May 1999, at 11: 'The humanitarian catastrophe [the West's war against Serbia] was designed to avert has merely been intensified.'

[41] See, eg UNHCR/OSCE, *Overview of the Situation of Ethnic Minorities in Kosovo* (1999).

civilian target, that is not arguably related to one of these objectives and therefore a 'legitimate' target?

Another troubling aspect of the Kosovo crisis was the massive disparity in power between NATO and Yugoslavia and the overwhelming and irresistible high-technology nature of NATO's assault. On one side of the conflict was Yugoslavia, one of the West's smaller and poorer nations, with 11 million people and an economy already decimated and impoverished by ten years of NATO sanctions. On the other side were 19 of the world's most populous, richest, and technically advanced nations, with a combined population around 40 times that of Yugoslavia, about half the world's gross national product, an industrial capacity and gross national product perhaps 400 times greater than those of Yugoslavia, and able to deploy the world's most sophisticated and powerful weapons.[42] Moreover, NATO's high-technology, remote assault was carried out through means against which Yugoslavia was virtually powerless to defend itself, including long-range missile attacks and bombings at 15,000 feet. A *New York Times* article described an American B-2 pilot taking off from his base in Missouri, dropping 12 tons of bombs over Yugoslavia and then returning home to cut the grass and order dinner for his family from Pizza Hut.[43] The disparity in casualties was similarly staggering. There were no combat deaths on the NATO side, while Yugoslav casualties were, according to NATO, in the tens of thousands.

There is nothing in international law which suggests that one side in a conflict cannot have overwhelming superiority, that it must suffer proportionate casualties, or that a fight must be 'fair'. Nonetheless, some have argued that NATO's high-altitude bombing and long-distance missile campaign, clearly designed to minimize the risk of NATO casualties, was inconsistent both with NATO's professed objective of halting the atrocities against the Kosovars and of avoiding Yugoslav civilian casualties. For example, Steven Erlanger, *New York Times* Bureau Chief in the Balkans, reported:

Here I feel some shame. Looked at from beneath the bombs, NATO's conduct can seem cowardly. The Serbs knew they were powerless to prevent NATO from doing what it pleased, but they have been insulted by the invisibility of the enemy. They sense that it is a way of pretending that their lives are expendable, the 'collateral damage' of NATO's desperate effort to retain credibility in a mismanaged war.[44]

---

[42] Rough estimates based on statistics on population and gross national product in the *World Almanac* and *Book of Facts 1999*, which lists Yugoslavia's population at about 11.2 million and its 1995 GNP at $20.6 billion; the US population alone is listed at 270 million, and its 1997 GNP at $8.11 trillion. According to the *Wall Street Journal*, 7 June 1999, the NATO countries account for about half the productive capacity of the planet, while Yugoslavia's GNP is equal to about 1/50th the US defence budget.

[43] T Ricks, 'For These B-2 Pilots, Bombs Away Means Really Far, Far Away', *Wall Street Journal*, 19 April 1999, at 1: 'When he got home, recalls this blond son of the midwest, "my wife kissed me and she said 'You need to mow the lawn. I'll go get the kids". After he did his chores, "we ordered out from Pizza Hut".'

[44] S Erlanger, 'Beneath the Falling Bombs', *New York Times Magazine*, 11 June 1999, at 86.

Likewise, the author of a letter to the *Wall Street Journal* noted the 'moral ambiguity' of NATO's air strategy and its 'self-congratulation' at having no combat casualties:

We suffered no casualties because, except to an almost insignificant extent, we did not engage enemy forces. Rather, we heavily damaged infrastructure essential both to the military and to the civilian economy, causing immense suffering and death to women, children and other noncombatants—both Serbs and Kosovars—who are defenseless and wholly powerless to influence the depredations taking place in Kosovo.

Avoiding military casualties by inflicting death and suffering on innocent civilians can only weakly be argued as the better of terrible alternatives, considering that it totally failed to halt the dreadful ethnic cleansing in Kosovo....[45]

Thus, while NATO governments have viewed the bombing as a demonstration of NATO's concern for human rights, at least some other governments and peoples have viewed it very differently: as the brutal bullying into abject submission by NATO and an increasingly imperial US of a very weak country. For example, the *People's Daily*, in China, called the bombing part of an American 'global strategy for world hegemony', an 'aggressive war' that was groundless in morality or law and 'a new form of colonialism' which relied on pretexts such as human rights to turn other countries into dependents.[46] Indeed, some question whether Kosovo was really a 'war' at all. To some critics, it was more in the nature of a 'punitive expedition', reminiscent of those conducted by Imperial Rome, with its client subservient 'allies', to punish a small country and people who refused to bow to Rome's will and to capture its recalcitrant leaders and parade them in chains through Rome (for Rome read, The Hague).

The Kosovo crisis suggests that, if we are to permit or at least tolerate humanitarian interventions, we may wish to rethink the ways our laws of war should apply in such situations. Certainly coercion is the name of the 'war game', and so-called 'humanitarian interventions' may be no different. Indeed, perhaps there is a bit of truth in the theory that, if the military had been 'unleashed' to launch a more brutal and overwhelming assault, Yugoslavia might have yielded more quickly, and fewer lives might have been lost. Nevertheless, there remains a fundamental inconsistency between the concept of humanitarian intervention and the techniques of the remote, high-technology killing of large numbers of people, including many innocent civilians. One might refer to the troubling remark attributed to a US infantry officer during the Vietnam War: 'We had to destroy the village in order to save it'.[47] There is something inherently repugnant about the idea of 'bombing for peace'.

---

[45] Letter from C McCrea Sr, *Wall Street Journal*, 17 June 1999, at A27. See also, eg 'On Killing from beyond Harm's Way', *New York Times*, 18 April 1999, at wk 4.

[46] *New York Times*, 18 May 1999, at A9. See also C Bodeen, 'Chinese President Claims US Seeking World Dominance', *Wisconsin State Journal*, 14 May 1999, at 9A, and *New York Times*, 6 June 1999, at 114.

[47] See Bilder, 'Rethinking Human Rights' n 2 above.

More ominously, poorer non-Western countries may begin to wonder whether the laws of war are simply another tool of Western hegemony that permits the kind of remote-killing high-technology warfare the wealthy, industrialized states can conduct, but bars the only kinds of measures and weapons that poorer and weaker countries can afford to obtain or use in defence. Indeed, several commentators have warned that Kosovo could fuel the proliferation of nuclear, chemical, and biological weapons and land mines as less powerful and less technologically advanced nations desperately seek the means to counter the potential threat of US and NATO high-technology and otherwise irresistible Kosovo-like punitive interventions.[48]

4. Kosovo and International Criminal Law

On 27 May 1999 the International Criminal Tribunal for Former Yugoslavia indicted President Slobodan Milosevic, Serbia's minister of internal affairs, the chief of staff of the Yugoslav armed forces, and Yugoslavia's deputy prime minister on war crimes charges, accusing them of authorizing a military campaign against civilians in Kosovo. They faced charges of murder, deportation and prosecution in violation of the laws and customs of war. The indictment alleged that, since the beginning of 1999, Milosevic and his aides had orchestrated and led 'a campaign of terror and violence directed at Kosovo Albanian civilians' that resulted in nearly 800,000 people forced at gunpoint from their province and the documented murder of over 340 civilians in towns and villages across Kosovo. This was the first time an international tribunal indicted an acting head-of-state for international crimes. The landmark indictment followed the adoption by 120 countries in Rome on 18 July 1998 of a treaty to establish an International Criminal Court (ICC) with jurisdiction to try war crimes, crimes against humanity and genocide,[49] and the UK's House of Lords and Home Secretary's decision in March and April 1999 that Spanish Judge Baltasar Garzon could continue to seek Chilean General Augusto Pinochet's extradition from the UK to Spain to face charges that he had authorized the use of torture in Chile.[50] All of these events have been widely hailed by the international human rights community as 'joys': the dawn of a new era in which the

---

[48] See, eg S Schmemann, 'Now, Onwards to the Next Kosovo, if There is One', *New York Times*, 6 June 1999, at wk 1, where Susan Woodward, an expert on the Balkans at the Brookings Institution, is quoted as saying: 'People will not say, "I will think twice before I do horrible things". Rather they will think, "I better prepare better defensively against external interventions of that kind".'

[49] See A Stanley, 'US Dissents, but Accord is Reached in War-Crime Court', *New York Times*, 18 July 1998, at A3; N King Jr, 'Nations Create War-Crimes Court despite US Protest', *Wall Street Journal*, 20 July 1998, at 8.

[50] *Regina v Bartle and the Commissioner of Police for the Metropolis ex parte Pinochet*, House of Lords Decision of 24 March 1999, 38 ILM(1999) 581.

impunity of tyrants will end and gross violators of human rights, no matter their rank or status, will be held accountable and brought to justice. The arrest and subsequent extradition of Milosevic probably constituted a crowning event in a long chain begun in Nuremberg.

The case in support of international criminal courts and universal jurisdiction is long standing and compelling. '[C]rimes against international law are committed by men, not by abstract entities', found the judgment at Nuremberg, 'and only by punishing individuals who commit such crimes can the provisions of international law be enforced.'[51] Certainly, there is much to the contention that, if we want and expect the prohibitions of international human rights and humanitarian law to be taken seriously and prospective tyrants or genociders to be deterred, we must possess legal procedures and institutions that can credibly, fairly, and effectively bring such gross violators to justice on behalf of the international community. Moreover, international criminal courts and prosecutions have a symbolic importance, showing that there is a credible international law and that the international community is prepared to protect human rights and hold those who engage in gross violations accountable. All of these developments are clearly a major step in that direction. Louise Arbour, the former Chief Prosecutor for the ICTY and now the High Commissioner for Human Rights, has said that, the creation of the ICTY and its companion International Criminal Tribunal for Rwanda, together with the adoption of the Rome statute for the ICC, 'are probably the greatest, most imaginative achievements in the enforcement of fundamental human rights since Nuremberg and Tokyo'.[52]

There has been general acclaim for these and other recent international criminal law developments, but they are not without problems.

First, will the ICTY's indictments and judgments be widely accepted in the long term within the international community as genuinely impartial and non-political? President Clinton and other NATO and Western commentators hailed the indictment of Yugoslavia's leadership as a victory for justice, a vindication of NATO's position and a major step forward for human rights. But others have taken a very different view. Thus, some critics have charged that the ICTY is dominated by the US and NATO, that it is composed largely of judges from NATO countries, that its indictments have been overwhelmingly against Serbs, and that the indictment of Milosevic and his aides followed a chorus of threats by NATO leaders that, should he continue his resistance, he would be indicted. Consequently, these critics have viewed the indictment as simply an attempt by NATO, through the Tribunal, to increase the personal pressure on Milosevic, turn his people against him and reinforce the credibility of NATO's claim that the bombing was morally necessary and justified.

---

[51] 'Judgment of International Military Tribunal (Nuremberg) for the Trial of German Major Criminals (30 September and 1 October 1946)', 41 AJIL (1946) 172.

[52] 'UN Prosecutor Applauds Innovations', National Law Journal, 16 November 1998, at A11.

For example, the *New York Times* reported that the indictment would confirm the suspicions of most Serbs that the tribunal is prejudiced against them and not an independent court.

'It is a politically motivated decision that renders the tribunal an accomplice to NATO as an aggressor', Yugoslavia's delegate to the UN told the BBC. China's deputy representative on the UN Security Council called the indictment 'politically motivated'.[53] While one *New York Times* article reported that 'American officials insisted that the United States had not pressured the then Chief Prosecutor of the Tribunal, Louise Arbour, to delay or hasten the indictment of Mr. Milosevic',[54] a companion article noted that, 'Although the tribunal is avowedly apolitical, its decision to indict Mr. Milosevic comes at a time when a sea change has occurred in the attitude of western governments towards the Serbian leaders'.[55] Others have made a more nuanced criticism, suggesting that, even if the Court is impartial, the US can control the Court's actions simply by supplying or refusing to supply the tribunal with information essential to an indictment and that the US had only done this in regards to the case against Milosevic, because it felt that it was politically useful at that time to have him labelled a 'war criminal'. Presumably this proved effective; Milosevic began invariably to be referred to by the US government and the US press as 'the indicted war criminal Milosevic'.

Thus, whatever may be our own level of confidence in the ICTY's integrity and impartiality, Kosovo may have reinforced concerns, particularly among non-Western countries, that at least ad hoc international criminal courts such as the ICTY—with judges whose appointment necessarily depends on the approval of the major powers—can never be truly apolitical and impartial, but will inevitably become simply another weapon used by great powers against the weak. Indeed, as the US reaction to the *Nicaragua* case in the ICJ clearly demonstrates, the US itself shares concerns about the impartiality and possible political bias of international judges, and it has reportedly been similarly concerned about the powers and possible bias of the ICC and its prosecutor. Do we really want an international criminal court empowered to issue secret indictments ordering the arrest and abduction to The Hague of anyone its particular judges and prosecutors choose? The US, while strongly supporting the ICTY's actions against people it does not like, has been quite clear that no international court should ever try to do this to a US citizen.

Secondly, is there a danger that the ICTY or any international criminal court—either for political reasons, or simply because of the limited powers and resources of the court—will inevitably engage in selective, even random, prosecution, and can such selective prosecution *ever* be just? A very sad book, *The*

---

[53] *New York Times*, 27 May 1999, at A12.
[54] Ibid.
[55] Ibid.

Execution of Private Slovik,[56] examines the story behind the US's execution during World War II of a US soldier who had deserted: in fact, the only one out of many thousands of deserters who was executed by the US for desertion during that war. General Eisenhower decided that, to discourage desertion, someone should be made an example, and Private Slovik was the individual the lightning hit. The ICTY was long accused of indicting only 'small fry' war criminals—the Dushan Tadics—rather than government leaders. Then, Ms Arbour's policy changed so that she sought to prosecute only leaders. Does this mean that the smaller fry will now go unpunished? Is it fair for the ICTY to try Serbs, but no Croats or Muslims, and then (as some suggest was the case), when criticized for this, to indict a few 'token' Croats or Bosnian Muslims? Is it likely that such an international court would ever indict a Western, Chinese, or Russian official or even a US soldier, and, if so, what would be the reaction of these countries? In an article in the *New York Times*, a Balkan expert questioned the ICTY's failure to indict Franjo Tudjman of Croatia, who is widely thought to have been responsible for the ethnic cleansing of hundreds of thousands of Serbs in Croatia and other atrocities and who, the writer argued, was fully as monstrous as Milosevic; the writer also suggested that the ICTY's failure may in part be due to the fact that the US had not supplied evidence against Tudjman because he was a useful ally.[57] Likewise, General MacArthur reportedly refused to permit the indictment of Emperor Hirohito at the Tokyo trials, despite much evidence that the Emperor was significantly involved in the relevant Japanese aggressive policies, because MacArthur believed that such an indictment would complicate the US occupation of Japan.[58] Obviously, a criminal law system can only accomplish so much; the fact that we cannot find and punish *all* criminals does not mean we should not try to punish those we *can* reach and capture. But to punish only a very few politically or randomly chosen individuals may in practice not only have little deterrence effect, but also weaken respect for international courts and international law.

Thirdly, did the indictment of Milosevic and his top aides help or hurt in bringing an end to the Kosovo conflict? The answer to that question is one that is probably better left to historians once all the facts have become available and archival work can proceed. But it is certainly true that, in retrospect, one can see Milosevic's indictment as an important step in prompting a realization by pragmatic forces within Serbia that he stood once and for all in the way of what was ultimately an inevitable *rapprochement* with the West. On the other hand, in the short term the indictment probably polarized an already deeply antagonized society. That the consequences of the indictment turned out not to be more dramatic, is perhaps attributable less to law's deterrent effect than to the fact that Serbia's military nuisance

---

[56] WB Huie, *The Execution of Private Slovik* (1954).

[57] P Maass, 'Let's not Forget Milosevic's Partner in Crime', *New York Times*, 31 May 1999, at A13.

[58] See, generally, JM Dower, *Embracing Defeat: Japan in the Wake of World War II* (1999).

power had by then already been effectively circumscribed. Most importantly, the fact that the indictments focused on a few individuals risked treating merely the symptoms of political violence. It is certainly the case, for example, that of those who rushed to fill the power vacuum left by Milosevic, many were by no means free of the kind of aggressive nationalism that triggered the former Yugoslavia's many wars—although their inclinations were admittedly more democratic and moderate. Be that as it may, Yugoslavia's transition from the pariah of Europe into a fully-fledged partner is still at this stage far from complete and the legacy of the NATO strikes has proved a hard one to manage for Yugoslav politicians seeking to ally with the West while courting public opinion at home.

And what of the lesser war criminals? Media reports in the aftermath of the war indicated that the US and NATO, with the cooperation of NGOs, were planning a massive campaign to identify and prosecute all those in Kosovo allegedly responsible for the atrocities—a process that could have been very costly and disruptive and continued for years.[59] Certainly, since the moral and legal positions of both the Kosovars and NATO had been based on the premise of vast and horrific Serb atrocities, there was considerable pressure for NATO to validate the premise. In actual fact, NATO has turned out to move with as much caution when it came to making arrests in Kosovo, as it had displayed, for example, in Bosnia. By the time Milosevic had been ousted, it became understood that aside from the major criminals, the Yugoslav Republic should deal with its war criminals itself.[60] While this is a natural solution in view of the new regime's professed intention to break with the pattern of impunity of the past, it has also raised worries that the resulting investigations and trials might lead to discreet cover-ups, and at any rate an examination of Serbia's responsibilities that was substantially more lenient than might have otherwise been desirable. It may be, however, that this was the price to pay for a settlement—and it is by no means clear that much would be gained by aggressively pushing an already fragile regime to do even more in that direction.

Finally, one question that remains open for the future is whether the indictment of Milosevic and others by the ICTY will in fact deter future human rights violations by others? Perhaps, but one may be sceptical. It is possible that only leaders of smaller and militarily weak countries likely to fall into the bad graces of the US or NATO may regard themselves as potentially at serious risk.

More broadly, there is a clear need to re-examine the whole notion of the approaches of criminal law to massive human rights disasters.[61] These approaches

---

[59] See, eg C Trueheart, 'War Crimes Court Set for Kosovo Probe', *Washington Post*, 10 June 1999, at A22; 'FBI Plans to Begin its Inquiry at Once', *New York Times*, 12 June 1999, at A8; 'Investigators from Many Nations to Begin Search for War Crimes', *New York Times*, 15 June 1999, at A16.

[60] See C Gall, 'Serbia Finds Where Bodies Are Buried, and Investigates', *New York Times*, 31 July 2001, at A3.

[61] There has been an extensive recent literature on this issue. Compare, eg M Minow, *Between Vengeance and Forgiveness: Facing History after Genocide and Mass Violence* (1998); N J Kritz,

may now be widely perceived, especially by non-Western countries and peoples, as unfair, simply as another tool of US neo-imperialism. Moreover, the scope and the complexity of the violations involved may make criminal trials of all those responsible unmanageable at least in terms of due process. For example, in Rwandan jails there were reportedly over 130,000 people accused of participation in genocide, but the Rwandan legal system is almost non-existent and incapable of fairly and promptly dealing with these people, and the ad hoc International Criminal Tribunal for Rwanda certainly cannot handle all these cases. The Gacaca courts have taken some of the burden off the tribunal, but their achievements remain to be seen. Trials in Kosovo courts, despite the presence of 'international' judges, have depressingly revealed the extent of prejudice that still permeates the population, and the ease with which courts can become instruments to settle political scores.[62]

The ICC also poses problems. At the moment, it seems clear that the US, despite its fervent advocacy and support for the ICTY, will not ratify the Rome ICC treaty so long as the treaty continues to permit the ICC's potential exercise of jurisdiction against non-parties and so long as it seems possible that the Court can try any US citizen. Despite hopes raised by the signing of the treaty by the Clinton administration, various actions taken by the Bush administration and the Congress, including the adoption of legislation designed to ensure that no American serviceman is ever tried by the ICC, seem to indicate that there will be little sympathy for the ICC in the absence of a major change of heart on the part of a new administration after 2009.

The *Pinochet* case raised equally controversial and complex issues. Many people, but particularly the relatives of victims of the Pinochet regime, were rejoicing that a brutal dictator might finally get his just desserts and that the so-called 'culture of impunity' had at least been dented. Others argued that Judge Baltasar Garzon's action was irresponsible and a harmful precedent. They questioned the right of Spain to upset an accommodation that the Chilean people had reached and thus to risk throwing Chile into political conflict. They were also asking why this Spanish judge took it upon himself to interfere in another country's and another people's problems? Why did he feel uniquely entitled to decide how such wrongs should be righted, gaining global media attention in the process, but leaving the Chilean people to sort through the outcome? Why is Spain not focusing instead on its own human rights problems, including those revolving around Basque separatism and the human rights violations during the Franco years? If

---

Transitional Justice: How Emerging Democracies Reckon with Former Regimes (1995); SR Ratner and JS Abrams, *Accountability for Human Rights Atrocities in International Law: Beyond the Nuremberg Legacy* (1997); A Neier, *War Crimes: Brutality, Genocide, Terror, and the Struggle for Justice* (1998); C Joyner, 'Redressing Impunity for Human Rights Violations: The Universal Declaration and the Search for Accountability', 26 Denver J. of Int'l Law & Pol. (1998) 591.

[62] G Powles, 'The Quality of Justice', *The Times*, 8 March 2000 (deploring ethnic bias in Kosovo courts).

Spain can exercise such universal jurisdiction on the initiative of a subordinate judge, what is to prevent every other country—Iran, China, Cuba, Afghanistan, or Nauru—from doing the same? Here, the critics might (and often do) lay out a list of the potential alleged 'human rights violators' beginning with President Clinton, US General Clark, and Henry Kissinger. Or, will this simply be another situation in which there is one law for the strong, and another for the weak, and only leaders in smaller countries such as Chile need fear such actions? Is this what nations intended when they established the concept of universal jurisdiction (that is, at a time when the chief aim was not to displace national jurisdiction, but rather to permit punishment of pirates and slave traders beyond the reach of most effective national jurisdictions)?

More broadly, the critics ask, how can countries that may wish to put matters to rest through mechanisms such as truth commissions move on if foreign judges can interfere with their preferred methods of reaching settlements? Will military regimes be willing to give up power and permit peaceful transitions to democracy if they cannot rely on the permanence of agreed national amnesties? What about legal principles that are founded on the finality of measures—such as *res judicata*, *stare decisis* and *pacta sunt servanda*? Don't we need a way of permitting countries to reach such compromises without other countries or even the international community interfering? Recent cases, such as the international community's protracted efforts to find an acceptable solution to deal with crimes committed in Sierra Leone, show both that these problems have not lost any of their vigour and that new and innovative solutions are still possible.

5. Kosovo and International Political Stability

Kosovo also raised difficult questions about the relationship of human rights efforts to other important goals such as international cooperation, peace and stability.

NATO maintained that its humanitarian intervention in Kosovo strengthened peace by preventing Yugoslavia's ethnic conflict from having a 'domino effect' and spilling over and disrupting the peace and security not only of neighbouring countries, but of all of Europe. NATO also argued, more broadly, that its action helped foster stability by increasing the pressure for the ouster of Milosevic and the establishment of democracy in Yugoslavia and by deterring other potential Milosevic-like tyrants in other countries from committing human rights violations that may similarly disrupt international peace.

Only time will tell whether NATO's confidence is justified. But on the downside, NATO's actions appeared to have caused a serious chill in its relations with China, Russia, and some other non-Western countries. While NATO portrayed Kosovo as an unselfish humanitarian crusade, Russia and China viewed it as brutal and naked aggression against a weaker sovereign state and a violation of both the UN Charter and international law. Commenting on the very different perceptions that surrounded the Kosovo operation, a *Los Angeles Times* article quoted a Russian newspaper editor: 'In the West the Kosovo story is about ethnic cleansing and refugees and a Serb dictator. Here the Kosovo story is NATO air strikes and their destruction'.[63] The article continued: '...there is no doubt in the Russian mind that NATO is not setting things right in Kosovo but merely compounding the wrongs....'.[64] In a news analysis on Serb and Russian reaction just after the Kosovo peace agreement, the *New York Times* reported that in Yugoslavia, 'There is significant bitterness toward Mr. Milosevic but there is much more directed at what many Serbs consider American arrogance and hypocrisy, where the language of human rights has clothed the naked exercise of power'.[65] The article quoted the reactions of ordinary Russians such as: '...the logic of "we'll stop bombing if you leave your country" is very difficult to understand'; 'people think the United States is owner of the world'; 'It is simply that the world is set up in such a way that the strong beat up on the weak; there's a double standard and the strong are always right'; and 'Both sides are at fault, but NATO is worse.'[66]

Russia appeared to have been particularly angry that, despite its historic ties with Serbia, it was ignored or treated with disdain by NATO and that NATO seemed to regard it of little importance. The reaction of China was, of course, exacerbated by the bombing of the Chinese embassy in Belgrade, to which China reacted with fury. The leaders of both countries were well aware that NATO bypassed the UN to avoid a veto. Of course, both Russia and China had then, and still do today, human rights and ethnic problems and could readily have identified with Yugoslavia. The result was at least a temporary fuelling of Russian and Chinese distrust of the US and of NATO, damage to Western efforts to establish cooperation with and encourage respect for human rights, a strengthening of conservative, hard line elements in both countries, a pronounced chill in relations, and an increase in international tensions.[67]

Eventually, NATO altered its policy towards Russia, and some commentators suggested that it was the Russians who, by backing the Petersberg settlement and thus helping NATO avoid a ground invasion of Kosovo, really 'pulled NATO's chestnuts out of the fire'. Certainly, the involvement of Russia in the peace agreement, the inclusion of at least some Russian troops in the Kosovo force and the repeated US apologies to China for the embassy bombing helped relax tensions.

---

[63] M Reynolds, 'Crisis in Yugoslavia: Sullen Russia Feels Snubbed by the West', *Los Angeles Times*, at 12.

[64] Ibid.

[65] *New York Times*, 6 June 1999, at p 11.

[66] Ibid.

[67] For example, the headline of a local US paper read, 'Russia Turns Angry, Bitter: NATO's Slights May Fuel New Cold War', *Wisconsin Capital Times*, 31 May 1999, at 1.

The issue here is an old one: the role of human rights in foreign policy and the tensions between morality and pragmatism and between human rights and peace. Some argue that we can never compromise on morality, that it is a moral obligation to pursue human rights objectives, even if this might involve foreign policy risks and dangers to peace. Indeed, some maintain that there is a close link between human rights and peace, that more liberal democracies, respectful of human rights, do not engage in aggression and that, consequently, we can only hope to have secure and longlasting peace if we actively support human rights despite the risks. Others argue for a more pragmatic attitude. They maintain that, while human rights may be an appropriate and important component of national foreign policies and of the approaches of international organizations, human rights are not the only component, and other policy interests, such as security or detente, may be equally or even more important. They believe that countries seeking to promote human rights must be prepared to moderate these efforts and to make compromises if it becomes evident that the efforts are deeply resented by other countries, may hinder cooperation and social liberalization, or may lead to increased tensions. They think that there is little sense in pressing other countries on human rights if these efforts are not only likely to be unsuccessful, but to lead to conflict. In the S, Henry Kissinger has long been a particularly prominent, thoughtful, and articulate proponent of this position in the context of US relations with the Soviet Union and China and then in terms of Kosovo.[68] He pointed out long ago that nuclear war would be the ultimate denial of all human rights.[69]

Perhaps NATO's intervention in Kosovo was the correct action and morally unavoidable, but it reminds us that human rights efforts may also have a cost. To the extent that humanitarian interventions such as the one in Kosovo may move us towards a more hostile, confrontational, and dangerous world, the cost may be a very high one.

6. Kosovo, the Media, and NGOs

The Kosovo crisis raised interesting, but also troublesome questions concerning the role of the media and NGOs in international human rights efforts, particularly humanitarian emergencies.

No one doubts the enormous, even crucial contribution of NGOs to international human rights efforts. NGOs have spurred the development of the

---

[68] See H Kissinger, 'The New World Disorder', *Newsweek*, 31 May 1999, at 41: 'The ill-considered war in Kosovo has undermined relations with China and Russia and put NATO at risk', and H Kissinger, 'As the Cheers Fade', *Newsweek*, 21 June 1999, at 48.

[69] See, eg then Secretary of State Kissinger's address, 'Moral Purposes and Policy Choices', at the Third Pacem in Terris Conference, Washington, DC, 8 October 1973, reprinted in 69 Department of State Bulletin 525 (1973).

international human rights concept and the related treaties and institutions and have played a central and vital role in making the international human rights system work. Indeed, without NGOs, the system may not have worked at all. NGOs deploy a level of commitment, expertise, energy, imagination, and initiative unmatched by any government. They alone are able to mobilize the public and political support necessary to sustain government interest and concern. They alone have the resources and facilities effectively to monitor global human rights developments, identify problems and bring them to the attention of the public, governments, and international organizations, and, in particular, give otherwise helpless people and groups access to remedies and to justice. Moreover, they can operate both at a grass roots level and through informal international networks that transcend national barriers. Consequently, many proposals for reform focus on finding ways to increase the role of NGOs in international institutions and more fully to utilize their resources and expertise.

One of the most important developments in recent years is the emergence of NGOs as independent actors in international affairs, establishing and implementing their own international policy initiatives and effectively compelling or vetoing government policy. Perhaps one of the most notable recent examples has been the NGO International Campaign to Ban Land Mines, which, over US and some other great power objections and within only a few years, succeeded in persuading 133 countries to conclude at Ottawa the 1997 Land Mine Treaty barring the production, use, and export of land mines.[70] The campaign was awarded the 1997 Nobel Peace Prize for its efforts. NGOs have played a similarly key role in other areas of human rights, including their substantial input at the Beijing Conference on Women[71] and, particularly, the Rome conference which concluded the treaty to establish an International Criminal Court.[72]

The crucial role of the media is also obvious. Without media attention, it is hard to educate people about the significance of international human rights efforts, to make governments or the public aware of serious human rights issues, or to mobilize public and government support for important human rights initiatives.

However, Kosovo and more recent crises such as the invasion of Iraq suggest that the media and NGOs sometimes play a more controversial and arguably less helpful role, for it is evident that, because of their extensive resources and widespread reach, the media and NGOs have a great capacity to shape public opinion and thus influence government action. This seems to be especially the case in situations involving alleged human rights deprivations or humanitarian crises, which have an inherent ability to attract public sympathy and outrage. There can be little doubt that the reporting by the media and NGOs of human rights atrocities in Bosnia and Kosovo and of the ethnic cleansing of Kosovars—the torrent of

[70] See <http://www.icbl.org>.
[71] Beijing Declaration and Platform of Action, A/CONF. 177/20 (1995) and A/CONF. 177/20/ Add.1 (1995).
[72] Rome Statute of the International Criminal Court, UN Doc A/CONF.183/9 (1998).

images of unending columns of refugees and of atrocities—was crucial in creating and maintaining public support, at least in the West, for NATO's ultimatum to Milosevic, the subsequent bombing, and NATO's drawn out refusal to negotiate or compromise with the Yugoslav authorities throughout the 11-week crisis. In an article in the *New York Times* subtitled 'We Let Television Cameras Choose Our War', columnist Max Frankel argued that the willingness of the American people to go to war was due not to the arguments put forward by the administration but because of the television pictures of almost unfathomable atrocity.

Those scenes of huddled masses burned out of their homes and driven into exile aroused our sympathy and overrode all obligations to respect Serbia's sovereignty. Once the cameras went into action, and the President promised only surgical, aerial combat, no UN treaties or Russian entreaties could keep us out. And once 'in', as the slogan went, we had to 'win', whatever that meant.

Brushed aside were the slogans of the former anti-war movements that America was not 'the world's policeman', that we had no business interfering in other nations' civil wars. A few critics clucked about our inconsistency—our failure to get similarly aroused about even worse barbarities in Cambodia, East Timor, Liberia, Sudan, Algeria, Rwanda. Did Asian and African slaughters not qualify for a US response?

What those challenges fail to grasp is that our responses, or lack of responses, are not based on consistency of policy. They're based on the tube....'[73]

Karl Zemanek, in his 1997 Hague Lectures, also commented thoughtfully on the ways in which this 'new force' of the media and the internet influence the international system:

One such way is opened by the widely available information about international affairs and, in particular, about grave violations of international law which lead to severe political crises. That this information is selective and depends mainly on the presence of mass media representatives on the spot does not diminish its impact, even when it has been stated jokingly, but not without reason, that an international crisis is only perceived as one if it is covered by CNN.

Nonetheless, incomplete as such coverage may be, it has caused significant change. International law is no longer an esoteric playground for diplomats and scholars. Its effectiveness is judged by a wide public audience which—as it now turns out, unfortunately—has never been informed of its true nature....

Not only do the media shape the public outlook on the effectiveness of international law, they actually influence national or international decisions in a crisis by the tone which they choose for their reporting. They may thus emphasize or de-emphasize a particular event. In democratic States public pressure on the government may be generated through gruesome television images or lurid radio and newspaper stories. As a result, government decisions on grave international matters are often not determined by the so-called 'reason of State' or by reference to international law but by computing the public support they will find. The vacillation of the States which contributed contingents to UNPROFOR

---

[73] M Frankel, 'Word & Image: Our Humanity v their Sovereignty', *New York Times Magazine*, 2 May 1999, at 36.

[United Nations Protection Force] and the changing attitude of the United States towards their engagement in Somalia, depending on whether dying children or wounded 'Blue Helmets' were shown on television, come to mind as recent examples.[74]

There is, of course, much to the argument that events such as the atrocities in Kosovo *should* be brought forcefully and dramatically to the attention of the public and of governments and that it is entirely appropriate and praiseworthy for NGOs and the media to urge governments to do something about such situations. But there is also a risk that, as Frankel and Zemanek suggest, such efforts may sometimes involve exaggerations, distortions, or even falsifications of a situation, creating public emotions and pressures which compel unwise government action or inaction. One is reminded of the famous episode in US history when the newspaper magnate William Randolph Hearst, through his newspaper's warmongering and repetition of the slogan 'Remember the Maine!' (a US battleship which unexpectedly sank in Havana harbour under mysterious circumstances in February 1898), created an outpouring of public fervour which literally pressured the US government into the Spanish-American war.[75] Moreover, there is obviously a reverse effect as well; governments and their spokespersons—particularly their so-called 'spin doctors'—have an incentive and are not averse to deliberately using the media and NGOs to create or sustain a public climate supportive of government policy. It seems evident that NATO, properly or improperly, was doing this in Kosovo.

There is another concerning aspect evident in recent crises: the use of the technique of 'demonization'. Unfortunately, neither the Kosovo crisis, nor Milosevic, nor Saddam Hussein are unique in our troubled world; one can find many past and present examples of atrocities and individuals which match or exceed these in horror—Rwanda, the Sudan, Liberia, Angola, Sierra Leone, and, not so long ago, Vietnam. However, it is noteworthy that NATO leaders, the media, and NGOs, from the earliest days of the crisis, chose to characterize the situation in Kosovo as 'genocide' or a 'holocaust' and referred to Milosevic as 'a monster' or 'a Hitler'. The cover of *Newsweek* on 19 April 1999 featured Milosevic's face surrounded by raging hellfires and the title 'The Face Of Evil' in large letters and Margaret Thatcher called him 'The Butcher of Belgrade'.[76] A similar process of demonization occurred, in the

---

[74] K Zemanek, 'The Legal Foundations of the International System: General Course on Public International Law', 266 Rd C,(1998), at 40–42. Also see, eg Carnegie Commission on Preventing Deadly Conflict, *Media Coverage: Help or Hindrance in Conflict Prevention?* (1997) and TG Weiss and RI Rotberd (eds), *From Massacres to Genocide: The Media, Public Policy and Humanitarian Crisis* (1996).

[75] See, eg W Goodman, 'Remember the Maine, and So They Did', *New York Times*, 23 August 1999, at B6.

[76] M Thatcher, 'The West Must Answer Evil with Strength', *Wisconsin State Journal*, 6 June 1999, at A26; Prime Minister Tony Blair reportedly also used the term 'Butchers of Belgrade' in a front page article in the *Sunday Mirror*. See also *New York Times*, 10 May 1999, at 8, and, eg S Sontag, 'Why are We in Kosovo?', *New York Times Magazine*, 2 May 1999, 50, at 55: 'There is radical evil in the world, which is why there are just wars.'

US media at least, with respect to other US 'enemies' such as Saddam Hussein and Fidel Castro. Moreover, while NATO maintained that its war was solely against Milosevic and not the Yugoslav people, a gradual, but inevitable process of demonization of the Serbian people as a whole also probably occurred. For example, the *New York Times* columnist Anthony Lewis wrote: 'The Serbian people will suffer, but so they must for the tyranny they have repeatedly endorsed'.[77] In another *New York Times* article, the newspaper's Balkan correspondent, Steven Erlanger, commented that his role demanded 'that I defend the half-truths uttered by the NATO spokesman, Jamie P. Shea', and that he 'try to present them as real, and not as caricatures from some movie about American good and Nazi evil'.[78]

Clearly, demonization seems effective in engaging and mobilizing public emotions in support of particular, perhaps worthy, policies. But it can also stifle rational debate, constrain policy choice and forestall compromise, for how can one compromise with evil? Attempts to manipulate public emotions by deliberately demonizing individuals or peoples are an insult to our humanity, demeaning and contemptuous of our intelligence and inconsistent with our democratic traditions. Moreover, this is the very sort of deliberate manipulation of prejudice and hatred that we have condemned in the Nazi, Serbian, and other governments.

The charge has been made that many NGOs do not really reflect broader public and national goals and that their great influence risks distorting national policy. NGOs are frequently criticized for not being transparent or accountable. Despite their sometimes vast memberships and considerable financial resources, they are often accused of having only narrow agendas and of being effectively controlled by special interests—human rights entrepreneurs who are 'doing well by doing good'. Non-Western critics say that NGOs tend to represent the values of the privileged classes in the West and fail to reflect other cultures, classes, or perspectives.

It has been suggested, for example, that NGO humanitarian activities in Somalia and the Sudan and among the Hutu refugees from Rwanda in Zaire helped sustain those conflicts and killings and that Western anti-slavery NGOs which buy slaves in order to free them have encouraged Sudanese entrepreneurs to go into the business of enslaving women and children so that these people can then be sold to the NGOs. An article in *The Atlantic Monthly* entitled 'The False Promise of Slave Redemption', discussing especially the situation in the Sudan, commented:

...some Africans say that Westerners are a large part of the problem; nearly everything the activists do makes matters worse....

---

[77] A Lewis, 'Proof of the Pudding', *New York Times*, 5 June 1999, at A25. Also see A Lewis, 'The Question of Evil', *New York Times*, 22 June 1999, at A31.

[78] See Erlanger, 'Beneath the Falling Bombs', n 44 above. Also see, eg AM Rosenthal, 'Fruits of Victory', *New York Times*, 11 June 1999, at A31: 'We have seen our country launch a war, first by futile ultimatum, then by a slovenly planned war that from the beginning brought more suffering to Kosovars and Serbian civilians than to Milosevic and his thugs. Far too many Americans wrote and talked of Serbs...as if they were bugs.'

...the financial incentives of slave redemption are so powerful that they encourage the taking of slaves. 'We've made slavery more profitable than narcotics', one former slave redeemer says.[79]

Some US commentators argue that NGO representatives at the Rome Conference played a mischievous role by preventing a US-sponsored compromise concerning the Court's jurisdiction that might arguably have allowed US participation in the ICC. Similar charges have been made about the alleged refusal of NGOs to permit compromises for the Land Mine Treaty that might have permitted the US to join, and about the alleged tensions caused by the extensive NGO presence in Chiapas, Mexico, that, some suggest, made matters worse there during the insurrectionist disturbances. More broadly, some critics claim that the dependence of NGOs on contributions leads the NGOs to exaggerate or 'hype' humanitarian crises in order to attract more contributions, that in some cases they engage in unseemly or wasteful competition for prestige, media coverage, or humanitarian assistance money and that NGO staffs are often inefficient and help themselves before they help crisis victims.

PJ Simmons has summed up some of these criticisms:

Embracing a bewildering array of beliefs, interests and agendas, [NGOs] have the potential to do as much harm as good. Hailed as the exemplars of grassroots democracy in action, many NGOs are, in fact, decidedly undemocratic and unaccountable to the people they claim to represent. Dedicated to promoting more openness and participation in decision-making, they can instead lapse into old fashioned group politics that produces gridlock on a global scale.[80]

And she concludes that

the real challenge is to figure out how to incorporate NGOs into the international system in a way that takes account of their diversity and scope, their various strengths and weaknesses and their capacity to disrupt as well as create.[81]

On the whole, NGOs do a great deal of good and are essential to our human rights efforts, but we ought to think more about what their most useful and appropriate role should be and how we can ensure that they can do this well.

---

[79] R Minite, 'The False Promise of Slave Redemption', *Atlantic Monthly*, July 1999, 63 at 63–5; 'The Price Tag of Freedom', *Newsweek*, 3 May 1999, at 50, and, generally, D Rieff, 'The Humanitarian Illusion', *New Republic*, 16 March 1998, at 30; P Spiro, 'New Global Potentates: Non-governmental Organizations and the "Unregulated" Marketplace', 18 Cardozo L Rev (1996) 957; R Bonner, 'Aid for Sudan's Hungry Keeps War well Fed', *New York Times*, 11 October 1998, at 14.

[80] PJ Simmons, 'Learning to Live with NGO's', 112 *Foreign Policy* (1998) 84.

[81] Ibid. See, generally, P Lewis, 'Not Just Governments Make War or Peace', *New York Times*, 28 November 1998, at A19; D Sagge (ed), *Compassionate Calculation: The Business of Private Foreign Aid* (1996); J Matthews, 'Power Shift', 76 *Foreign Affairs* (1997) 50; TG Weiss, *Military-Civilian Interactions: Intervening in Humanitarian Crises* (1999); M Maren, *The Road to Hell: The Ravaging Effects of Foreign Aid and International Charity* (1997).

7. Kosovo, Sovereignty, and Ethnic Conflict

It has become common to hear that the concept of sovereignty is passé and that the state is 'withering away'; at most it is an administrative convenience, increasingly irrelevant in a 'globalized' world. The human rights idea and the concept of rights as 'trumps' challenge fundamentally the idea of sovereignty and thus, in effect, the state system. Sir Hersh Lauterpacht long ago referred to the inherent '[contradiction] between the supremacy of the law within the state and the notion of fundamental human rights'.[82] In the light of developments such as Kosovo, *The Economist* concluded that

sovereignty is no longer absolute but conditional.... Eventually all government claims to sovereignty may depend on whether it respects the basic human rights of its citizens.

That is the way in which international law is slowly moving....[83]

At a session of the UN Commission on Human Rights, then UN Secretary General Kofi Annan said that the protection of human rights 'take[s] precedence over concerns of state sovereignty.... As long as I am Secretary-General [the United Nations] will always place human beings at the center of everything we do.'[84]

Kosovo will perhaps best be remembered for putting an exclamation mark on these pronouncements. NATO paid little heed to Yugoslavia's claim that it had a sovereign right to determine what happened within its own country and said that it, rather than Yugoslavia, was entitled to occupy Kosovo and determine its future. On the other hand, while NATO clearly endorsed Kosovo's autonomy, it also repeatedly acknowledged Yugoslavia's abstract claim of sovereignty over Kosovo, thus burdening efforts to reconstruct Kosovo with a seemingly indefinite ambiguity as to its status. NATO was reluctant to recognize the claim of the Kosovars to secession, particularly a secession which would have led to union with Albania in a greater Albania.

These facts deserve comment. First, reports of the death of the state and of sovereignty are somewhat exaggerated—the US Congress or the government of the People's Republic of China would be the first to point this out. Second, we must re-imagine sovereignty and the role and function of the state in our increasingly globalized world. The UN is *not* at this time an effective world government; as yet, we have nothing credible to take the place of the state system. So, we may wish to pause before we meddle too much with the notion of sovereignty. Indeed, some kinds of problems are best dealt with by individual countries on their own. Each community knows its situation the best, and the community is the group

---

[82] Quoted in JP Humphrey, *Human Rights and the United Nations: A Great Adventure* (1984), at 38.

[83] 'A Survey of Human Rights Law', *The Economist*, 5 December 1998, at 15.

[84] See n 23 above.

which must live with the consequences of the decisions which affect it. This might be expressed as follows:

> The concept that good government requires that the subjects of any governance system have at least some protected area of freedom from overbearing authority is a cherished feature of all liberal and non-totalitarian societies, reflected not only in democratic trad-itions of personal liberty, but in the structure of the US and other federal systems, and, at the international level, in the concept of domestic jurisdiction embedded in Article 2(7) of the UN Charter.
>
> ....
>
> The idea of sovereignty in at least one sense reflects this claim of a particular political community to the freedom to be left alone to do what it considers best—its own thing![85]

Third, one should think long and hard before interfering in other people's prob-lems, and this is also true of ethnic conflicts.[86] NATO claimed that it had a moral duty to act to save the Kosovars, and perhaps history will prove this correct. Nonetheless, the consequences and implications of NATO's intervention for the Kosovars and Serbs, for other ethnic conflicts and for international law may be long-lasting and significant. In Kosovo itself, far from solving the ethnic prob-lem, NATO's intervention probably exacerbated it: efforts by the ethnic Albanian population to intimidate remaining Serbs into leaving the province are a painful reminder of the rapidity with which the oppressor–oppressed dichotomy can be reversed. Certainly the bombing and ethnic cleansing which occurred before and in the wake of NATO's campaign deeply scarred memories and altered the rela-tionship between the Kosovars and the Serbs, leaving a legacy of bitterness and hatred that only time and huge efforts by the international community may one day soothe.

Kosovo has obviously established a troubling precedent. Ethno-nationalism is a rampant and often 'dark' force in the present world, and insurgent separatist groups—the Kurds, Chechnyans, Ibos, Tamils, Basques, IRA, East Timorese, Guatemalan Indians, Kashmiri Muslims, and many others—have met with similarly brutal government countermeasures and oppression, including mass killings and ethnic cleansing. Presumably, these insurgent groups would wel-come a 'humanitarian crisis', such as that in Kosovo, whereby NATO or some other collection of sympathetic countries would intervene as their allies. And the governments against which such insurgent groups are conducting their guerilla,

---

[85] R Bilder, 'Perspectives on Sovereignty in the Current Context: An American Viewpoint', 20 Canada-United States Law Journal (1994) 9, at 17.

[86] See, eg R Steel, 'Playing Broker has its Pitfalls', *New York Times*, 25 February 1999, at A2, which suggests that it is 'not in America's interest to encourage disgruntled ethnic groups to dis-member sovereign states'. For a subsequent comment by President Clinton, see J Brooke, 'Clinton Jolts Canadians with a Plea on Federalism', *New York Times*, 10 October 1999, at 7, which reports that, at a forum in Canada on federalism, President Clinton said that, if every major racial and ethnic group were to win independence, 'we might have 800 countries in the world and have a very difficult time having a functioning economy.... Maybe we have 8,000—how low can you go?

often terrorist, activities must be pondering whether they too might one day become the target of a 'humanitarian intervention'.

What are the criteria for humanitarian interventions which we can expect to be employed in the future by NATO, other non-UN country-groups, or the international community? How will NATO or the international community distinguish Kosovo from other similar conflicts? According to the distance from NATO's borders? According to the extent of the atrocities committed and the degree to which the outside world perceives the insurgents as victims? According to the weakness and unpopularity of the 'opposing' government? According to whether CNN or another media entity considers the situation newsworthy or an influential NGO views the situation as fitting for its particular attention? Will the Kosovo precedent encourage other separatist or terrorist movements or ethnonationalist 'entrepreneurs' to attempt to gain international publicity, sympathy and military support? Will it foster a strategy of staging or deliberately provoking atrocities to gain media attention and international sympathy? Is it fair and can we defend a legal doctrine which legitimates support for one separatist group, but not for another, for the Kosovars, but not the Kurds, Tamils, Basques, Kashmiri Muslims, East Timorese, Chiapans, Guatemalan Indians, and so on and on?

Finally, what did Kosovo signify in terms of the international law of self-determination? An extensive literature already exists on the scope and meaning of the principle of self-determination of 'peoples'.[87] For obvious reasons, many governments oppose recognizing that the right of self-determination applies to 'peoples' within existing states as contrasted with 'peoples' in overseas colonies of states.

'Nothing in the foregoing paragraphs shall be construed as authorizing or encouraging any action which would dismember or impair, totally or in part, the territorial integrity or political unity of sovereign and independent states' is the way this is expressed in the General Assembly's 1960 Declaration of Self-Determination and the 1970 Declaration on Friendly Relations, albeit with the significant proviso that such states should be representative of the entire people, observe equal rights and not discriminate.[88] However, Kosovo certainly suggests that, if an ethnic group constitutes a substantial majority or can, over time, become one through immigration or more rapid population growth, or if a case can be made that the ethnic group lacks representation, is discriminated against, or is oppressed, then it is entitled to at least autonomy, and the international community may actively support its claims in this regard. Thus, practically, as well as legally, Kosovo seems likely to encourage further separatist demands and perhaps

---

[87] See, generally, eg H Hannum, *Autonomy, Sovereignty and Self-Determination: The Accommodation of Conflicting Rights* (1990).

[88] See, eg, Declaration on the Granting of Independence to Colonial Territories, GA Res. 1514 (XV) (1960); UN Declaration on Principles of International Law Concerning Friendly Relations among States in Accordance with the Charter of the United Nations, General Assembly, A/Ros 2625 (XXV) (1970), GAOR, 25th Session, Supplement 28, at 121.

the conflicts, chaos and human rights violations all too often accompanying such demands.

There is certainly little agreement over whether, in these circumstances, the dismemberment or fragmentation of states is a good or a bad outcome. Certainly, in principle, a 'people'—however this may be defined—should be entitled to govern themselves and manage their lives without discrimination or oppression. But political unity and pluralist accommodation are also valid goals. At what point do we say to ever-smaller claimant separatist groups 'enough is enough'?

International lawyers have not yet been able to develop techniques capable of accommodating or dissipating inter-ethnic or inter-religious tensions, providing for power sharing and promoting tolerance and respect. Unfortunately, as Kosovo shows, '[n]o system of coexistence can work unless the people involved have peaceful intentions'.[89]

8. Kosovo and the Future of International Human Rights Law

What was Kosovo? Two steps forward for international human rights or one step back?

Kosovo was at least an important symbolic landmark: the first time that some of the world's major powers asserted a collective duty to act forcefully and undertake risks solely to prevent or redress gross violations of human rights, and the first time an international tribunal indicted an acting government leader for international crimes. As suggested in a 1969 article

even if government professions of support for human rights aims are often insincere, such activities are nevertheless sowing seeds which are gradually sifting down and taking root in popular attitudes. One generation's hypocrisy may be the next generation's fighting creed.[90]

The power of inertia, precedent, and 'path-determinacy' is remorseless. But the UN-mandated intervention in East Timor has already made it clear that, although the US and NATO powers may attempt in the future to make Kosovo a special case and to ignore, fail to respond to, or even abet similar human rights disasters in other places, it will be harder and more embarrassing for them to do so.

Yet, NATO's intervention in Kosovo has raised concerns as well. These include:

- The threat of serious damage to the integrity and credibility of the UN and international law: the rocks upon which any viable international human rights programme and effort must inevitably rest.

---

[89] R Lapidoth, *Autonomy: Flexible Solutions to Ethnic Conflict* (1997), at 205.
[90] Bilder, n 2 above at 217.

- The threat of the further politicization of human right concepts, efforts, and institutions and the risk that these may now be even more strongly perceived by the non-Western world as simply pretence and a tool of Western hegemony.

- Finally, the harm in Kosovo and Yugoslavia, including the quasi-destruction of the multi-ethnic community in Yugoslavia, with enormous human and material cost to each group, the humiliation and impoverishment of all people in Yugoslavia, the crippling of the country as an effective member of the international community, the problem of reverse ethnic cleansing by returning Kosovars of the Serbs and Roma, and a lengthy, bitter, painful, and very costly, period of international stewardship in the region.

Certainly, since the US and NATO justified their bombing of Yugoslavia and the occupation of Kosovo on humanitarian grounds, it has become particularly important for them to conscientiously fulfil their legal duties as occupying authority to forestall retaliatory atrocities or reverse ethnic cleansing.[91]

Was the bombing necessary to obtain Milosevic's agreement to the terms he finally accepted? The US and NATO leadership says it was. US General Short, who ran the NATO air campaign, has said that it was the bombing alone that forced Yugoslavia to accept the Petersberg agreement and has claimed that 'NATO got every one of the terms it had stipulated in Rambouillet and beyond Rambouillet'.[92] But others, including former Secretary of State Henry Kissinger,[93] have raised questions in this respect, pointing out that the peace plan to which Yugoslavia ultimately agreed[94] was significantly less demanding than Secretary of State Albright's original ultimatum at Rambouillet. In fact, the terms of the final peace plan appear to have met many of the major Yugoslav concerns which NATO had refused to grant at Rambouillet. For example, under the Petersberg agreement: (1) Kosovo continued to be part of Yugoslavia and was not, as under the Rambouillet ultimatum, permitted to declare independence in three years, (2) NATO troops were restricted to Kosovo and could not, unlike Rambouillet, enter Serbia, (3) NATO's mission was subject to authorization and control by the UN Security Council and thus to a Russian or Chinese veto, and (4) unlike Rambouillet, at least some Yugoslav troops were permitted to re-enter Kosovo to guard border crossings and certain cultural sites. Indeed, the *New York Times* reported that some have questioned whether Kosovo was a firm 'victory'. The article cited statements such as:

'For us to go in there and do what we have done is unconscionable', said Representative Randy Cunningham of California. 'We have killed civilians. That is not a war. Hundreds of thousands of people are refugees. That is not a victory.'

....

---

[91] See letter from R Bilder, *New York Times*, 11 June 1999, at A30, reprinted as 'Any Reverse Ethnic Cleansing Must be Punished', *Wisconsin Capital Times*, 23 June 1999, at 1A.

[92] C Whitney, 'Air Wars Won't Stay Risk-Free, General Says', *New York Times*, 18 June 1999, at A16.

[93] Kissinger, 'As the Cheers Fade', n 68 above at 48. Also see letter from A Kuperman, 'Kosovo Deal Represents "Botched Diplomacy",' *USA Today*, 14 June 1999, at 18A.

[94] See 'Agreement on the Principles (Peace Plan)', n 1 above.

Representative Mark E. Sander of South Carolina declared, 'After 11 weeks of bombing we have a settlement we probably could have achieved at the beginning. If this is victory, what would defeat look like?'

. . . .

Leslie Gelb, President of the Council on Foreign Relations, said, 'The feeling is the situation was very bad to begin with and NATO and the Clinton Administration made it worse, and much to the surprise of the critics, they came out with a deal far better than anyone expected. But they got it at a hell of a heavy cost'.[95]

It may be true that there was no alternative to NATO's action and that, in the light of the Holocaust, the Cambodian and Rwandan genocides and other tragedies, and particularly the past atrocities and bad faith of Yugoslavia in Bosnia, one could not in all decency simply stand by. Perhaps 'radical evil' exists. The sight of the endless columns of refugees made one feel that it was impossible not to do something. Could we allow international law to keep us from doing what seemed morally correct in the face of such a disaster? As Jean Valjean argued in *Les Miserables*: Is law relevant to a situation of clear necessity?

Nevertheless, international law and the UN Charter crystallize and reflect norms that embody common values and long-term interests, and we ignore them at our peril. Policies which involve 'bombing for peace', 'killing for human rights', 'ethnically cleansing the ethnic cleansers' do not seem like satisfactory, moral, or responsible solutions. It is hard to believe that, with all the enormous talent, wealth, and power at the disposal of the US and the other NATO countries, they could not have found a better way of resolving the Kosovo crisis.

Does the future hold the promise of more or less 'Kosovos'? The test will be whether the US and NATO are prepared to intervene against a country engaging in massive atrocities which is a significant economic market, is of little strategic importance, or has the capacity to fight back. Perhaps Kosovo represented, as NATO claimed, a 'just and necessary' war. But, in the wake of Kosovo, the international community may wish to consider more carefully the legality, usefulness, reach, and potential consequences of this 'new interventionism'. If we are to act in such humanitarian crises—as we certainly should—we must develop doctrines and modalities that help us accomplish this collectively, effectively, and justly.

---

[95] *New York Times*, 11 June 1999, at A15.

5

Legality Verses Legitimacy: Can Uses of Force be Illegal but Justified?[*]

Anthea Roberts[**]

1. Introduction

To many commentators, unilateral humanitarian intervention poses the dilemma of what states should do when there is a great divide between what international law requires and what morality dictates. This issue was brought into sharp relief by NATO's bombing campaign in Kosovo in 1999. Most western international lawyers concluded that NATO's use of force was both morally justified and incompatible with international law. In short, NATO's actions were 'illegal but justified'. Due to a fear that recognizing a right of unilateral humanitarian intervention would lead to abuse, many advocated that such uses of force should remain illegal but that the law should turn a blind eye to breaches in particular cases, such as Kosovo.

Variations of this approach have been adopted by a number of prominent scholars, including Simma and Franck. Simma argues that there are sometimes 'hard cases' where political and moral considerations leave states no choice but to act outside the law. However, he contends that NATO's intervention in Kosovo should be treated as an ad hoc exception rather than a precedent for establishing a new rule allowing for unilateral uses of force.[1] Franck argues that unilateral humanitarian intervention is and should remain illegal.[2] However, he contends that the doctrine of mitigation should be employed in such cases so that

[*] Editors' Note: This Chapter, edited by the author in 2008, was originally written in mid-2003. It focuses on unilateral humanitarian intervention in Kosovo as a case study, but the argumentative approach it critiques has enduring relevance for the use of force more generally. The Editors have incorporated references to some of the post-2003 literature in the footnotes.

[**] I would like to thank Neil Walker, Joseph Weiler, Alan Roberts, Jesse Clarke, Sandesh Sivakumaran and Roy Schondorf for their helpful comments on earlier drafts of this paper.

[1] B Simma, 'NATO, the UN and the Use of Force: Legal Aspects' (1999) 10 EJIL 1 at 1 and 22.

[2] T Franck, *Recourse to Force: State Action Against Threats and Armed Attacks* (2002) 174–191.

'technically illegal but morally justified actions' are met with minimal rebuke in recognition of the mitigating circumstances.[3]

This chapter critiques the notion of uses of force being 'illegal but justified'. It does not focus on whether NATO's intervention was actually illegal or whether it was in fact justified. Instead, it uses Kosovo as a case study for analyzing attempts by scholars and states to simultaneously embrace both conclusions. The 'illegal but justified' approach provides an intuitively attractive way of maintaining the prohibition on unilateral uses of force while permitting justice in individual cases. However, it is ultimately not a sustainable position given the role of state practice in developing international law. This approach also shifts the focus away from questions of legality and towards questions of legitimacy, which can undermine the law and risk manipulation.[4]

2. The Dilemma of Humanitarian Intervention

A. The Law Prior to Kosovo

Article 2(4) of the Charter of the United Nations (UN) prohibits the threat or use of force against any state, subject to two exceptions: individual or collective self-defence in response to an armed attack, pursuant to Art 51; and uses of force authorized by the Security Council under Ch VII following a determination of the existence of a threat to the peace, breach of the peace, or act of aggression.

Unilateral humanitarian interventions do not fit easily within either exception. 'Humanitarian intervention' describes the use of force by one or more states in another with the aim of preventing major human rights violations. Human rights abuses committed within one state are unlikely to amount to an 'armed attack' on another state, so unilateral humanitarian intervention cannot usually be justified as self-defence. Although the Security Council may authorize *collective* humanitarian intervention under Ch VII if the situation constitutes a threat to international peace and security,[5] *unilateral* humanitarian intervention occurs when the Security Council has not authorized intervention. Unilateral humanitarian intervention is thus prima facie a violation of the Charter.

---

[3] Ibid., at 184. For a more general discussion of the dilemmas posed by issues of humanitarian intervention for the international lawyer, see M Frank, 'The Dilemmatic Structure of Humanitarian Interventions', in G Meggle (ed), *Ethics of Humanitarian Interventions* (2004) 97.

[4] For a critique of the potential damage done to the international system in shifting from a discourse of legality to one of values in justifying intervention, see generally D Chandler, *From Kosovo to Kabul and Beyond* (2005).

[5] Refugee flows across national borders as a result of humanitarian crises may constitute a threat to international peace and security: see eg SC Res. 819 (1993), SC Res. 824 (1993), SC Res. 836 (1993) (Balkans) and SC Res. 918 (1994), SC Res. 929 (1994) (Rwanda). Serious, systematic or widespread abuses of international humanitarian law may also contribute to a threat to international peace and security: see eg SC Res. 808 (1993), SC Res. 827 (1993) (Yugoslavia) and SC Res. 1264 (1999) (East Timor).

Before Kosovo, a possible doctrine of unilateral humanitarian intervention had been mooted, but never gained sufficient support to be accepted. A number of instances were cited in support of such a doctrine, including India's 1971 invasion of East Pakistan to facilitate the secession of Bangladesh; Tanzania's 1978 intervention in Uganda to end the rule of Idi Amin; Vietnam's 1978–9 invasion of Kampuchea to overthrow the Khmer Rouge; the actions of the Economic Community of West African States (ECOWAS) in Liberia in 1990 and Sierra Leone in 1997; and the United States, United Kingdom, and France setting up no-fly zones and safe-havens to protect the Kurds and Shiites in Iraq in 1991.[6] Despite each case involving some humanitarian justifications, the states using force tended to rely primarily on other legal justifications, such as claims of self-defence or interpretations of existing or subsequent Security Council resolutions.[7]

B. NATO's Use of Force in Kosovo

The humanitarian intervention debate was re-ignited in 1999 with NATO's use of force in Kosovo. During the 1990s, the former Yugoslavia was ravaged by terrible ethnic conflicts. In 1998, the Security Council adopted three resolutions in which it condemned the actions of the Federal Republic of Yugoslavia (FRY), declared the situation to be a threat to peace and security and referred to an 'impending humanitarian catastrophe'.[8] However, the Security Council did not authorize the use of force against FRY. After peace negotiations failed in March 1999, NATO began an eleven-week campaign of air strikes against FRY without seeking Security Council authorization, presumably because China

---

[6] See generally Franck, above n 2 at 155–62; C Gray, *International Law and the Use of Force* (2000) 28–31, 191–3, 218–27; M Weller (ed) *Regional Peace-Keeping and International Enforcement: the Liberian Crisis* (1994) 73; C Gray, 'After the Ceasefire: Iraq, the Security Council and the Use of Force' (1994) *British Yearbook of International Law* 135; J Stromseth, 'Iraq's Repression of Its Civilian Population: Collective Responses and Continuing Challenges' in L Damrosch (ed) *Enforcing Restraint: Collective Intervention in Internal Conflicts* (1993) 100.

[7] On this, see J Welsh, 'Taking Consequences Seriously: Objections to Humanitarian Intervention', in J Welsh (ed) *Humanitarian Intervention and International Relations* (2006) 52 at 55–57. For a more detailed analysis of state practice in the field of humanitarian intervention prior to 1999, see Olivier Corten's contribution to this volume.

[8] In March 1998, the Security Council passed Resolution 1160, in which it, inter alia, condemned the use of excessive force by the Serbian Police and imposed an arms embargo (SC Res. 1160 (1998)). This resolution was adopted under Ch VII but the Security Council did not expressly determine that the situation was a threat to international peace and security. In September 1998, the Security Council adopted Resolution 1199, in which it affirmed that the situation in Kosovo constituted a threat to peace and security in the region (SC Res. 1199 (1998)). The Security Council demanded certain actions in order to avert the 'impending humanitarian catastrophe' and resolved that it would consider further action if concrete measures were not taken to comply with requirements. In October 1998, FRY signed agreements including an undertaking to comply with Resolutions 1160 and 1199. The Security Council endorsed these agreements in SC Res. 1203 (1998). China and Russia both abstained from voting but made it clear that they did not view this Resolution as authorizing the use of force (S/PV 3937 (1999) at 12 (Russia) and 14–5 (China)).

and Russia would have vetoed any such resolution. The NATO states argued that their actions were justified because FRY had violated previous Security Council resolutions and force was necessary given the impending humanitarian catastrophe.

Russia responded to the bombings by demanding an immediate convening of the Security Council, in which Russia, China, Belarus and India condemned the bombings.[9] Russia sponsored a resolution condemning NATO's use of force as a flagrant violation of the UN Charter and demanding the immediate cessation of NATO aggression,[10] but it was defeated by twelve votes to three.[11] A few months later, in June 1999, an agreement was brokered between NATO and FRY to end the conflict and bombings.[12] The Security Council then passed Resolution 1244, which did not refer to the legality of NATO's use of force, but welcomed the agreement and made the UN a partner with NATO in the interim administration of Kosovo.[13]

C. Responses to Kosovo

Kosovo deeply challenged conceptions of right and wrong under international law.[14] Respecting the prohibition on unilateral uses of force seemed to be a case of good law producing bad results, while creating an exception for unilateral humanitarian intervention appeared to be an example of hard cases making bad law. Many commentators ended up adopting the ambivalent position that NATO's use of force was formally illegal but morally justified.[15] For example, Cassese concluded that 'from an ethical viewpoint resort to armed force was justified. Nevertheless, as a legal scholar I cannot avoid observing in the same breath that this moral action is contrary to current international law.'[16] Similarly, the Independent International Commission on Kosovo found that NATO's intervention was illegal based on

---

[9] SCOR, 3988th Mtg, 24 March 1999, 12–13 (China), 13 (Russia), 15 (Belarus) 15–16 (India); S/1999/320 of 24 March 1999.

[10] S/1999/328, 26 March 1999.

[11] SCOR, 3989th Mtg, 26 March 1999, 6. The five NATO states voted against the resolution (the United Kingdom, Canada, France, the Netherlands, and the United States) along with Argentina, Bahrain, Gabon, the Gambia, Malaysia, and Slovenia. Only China, Namibia, and the Russian Federation supported the draft resolution.

[12] S/1999/649.

[13] SC Res. 1244 (1999); SCOR, 4011th Mtg, 10 June 1999, 9.

[14] For example, Reisman states that 'no lawyer, whatever his or her conclusion as to the lawfulness of NATO's action in Kosovo, can look back on the incident without disquiet': M Reisman, 'Kosovo Antinomies' (1999) 93 AJIL 860 at 860.

[15] M Koskenniemi, '"The Lady Doth Protest Too Much": Kosovo, and the Turn to Ethics in International Law' (2002) 65 MLR 159 at 162. For example, L Henkin, 'Kosovo and the Law of "Humanitarian Intervention"' (1999) 93 AJIL 824 at 826; J Charney, 'Anticipatory Humanitarian Intervention in Kosovo' (1999) 93 AJIL 834 at 838.

[16] A Cassese, '*Ex iniuria ius oritur*: Are We Moving towards International Legitimation of Forcible Humanitarian Countermeasures in the World Community?' (1999) 10 EJIL 23 at 25.

existing international law but legitimate based on an emerging international moral consensus.[17]

Two important contributions to this debate came from Bruno Simma and Thomas Franck. In an article written shortly before the NATO intervention in Kosovo, Simma argues that only a thin red line separated NATO's use of force from international legality.[18] He notes that NATO had attempted to get as close to compliance with international law as possible by making their actions conform to the sense and logic of existing Security Council resolutions and by characterizing the intervention as necessary to avert a humanitarian catastrophe. Despite this, Simma concludes that NATO's intervention in Kosovo was illegal due to the lack of Security Council authorization.

Simma nonetheless argues that, in certain cases such as this one, political and moral considerations might leave no choice but to act outside the law. Such exceptions are dangerous because they have the potential to erode collective security by creating a precedent for bypassing the Security Council. However, he contends that this risk could be reduced by identifying factors that made NATO's intervention ad hoc and singular, which would minimize its precedential status. Simma concludes that to 'resort to illegality as an explicit *ultima ratio* for reasons as convincing as those put forward in the Kosovo case is one thing. To turn such an exception into a general policy is quite another.'[19]

In a similar vein, Franck argues in a book published in 2002 that the claim that unilateral humanitarian intervention is 'illegal but justified' can be understood by importing the domestic concept of mitigation into international law.[20] Following his approach, mitigating circumstances do not change the illegality of an action but they may affect its consequences, for example, by leading to the imposition of a nominal or reduced punishment. Franck, writing with Rodley, argues that:

In exceptional circumstances... a large power may indeed go selflessly to the rescue of a foreign people facing oppression. But surely no general law is needed to cover such actions... [I]n human experience, it has proven wiser to outlaw absolutely conduct which, in practical experience, is almost invariably harmful, rather than to try to provide general exceptions for rare cases. Cannibalism, given its history and man's propensities, is

---

[17] Independent International Commission on Kosovo, *Kosovo Report: Conflict, International Response, Lessons Learned* (2000) 164.

[18] Simma, above n 1 at 1, 6.

[19] Ibid., at 1 and 22.

[20] Franck, above n 2 at 184. Mitigation has been a recurring theme in Franck's work on unilateral humanitarian intervention for the past thirty years, which he recently developed in greater detail in *Recourse to Force*. See T Franck, 'Interpretation and change in the law of humanitarian intervention' in J Holzgrefe and R Keohane (eds) *Humanitarian Intervention: Ethical, Legal and Political Dilemmas* (2003) 204; T Franck, 'Lessons from Kosovo' (1999) 93 AJIL 857; T Franck and N Rodley, 'After Bangladesh: The Law of Humanitarian Intervention by Military Force' (1973) 67 AJIL 275 at 290–91.

simply outlawed, while provision is made to mitigate the effect of this law on men adrift in a lifeboat.[21]

Franck bases his analysis on two famous cannibalism cases: *Regina v Dudley and Stephens* and *US v Holmes*.[22] In the first, two sailors killed and ate the cabin boy in order to survive after being shipwrecked. In the second, crewmembers on an overcrowded lifeboat threw some passengers overboard in order to prevent the lifeboat from sinking. In each case, the defendants were found guilty of murder. The courts did not recognize necessity as a defence of either justification or excuse but they gave very lenient sentences or recommendations for clemency in recognition of the mitigating factors.

Franck argues that 'technically illegal but morally justified actions' such as unilateral humanitarian intervention have often passed without comment, with tacit approval, or with only minimal rebuke by the political and judicial institutions of the UN.[23] Thus he concludes that the organs of the UN have, in practice, acted similarly to the courts in the cannibalism cases by adopting an approach akin to mitigation in cases like Kosovo.

3. A Critique of the 'Illegal but Justified' Approach

The 'illegal but justified' approach appears to be motivated by a desire to have the best of both worlds: to maintain the prohibition on unilateral uses of force while allowing worthy interventions to occur without rebuke. But does the approach succeed at its goal? I contend that the 'illegal but justified' approach does not maintain the integrity of the general prohibition on the use of force. It is also not clear that it achieves the policy of allowing intervention in extreme cases while minimizing abusive claims. Before moving to these substantive arguments, however, I begin by examining some of the loaded terminology that often clouds this debate.

A. Loading the Language

Proponents of the 'illegal but justified' approach often use weighted terminology to present their claim in a more favorable light. For example, Franck claims that mitigation may be 'particularly appropriate when a *technically illegal* action has occurred in unforeseeable and extraordinarily grave circumstances threatening the very public order law seeks to uphold.'[24] A number of scholars insert a qualifying word before the term 'illegal', such as 'formally' or 'technically' illegal, in

---

[21] Franck and Rodley, above n 20 at 290–1.
[22] (1884) LR 14 QBD 273; (1842) 26 Fed Cas 360, 1 Wall Jr 1.
[23] Franck, above n 2 at 184.
[24] Ibid., at 185 (emphasis added).

order to soften the problem of illegality or to suggest that it is merely a formal issue.[25] However, the notion that the use of force, even for a good cause, may be merely 'technically' or 'formally' illegal is highly suspect.

Article 2(4) of the Charter of the UN prohibits the 'threat or use of force against the territorial integrity or political independence of any state, or in any other manner inconsistent with the purposes of the United Nations'. Some argue that unilateral humanitarian intervention does not breach Art 2(4) because it is not directed against the 'territorial integrity or political independence of any state',[26] but this view has not been generally accepted.[27] Others argue that humanitarian intervention is not 'in any other manner inconsistent with the Purposes of the United Nations' because one of the aims of the UN is promoting and encouraging respect for human rights.[28] However, the first purpose of the UN listed in Art 1 is 'to maintain international peace and security'[29] and it appears doubtful that the drafters regarded human rights as equal in importance to peace.[30] Hence, unilateral uses of force are not illegal because

[25] A recent example of this is Slaughter's claim that NATO's intervention in Kosovo in 1999 and the United States' invasion of Iraq in 2003 were 'formally illegal' but that there were good arguments for going around the law in both cases: A Slaughter, 'Good Reasons for Going Around the UN', *New York Times*, 18 March 2003.

[26] See A D'Amato, *International Law: Process and Prospects* (1987) 57–73; F Teson, *Humanitarian Intervention: An Inquiry into Law and Morality* (1997) 150–51; M Reisman with the collaboration of M McDougal, 'Humanitarian Intervention to Protect the Ibos' in R Lillich (ed), *Humanitarian Intervention and the United Nations* (1973) 177.

[27] For example S Chesterman, *Just War or Just Peace?* (2001) 49–52; I Brownlie, *International Law and the Use of Force by States* (1963) 267–8; O Schachter, 'The Legality of Pro-democratic Invasion' (1984) 78 AJIL 649 at 649; J Charney, above n 15 at 835; M Akehurst, *A Modern Introduction to International Law* (P Malanczuk (ed), 7th rev. edn, 1997) 309–11. See also Declaration on Principles of International Law Concerning Friendly Relations and Cooperation Among States in Accordance with the Charter of the United Nations, GA Res. 2625 (XXV) (1970) ('No State or group of States has the right to intervene, directly or indirectly, for any reason whatever, in the internal or external affairs of any other State. Consequently, armed intervention and all other forms of interference or attempted threats against the personality of the State or against its political, economic and cultural elements, are in violation of the law'); *Corfu Channel* case [1949] ICJ Rep 4, 29, 35; [1948] ICJ Pleadings, *Corfu Channel* case, vol 3, 296 (rejecting the United Kingdom's argument that conducting a mine sweeping operation in Albanian waters had not violated Albania's territorial integrity or political independence).

[28] Arts 1(3), 55–56. On this point, and for a detailed discussion of UN law and practice in relation to humanitarian intervention more generally, see Adam Roberts, 'The United Nations and Humanitarian Intervention', in J Welsh (ed) *Humanitarian Intervention and International Relations* (2006) 71 at 73.

[29] Art 2(3) of the UN Charter also obliges member states to settle their international disputes by 'peaceful means in such a manner that international peace and security, and justice, are not endangered'.

[30] The *travaux preparatoires* also make clear that these additional phrases were intended to make the prohibition watertight rather than to allow room for exceptions. The first phrase was inserted during the San Francisco Conference because a number of smaller states wanted to emphasize the importance of protecting these elements rather than because they wanted to allow uses of force in other circumstances. See 6 UNCIO 304. As for the second phrase, the US Delegate stated that the intention of the drafters was to create 'in the broadest terms an absolute all-inclusive prohibition' and that 'the phrase "or in any other manner" was designed to insure that there should be no loopholes.' See 6 UNCIO 335.

they breach a technicality; they are illegal because they breach a fundamental Charter obligation.

This leads to the claim that unilateral action may be permissible in response to 'unforeseeable' or 'unanticipated' circumstances.[31] Yet are humanitarian crises and Security Council inaction really unforeseeable? Franck notes that unilateral humanitarian intervention was mooted at the time of drafting but not incorporated into the Charter.[32] Likewise, the fact that the veto could be used to frustrate the majority will of the Security Council was evident at the time the power was created. In terms of foreseeability, a distinction might also be drawn between the first time unilateral humanitarian intervention occurs and future reliance on the same doctrine. It may be justifiable to act unilaterally the first time a crisis arises, particularly if there was no time to renegotiate international law in the face of that crisis. But the same would not be true the next time such a conflict arises if states have deliberately failed to seek the creation of an exception in the meantime.

Another common claim is that unilateral humanitarian intervention may be permissible when the Security Council is 'paralyzed' by the threat or use of the veto.[33] 'Paralyzed' is a strong and pejorative word that implies that the Security Council has been unable to act when it should have acted.[34] However, just because the Security Council does not adopt a resolution because of the veto does not mean that the Security Council is paralyzed or dysfunctional.[35] There is a difference between the Security Council being generally unable to act because of the veto, as occurred during the Cold War, and the Security Council being unwilling to act in a particular situation. Since the end of the Cold War, the Security Council has passed many resolutions, including some clearly authorizing the use of force in humanitarian crises.[36] If a permanent member uses the veto because it believes force would be inappropriate, that is precisely the role for which the veto was intended.[37]

Proponents also argue that 'extreme necessity' may sometimes mitigate the consequences of violating the Charter prohibition on the use of force.[38] However,

---

[31] Franck, above n 2 at 185, 190.

[32] Ibid., at 136.

[33] Ibid., at 181; Reisman, above n 14 at 860.

[34] R Wedgwood, 'NATO's Campaign in Yugoslavia' (1999) 93 AJIL 828 at 834 (arguing that the veto has often thrown a 'monkey wrench' in the machinery of collective security and that one should be careful about insisting on 'procedural perfectionism' when there are important moral issues at stake).

[35] D Joyner, 'The Kosovo Intervention: Legal Analysis and a More Persuasive Paradigm' (2002) 13 EJIL 597 at 608.

[36] For example the Security Council authorized the use of force for humanitarian purposes in Somalia and Haiti: see S/RES/794 of 3 December 1992 (Somalia) and S/RES/940 of 31 July 1994 (Haiti).

[37] R Falk, 'Kosovo, World Order, and the Future of International Law' (1999) 93 AJIL 847 at 850; Joyner, above n 35 at 608.

[38] Franck, above n 2 at 190; see also Simma, above n 1 at 1 and 22.

the *Articles on State Responsibility* provide that a state may not invoke necessity as a ground for precluding wrongfulness unless: (i) the act was the only means of safeguarding an essential interest against a grave and imminent peril; and (ii) the act did not seriously impair an essential interest of the state to whom the obligation was owed or the international community as a whole.[39] The use of force is likely to impair an essential interest of the state whose territory is violated. Necessity may also not be invoked as a ground for precluding the wrongfulness of a violation of a peremptory norm.[40] Commentators split on whether the prohibition on the use of force is a peremptory norm,[41] or whether that status is limited to the prohibition on acts of aggression.[42] If the former, this might prevent resort to necessity.

Necessity also requires that the action taken be the 'only means' of safeguarding an essential interest.[43] This is a high burden. Simply demonstrating that the Security Council will not be able to act does not necessarily mean that all peaceful means for resolving the dispute have been exhausted. I am not in a position to know if there were other options available to NATO. However, Pellet argues, for example, that it would be possible to work within the UN system by reviving the 'Uniting for Peace' Resolution,[44] which requires the General Assembly to consider the matter if the Security Council fails to exercise its primary responsibility for the maintenance of international peace and security due to lack of unanimity by the permanent members.[45] This Resolution is controversial and some commentators are critical of this approach.[46] NATO may have decided that a Uniting for Peace Resolution would have taken too long or that it would be

---

[39] International Law Commission, *Articles on State Responsibility*, Art 25(1); see also *Gabčikovo-Nagymaros Project (Hungary/Slovakia)* ICJ Reports 1997, 7 at 40–41.

[40] International Law Commission, *Articles on State Responsibility*, Art 26.

[41] American Law Institute, *Restatement (Third) of the Foreign Relations Law of the United States* (1987) para 102, Comment k. See also the *Nicaragua* case, where the International Court of Justice referred to the conclusion of the International Law Commission that the Charter's prohibition on the use of force was a conspicuous example of a peremptory norm: *Case Concerning Military and Paramilitary Activities in and against Nicaragua (Merits)* [1986] ICJ Rep 14, 100 at para 190 citing the Report of the International Law Commission, 18th Session [1966] 2 *Yearbook of the International Law Commission* 172 at 247.

[42] See J Crawford, *The International Law Commission's Articles on State Responsibility: Introduction, Text and Commentaries* (2002) 188. For a general discussion on the ILC's approach to the defence of necessity and its potential application to humanitarian intervention, see in I Johnstone, 'The Plea of "Necessity" in International Legal Discourse: Humanitarian Intervention and Counter-terrorism', 43 Columbia Journal of Transnational Law (2005) 337 at 352–65.

[43] Similarly, under domestic law, the defence of necessity usually requires that there was no reasonable legal alternative to disobeying the law. P Knoll, *Criminal Law Defences* (1987) 127 (para 241).

[44] A Pellet, 'Brief Remarks on the Unilateral Use of Force' (2000) 11 EJIL 385 at 390. See also Scott who argues that the General Assembly may *recommend* (rather than authorize) enforcement actions that go beyond the traditional exceptions of self-defence and Security Council authorization: C Scott, 'Interpreting Intervention' (2001) *The Canadian Yearbook of International Law* 333 at 362–3.

[45] GA Res. 377(V), 3 November 1950.

[46] For example, Joyner, above n 35 at 612–13.

unlikely to receive sufficient support. However, if those calculations were being made, they are relevant to assessments of legitimacy and necessity.

The same criticism is also applicable to Prime Minister Blair's statement that the choice in Kosovo was between the world doing something and doing nothing.[47] One must always do something or do nothing; that is a genuine dichotomy. However, even in the absence of air strikes, the level of international military and monetary interventions in the former Yugoslavia before 1999, coupled with the clear threat of air strikes by NATO, could hardly be characterized as 'doing nothing'.[48] Moreover, Blair defined 'doing something' as unilateral humanitarian intervention in the form of air strikes, thus portraying the choice as being between engaging in air strikes and doing nothing. This is a false dichotomy because it excludes other possibilities for action and gives the option of air strikes a false sense of necessity.[49]

Finally, Simma claims that sometimes there may be 'no choice but to act outside the law' and Franck contends that states may, in exceptional circumstances, act 'off the Charter' while leaving the Charter norms 'intact'.[50] Acting 'outside the law' and 'off the Charter' are euphemisms for *breaking* the law. Like claims about unilateral humanitarian intervention being 'technically' or 'formally' illegal, these phrases downplay the reality that such uses of force breach a fundamental Charter provision. Allowing states to bypass the Security Council may have a major impact on the binding force of the Charter and respect for the Security Council more generally. Moreover, acting off the Charter does not leave Charter norms 'intact'. It is true that if states simply breach the Charter, then they leave the Charter norms intact by not attempting to stretch the interpretation of the law to fit the situation. But by acting off the Charter, these norms are broken rather than bent. To the extent that the prohibition may be left intact, it is also rendered irrelevant to the decision of whether or not to use force.

B. Declaration of Illegality?

The next question to consider is how well does the doctrine of mitigation translate from domestic law to international law. Domestic analogies form a rich resource

---

[47] See Chesterman, above n 27 at 220.

[48] A Orford, 'Locating the International: Military and Monetary Interventions after the Cold War' (1997) 38 Harvard International Law Journal 443 at 449, 459.

[49] For example, Falk argues that the NATO states could have used more flexible diplomacy in negotiating with FRY before the bombings, such as not excluding Russian diplomats from the negotiations and not offering terms to which FRY would clearly never agree. Falk, above n 37 at 850, 854. Joyner argues that greater pressure might have been placed on China and Russia to abstain from voting instead of vetoing an authorization to use force, and that Russia and China could have made statements to the effect that their abstentions did not amount to approval of the action and did not form a precedent for future humanitarian interventions. Joyner, above n 35 at 615.

[50] Simma, above n 1 at 1, 22; Franck, above n 2 at 190.

from which scholars can draw in order to explain problems, resolve conflicts, and progressively develop international law.[51] However, care should be taken when using domestic analogies because there are fundamental differences between the international and domestic legal systems. For example, disputes about the law and punishments for breaking the law are more likely to be determined by courts in domestic systems than in the international legal system because international law lacks courts with compulsory jurisdiction. Similarly, breaches of the law may have different legal significance in international and domestic systems because international law is often developed through breaches of existing law.

A declaration of illegality plays an important role in the doctrine of mitigation because it reaffirms the general prohibition in question. In the cannibalism cases, the courts found the defendants guilty of murder and clearly stated that murder remained criminal even in cases of extreme necessity. The international equivalent of this might be a clear consensus among a majority of states, or a statement by the International Court of Justice (ICJ), Security Council, or General Assembly, that a particular use of force was illegal. The most commonly cited international example of the 'illegal but justified' approach is the judgment of the ICJ in the *Corfu Channel* case.[52] In that case, the United Kingdom conducted a minesweeping operation in Albanian waters after mines damaged its warships. The Court held that, despite Albania's failure to fulfill its obligations, the United Kingdom's action was illegal because it violated Albania's sovereignty, but the only remedy it gave was a declaration of illegality.[53]

One problem with applying this mitigation model to unilateral humanitarian intervention is that a declaration of illegality is often not forthcoming. The ICJ, the Security Council, and the General Assembly are not obliged to pass judgments on all violations of peace and security.[54] NATO's intervention in Kosovo provides a good example of this phenomenon. The Independent International Commission on Kosovo concluded that the intervention in Kosovo fell into a 'gray zone' where neither approval nor censure was forthcoming.[55] Only a few states contended that NATO had violated Art 2(4) of the Charter,[56] while some expressed doubts about the legality of the intervention but were still prepared to support it.[57] The Non-Aligned Movement rejected the legality of unilateral humanitarian

---

[51] For example, principles from domestic contract law are sometimes used to inform treaty interpretation, while notions such as equity have been used to resolve disputes between states. For example H Lauterpacht, *Private Law Sources and Analogies of International Law* (1927).

[52] *Corfu Channel* case [1949] ICJ Rep 4.

[53] Ibid., at 35.

[54] For example, after Tanzania used force in Uganda in 1978, the UN Secretary-General and the Security Council simply avoided dealing with complaints made by Uganda and Libya about Tanzania's use of force: see Franck, above n 2 at 143–5.

[55] Independent International Commission on Kosovo, above n 17 at 174.

[56] For example, SCOR, 3988th Mtg, 24 March 1999, 12–13 (China), 13 (Russia), 15 (Belarus), 15–16 (India); S/1999/320 of 24 March 1999.

[57] SCOR, 4011th Mtg, 10 June 1999, 17 (Brazil); SCOR, 4011th Mtg (Resumption), 10 June 1999, 4 (Costa Rica).

intervention in a ministerial meeting in September 1999.[58] However, the vast majority of states did not declare NATO's action to be legal or illegal.

The reaction of the Security Council was also ambiguous. Russia's proposed resolution condemning NATO's use of force failed by twelve votes to three.[59] Some commentators claim that this demonstrates that twelve members believed NATO's actions were legal, while others argue that the voting was motivated by other factors.[60] After an agreement was brokered to end the conflict, the Security Council passed Resolution 1244 by 14 votes in which it welcomed the political agreement ending the conflict and made the UN a partner with NATO in the administration of Kosovo.[61] Some states saw this Resolution as amounting to *ex post facto* approval,[62] while others disagreed.[63] Whether or not these resolutions demonstrate that the intervention was made legal *ex post facto*, it is clear that they did not amount to a declaration that NATO's use of force was illegal.

In the absence of Security Council condemnation, no state or group of states requested an immediate meeting of the General Assembly to declare illegal NATO's use of force.[64] In the case brought by Yugoslavia against some of the NATO states, the ICJ made no declaration that NATO's use of force was illegal.[65]

But does a lack of a declaration of illegality really matter? The answer is yes. Such declarations are important under the doctrine of mitigation because they reinforce the general prohibition in question. If there is no clear statement that unilateral humanitarian intervention is illegal, that opens the door to claims that there is or should be a legal exception to the prohibition on the use of force in extreme humanitarian crisis. Naturally, the development of such a norm will not occur as quickly as if states openly endorsed such a norm as a legal exception to the prohibition on unilateral force. But debate will occur either way in the absence of a declaration of illegality.

---

[58] UN Press Release GA/SPD/164.

[59] SCOR, 3989th Mtg, 26 March 1999, 6.

[60] See C Gray, above n 6 at 163; P Hilpold, 'Humanitarian Intervention: Is There a Need for a Legal Reappraisal?' (2001) 12 EJIL 437 at 460.

[61] SC Res. 1244 (1999); SCOR, 4011th Mtg, 10 June 1999, 9.

[62] China abstained from voting on Resolution 1244 on the basis that NATO had seriously violated the Charter and the Resolution ratified NATO's use of force. See also the argument made by Belgium in the *Legality of the Use of Force (Yugoslavia v Belgium)*, Request for the Indication of Provisional Measures, Oral Pleadings, available at <http://www.icj-cij.org>; and the argument made by Slovenia in the Security Council: SCOR, 3989th Mtg, 26 March 1999.

[63] Russia, when voting in favour of the resolution, stated that it was pleased that NATO had recognized that the Security Council was the body with primary responsibility for the maintenance of peace and security. See Gray, above n 6 at 35.

[64] Cassese, above n 16 at 29. Cassese concludes from this that the overwhelming majority of states did not oppose NATO's use of force: A Cassese, 'A Follow-Up: Forcible Humanitarian Countermeasures and *Opinio Necessitatis*' (1999) 10 EJIL 791 at 792.

[65] *The Legality of the Use of Force, (Yugoslavia v Belgium, Canada, France, Germany, Italy, Netherlands, Portugal, Spain, United Kingdom, United States of America)*, available at <http://www. icj-cij.org>.

It is also questionable whether a declaration of illegality that is not backed up by a sanction should be considered to amount to a finding that the action was illegal but justified. Some examples may be cited in support.[66] Yet the Security Council often condemns actions of states without imposing sanctions where it would be difficult to conclude that it believed the actions to be illegal but justi-fied.[67] Similarly, states often express concern about, or condemnation of, human rights abuses in other states without imposing sanctions. These statements serve an important purpose in passing judgment on, and shaming, another state and the lack of a sanction does not mean that the conduct is necessarily viewed as 'illegal but justified'.

The notion of mitigation works best in the domestic system where punish-ments usually follow a declaration of illegality and a range of punishments are available. However, in the international community, declarations of illegality are often not forthcoming, and punishments such as economic sanctions and military actions tend to be reserved for extreme cases where there is little debate about justification.

C. Mitigation or Justification?

Franck claims that unilateral humanitarian intervention should be analyzed under the doctrine of mitigation rather as a defence of justification. In *Regina v Dudley and Stephens* and *US v Holmes*, the courts did not recognize necessity as a defence to murder, but they responded with very lenient sentences or recom-mendations for clemency. Franck argues that these decisions reflect a distinction between unlawfulness and culpability. The necessity for action does not render an otherwise illegal action legal (justification) but it may reduce the culpability of the actor and thus lead to a reduced penalty or no penalty (mitigation).[68]

---

[66] For example, in 1960, Argentina lodged a complaint with the Security Council after Israel abducted Eichmann from Argentina. SCOR, 865th Mtg, 22 June 1960, 2–7; S/4334 of 8 June 1960. The Security Council passed Resolution 138 stating that the sovereignty of Argentina had been infringed and requesting Israel to make 'appropriate reparations'. SC Res. 138 of (1960). However, the Security Council noted that it was mindful of the concern that Eichmann be brought to justice and it did not impose any penalties on Israel. Thus, it is arguable that the Security Council considered Israel's action to be illegal but justifiable. Franck, above n 2 at 114.

[67] For example, in 1981, Israel bombed a nuclear reactor in Iraq, alleging that its use of force was justified as pre-emptive self-defence because the site was being used to develop nuclear weapons. The Security Council adopted a resolution in which it strongly condemned Israel's use of force and affirmed Iraq's right to sovereignty and to develop a peaceful nuclear capacity. SC Res. 487 (1981). The General Assembly also adopted a resolution, by a strong majority, condemning the use of force and warning against the repetition of such force. GA Res. 36/27 (1981) (109 votes in favour, the United States and Israel against, and 34 abstentions). Despite the absence of sanctions, most schol-ars would not accept that these bodies considered Israel's actions justified. For example, Franck, above n 2 at 106.

[68] Franck notes that there are differences between domestic systems as to whether necessity excuses a crime or mitigates its consequences, but all systems recognize the obligation of the law to do one or the other. Franck, above n 2 at 180.

Following Franck's approach, Art 51 would provide a good example of a justificatory defence because it allows states to use force in self-defence without
being guilty of violating the prohibition on the use of force in Art 2(4). By contrast, unilateral humanitarian intervention would be analyzed as an excuse or
mitigating circumstance rather than as an exculpatory defence. Following this
approach, the general prohibition on the use of force, including the prohibition
on unilateral humanitarian intervention, would be maintained but, in certain
instances, the punishment for states intervening to stop humanitarian crises
would be mitigated.

A number of other scholars have identified or adopted a similar approach.[69]
Stromseth calls this the 'excusable breach' approach, where unilateral humanitarian intervention remains technically illegal under the Charter but may be
morally and politically justified in certain exceptional circumstances.[70] The
Danish Institute of International Affairs refers to this approach as a 'safety valve'
or an 'emergency exit' from the rules of the Charter in cases when intervention
is justified or legitimate.[71] Similarly, Chesterman and Byers, writing together,
argue that Kosovo should be analyzed under a theory of 'exceptional illegality',
where arguments about legitimacy amount to pleas in mitigation.[72]

While this mitigation analysis seems intuitively plausible, the distinctions
between justification, excuse, and mitigation are blurry in the international
system. In comparative criminal law, a distinction is drawn between defences
of justification and excuse.[73] Consider a situation where X shoots Y. If X claims

---

[69] For example, D Hovell, 'Necessity: the Mother of In(ter)vention?' (unpublished manuscript,
2000) (arguing that the doctrine of necessity might be used to excuse breaches of the prohibition
on the use of force when there are strong humanitarian justifications for intervention); J Lobel and
M Ratner, 'Bypassing the Security Council: Ambiguous Authorizations to Use Force, Ceasefires
and the Iraqi Inspection Regime' (1999) 93 AJIL 124 at 136–7 (arguing against bypassing the
Security Council but admitting that, in extreme cases such as genocide, it may be preferable for the
formal law to be violated).

[70] Stromseth notes that this notion of 'excusable breach' is somewhat different to criminal
law concepts of 'excuse' and is closer, but not completely analogous, to justificatory defences:
J Stromseth, 'Rethinking humanitarian intervention: the case for incremental change' in
J Holzgrefe and R Keohane (eds) *Humanitarian Intervention: Ethical, Legal and Political Dilemmas*
(2003) 232 at 243 (fn 38).

[71] Danish Institute of International Affairs, *Humanitarian Intervention: Legal and Political
Aspects* (1999) 27, 99, 112, 116–18, 127–8. For a more recent statement of a similar position,
based upon Franck's work, see eg B Lepard, 'Jurying Humanitarian Intervention and the Ethical
Principle of Open-Minded Consultation', in T Nardin and M Williams (eds) *Humanitarian
Intervention* (2006) 217 at 237.

[72] M Byers and S Chesterman, 'Changing the rules about rules? Unilateral humanitarian intervention and the future of international law' in J Holzgrefe and R Keohane (eds) *Humanitarian
Intervention: Ethical, Legal and Political Dilemmas* (2003) 177 at 198–201.

[73] This distinction is crucial in many civil law countries. For example, German law makes
a distinction between the wrongfulness of the act (rechtswidrigkeit) and the culpability of the
actor (schuld). While both theories are evident to some extent in defences in common law countries, these systems do not tend to recognize the distinction in any systematic way. In favour
of the recognition of this distinction, see A Eser, 'Justification and Excuse: A Key Issue in the
Concept of Crime' in A Eser and G Fletcher (eds) *Justification and Excuse: Comparative Perspectives*

that her action was fully warranted in the circumstances, for example because she acted in self-defence, then she offers a justificatory defence. Alternatively, if X admits that what she did was wrongful but claims that she was not to blame, for example because she acted under duress, then she offers an excuse. Whereas justifications go to the acceptability of the conduct, excuses are directed towards the accountability of the defendant.[74]

In addition, a defendant who is found guilty can also raise a claim of mitigation at the sentencing stage. Mitigation does not affect the illegality of an action but rather seeks to moderate the consequences that flow from that illegality. Thus a defendant may be convicted for having committed an illegal act, but if the circumstances mean that the defendant was less blameworthy than others who commit similar offences, the defendant may receive a reduced sentence or no penalty.

The first problem with Franck's mitigation analysis is that while necessity was not treated as an excuse or justification in *Dudley* or *Holmes*, it has now been recognized as a defence of excuse or justification in many jurisdictions.[75] Franck deals with this point by stating that all legal systems deal with necessity under

---

(1987) 17; G Fletcher, 'The Right and the Reasonable' in A Eser and G Fletcher (eds) *Justification and Excuse: Comparative Perspectives* (1987) 67. Against the recognition of this distinction, see K Greenawalt, 'The Perplexing Borders of Justification and Excuse' in M Corrado (ed) *Justification and Excuse in the Criminal Law* (1994) 341 at 341.

[74] G Fletcher, above n 73 at 76–8; G Fletcher, 'Introduction from a Common Law Scholar's Point of View' in A Eser and G Fletcher (eds) *Justification and Excuse: Comparative Perspectives* (1987) 9 at 11; R Schopp, *Justification Defences and Just Convictions* (1998) 1–3.

[75] For example, s 3.02 of the 1985 American Law Institute's Model Penal Code provides that 'Conduct that the actor believes to be necessary to avoid a harm or evil to himself or to another is justifiable, provided that: (a) the harm or evil sought to be avoided by such conduct is greater than that sought to be prevented by the law defining the offense charged': American Law Institute, *Model Penal Code: Official Draft and Explanatory Notes* (1985) 42–3. In Canada, the Supreme Court has held that necessity is a defence of excuse rather than justification: *Perka v The Queen* [1984] 2 SCR 232; *R v Hibbert* [1995] 2 SCR 973. Article 122–7 of the French Penal Code provides that '[a] person is not criminally responsible if that person, facing an actual or imminent danger threatening himself, herself, or another, or property, performs an act necessary for the preservation of person or property, unless there is a disproportion between the means employed and the seriousness of the threat': *The French Penal Code of 1994 (as amended as of January 1, 1999)*, translated by E Tomlinson (1999) 39. The Penal Code of the Federal Republic of Germany provides: '34. Necessity as Justification: Whoever, while faced with an imminent and otherwise unavoidable danger to life, limb, freedom, honor, property or another legal interest, commits an act to avert the danger from himself or another, does not act unlawfully if, upon weighing the conflicting interests, in particular the affected legal interests and the magnitude of the danger threatening them, the protected interest substantially outweighs the one prejudiced. This applies, however, only to the extent that the act is a proportionate means to avert the danger. 35. Necessity as Excuse: (1) Whoever, while faced with an imminent and otherwise unavoidable danger to life, limb, freedom, honor, or property, commits an unlawful act to avert the danger to himself, a relative or person close to him, acts without guilt. This does not apply to the extent that the perpetrator could be expected under the circumstances to assume the risk, in particular, because he himself caused the danger or stood in a special legal relationship; however the punishment may be mitigated pursuant to s 49(1) if the perpetrator was not required to assume the risk with respect to a special legal relationship. (2) If the perpetrator during the commission of the act mistakenly assumes that circumstances exist which would excuse him under paragraph 1, he only will be punished if he could have

excuse or mitigation. However, there is a real theoretical difference between the two, and there is an even greater difference with the defence of justification.

Mitigation and excuse are premised on the wrongfulness of the action, while justification is based on its rightfulness. Franck claims that unilateral humanitarian intervention is 'illegal but justified' and that such interventions should be analyzed under the doctrine of mitigation. The use of the word 'justified' is confusing in this context. On the one hand, Franck wishes to claim that certain interventions are morally *justified*, but on the other hand, he does not want to analyze such interventions under the defence of *justification*. It may be more appropriate to describe this approach as unilateral humanitarian intervention being 'illegal but excused' or 'illegal but mitigated'. Yet would that really capture the essence of the claim?

Analyzing unilateral humanitarian intervention as an excuse or mitigating circumstance is problematic because many do not accept the wrongfulness of such actions. If such interventions are morally right or at least morally permissible, why should we maintain that they are illegal? Maintaining a prohibition on actions that most people deem morally right may bring the law into disrepute. Indeed, a number of scholars argue that necessity should be analyzed as a defence of justification because choosing the lesser of two evils promotes overall well-being, so the action is not wrongful.[76] Similarly, the *Articles on State Responsibility* treat necessity as a ground for precluding the wrongfulness of an act, rather than simply as a ground for excusing or reducing culpability.[77]

In practice, it may be difficult to identify any difference between mitigation and justification if one is arguing that mitigation should lead to states being subject to no penalty rather than a reduced penalty if they intervene on humanitarian grounds. If the intervention was 'justified' and the intervening state is not going to be punished, how does that differ from an exculpatory defence like self-defence? The difference may lie in the fact that unilateral humanitarian intervention would still be 'technically illegal'. However, if declarations of illegality tend not to be forthcoming, how can we tell the difference between mitigation and justification if both result in no penalty? Even Franck admits that, in the practice of the UN political organs, 'the distinction between

---

avoided the mistake. The punishment shall be mitigated pursuant to s 49(1).' *The German Penal Code (as amended as of December 19, 2001)*, translated by S Thaman (2002) 12.

[76] For example, Horder claims that necessity cases involve a moral imperative to act, as the wrongdoing is committed in order to avoid some greater evil: J Horder, 'Self-Defence, Necessity and Duress: Understanding the Relationship' (1998) 11 Canadian Journal of Law and Jurisprudence 143 at 143, 155–6. Williams defines necessity as an assertion that conduct promotes some higher value than the value of literal compliance with the law: G Williams, *Criminal Law: The General Part* (1953) 567. Berger argues that the defence of necessity should be understood as a justification rather than an excuse or an issue of moral involuntariness: B Berger, 'A Choice Among Values: Theoretical and Historical Perspectives on the Defence of Necessity' (2002) 39 Alberta Law Review 848 at 856.

[77] International Law Commission, *Articles on State Responsibility*, Art 25(1).

what is justified (exculpated) and what is excusable (mitigated) is so fine as to be of pure (yet also considerable) academic interest'.[78]

D. Exception or Precedent?

The real motivation behind analyzing unilateral humanitarian intervention under mitigation rather than exculpation appears to be a desire to minimize the precedential effect of cases like Kosovo. According to Franck, analyzing unilateral humanitarian intervention as a mitigating circumstance means that it would not create a right or an obligation to intervene but rather would be seen as 'purely circumstantial and discretionary relief'.[79] In a similar vein, Simma spells out some factors that made NATO's decision to intervene in Kosovo ad hoc and distinctive and argues that Kosovo should be regarded as a 'singular case' from which 'no general conclusions' ought to be drawn.[80]

Franck and Simma are not alone in attempting to downplay the precedential value of Kosovo. For example, the US government did not articulate a legal justification for NATO's intervention based on a right to unilateral humanitarian intervention. Instead, the US Secretary of State stated that the intervention was 'a unique situation *sui generis* in the region of the Balkans' and that 'it is important not to overdraw the various lessons that come out of it'.[81] Similarly, the Federal Republic of Germany was very concerned to stress that NATO's intervention should not set a precedent for similar interventions in the future. For example, the Foreign Minister of Germany stated before the Parliament of the Federal Republic of Germany (*Bundestag*) that the 'decision of NATO [on air strikes against FRY] must not become a precedent. As far as the Security Council monopoly on force is concerned, we must avoid getting on a slippery slope.'[82]

The reluctance to develop a general doctrine of unilateral humanitarian intervention can be explained by a number of factors. Many smaller or less powerful states may fear endorsing a doctrine that would give more power to larger states to intervene in their domestic affairs.[83] Even if states recognize that the Security Council may have too many inhibitions about using force, they may fear that regional organizations such as NATO would have too few.[84] All of

---

[78] Franck, above n 2 at 191.

[79] Ibid., at 190. See also Franck, 'Lessons from Kovoso' above n 20 at 859 (arguing that '[e]very nation has an interest in NATO's actions being classified as the exception, not the rule' and that 'NATO's action in Kosovo is thus best seen as an exception from which may be derived a few useful lessons for the future, rather than as the future itself').

[80] Simma, above n 1 at 14.

[81] US Secretary of State Madeleine Albright, Press Conference with Russian Foreign Minister Igor Ivanoc, Singapore, 26 July 1999 quoted by Chesterman, above n 27 at 216.

[82] *Deutscher Bundestag, Plenarprotokoll* 13/248, 16 October 1998 at 23129 quoted in Simma, above n 1 at 13.

[83] Adam Roberts, 'NATO's "Humanitarian War" over Kosovo' (1999) 41 Survival 102 at 120.

[84] J Laurenti, 'NATO, the UN, and the Use of Force' quoted by Simma, above n 1 at 20.

the permanent members have an interest in maintaining the importance of the Security Council so that their veto remains potent.[85] Russia and China may fear that unilateral humanitarian intervention might lead to interventions in their own domestic affairs, such as Chechnya and Tibet.[86] The NATO states may wish to be able to intervene in certain cases without creating a general principle that could be used by other states to justify intervention.[87] States may also fear that a right to intervene would gradually turn into a duty to intervene or a 'responsibility to protect'.[88]

Although many states and academics refer to Kosovo as a singular case, it is too much to hope that this 'dramatic departure' from the Charter will remain an exception.[89] Once states realize that they can resort to force without facing censure, except for some nominal reprimand, what is to stop them acting likewise when they face similar situations in the future?[90] If humanitarian crises are likely to arise again, and interventions consistently fail to give rise to a sanction, has not Kosovo carved out an exception to the prohibition in cases of extreme humanitarian crises? Is this not really more analogous to carving out an exculpatory defence rather than merely relying on mitigation? Characterizing humanitarian intervention as an 'exception to the rule' or as a 'mitigating circumstance' may simply amount to a legal fiction designed to temporarily ease the concerns of precedent, conscious members of the international legal community.

The distinctions between mitigation and exculpation, and exceptions and precedents, are difficult to sustain in international law for the simple reason that state practice helps to create international law. The Charter prohibition on the use of force may be modified by subsequent state behavior in one of two ways. First, the prohibition may be modified by the emergence of a new norm of customary international law supporting a right to unilateral humanitarian intervention.[91]

[85] Wedgwood, above n 34 at 832.

[86] According to China's ambassador to the Security Council, the 'human rights over sovereignty approach' serves to promote hegemonism under the pretext of human rights. SC Res. 1244 (1999), SCOR, 4011th Mtg, 10 June 1999, at 9.

[87] Wedgwood, above n 34 at 829 (arguing that the United States government justified the action on the basis of a mixture of facts and principles in order to qualify a universal or wideranging theory that might prove less attractive in other hands).

[88] Report of the International Commission on Intervention and State Sovereignty, *The Responsibility to Protect* (2001). On the outcome of the 2005 World Summit, in which states ostensibly committed themselves to such a 'responsibility', see A Bellamy, 'Whither the Responsibility to Protect? Humanitarian Intervention and the 2005 World Summit', 20 Ethics and International Affairs (2006) 143. See also K Tan, 'The Duty to Protect', in T Nardin and M Williams (eds), above n 71 at 84.

[89] Cassese, above n 16 at 25. Chesterman in particular is skeptical of the 'exception to the rule' thesis because exceptional responses can quickly become rules. Chesterman, above n 27 at 217.

[90] Franck, above n 2 at 182 (acknowledging that Kosovo was not, unfortunately, an 'exotic happenstance'); Reisman, above n 14 at 862 (arguing that if the circumstances arise again, unilateral humanitarian intervention must also occur again).

[91] In the *Nicaragua* case, the Court found that there was a general customary prohibition on the use of force but that '[r]eliance by a State on a novel right or an unprecedented exception to the [customary] principle might, if shared in principle by other States, tend towards a modification of

Second, subsequent practice has the capacity to create an authoritative interpretation of the Charter.[92] Even if the prohibition on the use of force is a peremptory norm,[93] it may still be modified by another peremptory norm, such as the prohibition on genocide,[94] though such modification might not be available in less compelling cases.

Whether practice forms an authoritative interpretation or a customary modification of the Charter, one must examine the *actions* and *justifications* of intervening states as well as the *reactions* of other states and bodies of the UN to determine if there has been a change in the law. Drawing on domestic analogies, some commentators contend that a breach of the law does not necessarily undermine the existence of the law—after all, the domestic prohibition on murder is not undermined by some individuals committing murder.[95] However, this is a false analogy because, in domestic systems, national legislative bodies have the power to make the law and individuals are obliged to follow the law. Individuals cannot change the law simply by refusing to comply with the law because they do not have law-making authority.[96] By contrast, states are *legislators* and *subjects* of international law. When a state acts contrary to an existing norm, in one sense

---

customary international law.' *Case Concerning Military and Paramilitary Activities in and against Nicaragua (Merits)* 1986 ICJ Rep 14 at 109 (para 207) (June 27).

[92] The *Vienna Convention on the Law of Treaties* provides that treaties may be interpreted in light of 'any subsequent practice in the application of the treaty which establishes the agreement of the parties to its interpretation'. *Vienna Convention on the Law of the Treaties* 1969, Art 31(3)(b). A good example of this process is the interpretation of Article 27(3) of the Charter, which provides that non-procedural decisions of the Security Council shall be made by an *affirmative* vote of nine members including the *concurring* votes of the five permanent members. While this appears to require the affirmative votes of all five permanent members, in practice, the Security Council has consistently interpreted abstentions by permanent members as not amounting to a veto. *Legal Consequences for States of the Continuing Presence of South Africa in Namibia (South West Africa) notwithstanding Security Council Resolution 276 (1970)* [1971] ICJ Rep 16 at 22, para 22. See also B Conforti, *The Law and Practice of the United Nations*, (2nd edn, 2000), 65–8; S Bailey and S Daws, *The Procedure of the UN Security Council* (3rd edn, 1998) 250–51; Chesterman, above n 27 at 59.

[93] American Law Institute, *Restatement (Third) of the Foreign Relations Law of the United States* (1987) para 102, comment k. See also the *Nicaragua* case, where the ICJ referred to the conclusion of the International Law Commission that the Charter's prohibition on the use of force was a conspicuous example of a peremptory norm: *Case Concerning Military and Paramilitary Activities in and against Nicaragua (Merits)* [1986] ICJ Report 14, 100 at para 190 citing the Report of the International Law Commission, 18th Session [1966] 2 *Yearbook of the International Law Commission* 172 at 247.

[94] Article 53 of the *Vienna Convention*. D Kritsiotis, 'Re-Appraising Policy Objections to Humanitarian Intervention' (1998) 19 Michigan Journal of International Law 1005 at 1040–46. For the *jus cogens* status of the prohibition on genocide, see the American Law Institute, *Restatement (Third) of the Foreign Relations Law of the United States* (1987), vol 2, 161, para 702; M Shaw, 'Genocide in International Law' in Y Dinstein (ed) *International Law at a Time of Perplexity* (1989) 797; I Brownlie, *Principles of Public International Law* (5th edn, 1998) 515.

[95] For example Sohn, 'The International Law of Human Rights: A Reply to Recent Criticisms' (1981) 9 Hofstra Law Review 347 at 350.

[96] A Weisburd, 'Customary International Law: The Problem of Treaties' (1988) 21 Vanderbilt Journal of Transnational Law 1 at 31.

the action is a breach because the state is judged as a subject of international law. But, in another sense, the action is a seed for a new law because the state acts as a legislator of international law.

Brownlie draws a similar analogy between unilateral humanitarian interventions and euthanasia.[97] Euthanasia is unlawful in most states, partly due to the risk of such a right being abused if it were made lawful. However, in clear cases, such as a father smothering his severely abnormal child after years of devoted care, the circumstances may be considered in mitigation of the offence. While the father would not be immune from prosecution or punishment, and euthanasia would remain absolutely prohibited, in practice the state may decide not to prosecute the father. By analogy, Brownlie argues that states or UN bodies may choose not to condemn unilateral humanitarian interventions, in recognition of the mitigating circumstances for action, without undermining the general prohibition on the use of force.[98] However, this domestic analogy is problematic because states are both *legislators* and *enforcers* of international law. In practice, it is difficult to determine the difference between state and institutional practice amounting to discretionary 'non-prosecution' (leaving the existing law intact) and amounting to acceptance of, or acquiescence in, the modification of the rule (leading to changes in the law).

The radically decentralized nature of international law means that a breach may modify existing law if other states emulate or acquiesce in the breach, rather than enforcing the existing norm.[99] Far from having no precedential value, NATO's intervention in Kosovo and the reactions of other states, individually and through the organs of the UN, have the capacity to modify the prohibition on the use of force. The fact that states did not generally condemn NATO's intervention as illegal means that the legality of unilateral humanitarian intervention has come into question. If there are more instances of states unilaterally intervening for humanitarian reasons, coupled with other states and institutions failing to condemn such interventions, then humanitarian intervention may emerge as a new right under international law (though it will certainly not develop as quickly as if states openly asserted such a right).

E. Behavioural Claims and Policy Considerations

Franck and Simma appear to agree that there are extreme cases where the use of force is justifiable, particularly when supported by a widely shared moral

---

[97] I Brownlie, 'Thoughts on Kind-Hearted Gunmen' in R Lillich (ed), above n 26 at 146.

[98] Ibid., at 146.

[99] *North Sea Continental Shelf* cases *(FRG v Den.; FRG v Neth.)* 1969 ICJ Rep 3 at 44 (20 February) per Judge Lachs (dissenting) at 230–31; M Akehust, 'Custom as a Source of International Law' (1974–5) *British Yearbook of International Law* 1 at 37; A Weisburd, 'The Effect of Treaties and Other Formal International Acts on the Customary Law of Human Rights' (1995–96) 25 Georgia Journal of International and Comparative Law 99 at 107.

consensus. However, they also recognize the need to guard against states using the banner of humanitarian intervention as a pretext for ulterior and abusive purposes. This 'illegal but justified' approach seems to be premised on two assumptions. First, that keeping unilateral humanitarian intervention illegal will not prevent states from intervening in cases of extreme necessity where many states would agree that intervention is morally justified. Second, that maintaining the general prohibition on the use of force is less open to abuse than creating a legal exception for unilateral humanitarian intervention. Thus there seems to be a desire for states to be able to act when they should act, but not be able to act when they should not.

Are these behavioral assumptions defensible and how can we tell whether states should or should not intervene? I am not in a position to answer those questions, but I also believe that they are not easily answered.

First, does the prohibition on unilateral humanitarian intervention prevent states from acting when they otherwise should intervene? Despite the prohibition, states have used force to achieve humanitarian ends on a number of occasions as described above, often with little or no condemnation. Chesterman argues that states do not fail to engage routinely in humanitarian intervention just because such interventions are illegal.[100] They fail to intervene because the use of force is expensive, the conflicts often do not involve the essential interests of other states, and many states are anxious to avoid casualties to their own forces. States may not always intervene where they *should* intervene, but this does not mean that the prohibition on the use of force prevents states from intervening when they otherwise *would* intervene.

However, simply proving that states have resorted to unilateral humanitarian intervention in extreme cases does not prove that states do not weigh the illegality of their actions in determining whether to intervene. The prohibition may mean that states will only be prepared to use force in cases that are so extreme that the intervention is unlikely to be condemned. But this does not mean that humanitarian intervention would be inappropriate in less extreme cases. States may intervene when the conflict touches upon their own interests or where there is public outcry in response to extensive media coverage, as arguably occurred in Kosovo and Somalia. In other circumstances, states may conveniently put forward the prohibition on the use of force as a justification for not intervening. If there were a right to unilateral humanitarian intervention, there may be more pressure on states to intervene when they were in a position to do so, possibly reducing the present selectivity of interventions.

Furthermore, not all states or groups of states may feel able to breach the prohibition on the use of force. NATO may have felt empowered to break the law because the decision was taken by 16 member states (a greater number than are in the Security Council), including a number of economic powers and three

---

[100] Chesterman, above n 27 at 231.

permanent members of the Security Council.[101] However, would individual states and other groups of states feel able to intervene in breach of the prohibition on the use of force? It may be possible for a regional organization to take action provided none of the permanent members of the Security Council objects, such as occurred with ECOWAS's interventions in Liberia and Sierra Leone. But it would be hard to imagine many states or groups of states being able to undertake such measures *against* the wishes of some of the permanent members of the Security Council. Thus, prohibiting unilateral humanitarian intervention may limit which states or groups of states can undertake such actions.[102]

Second, does keeping unilateral humanitarian intervention illegal reduce the likelihood of states making abusive claims? Franck argues that Kosovo should be seen as an exception, not the rule, because allowing states to use force to stop what they believe to be an extreme violation of human rights in another state 'could launch the international system down the slippery slope into an abyss of anarchy.'[103] Chesterman likewise argues that interventions would be more likely if a right to unilateral humanitarian intervention were developed, but that these would represent an increase in the number of bad faith interventions.[104] He concludes that it is '*more* dangerous to hand states a right—even of such a limited nature—than simply to assert the cardinal principle of the prohibition on the use of force and let states seek a political justification for a particular action if they find themselves in breach of that norm.'[105]

It is true that established exceptions, such as self-defence, have been invoked by states in bad faith.[106] It is also true that any criteria given for when an exception can be used are likely to be stretched over time. For example, states have argued that, in the nuclear age, the concept of an 'armed attack' in Art 51 should include a notion of an anticipated armed attack, because a state should not have to risk being destroyed before it is able to defend itself. This means that self-defence could be used to justify anticipatory self-defence, even though a pre-emptive strike may be hard to distinguish from an act of aggression. In the same

---

[101] Wedgwood argues that NATO's decision deserves greater deference than purely unilateral action, meaning action undertaken by only one state: see Wedgwood, above n 34 at 833.

[102] Chinkin argues that Kosovo shows that the West continues to script international law, noting that the most frequently cited examples of humanitarian intervention involve western states acting in non-western states (Iraq, Somalia, and Haiti), as though they were conducting a 'civilizing mission'. Chinkin, 'Kosovo: A "Good" or "Bad" War' 93 AJIL (1999) 841 at 846.

[103] Franck, above n 2 at 171–2; Franck, 'Lessons from Kovoso' above n 20 at 859.

[104] Chesterman, above n 27 at 231.

[105] Ibid., at 231.

[106] For example, in 1968, the Warsaw Pact's armed forces entered Czechoslovakia in order to replace Dubcek's liberalizing regime with a hard line communist regime. The USSR justified this intervention on the basis of collective self-defence against anti-communists. This justification was widely rejected and the intervention only escaped Security Council condemnation because the USSR vetoed the resolution. S/8761 sponsored by Brazil, Canada, Denmark, France, Senagal, the United Kingdom, and the United States. The resolution was supported by ten states, three states abstained, and the USSR and Hungary voted against the resolution. See Franck, above n 2 at 73–5.

way, a right to unilateral humanitarian intervention could be used in bad faith and any criteria for such a right might be weakened over time.

However, the fact that an exception to the prohibition on the use of force would be open to abuse does not prove that creating an exception would be more dangerous than maintaining the absolute prohibition. Even though unilateral humanitarian intervention is illegal, Franck is at pains to show that states have engaged in such interventions anyway, in some cases with dubious motivations.[107] Making unilateral humanitarian intervention illegal may simply mean that abusive uses of force are justified under another name, such as self-defence. Franck acknowledges the fear that mitigation could lead to a slippery slope and create the potential for abusive claims. However, he argues that there have been many abusive claims of self-defence but that does not mean self-defence should not be recognized as an exception.[108] Why then does he not wish to recognize a legal exception for unilateral humanitarian intervention?

It may be that keeping unilateral humanitarian intervention illegal is likely to have an impact on the burden and standard of proof for intervening in particular cases. Franck argues that unilateral humanitarian intervention should remain outside the law, rather than be recognized as an exception within the law, so that the onus of proof is left 'squarely with those seeking a dispensation from the general rule'.[109] But even if unilateral humanitarian intervention were recognised as a legal exception, the burden of proving that a particular action should fall within that exception would still lie, at least initially, with the intervening party.[110] The real difference between making unilateral humanitarian intervention illegal and making it a legal exception relates to the standard and type of proof intervening states will have to satisfy. If unilateral humanitarian intervention remains illegal, then the bar will be set very high, forcing states to show that a particular humanitarian crisis justifies departing from the law. By contrast, if unilateral humanitarian intervention is recognised as an exception, then the bar will be lower because states will need to show only that their actions come within the exception. Moreover, the legal status of unilateral humanitarian intervention will impact upon whether a primarily legal paradigm is used to justify interventions or a moral/political one. Keeping unilateral humanitarian intervention illegal but saying that it may nonetheless sometimes be justified leads to a shift in paradigm in international law away from legality and towards some notion of legitimacy.

---

[107] Franck, above n 2 at 142, 150 (citing, for example, that India's motives in intervening in East Pakistan were 'not exactly above suspicion', while Vietnam's invasion of Kampuchea clearly served geopolitical purposes).

[108] Ibid., at 185–6.

[109] Ibid., at 190.

[110] It may be arguable that the intervening states would simply need to show a prima facie case that their intervention was humanitarian and then the burden would shift to opposing states. However, burdens of proof are not so mechanically applied in the international arena, particularly in political bodies such as the Security Council and the General Assembly.

4. The Movement from Legality to Legitimacy

A. Changing the Paradigm of Debate

If unilateral humanitarian intervention is seen as a legal exception to the prohibition on the use of force, then primarily legal justifications will be used to defend
interventions. Alternatively, if it is seen as an action outside the law, then primarily moral and political arguments will be used. Franck has previously endorsed
using political rather than legal justifications to defend humanitarian interventions, stating in 1973:

> I would prefer to advise politicians contemplating such intervention to look to political
> rather than legal justifications and mitigation. Political leaders who are contemplating
> unilateral military intervention should not be encouraged to believe that international
> law is firmly on their side. It is not. At best, it is unclear. They could still take their
> chances on a cogent political justification being accepted as genuine by the international
> community.[111]

The difference in paradigm was evident in the justifications given by the
NATO states for their intervention in Kosovo. The Secretary General of NATO
stated '[w]e must stop the violence and bring an end to the humanitarian catastrophe now taking place in Kosovo. We have a *moral duty* to do so.'[112] In the
provisional measures hearing before the ICJ, only Belgium justified the action
on the basis of a possible legal right to humanitarian intervention.[113] Other states
chose to frame their justifications without reference to specific legal language and
principles, for example by referring to the need to stop a humanitarian catastrophe without referring to the doctrine of humanitarian intervention.[114]

Not all people or all states share the same moral and political values, however.
In an attempt to avoid this problem, Franck endorses a utilitarian analysis to
determine whether a particular intervention is legitimate, stating 'it is necessary to
compare potential outcomes of action and inaction in precise circumstances'.[115]
He concludes that the 'ultimate test of a humanitarian intervention's legitimacy
is whether it results in significantly more good than harm'.[116] Yet this does not
resolve the problem of divergences between people's moral and political values.
Utilitarianism aims at maximising the greatest good for the greatest number, but

---

[111] T Franck, 'Conference Proceedings: Part II The Present' in Lillich (ed), above n 26 at 64. See
also Chesterman, above n 27 at 227 (arguing that 'certain acts are against the law, but the decision
of whether to condemn them is outside the law').

[112] NATO Press Release, 041, 14 March 1999 (emphasis added).

[113] *The Legality of the Use of Force, (Yugoslavia v Belgium, Canada, France, Germany, Italy,
Netherlands, Portugal, Spain, United Kingdom, United States of America)*, Oral Pleadings, available
at <http://www.icj-cij.org>.

[114] D Kritsiotis, 'The Kosovo Crisis and NATO's Application of Armed Force Against the Federal
Republic of Yugoslavia' (2000) 49 *International and Comparative Law Quarterly* 330 at 343.

[115] Franck, above n 2 at 188.

[116] Ibid., at 189.

what counts as 'good' is highly contested in a pluralistic world. Problems of ethics are not simply problems about how to determine the optimal scheme for securing the greatest good; rather, one of the central problems is identifying what should count as 'the good' in the first place.

Even if we were to accept a utilitarian approach, it is difficult to apply in practice because it deals with counterfactuals. It is impossible to know whether a situation would have been better or worse had states intervened to stop a humanitarian crisis or not. Systematic analysis of the welfare consequences of intervention and non-intervention are not generally available, so determining whether a particular intervention was or will be justified is largely a matter of guesswork.[117] It may be easier to determine after an intervention whether a particular use of force in fact helped the humanitarian crisis. Indeed, one reason that India, Vietnam, and Tanzania's actions are often accepted as good examples of humanitarian intervention is that they are generally considered to have produced positive outcomes. However, it may be extremely difficult to determine whether a use of force will work before intervention occurs, so these sorts of *ex post facto* conclusions may not provide very useful *ex ante* guides for actions.

I lack the empirical data from which to analyse whether NATO's intervention was justified, as it is generally assumed to have been. There were, however, criticisms of the intervention on this basis. For example, Adam Roberts notes that the air campaign did not in the short term stop, and may even have exacerbated, violence in Kosovo.[118] NATO also employed air strikes in order to minimize casualties to its forces so as to maintain domestic support for the intervention. Air strikes shifted the risk of war from the intervening states to the civilian population within the former Yugoslavia.[119] If one were employing true utilitarian calculations, then the calculation should have included whether it was worth flying lower in order to hit targets more accurately and reduce civilian casualties at the risk of some NATO pilots being shot down.[120] But would there have been any intervention at all if such utilitarian calculations had been employed?

Another problem with this utilitarian analysis lies in a failure to distinguish between act-utilitarianism and rule-utilitarianism.[121] Act-utilitarianism focuses on the utility of individual actions, so a specific act is just if its consequences are more favorable than those of any other available action. By contrast, rule-utilitarianism focuses on the utility of general rules, so a specific act is just if it conforms to a rule that would produce the most favorable consequences if it

---

[117] J Holzgrefe, 'The humanitarian intervention debate' in J Holzgrefe and R Keohane (eds) *Humanitarian Intervention: Ethical, Legal and Political Dilemmas* (2003) 15 at 25, 50–51.

[118] Roberts, above n 83 at 103.

[119] Chesterman, above n 27 at 222–3; Falk, above n 37 at 855–6.

[120] Koskenniemi, above n 15 at 166.

[121] R Frey, 'Act-Utilitarianism' in H LaFollette (ed) *The Blackwell Guide to Ethical Theory* (2000) 165; B Hooker, 'Rule-Consequentialism' in H LaFollette (ed) *the Blackwell Guide to Ethical Theory* (2000) 183; J Smart, 'An Outline of a System of Utilitarian Ethics' in J Smart and B Williams, *Utilitarianism: For and Against* (1973) 3 at 9.

were generally adopted. The difference between act-utilitarianism and rule-utilitarianism is often illustrated by the dilemma of whether individuals should keep their promises. According to act-utilitarianism, a person should keep a particular promise if the consequences of keeping that promise are better than the consequences of breaking it. According to rule-utilitarianism, a person should keep a promise if the existence of a general rule that people keep promises would produce better consequences than the absence of such a rule.

Proponents of the 'illegal but justified' approach seem to be attempting simultaneously to embrace an act-utilitarian and rule-utilitarian approach. On the one hand, they adopt an act-utilitarian approach by assessing the legitimacy of a particular unilateral humanitarian intervention based on a comparison of the consequences of action and inaction in the particular circumstances. On the other hand, they adopt a rule-utilitarian approach by concluding that the law should not be changed to provide a general right to unilateral humanitarian intervention because of the dangers associated with allowing states to unilaterally decide when to use force.[122] The 'illegal but justified' approach seeks to have the best of both worlds where the action is justified under act-utilitarianism, but the rule is justified under rule-utilitarianism.

This approach does not, however, provide a good guide for actions. When faced with a humanitarian crisis, should a state adopt an act-utilitarian approach and intervene, or a rule-utilitarian approach and not intervene? Drawing a strict division between justifications for actions and for rules is also flawed. Under international law, state practice forms the basis of customary international law. If the international community turns a blind eye to unilateral humanitarian intervention when such intervention would promote more good than harm in the individual case, then that is going to undermine the general prohibition on the use of force and help to establish an exception for humanitarian intervention. Laws are also intended to create general rules that govern all foreseeable circumstances, in order that like cases are treated alike, so appeals to act-utilitarianism may be 'inimical to the rule of law'.[123]

Even if one were to adopt an act-utilitarian approach to unilateral humanitarian intervention, the frame of reference employed for assessing the good and harm arising from such interventions is often too narrowly focused. For example, Franck frames the question as whether Kosovo would have been better off had there been no intervention or whether Cambodia would have been better off if Vietnam had left Pol Pot in power.[124] But one also needs to consider the systemic damage done to the rule of law by allowing states to breach the Charter. Respect for the Charter and the Security Council may be diminished if they are

---

[122] Franck, above n 2 at 171–2, 189; Simma, above n 1 at 1, 22.

[123] Holzgrefe, above n 117 at 23. Indeed, in Fuller's account of the internal morality of law, the worst problem in a legal system is the failure to achieve rules at all, so that every issue is decided on an ad hoc basis. L Fuller, *The Morality of Law* (1964) 39 and 46–9.

[124] Franck, above n 2 at 188–9.

seen not to protect against harms such as genocide. But allowing states to breach the Charter in 'worthy' cases may undermine the general prohibition on the use of force and provide a precedent for states to similarly disregard the Charter in less worthy cases. Indeed, it was harder for supporters of NATO's intervention in Kosovo to assert the sanctity of the UN Charter when faced with the United States and United Kingdom acting without clear Security Council authorization in Iraq in 2003.

B. Legality Versus Legitimacy?

Characterizing NATO's intervention in Kosovo as formally illegal but morally justified involves an underlying shift in the discourse of international law from legality to legitimacy. According to Pellet, the debates on unilateral humanitarian intervention can be summarized in two questions: when is unilateral action lawful; and if it is unlawful, can it nonetheless be legitimate?[125] The Independent International Commission on Kosovo concluded that NATO's use of force was illegal but legitimate and that an emerging doctrine of unilateral humanitarian intervention should be developed to close the gap between legality and legitimacy. The Commission situated this conclusion in an ambiguous gray zone between an extension of international law and a proposal for an international moral consensus: '[i]n essence, this gray zone goes beyond strict ideas of *legality* to incorporate more flexible views of *legitimacy*.'[126]

This shift in discourse begs two questions: what is legitimacy; and what is the relationship between legality and legitimacy? The term 'legitimacy' is both overused and under-defined in international law. Legitimacy is sometimes used as a descriptive or attitudinal concept concerned with an almost sociological investigation into commonly held subjective beliefs. Here the relevant question is whether a certain action or law is *accepted* as legitimate. At other times, legitimacy is used as a normative or evaluative concept that provides a set of criteria against which to assess actions and laws. Here the relevant question is whether a particular action or law is *acceptable* based on normative criteria. In addition to being a word with many meanings, legitimacy is also a word with many applications. Various criteria of legitimacy are applied to a wide range of phenomena, including actions, processes, individual laws, and the international legal system as a whole.

---

[125] Pellet, above n 44 at 385.
[126] Independent International Commission on Kosovo, above n 17 at 164 (emphasis added). It is worth noting here that Franck himself has recently reaffirmed a similar position, arguing that '...necessity and common sense have a role in tempering the law, in narrowing the gap between legality and legitimacy, between the letter of the law and its spirit, between normativity and morality'. See T Franck, 'Legality and Legitimacy in Humanitarian Intervention', in T Nardin and M Williams (eds), above n 71. See also Wedgwood, above n 34 at 834 (arguing that there were good reasons to go around the Security Council in the Kosovo case as '[l]egitimacy—and legality—represent a complex cultural process not confined to the Council chamber').

Legitimacy is a flexible concept. According to the Danish Institute for International Affairs, the concept of legitimacy is less precise than legality because there is no undisputed authority mandated to evaluate legitimacy and no agreed procedure for doing this.[127] Thus, there is a certain amount of 'fudge' room when commentators move from discussions about legality to discussions about legitimacy because it is not clear what exactly the latter represents. Despite this uncertainty, what seems to be reasonably clear is that when commentators juxtapose legality and legitimacy, they are somehow attempting to contrast notions of strict legal positivism with more substantive notions of morality.[128] This reasoning forces one to consider ethical principles and legal approaches in opposition to each other. In this way, the 'legality versus legitimacy' debate divorces the two concepts and places them on different spectrums.

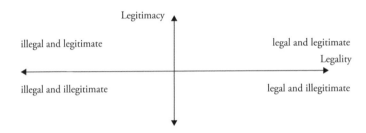

One way to represent the 'legality versus legitimacy' debate is to place legality and legitimacy on two axes (see diagram above). As there are two variables involved, actions can be legal and legitimate, illegal and illegitimate, legal and illegitimate, and illegal and legitimate. Commentators seem to be generally comfortable when they consider that legitimacy and legality coincide, such as when an action is legal and legitimate or illegal and illegitimate. For example, it could be argued that Iraq invading Kuwait was illegal and illegitimate, whereas the response of collective self-defence undertaken in Operation Desert Storm was legal and legitimate. However, problems arise when legality and legitimacy appear to conflict, such as when an action is considered to be legal and illegitimate or illegal and legitimate. For example, it is arguable that unilateral humanitarian intervention is illegal but legitimate, whereas the use of the veto to stop collective humanitarian intervention is legal but illegitimate.[129]

---

[127] Danish Institute of International Affairs, above n 71 at 24.

[128] For example, Buchanan argues that the moral justifiability of illegal humanitarian intervention is often seen as a choice between fidelity to law or to basic moral values. A Buchanan, 'Reforming the international law of humanitarian intervention' in J Holzgrefe and R Keohane (eds) *Humanitarian Intervention: Ethical, Legal and Political Dilemmas* (2003) 130 at 131.

[129] For example, Pellet argues that there can be 'no doubt that the NATO action in Kosovo can (and must) be seen as legitimate, while, on the other hand, the jamming of the Security Council by China and Russia cannot'. Pellet, above n 44 at 385.

The loaded terminology used to describe unilateral humanitarian intervention that was discussed above likely results from a feeling that legality and legitimacy have diverged. Using descriptions such as 'technically illegal' may reflect a feeling that just because something is illegal does not necessarily mean that it is illegitimate. Similarly, referring to the Security Council as 'jammed' or 'paralyzed' due to the veto reflects a feeling that the use of the veto may be legal but is not always legitimate.

However, polarizing legality and legitimacy in this way places limits on the way in which we construct and evaluate the debate over unilateral humanitarian intervention. First, the legality versus legitimacy debate leads one to formulate the choices presented by unilateral humanitarian intervention in dichotomous terms that exclude other potential avenues from consideration. Proponents of unilateral humanitarian intervention seek to contrast 'unilateral humanitarian intervention' (illegal but legitimate) with 'inhumanitarian non-intervention' (legal but illegitimate).[130] However, these are not necessarily the only options available, which is why opponents of unilateral humanitarian intervention seek to portray the choice as being between unilateral action (illegal but legitimate) and Security Council authorized collective action (legal and legitimate).[131]

Second, juxtaposing legality and legitimacy unfairly represents the choice as being between legal formalism and substantive morality. This approach fails to recognize that current notions of legality incorporate strong elements of substantive and procedural legitimacy. The prohibition on the use of force has substantive moral value because it recognizes the value of state sovereignty and helps to keep the peace and prevent aggression. Requiring states to follow procedures such as Security Council authorization also provides a forum for collective decision-making rather than allowing states to act unilaterally based on their own interests. On the other side of the equation, the moral value of intervening may not always be clear-cut as many cases involve mixed motivations about whether and how to intervene. Unilateral humanitarian intervention is not comparable to an ambulance running a red light at a deserted intersection on the way to the hospital;[132] it is more akin to allowing drivers with sick passengers to unilaterally decide whether to follow road rules in peak hour traffic.

Finally, attempting to strictly separate legality from legitimacy is problematic because one of the functions of the law is to help delimit legitimate actions from illegitimate actions and thus help guide behaviour. According to Joyner, the law was 'originally conceived for the purpose of legitimizing action deemed proper and delegitimizing action deemed improper by society, and to argue that law

---

[130] Chesterman, above n 27 at 236.

[131] For example, Chesterman argues that 'unilateral enforcement is not a substitute for but the opposite of collective action'. Chesterman, above n 27 at 222–3. See also Falk, above n 37 at 855–6.

[132] This is one of the classic examples used in discussions of a defence of necessity: see eg *Perka v The Queen* [1984] 2 SCR 232 at 242.

and legitimacy are divorced concepts is to undercut law's primary function'.[133] Separating legality from legitimacy may undermine the relevance of the law, as the law might require illegitimate actions and prohibit legitimate ones. It also encourages a static conception of the law where actions remain legal or illegal regardless of their legitimacy. Laws that are devoid of normative content may not provide effective guides for actions, while appealing to notions of 'legitimacy' may also not provide adequate guidance for actions if no definition of or criteria for legitimacy are forthcoming.

C. Motivations Behind the Movement to Legitimacy

Given the uncertainty behind the meaning of legitimacy and its relationship to legality, why do international lawyers turn to notions of legitimacy when discussing unilateral humanitarian intervention? I suggest that there are three reasons, each of which shows a different understanding of the relationship between legality and legitimacy.

First, legitimacy may be resorted to as an escape from law altogether. Powerful actors may seek to move the debate from questions of legality to questions of legitimacy because the current legality does not suit their interests and they believe they have a better chance of defining what is and is not legitimate. This shift to legitimacy is done with a view to creating exceptions to the law: there is a 'fundamental difference between recognizing an exception to one rule of law based upon another rule of law and recognizing an exception to the law itself'.[134] Instead of articulating a rule of unilateral humanitarian intervention where any state could act if certain criteria were met, powerful states may wish to keep such interventions illegal so that only they could justify using force where they determine intervention to be legitimate. For example, Byers and Chesterman argue that the United States may be attempting to create 'new, exceptional rights for the United States alone' rather than trying to change international law more generally, and that this 'exceptional legality' approach might eventually lead to one set of legal processes for the single superpower and another for all other states.[135]

Second, legitimacy may be used to supplement strict notions of legality in an attempt to maintain the integrity of the law while at the same time responding to the need for justice in individual cases. By declaring unilateral humanitarian intervention to be 'illegal but justified', proponents are endorsing a black and white view of legality where an action is either legal or illegal. However, they are able to supplement this black and white conclusion with a 'shades of gray' concept of legitimacy. While legality and illegality are either/or alternatives, legitimacy exists along a spectrum because laws and actions may be more or less

---

[133] Joyner, above n 35 at 610.   [134] Joyner, above n 35 at 609.
[135] Byers and Chesterman, above n 72 at 195–8.

legitimate depending on the circumstances.[136] Unilateral humanitarian intervention involves a complex balancing of important and conflicting principles such as human rights, state sovereignty, justice in individual cases, and respect for the rule of law. The illegal but justified approach seeks to maintain the strict legal prohibition on the use of force, while at the same time using the more flexible concept of legitimacy in order to better represent the complexity of the issues involved.

Third, legitimacy may be resorted to with a view to critiquing the law and progressively developing it. Legitimacy provides a useful standpoint from which to assess the legal system and to see whether existing laws should remain the same or be modified. For example, the Independent International Commission on Kosovo concluded that NATO's intervention in Kosovo was illegal but justifiable, but it recognized that such a gap was problematic because it could weaken the authority of and respect for the law. The Commission thus held that we should work diligently towards closing the gap between legality and legitimacy in order that the law more accurately reflects moral demands.[137] Similarly, the Danish Institute for International Affairs acknowledges that legitimacy cannot answer the question of the legality of a certain action but argues that it may give some idea about the desirability and possibility of future change in international law.[138]

Whereas the second approach views legality as an either/or alternative, the third approach focuses on legality and illegality gradually changing overtime. Consider a spectrum ranging from clear illegality at one end, to clear legality at the other end, with various shades of gray in between. Following the third approach, the legitimacy of an action would have the effect of helping to shift an action from being clearly illegal towards being legal. For example, Falk argues that, in the context of NATO's intervention into Kosovo, 'the most helpful form of legal appraisal is one of degree, conceiving of legality and illegality by reference to a spectrum. The more "reasonable" the response, the closer to the legality end of the spectrum.'[139] As every breach of a law contains the seed for a new legality, each time a state breaches the law and others acquiesce because they view the breach as legitimate, it becomes easier for the next state to disobey the rule until eventually a new line of conduct or a new interpretation of a treaty replaces the old.[140] In the meantime, unilateral humanitarian intervention may be situated in a gray zone between clear illegality and clear legality.[141]

---

[136] M Koskenniemi, 'Book Review: The Power of Legitimacy Among Nations' (1992) 86 AJIL 175 at 176. For example, the Independent International Commission on Kosovo enumerates a number of principles that could enhance or diminish the legitimacy of a unilateral intervention, such as whether the use of force enjoyed some measure of collective support or not: Independent International Commission on Kosovo, above n 17 at 194–5. See also Danish Institute of International Affairs, above n 71 at 24.

[137] Independent International Commission on Kosovo, above n 17.

[138] Danish Institute of International Affairs, above n 71 at 24.

[139] Falk, above n 37 at 852.

[140] A D'Amato, *The Concept of Custom in International Law* (1971) 97–8.

[141] By analogy, in the *Nuclear Weapons* Advisory Opinion, the ICJ similarly held that the threat or use of nuclear weapons was neither permitted nor prohibited under international law. *Legality of*

There are pros and cons to analyzing legality on a spectrum. The approach may be useful in reflecting the current uncertainty of the law and giving some indication of the law's likely future development. It may also focus our attention on the explicit policy questions of whether unilateral intervention should be legal and, if so, in what circumstances. Within the gray zone, legitimacy may be relevant to the progressive development of the law by helping to decide individual cases, which in time may create patterns of conduct that become settled law. However, analyzing legality on a spectrum is less helpful in practice when one wishes to determine whether a given intervention is or is not legal at a particular point in time. There is also a risk that legitimacy could be used to move controversial issues, such as unilateral humanitarian intervention, into the gray zone permanently or semi-permanently, thus moving them from the legal to the political sphere on an enduring rather than temporary basis.

Even if one accepts a black and white approach to legality, where an action is always legal or illegal at a given point in time, it would be unwise to expect that unilateral humanitarian intervention would ever move from being always illegal to always legal. To the extent that drawing on domestic analogies may be of use, we can see that domestic prohibitions are often black and white (in the sense that conduct is illegal or illegal), but that the rules are highly textured. Domestic law differentiates between different mental states (*mens rea*), such as premeditation, intention, recklessness, and negligence, leading to distinctions such as murder and manslaughter. Prohibited conduct is also subject to a number of complete and partial defences, such as self-defence, defence of others, and provocation. There is also differentiation between the *actus reus* for different crimes, such as battery and aggravated battery. These factors combine to provide a highly textured law capable of applying to a wide range of circumstances.

By comparison, the Charter gives the impression of a uniform prohibition on the use of force, subject to only two narrow exceptions. Following this logic, Iraq's invasion of Kuwait and NATO's use of force in Kosovo would appear to be equally reprehensible because both are violations of Art 2(4) and neither fit within the existing exceptions. However, many states view these situations as qualitatively different. While the Charter prohibition on the use of force appears to be black and white, state practice since 1945 has softened and textured the prohibition through the recognition of a variety of exceptions and sub-exceptions. Even when a use of force is considered to be illegal, many factors are relevant to assessing the gravity of that use of force, including the motivations for intervention (for example, aggression or humanitarian intervention) and the level of harm caused (for example, temporary or permanent infringement of sovereignty). These factors play a role in determining the likelihood and gravity of

the *Threat or Use of Nuclear Weapons*, Advisory Opinion, ICJ Rep 1996, at 266, paras 105(2)(A) and (B). President Bedjaoui argued that the old rule permitting nuclear weapons had become defunct but a new rule prohibiting them had not yet fully come into existence. Declaration of President Bedjaoui, ibid. at 272, para 16.

condemnations following a use of force, which also play a role in developing customary international law.

Franck identifies a spectrum of responses to different violations of the prohibition on the use of force.[142] It seems that states are in fact responding to breaches of the prohibition on the use of force as though it were a differentiated prohibition rather than a uniform one. However, Franck fears that recognizing this reality as a matter of law might provide states with greater opportunities to find loopholes and circumvent the prohibition on unilateral force. Suggesting any set of criteria for an exception to the use of force based on unilateral humanitarian intervention is problematic because they would inevitably be both over-and under-inclusive.[143] However, the alternative seems to be to suggest no criteria on the basis that 'necessity knows no law'.[144] According to Chesterman, attempts to formulate such criteria are flawed because 'the circumstances in which the law may be violated are not themselves susceptible to legal regulation.'[145] Yet, is the absence of criteria genuinely less susceptible to abuse than the existence of criteria? Or is it simply less susceptible to the identification of abuse?

Holding that uses of force can be illegal but justified has set a precedent for states to bypass Security Council authorization and still claim that their use of force is legitimate. This has wider implications than simply affecting the law on unilateral humanitarian intervention. For example, when the United States and United Kingdom were unable to obtain a new Security Council resolution explicitly authorizing the use of force in Iraq in 2003, they nonetheless claimed that their actions were legitimate. This claim was dubious given that world opinion appeared to be generally against going to war with Iraq, at least at that time and on the terms proposed. However, Slaughter argued that the attack on Iraq might come to be seen as 'illegal but legitimate' based on the Kosovo precedent.[146] Slaughter contended that, although the use of force may have been 'formally illegal', it may nonetheless come to be viewed as legitimate in the eyes of the international community if irrefutable evidence of the existence or development of weapons of mass destruction was discovered or if the Iraqi people welcomed

---

[142] According to Franck, this spectrum ranges from *ex post facto* approval of some unilateral interventions, such as ECOWAS's intervention in Liberia, to silent acquiescence by the Security Council and General Assembly of interventions, such as Tanzania's ousting of Uganda's Idi Amin, to mild condemnation of some uses of force, such as India's intervention in Bangladesh, to reasonably clear disapproval of other uses of force, such as the United States' invasion of Grenada and Panama, and finally to the emphatic condemnation given by the Security Council to Iraq's invasion of Kuwait: Franck, above n 2 at 186.

[143] Koskenniemi, above n 15 at 167.

[144] Stromseth, above n 70 at 243. For example, Franck argues that the doctrine of mitigation provides 'purely circumstantial and discretionary relief', which occurs on a case-by-case basis and cannot be determined in advance by criteria. Franck, above n 2 at 171–2, 190.

[145] Chesterman, above n 27 at 230.

[146] Slaughter, above n 25. In similar fashion, many scholars have noted the important role that 'humanitarian' justifications came to play in maintaining public and international support for the US-led 'Operation Enduring Freedom' in Afghanistan in 2001. On this, see generally S Chesterman, 'Humanitarian Intervention and Afghanistan', in J Welsh (ed), above n 28 at 163.

the intervention. Similarly, Franck argued that the illegal invasion in Iraq may be retroactively legitimized by the UN if the Iraqi regime used weapons of mass destruction during the fighting or if British or American forces discovered hidden stocks of prohibited weapons.[147]

It may have been the very absence of criteria for determining legitimacy that helped to facilitate the use of the 'illegal but justified' approach in Iraq. Simply claiming that the intervention in Kosovo was 'exceptional' has not stopped Kosovo being used as a precedent for future uses of force. What it has done is to prevent many commentators from narrowly defining the Kosovo precedent to justify uses of force in certain circumstances only, such as when there are breaches of fundamental human rights and the decision to use force is taken by a regional organization with the support or acquiescence of a majority of the Security Council. The result may be that Kosovo has become a precedent for using force outside the Security Council whenever such force may be justified as 'legitimate', even though no criteria for or definition of legitimacy have been generally agreed upon. In this way, the 'illegal but justified' approach has provided a general mechanism for turning away from legality and towards legitimacy, setting legitimacy apart as an independent source of authority in international law that may be used to justify breaches well beyond the scope of unilateral humanitarian intervention.

5. Conclusion

NATO's intervention in Kosovo raised the dilemma of what states should do when there is a divide between the demands of international law and morality. A common response to this dilemma has been to argue that NATO's actions were 'illegal but justified'. However, while this approach provides an intuitively plausible way of reconciling legality and morality, it is ultimately not a sustainable position in international law. If unilateral humanitarian intervention is consistently met with acquiescence, then it will come to be recognized as an exception to the prohibition on the use of force. NATO's intervention cannot be downplayed as merely an exception to the rule rather than a precedent for a new rule for the simple reason that state practice helps to shape international law.

The 'illegal but justified' approach also shifts the focus away from questions of legality and towards questions of legitimacy. Attempting to completely divorce legality and legitimacy can ossify the law and undermine its relevance, which increases the risk of self-serving exceptionalism. Relying on legitimacy as an independent justification for action is also problematic because legitimacy is underdefined and open to manipulation by powerful actors. Thus, the 'illegal but

---

[147] T Franck, 'La Charte des Nations Unies est-elle un Chiffron de Papier?', *Le Monde*, 2 April 2003 (English translation, 'Has the United Nations Charter Become a Scrap of Paper?').

justified' approach endorses too black and white an understanding of legality and the use of force, tempered by a conception of legitimacy that is often so gray as to be wholly indeterminate. Instead of pursuing this path, a more dynamic understanding of international law needs to be developed so that the law is responsive to new circumstances and arguments.

It would be a mistake, however, to think that the problem of unilateral humanitarian intervention is simply a problem with the substantive law. Many of the problems concerning the use of force arise from a lack of procedural legitimacy of the collective security system. Giving the Security Council exclusive or primary power to authorize the use of force is problematic because of its small and unrepresentative membership and the veto power of the permanent members. Decisions about which humanitarian interventions are acted upon and which are ignored are routinely made on the basis of political interests rather than principled distinctions. Moreover, when states break the law on the use of force, they are often not subjected to condemnation or penalties, which results in a lack of accountability. Developing international law is not simply a question of fine tuning the substantive law. We also need to develop greater confidence in the inclusiveness, impartiality, and effectiveness of the institutional framework charged with applying that law.

6

Intervention in a 'Divided World': Axes of Legitimacy

*Nathaniel Berman**

Following World War I, which ended more than 83 years ago, the whole Islamic world fell under the crusader banner—under the British, French, and Italian governments. They divided the whole world... Those who refer things to the international legitimacy have disavowed the legitimacy of the Holy Book...

Osama Bin Laden, November 2001[1]

[The UN must] prove to the world whether it's going to be relevant or whether it's going to be a League of Nations, irrelevant.

George W Bush, September 2002[2]

And while it is difficult to see the world body go down the drain like its predecessor the League of Nations... it is equally difficult to see how the United Nations will regain the status and relative coherence it enjoyed before Operation Iraqi Freedom.

The Independent (Banjul) March 2003[3]

1. 'Status and Coherence'

A. The Internationalist Dream

It would be tempting to look back at the long post-Cold War decade as an era of the more or less steadily growing legitimacy of an activist internationalism—an

* This paper was funded, in part, with a Brooklyn Law School summer research stipend.
[1] Translation of Osama Bin Laden speech, broadcast on Al Jazeera television network on 3 November 2001, available at <http://news.bbc.co.uk/2/hi/world/monitoring/media_reports/1636782.stm>.
[2] Remarks by President George W Bush, available at <http://www.whitehouse.gov/news/releases/2002/09/20020919-7.html>.
[3] Baba Galleh Jallow, 'Of Iraqi Freedom, Democratic Contagion and Giant Mistakes', *The Independent* (Banjul), 24 March 2003.

era that began with '1989' and ended somewhere between '9/11' and the US invasion of Iraq. A representative example of this perspective was provided by a writer in a Gambian newspaper shortly after the start of the invasion of Iraq (the third of the three epigraphs to this paper).[4] The writer declared that the US attack would probably signal the demise of the 'status and relative coherence' previously enjoyed by the UN, condemning it to the fate of its predecessor, the League of Nations. This writer's views characterized much of pro-internationalist world opinion at the time of the American action.

If internationalism seems to such observers to have suffered a severe blow, the post-Cold War decade often appears to them by contrast as something of a golden age, in which internationalism had 'status' and 'coherence'. This contrast between the deep fractures of the present with a more harmonious recent past reflects the persistent dream of an international community with the status of a legitimate identity and the coherence of integrated ideals and practices. Above all, this dream is that of a community that would thoroughly integrate state power into internationalist principle—hence the gravity of the US invasion of Iraq. This internationalist dream has usually been articulated in the mode of absence—as a nostalgic lament for the loss of the community or a millenarian hope for its construction. It is a dream that particularly appeals to legal internationalists—and may account for the fact that writings addressed to the problem of 'The Disintegration of International Society'[5] and 'International Law in a Divided World'[6] have come to constitute a traditional genre favoured by some of the leading international lawyers over the past century. It may also account for the fact that a dichotomy between an international law founded on the principle of equality and one founded on the power of 'hegemonism' has seemed a useful analytical axis to widely divergent observers over the past several decades.[7]

It would not be difficult, however, to argue that remembering the long post-Cold War decade as a time of steadily, even if unevenly, growing internationalist legitimacy is a retrospective illusion. Words like Srebrenica and Rwanda should be enough to remind us of internationalism's *incoherence* during that period, due to the selectivity of its attentions; words like Kosovo should remind us of its uncertain *status*, due to the intermittence of respect shown by states to the need to subordinate their action to the authority of the formally constituted international community.

---

[4] Ibid.

[5] Georg Schwarzenberger, 'The Rule of Law and the Disintegration of the International Society', 33 AJIL 56 (1939).

[6] See, eg, Antonio Cassese, *International Law in a Divided World* (1986); Rosalyn Higgins, *Conflicts of Interest: International Law in a Divided World* (1965); Oliver Lissitzyn, 'International Law in a Divided World', 542 Int'l Conciliation 1 (1963).

[7] See, eg, Detlev F Vagts, 'Hegemonic International Law', 95 AJIL 843 (2001); UNGA Res. 103, A/Res/34/103 (14 December 1979). The 1979 GA Res. 103, entitled, 'Inadmissibility of Hegemonism in International Relations,' probably marks something of a high-water mark of Seventies Third Worldism in international fora.

To be sure, many who share the nostalgia for the long post-Cold War decade may readily acknowledge that it was a time of numerous swings in internationalist prestige. Yet criticism of post-Cold War internationalism is usually presented in the ameliorative mode. Challenges to the selectiveness of internationalists' attentions or the lack of inclusiveness of participation in their decision-making councils are usually intended to lead the international community to make good on its universal claims, rather than attack its foundation. Such criticisms, therefore, are not incompatible with treating the failures and disappointments of the long decade as the inevitable travails of a universal international community struggling to be born, however regrettable and even tragic those travails may have been.

Since the end of the long post-Cold War decade, however, the very ideal of the gradual transformation of the world into a community governed by widely-accepted internationalist principles and institutions has been subjected to a series of high-profile attacks. Perhaps the most well-known of these attacks issued from the very different quarters of Osama Bin Laden and George W Bush (the first and second epigraphs to this paper). As we shall see, where Bin Laden primarily attacked the *status* of internationalism due to its putatively illegitimate identity, Bush primarily attacked its *coherence*, due to the putative gap between its principles and its institutions. Like the internationalist writer in the Gambian newspaper, both of these challengers cited the League of Nations as an important reference, though each did so with very different intents. As a result of such attacks, the prospect of the ideological redivision of the world into competing 'legitimacies' has begun to appear to some internationalists as a grave danger, provoking a variety of discursive and practical strategies. Strategies designed to meet other challenges to internationalism in the past, such as those of Fascism in the 1930s, Communism during the Cold War, and the US during the Vietnam era, have begun to play a visible role.

In this paper, I propose that we reject the nostalgia for the long post-Cold War decade as both historically inaccurate and theoretically flawed. It would be easy, for example, to show that current challenges to internationalism—and the counter-attacks on them—were in full play throughout the long decade. More fundamentally, I propose that we reject the utopian dream of an international community that would finally have integrated power and principle. Activist internationalism will always appear to some as mere power for at least two reasons. First, ideological divisions in the world are not a product of a fall from grace, but of the human condition—periodic announcements of the 'end of ideology' notwithstanding. 'Status' challenges, attacking the putatively universal community as ideologically partisan, will therefore be a persistent feature of international debate. Secondly, the final integration of power and principle is impeded by the fact that internationalist principles and institutions are themselves deeply heterogeneous—rendering the achievement of 'coherence', even 'relative coherence', a provisional and contested affair. Internationalism, especially in its legal dimension, consists of a body of rules and institutions in which 'self-determination' must always confront 'sovereignty'; 'minority protection' must face 'individual rights'; 'free trade' must always confront the 'right to development'; the equality-principle that governs the General Assembly must always face the power-principle that governs the Security Council; and so on. Attempts at effecting 'coordination'[8] among these elements will never achieve more than a temporary consensus. The Bin Laden-style attacks on internationalism's status and the Bush-style assaults on its coherence are not exceptional, but only the latest instances of perennial challenges. Indeed, such challenges reveal much about the theoretical and practical elements of internationalist legitimacy—a legitimacy found not in a golden past or future, but provisionally wrested out of the divisions of the present, particularly out of the crucibles of the kinds of local conflicts whose pacification our era has implicitly identified as central tasks for any internationalism.

Taking the legitimacy of international intervention in local conflicts as my focal point, I argue that we reject the quest for an international community that would finally have achieved status and coherence. Rather, I advocate a focus on the situational, provisional aspect of legitimacy, on the way internationalist actors must continually seek to re-achieve legitimacy in relation to a variety of constituencies and in the face of ever-changing developments. In short, I argue for an understanding of internationalist legitimacy which is less foundational and more vulnerable, less static and more tentative, less certain and more messy.

B. Axes of Challenge, Axes of Competition

Those who challenge the legitimacy of dominant internationalist ideals and institutions usually present bids to legitimate competing alternatives. Those who attack the *status* of internationalism present an external critique of its identity as a whole, an identity they perceive as both specifiable and pernicious ('Crusader', 'Capitalist', 'Imperialist', 'American', etc). In keeping with the nature of their challenge, they usually propose a competing internationalism embodying a different identity ('Islamic', 'Communist', 'Third Worldist', 'multilateralist', etc). Bin Laden provides an example of this kind of critique and competing bid.

By contrast, those who attack the *coherence* of internationalism problematize the specifiability of its identity by highlighting the heterogeneity of its internal elements. They allege that these elements—discursive, practical, and institutional—have been wrongfully or irrationally articulated, wrongfully or irrationally assembled, or wrongfully or irrationally implemented. They may make a bid to establish a competing alternative structure by presenting a competing configuration of these elements—for example, by giving some element, such as self-determination or sovereignty, more weight relative to the other elements

---

[8] Cassese, n 6 above, at 160–63.

than it possesses in the prevailing regime, while still seeking to achieve coherence, through a new kind of coherence, between their favourite element and the others. They may, alternatively, reject the search for coherence and seek legitimacy for their perspective by defying the demand for satisfying the claims of all the elements. In opposition to the legitimacy of coherence, they may thus make a bid for a 'legitimacy through defiance'—a legitimacy that derives its power by overtly privileging certain elements and denigrating others.[9] George W Bush provides an example of this kind of legitimacy bid.

I argue that external critiques of internationalism's *status*—that is, the ideological rejection of the legal system *as a whole*—do not alone account for the most serious challenges to internationalism in the past century. Rather, the strength of these challenges stemmed from their ability to link this external opposition with an internal critique of internationalism's incoherence. In the past, for example, Nazi and Communist publicists sought to undermine the prevailing international legal order both by attacking its identity (for example, as 'Jewish' or 'Capitalist') *and* by heightening the tensions between heterogeneous principles as they related to particular local conflicts. The challengers' external critique, their attempt to delegitimate the system as a whole, weakened internationalists' authority to persuasively produce new configurations of these disparate concepts in response to new developments in local conflicts. At times, these challengers made bids for a competing legitimacy of coherence; at other times, they sought a legitimacy of defiance by fiercely denigrating previously hallowed principles and exorbitantly privileging others. This kind of linkage between external and internal critique, and between critique and competing legitimacy bids, has played a very powerful role at various junctures over the past century.

Such double challenges enable us to see, by contrast, the double source of internationalism's legitimacy. In periods of internationalist self-confidence, its internal tensions have been a great resource. It has been precisely international law's ability to marshal a range of seemingly conflicting ideas about personal and collective identity and about local and international political order that has enabled it to create its most audacious experiments. The boldest of these experiments include the international regimes to settle nationalist conflicts ranging from Upper Silesia, 1923, to Kosovo, 1999. A close study of such cases show internationalists' efforts at dynamically achieving and re-achieving legitimacy—by continually persuading relevant publics that the internationally sponsored regime was producing an evolving and coherent whole out of its heterogeneous elements in response to the changing exigencies of the local situation. These kinds of local, provisional successes established the identity of internationalism as a whole, not as that of a system with a fixed ideology, but as a work in progress, subject to constant revision through situational engagement. The revisability of these experiments was

---

[9] I have explored this phenomenon in detail in 'Legitimacy through Defiance: From Goa to Iraq', 23 Wisc J Int'l L (2005) 93.

made possible precisely by the heterogeneity of their elements, by the fact that no one configuration was logically inevitable. To be sure, this revisability also meant that power could never be finally integrated into principle, because principle was in the process of constant, and contestable, permutation.

A feature of such situational attempts to achieve legitimacy is a third kind of legitimacy problem, beyond status and coherence. Precisely at the moment of its successes, internationalism has been haunted by the spectres of its discredited past, exercises of internationalist power that have been more or less thoroughly delegitimated. During the long post-1989 decade, this kind of legitimacy problem took the form of the resurgence in public debate of nearly forgotten historical terms: terms like trusteeship, protectorate, proconsul, even recolonization. These terms were deployed by both detached observers and committed partisans of the post-1989 experiments in bold internationalism: at times with the knowing wink of the ironist, at times the high tones of the pedant, and at times the angry polemics of the militant.

Though lacking the overtness of systematic opposition and the shrewdness of internal critique, the resurgence of these historical references insidiously gnaws away at internationalist legitimacy. It tarnishes the cutting-edge ventures of internationalist idealism by pairing them with delegitimated forms of outdated power. Indeed, the long post-Cold War decade seems to have forced us to frankly confront the relationship between international law's two famously contradictory talents: making the world safe for the exercise of power, and making the world safe for the highest ideals of humanity. At least after Kosovo, no one engaged in internationalist theory or practice could deny that power and idealism were thoroughly intertwined, that pure idealism and pure realpolitik had become equally quixotic aspirations. Talk about the enforcement of human rights seemed to inevitably evoke talk about proconsuls and protectorates; talk about strategic projection of power seemed to inevitably evoke talk about international legality and cross-cultural understanding. What once seemed like international law's past (colonial or quasi-colonial institutions and doctrines) and what seemed like its future (human rights and community) now seemed destined to haunt each other.

I think that this third challenge to internationalist legitimacy is a salutary element in the dynamics of legitimacy that I am emphasizing here. The inevitable haunting of internationalism by the spectres of its unsavoury past makes any final achievement of legitimacy impossible, and forces internationalists to continually seek to prove their differentiation from those spectres. Rather than dream of a final integration of power by principle, I propose that we continually goad power-holders by comparing them to those in the past who are now viewed as unprincipled. Depriving those with power of any secure legitimacy should spur them on to avoid words and deeds deserving of the most ignominious illegitimacy.

This paper, then, seeks to understand international law's attempts to achieve legitimacy in response to three kinds of challenge—attacks on the status of its identity, critiques of the coherence of its words as well as its deeds, and attempts to associate it with spectres from its unsavoury past.

2. Status

In one of his video pronouncements not long after September 11, 2001, Osama Bin Laden made a bid to be the theorist of a new attack on the status of internationalism. In this speech, he opposed 'international legitimacy' to an incompatible and superior legitimacy.

> Those who claim that they are the leaders of the Arabs and continue to appeal to the United Nations have disavowed what was revealed to Prophet Muhammad, God's peace and blessings be upon him.
>
> Those who refer things to the international legitimacy have disavowed the legitimacy of the Holy Book and the tradition of Prophet Muhammad, God's peace and blessings be upon him.[10]

To be sure, this seems a weak bid, at a theoretical level—relying on a set of clichéd oppositions between secular law and religion, between international institutions and those of a particular tradition, between self-proclaimed leaders and their authentic counterparts, and so on. Nevertheless, the challenge made up in obsessional comprehensiveness what it lacked in theoretical subtlety. In this rather lengthy manifesto, Bin Laden gave an overarching interpretation of the far-flung events of the long post-Cold War decade under the single theme of the oppression of 'Islam' by the 'West'. Somalia, Palestine, Iraq, Bosnia, Chechnya, Kashmir, even poor East Timor: Bin Laden cited all these disparate conflicts only in order to subsume them under his one grand theme. The manifesto sought to delegitimate activist internationalism in all its forms—describing actions undertaken in the name of internationalist principles, such as the interventions in Somalia and East Timor, as mere acts of power by 'Crusader forces'.

Even leaving aside this last, atavistic reference, Bin Laden's narrative was ambitious in historical scope. Reaching beyond the 1990s to the twentieth century as a whole, he declared: 'Following World War I, which ended more than 83 years ago, the whole Islamic world fell under the crusader banner.'[11] With this quite specific historical frame, Bin Laden proposed nothing less than a systematic challenge to the entirety of modern internationalism. For the origins of internationalism's proudest achievements—including human rights, self-determination, and international institutions—lie precisely in its renewal at the end of World War I, exactly 83 years prior to Bin Laden's speech.

In thinking about current responses to this latest attack on the status of internationalism, it is useful to compare them with responses to the two other most

---

[10] Bin Laden, n 1 above.   [11] Ibid.

prominent attacks of this kind: the Fascist/Nazi challenge and the Communist/ Soviet challenge. These three challenges were radically different in political intent and historical context. Nevertheless, they share a set of formal similarities, among them a broad contempt for the legitimacy of the prevailing form of internationalism, a desire to unmask the self-proclaimed universal as particular, and a bid to establish an alternative international political identity with global aspirations, such as the German *Reich* or the Communist International.

The Fascist and Communist challenges prompted a variety of responses from legal internationalists, responses which may be divided into three broad categories: the *purist responses*, the *alternative community responses*, and the *higher law responses*. Each of these responses has had its counterparts in recent years, coming into prominence with Kosovo, but accelerating after 9/11 and the invasion of Iraq.

The *purist responses* consisted simply in the reassertion of the dignity and validity of international law and internationalist principles in the face of attacks and distortions by their enemies. Purism came in many political stripes, from mainstream treatises to Popular Front manifestos. For example, after the Italian invasion of Ethiopia, a group of right-wing French intellectuals issued a pro-Italian 'Manifesto in Defense of the West', mocking the League of Nations' 'false juridical universalism'.[12] In response, a group of leftist and liberal intellectuals responded, not with an equally politicized diatribe, but rather, with a 'Manifesto for the Respect of International Law'.[13] Among other things, this manifesto defended the League of Nations, which at that 'very hour' was 'justifying its existence in the eyes of all men of good will'—surely a formalist assertion in 1935 if ever there was one. The 'falseness' of the League's universality in 1935, like that of the UN in the first half of 2003, was undeniable as an empirical matter—whether or not that universalism could be defended as a matter of normative purism.

The *alternative community responses* were more complex and took a variety of forms. In the face of undeniable ideological division, they accepted that internationalist norms and institutions could not simply claim universal status. Rather, they frankly made a claim to the creation of partial international communities to replace the fractured universal community. Often this kind of effort involved favourably contrasting the antiformalist stance of the alternative community with the legal formalism of the prevailing system.

For example, some justified Munich, 1938, as the site of a concrete grappling with real problems, bypassing the formalistic impasses of the League. Such commentators argued that an international conclave embodying the 'spirit of Geneva'[14] had transpired in Munich, while only international law's dead letter

---

[12] Manifesto for the Defense of the West, *Le Temps* (4 October 1935), at 1 (all translations mine unless otherwise noted).

[13] Manifesto for the Respect of International Law, *Le Populaire* (5 October 1935) at 1.

[14] An Overshadowed Assembly, Editorial, *Times of London*, (3 October 1938) at 5.

remained in Switzerland. A similar discourse had begun to develop in 1935 to justify Franco-British plans to make a deal with Italy on Ethiopia.[15] In both of these cases, the alternative international community, though partial, united ideological allies and adversaries: the French, British, and Germans in Munich, the French, British, and Italians in the Ethiopia negotiations.

A different variant of the *alternative community response* focuses not on an informal coalition between ideological adversaries, but on an overt presentation of an ideological alliance as the true internationalist community, even if non-universal. This strategy was most fully deployed during the Cold War. The Soviets and the Americans each presented their respective partisan alliances as embodying true internationalism, at the expense of a UN viewed as either paralyzed or under the sway of the ideological adversary.[16] In these cases, the alternative community was a select group of states united by substantive values, as opposed to the merely formally grounded—and merely numerically universal—UN. A somewhat weaker form of this variant developed in the aftermath of Munich, in which some in France sought to forsake the irremediable fractures of Europe in favour of a '*repli impérial*'—not so much an assertion that the French empire represented the interests of the whole world, but that the empire, rather than Europe, constituted the centre of gravity of the French world.[17]

These *alternative community responses* were very elaborate precursors to the 'illegal-yet-legitimate' school of international lawyers in response to the Kosovo intervention[18]—and the far smaller 'illegal-yet-legitimate' school in response to

[15] For some versions of these plans, See 'Summary of the Franco-British Suggestions', 16 League of Nations OJ 1620 (August 1935); 'Note of the Committee of Five to the Ethiopian and Italian Representatives, September 1935', in Canadian Secretary of State for External Affairs (ed), *Documents Relating to the Italo-Ethiopian Conflict* (1936) 54; Text of the Suggestions for an Agreed Settlement of the Conflict, December 1935, in ibid. at 173. See also the ambivalent response of leading international lawyers to the proposals, eg G Scelle, 'La Politique extérieure française et la SDN', 10 *Année politique française et étrangère*, (1935) 292–3; Charles Rousseau, 'Le Conflit Italo-Ethiopien', 45 *Revue Générale de droit international public*, (1938) 61–2.

[16] Compare the US justification of the invasion of the Dominican Republic, 1965, with the Soviet justification of the invasion of Czechoslovakia, 1968. See Leonard Meeker, 'The Dominican Situation in International Law', 53 Dep't of State Bull (1965) 60; Pravda article on Czechoslovakia, 7 ILM, (1968) 1323. The US justification relied heavily on the Organization of American States, as an international community based on the substantive value of anti-communism; the Soviet justification relied heavily on the Warsaw Pact, as a community based on the substantive value of Marxism-Leninism. Both at least implicitly acknowledged the formal illegality of their actions under the Charter. It should perhaps be noted here that the 'United Nations' originated as such a partial international community: the coalition of forces arrayed against the Axis Powers.

[17] See, eg an editorial in the newspaper, *La République*, published a short time after Munich. Under the title 'From Munich to Our Colonial Empire', the editorial declared: 'Our own Central Europe is the African continent. Our country is too great for quarrels between Germans and Slavs ever-resurgent in the Balkans.' Quoted in Charles-Robert Ageron, 'A propos d'une prétendu politique de "repli impérial" dans la France des années 1938–1939', 12 Revue d'histoire maghrebine, (1978) 225.

[18] See, eg The Independent International Commission on Kosovo, *The Kosovo Report* (2000) 186.

the invasion of Iraq.[19] In fact, one can divide the recent 'illegal-yet-legitimate' responses into three groups, each with analogies to their historical precursors. Some versions resembled the Munich/Ethiopia method of constructing a pragmatic community of ideologically disparate states, a community which claims to embody the spirit of the formally legal institutions, while bypassing their procedures. Other versions resembled the Cold War Warsaw Pact/NATO method of constructing a partial community grounded in particular substantive values, designed to oppose an ideological adversary. In the case of Kosovo, the question of what kind of alternative community should replace the UN partly depended on individual publicists' attitude towards Russia: a state seen by some as amenable to pragmatic cooperation, while viewed by others as the potential leader of some vaguely perceived pan-Slavic ideology. Finally, the valorizations of an 'American empire' heard in some US policymaking quarters as the long decade ended, and particularly after September 11, may be viewed as an assertion that the US is the true embodiment of internationalism in our time, however few its allies—or as simply a *repli impérial* in the French style. 'Illegal-yet-legitimate' justifications of the US invasion have thus sometimes taken the form of presenting the US as the only effective agency of the true internationalist interest, an interest impeded and betrayed by the majority of the UN, and have sometimes taken the form of presenting US policy as a *repli Américain,* directed at safeguarding primarily the ideals of an American sphere of influence.

A third kind of response to the Fascist and Communist challenges, the *higher law responses,* consisted in attempts to surmount ideological division by hoisting law ever-further upwards to achieve a legitimate position above the fray. One can distinguish two strands in these responses, the principled strand and the functionalist strand. The principled variant seeks a set of principles, such as peace or minimal distributive fairness among relevant states, which their proponents portray as transcending deep ideological divides. This variant played an important role in the discussions of 'peaceful change' in the 1930s, in reaction to the Fascist/Nazi challenge. Of course, the transcendental principles put forward were historically contingent, to put it mildly. Among the principles of minimal distributive fairness at play in these discussions were notions about a fair distribution of colonial possessions between the colonial 'haves', France and Britain, and the colonial 'have-nots', Germany and Italy.[20]

The second, functionalist, strand seeks to ground the legitimacy of international law in interests that states share by virtue of their common condition *as states.*[21] Functionalist higher-law responses often argue for a long-term perspective. While

---

[19]   See, eg, Anne-Marie Slaughter, 'Good Reasons for Going Around the U.N', *New York Times,* 18 March 2003, at p. A31.

[20]   See, eg FH Leitner, 'Les problèmes généraux du "Peaceful Change"', in Fédération universitaire internationale, Problèmes du 'Peaceful Change' 78 (1936); JL Kunz, The Problem of Revision in International Law, 33 AJIL 54 (1939).

[21]   See, eg Lissitzyn, n 6 above, at 68–9.

acknowledging that ideological differences may fracture the international community for a while, they assert that the deeper interests that all states share will ultimately assert themselves. The two strands of the higher-law responses, the principled strand and the functionalist strand, are often interwoven in the work of a single author, together bolstering the claim that a legitimate international law can be established despite the appearance of a 'divided world'.[22]

To summarize these three responses to attacks on internationalism's status: where the *purist responses* reassert a pristine, universal international law against a deceitful double, and the *alternative community responses* accept the challenge of a divided world by constructing a partial alternative to the formally universal community, the *higher-law responses* seek to raise international law above the divided world and establish a relegitimated, if thinner, internationalism, beyond the superficial fractures of a given historical moment.

I would argue that none of these responses have been particularly persuasive in the past. I would also argue that the danger that their weakness posed to international law did not lie in its supposed need for an unassailable theoretical foundation. Rather, the danger lay in the damage the ideological challenges posed to international law's ability to present itself as a unitary and legitimate authority able to persuasively and dynamically reconfigure its heterogeneous internal elements to meet new local crises. For the Fascist and Communist challenges coupled their systematic opposition with a kind of challenge that the Bin Laden-type opposition has not yet pursued, that of internal critique.

3. Coherence

One of the secrets of international law's resilience over the past century has resided in its productive use of the tension between the heterogeneous elements of its doctrinal and institutional toolbox for responding to local conflicts. The elements of this toolbox—sovereignty and self-determination, minority protection and individual rights, local democracy and international tutelage, local and international tribunals, and so on—have different and often incompatible historical and conceptual foundations. Yet, it is precisely the fact that these legal tools do not cohere in any logically necessary fashion that has permitted the best legal innovators to distribute them differently in individual legal regimes, regimes that present themselves as custom-designed for the unique exigencies of particular local conflicts. And as such situations evolve, it is precisely the tensions between the legal tools that make possible the flexibility to redistribute their relative weight to meet changing needs—to re-achieve legitimacy through a new and different coherence of the elements. International law's strength in approaching local conflicts

---

[22] See, eg Cassese n 6 above, at 123–64.

thus does not depend on the provision of 'clear mandates'.[23] On the contrary, it depends on complex, heterogeneously composed mandates—and on the presence of an agile and legitimate implementer of those mandates, able to use the conflicts between the elements of the international regime as a resource for responding to changing or previously misunderstood features of the situation.

Nevertheless, the secret of international law's resilience is also its Achilles heel. The relative stability of the contents of this toolbox over the past century represents a potential source of blindness for internationalism insofar as it leads decision makers to place very different conflicts in similar conceptual frames. Equally dangerously, the heterogeneity of the tools has served the goals of those who seek to subvert both the local internationalist experiments and the system as a whole. The two major historical challenges to legal internationalism, Fascism and Communism, drew much of their strength from internally subverting the prevailing internationalism in particular cases—exploiting the tensions between the elements in local internationalist experiments to destroy the legitimacy of the prevailing internationalism as a whole.

Alongside their broad contempt for the system as a whole, these challenges thus drew much of their resources in particular cases from that very system. They combined external and internal critique, attacks on internationalism's status, and attacks on its coherence. For example, the Italian claim to Ethiopia and the German claim to Sudetenland were justified in terms of some of the core (albeit heterogeneous) concepts of the Versailles settlement—self-determination for some groups, international tutelage for other ('backward') groups, and minority rights for still other groups.[24] As a result, elite opinion makers in Western Europe, including international lawyers, often found it difficult to respond to these claims without conceding considerable conceptual and even political ground—or, in the words of one contemporary observer, found it difficult to do so 'without belying themselves'.[25] Thus, the Italians criticized the sovereignty of Ethiopia on the grounds that it was just as 'backward' and deserving of tutelage as territories under League Mandate or the colonial rule of the British and French; they claimed that the structure of the Ethiopian state flew in the face of the self-determination or minority rights of the country's non-Amharic peoples; and they claimed that Italian rule would embody the principle of internationalist tutelage. Some prominent liberal international lawyers found it difficult to defend the sovereignty of Ethiopia in light of these other principles. Having conceded much on the terrain of coherence, they responded on the terrain of status—contending that Fascist Italy could not properly represent the international community in the otherwise justified task of placing the

---

[23] See contra Report of the Panel on United Nations Peace Operations ('the Brahimi Report') (2000), available at <http://www.un.org/peace/reports/peace_operations/>.

[24] I discuss this at length in 'Beyond Colonialism and Nationalism? Ethiopia, Czechoslovakia, and "Peaceful Change"', 6 Nordic J of In'l L (1996) 421.

[25] P Teissonière, 'Faut-il résister aux violents?', 49 La Paix par le Droit, (1938) 13.

country under trusteeship. But the ideological divisions of the 1930s, and the accompanying external attacks on the international system, meant that it was no longer possible to achieve consensus on the identity of the true agents of the international community.

Similar examples can be drawn from the history of Communist challenges to legal internationalism. These included the early anticolonialism of left-wing Communists in the 1920s, which coupled an internal attack on the prima facie racism of the unequal application of self-determination with an external attack on the League of Nations as an 'association of imperialist pirates'.[26] Later examples include Soviet defences of their various unilateral interventions. These defences, which mirrored US justifications of analogous interventions, exploited the tensions between prevailing international norms, and linked this coherence challenge to an assertion about the status of the Warsaw Pact as an alternative international community.[27] Thus, over the course of nearly a century, legal internationalists have been confounded not by totalizing rejections of their system standing alone, but rather by the ability of the challengers to couple their ideological rejection with internal critique.

The strength of such challenges was thus due to the fact that internationalism's resilience has not resided in purist obliviousness, Manichaean divisions between competing international communities, or Herculean attainments of a higher law above partisan conflict. Rather, it has consisted in Legal Realist-style exploitation of contradictoriness and inconsistency as resources that facilitate case-specific complexity and flexibility. The significance of past ideological attacks on the status of internationalism as a whole stemmed from the damage they inflicted on internationalists' authority to persuasively reconfigure their disparate legal concepts in response to changing local conflicts—to establish new legitimacies of coherence. The challengers attacked the particular configuration of international legal elements laid down for particular conflicts by the prevailing international authorities; their external attacks crippled the ability of those authorities to establish new configurations.

Panicked responses to the current crisis in internationalist legitimacy, to the extent that they are provoked solely by the prospect of a new totalizing rejection of the system, are thus misplaced. Current status challenges, such as the Islamicist and US challenges, are likely to have a significant effect on activist internationalism only if the challengers attempt to undermine the system from within as well as from without. Consider, for example, the US administration of Iraq, which lacks status legitimacy in the eyes of most of the world. One could imagine a US occupation authority that was able to overcome its status illegitimacy and achieve a legitimacy of coherence through a skilful deployment of the various elements in the international toolbox for local conflicts. Of course, whether the actual US

---

[26] Quoted in Alan Rose, *Surrealism and Communism* (1991) 132.
[27] See Meeker and Pravda articles, n 16 above.

administration of Iraq will ever be able to achieve legitimacy in this way is, as of this writing, highly questionable.

Beyond the skill and intent of the American administrators, there are two key obstacles. First, the high degree of status illegitimacy of the US occupation makes the actions of the American administrators suspect both locally and internationally. Secondly, the US justification of the invasion of Iraq involved not only an attack on the status of internationalism embodied in the UN, but also—at least in some official pronouncements—a *defiant attack on the coherence* of international norms. The pronouncements I have in mind are those that suggest that the US was rejecting the legitimacy of coherence by denigrating some principles at the expense of others, rather than merely seeking a reconfiguration of their relative weights—in other words, making a bid to achieve *legitimacy through defiance*. Bids for legitimacy through defiance frankly seek approval for the boldness of their actions precisely by virtue of the fact that they defy some prevailing norms. Such bids thus may be viewed as seeking a *surplus legitimacy*—attempting to use the very legitimacy-deficit of their actions as a basis for a higher legitimacy.

A brief comparison between justifications of the use of force in Kosovo, 1999, and Iraq, 2003, can illuminate the distinctiveness of bids for legitimacy through defiance. Both uses of force were justified through exploiting the tensions between international legal principles. The principles restricting the use of force stated in the Charter were juxtaposed to principles permitting unilateral uses of force, such as humanitarian intervention and expansive notions of self-defence, purportedly grounded in customary law; the substantive obligations the Security Council imposed on particular states, Yugoslavia and Iraq, were juxtaposed to the Council's refusal to grant enforcement authority to other states. Both Kosovo and Iraq thus implicated conflicts among substantive principles, between treaty and custom, and between substance and procedure.

However, where the Kosovo justifications tended to make the effort to present a competing configuration of the prevailing international requirements, some of the US pronouncements on Iraq tended to denigrate, rather than reconfigure, the elements disfavouring the intervention. NATO pronouncements on Kosovo, for example, tried to show that the intervention represented a legitimate, even if novel, form of cooperation between the UN and NATO. In Bruno Simma's words:

Indeed, one is immediately struck by the degree to which the efforts of NATO and its member states follow the 'logic' of, and have been expressly linked to, the treatment of the Kosovo crisis by the Security Council. In an address delivered in Bonn on 4 February 1999, US Deputy Secretary of State Strobe Talbott referred to an 'unprecedented and promising degree of synergy' in the sense that the UN and NATO, among other institutions, had 'pooled their energies and strengths on behalf of an urgent common cause'; as to the specific contribution of the UN, he saw this in the fact that 'the UN has lent its political and moral authority to the Kosovo effort'.[28]

---

[28] Bruno Simma, 'NATO, the UN and the Use of Force: Legal Aspects', 10 EJIL 11 (1999). Simma rejects the legal soundness of this position.

Despite the seeming violation of formal legal norms in their accepted configuration, NATO officials attempted to make their actions appear to conform to the logic of the principles as a whole, once their relative authority had been reconfigured. In other words, they tried to present an alternative legitimacy of coherence.

By contrast, many of the US pronouncements prior to the invasion of Iraq frankly declared American intentions to defy the prevailing international legal system. The most overt example of this stance was provided by George W Bush in declaring that it was the UN that had to 'prove to the world whether it's going to be relevant or whether it's going to be a League of Nations, irrelevant'.[29] Bush thus made an open challenge to the status of the UN, attacking the legitimacy of its identity.

However, his challenge was not limited to its status aspect. Rather, it also focused on the coherence of the system's internal normative elements, frankly rejecting any obligation to accommodate them all. This aspect of the challenge frankly declared American intentions to ignore some prevailing norms, rather than to reconfigure the normative system. In particular, Bush attacked the UN's purported unwillingness to enforce the substantive obligations it had imposed on Iraq, and stressed the importance of the substantive obligations at the expense of the procedural norms for enforcement.

We will work with the UN Security Council for the necessary resolutions. But the purposes of the United States should not be doubted. The Security Council resolutions will be enforced—the just demands of peace and security will be met—or action will be unavoidable.[30]

Bush was thus asserting that the US would not be engaged in a simple act of flouting the UN, as he might have if he were only attacking the status of the UN. Rather, he announced that the US would be upholding some of its norms at the expense of others—linking his attack on the *status* of the UN, its identity as an 'irrelevant League of Nations', with an attack on the legitimacy of the *coherence* of its norms. And he sought legitimacy for the US action precisely by virtue of its bold willingness to violate certain norms, particularly procedural norms, in order to support others; this was a bid for a surplus legitimacy for brash, taboo-breaking behaviour by means of an attack on both the status and coherence of the international system.

To be sure, this bid for legitimacy through defiance generally failed outside the US and the substantive case for the invasion was based on a mass of false factual assertions. Nevertheless, it offers a clear example of such a bid. It is also important to note that bids for legitimacy through defiance have come from across the political spectrum at various times. There are few people who would not view them sympathetically in at least some circumstance—except perhaps for formalists of the '*pereat mundus, fiat jus!*' school.

---

[29] Bush, n 2 above.
[30] Ibid.

In the particular situation of the US in Iraq, however, this bid for legitimacy through defiance has presented serious difficulties for its protagonist. As I have noted, the US lacks international status legitimacy in Iraq due to the failure of its bid to secure support for the invasion through defying the international system. In the years since the invasion, it has tried to achieve a legitimacy of coherence by attempting to show the implementation of widely shared international values in its conduct of the occupation. Yet, the pre-war US attack on the coherence of international norms, as well as on the status of international institutions, has made its bids for a new legitimacy of coherence very fragile. Having sought a surplus legitimacy for its coherence-defying action in invading Iraq, it has been ill-equipped to seek the legitimacy of coherence in its self-proclaimed role as internationalist administrator of that country. Nor has the actual conduct of the American occupation of Iraq come close to providing the factual basis for such a legitimacy bid.

4. 'Our Law': Producing Unity through Heterogeneity

I have argued that the secret of internationalism's resilience over the past century has resided in its productive use of the tension between the heterogeneous elements of its doctrinal and institutional toolbox for responding to local conflicts. To portray a successful example of the production of legitimacy out of disparate concepts, I turn in this section to an incident from the early days of the UN Mission in Kosovo (UNMIK). It is in such attempts to manage local crises that the alchemy of international coordination of heterogeneous concepts can be seen in action. And yet, it is precisely here, when the alchemy has worked its unifying magic, that international law rediscovers its unsettling historical doubles—internationalist regimes doubled by the word 'protectorate', and internationalist administrators doubled by the word 'proconsul'.

The incident to which I turn presents a striking allegory of the dynamics of situational legitimacy, the provisional construction of internationalism in a particular context out of heterogeneous conceptions and practices. This incident was widely reported in the elite Western press, exemplified by this symptomatic account in *Le Monde*:

'A new Kosovo is beginning; we have changed the law', declared Mr. Kouchner to the judges and journalists who surrounded him at the meeting. It had been convened, they explain at UNMIK, after a cascade of resignation threats by those who formed the nucleus of the new 'independent and multiethnic' judicial system of Kosovo. A week ago, three judges from Prizren launched the movement. They rejected Section 3 of 'Regulation 1' (signed by Mr. Kouchner on July 25th to define his own powers), which declared that 'The laws applicable in the territory of Kosovo prior to 24 March 1999 shall continue to apply in Kosovo insofar as they do not conflict with [internationally recognized human rights standards].' A campaign was then launched by the KLA against what it interpreted as the maintenance in Kosovo of Yugoslav laws which were, in fact if not always in the text, an instrument of Serb repression in the province. Judges were then subjected to pressures to resign. Nipping this offensive in the bud, Bernard Kouchner apologized before 50 of the judges for having 'insufficiently consulted them, especially before publishing Regulation 1'. Assuring them that his mission is to 'permit the emergence of an autonomous administration', he promised not to take any further decisions without 'involving the people of Kosovo'. A working group, joined by international experts, will draft the law of Kosovo—*our law, which is neither Serb nor Yugoslav*', he emphasized. This work will be coordinated with the Council of Europe, which is supposed to present a first 'purge' of existing laws at the end of September.... The great majority of judges declared themselves satisfied with the statements of the UN 'proconsul' and promised to get to work to rapidly fill the legal void that has prevented the trials—but not the detention—of hundreds of people already arrested by KFOR in Kosovo.[31]

One would have had to invent this story if it hadn't been conveniently reported in the press. This real-life allegory contains all the quandaries of the robust internationalism of the long post-1989 decade. A UN administration established itself in a territory on the basis of a use of force of controversial legality. The appointment of a famous humanitarian as the head of the territorial administration symbolized the internationalist desire to transmute this questionable force into legitimate law, to absorb power into principle. In accordance with this desire, Kouchner's first act was to attempt this transmutation by establishing a *legal* framework 'to define his own *powers*'. This act was particularly urgent since the Kosovo Force, itself already an internationalist transmutation of NATO, had arrested hundreds of people outside of a legal framework. The 'new beginning of Kosovo,' declared Kouchner, was not the NATO intervention, but the fact that 'we have changed the law'—a pronouncement that was not an observation of fact, but rather, a bid for the construction of legitimacy.

Yet the question of what constituted legitimate legal change turned out to be a highly contestable matter. Kouchner appears to have first conceived his task as a matter of legal technique, the establishment of a neutral legal framework to permit the work of his administration to begin. He sought to achieve this goal by declaring that 'law' would now prevail over military force and by subjecting domestic law to the test of international human rights standards. In defining the meaning of 'law' as the law in effect before the start of the exercise of NATO power,[32] he chose the seemingly neutral approach of legal continuity, the protection of acquired rights. The Kosovo Liberation Army (KLA) and its allied judges, in response, challenged the notion that the question of a rule of 'law' was

---

[31] 'Vers une loi du Kosovo, ni serbe ni yougoslave', *Le Monde,* 17 August 1999 (emphasis in the original).

[32] The relevant portion of Regulation 1 reads: 'The laws applicable in the territory of Kosovo prior to 24 March 1999 shall continue to apply in Kosovo insofar as they do not conflict with [internationally recognized human rights standards], the fulfilment of the mandate given to UNMIK under United Nations Security Council resolution 1244 (1999), or the present or any other regulation issued by UNMIK.' UNMIK/REG/1999/1 Section 3 (25 July 1999).

simply a technical matter. By asserting that *this* 'law' had a partisan identity, that of Serbian supremacy, they rejected the neutrality of legal continuity. Nor were they satisfied with the purging filter of international standards, seeking, instead, a total rejection of the illegitimate Yugoslav legal source. Indeed, Kouchner's law, which pretended to the neutral identity of impartial technique, became for them a mere tributary of this partisan source.

This kind of attack on internationalist legitimacy may be interpreted as proceeding from an internal critique of the *coherence* of the elements of the Kosovo regime to an external critique of its *identity*. The internal critique was aimed at Kouchner's initial configuration of the famously conflicting elements in the UNMIK mandate: embodied in Resolution 1244's call for: (1) 'the *sovereignty*...of Yugoslavia'; (2) '*autonomy* and...*self-administration* for Kosovo,'; and (3) administration by '*international* civil and security presences'.[33] Given the many tensions latent in this multiple mandate, Regulation 1's provision banning legal rules incompatible with Resolution 1244 (in addition to those that conflicted with international human rights standards) provided ample room for internal critique from almost any perspective. The Albanian opposition rejected the version of coherence among 1244's elements embodied in Regulation 1's stance of technical legal neutrality. It accompanied this critique of Regulation 1's bid for a legitimacy of coherence with an alternative bid for a legitimacy of defiance—rejecting the notion that the principle of Yugoslav sovereignty should play any role at all. Finally, it implicitly delegitimated Kouchner's internationalist status as a whole, accusing it of partiality, demoting him from his identity above the fray to that of merely one player in the conflict.

While one may only imagine his private frustration, Kouchner's admirable public recovery from this 'snafu' shows that he understood precisely what was involved. Without internationalist status legitimacy, the delicate work of coordination among conflicting groups, let alone legal concepts, would be impossible. He immediately set about, therefore, to ground his authority in a different concept of legitimacy than the one with which he began his tenure. By reshaping his internationalist identity, he sought to relegitimate his status, thus making it possible for him to proceed with the work of reconfiguring the elements of the internationalist regime for Kosovo and make a new bid for a legitimacy of coherence.

Gathering the Albanian judges, he made an explicit appeal for an alliance with them. This appeal involved a different identity for international authority—no longer that of neutral technocracy, but rather, that of an ally, however asymmetrical, with a deserving population. He apologized for his failure to consult and promised henceforth to 'involve the people'—hardly necessary measures when he had conceived the matter at hand as merely technical. He encapsulated his new stance in his declaration that the law to be drafted would be '*our law, which is neither Serb nor Yugoslav*'.

---

[33] UN SC Res. 1244, S/RES/1244 (1999).

A thought-provoking and ambivalent phrase. For if the 'our' in 'our law' referred to the pure universality of internationalism (the royal 'our'), one would have rather expected the rest of the phrase to read 'neither Serb nor Albanian'— that is, it would be a neutral law, not ethnically marked. By contrast, 'neither Serb nor Yugoslav' might suggest that it would be Albanian. This would suggest that Kouchner was abandoning a bid for a universalist internationalism in favour of a partial community that frankly acknowledged its partiality. Yet, if Kouchner were purporting to be speaking solely as the representative of the Albanians, then the 'our' would have been sufficient—the 'neither...nor' phrase would seem a bit like protesting too much. In fact, the very structure of the phrase 'neither... nor' evoked impartiality, even though the terms that followed those conjunctions partly confounded that evocation.

The ambivalences of his phrase, I would argue, suggests that Kouchner sought to achieve his legitimacy by doing something other than asserting *either* neutrality *or* partisan identity. Rather, Kouchner's 'our' strove to effect a complex alliance of two seemingly conflicting sources of legitimacy, that of overarching international authority and that of Albanian nationalism. He sought to achieve his legitimacy through a paradoxical alliance between the two—an internationalism that wagers its legitimacy on its ability to respond to the deepest needs of nationalist partisans.[34]

At least in this crisis, Kouchner apparently succeeded. By reshaping the identity of his internationalism, he made credible his pledge to reconfigure the conflicting internal elements of the legal regime called for by Resolution 1244. The mass resignation of the judges was averted.

Kouchner eventually repealed Regulation 1, replacing it with Regulation 24. The new Regulation provided that Kosovo would be governed by the law in effect before 22 March 1989—that is, the law that prevailed during the period of Kosovo's autonomy within Serbia. This 1989 law cannot be said to be 'neither Serb nor Yugoslav' in a pure sense. Regulation 24 can, however, be seen as a reconfiguration of the internally heterogeneous mandate of Resolution 1244. 'Our law', as embodied in Regulation 24, would be neither solely Yugoslav nor solely Albanian—nor solely international. Rather, it would be a new configuration of conflicting elements, a new appeal for legitimacy made to the relevant publics.

To be sure, as Kouchner discovered, identifying the relevant publics may be a tricky matter to achieve in advance. Kouchner may have thought his public was a community of lawyers, perhaps international, perhaps Yugoslav, perhaps Kosovar. He may have thought his public was the UNMIK staff or the NGO world. He discovered, through its resistance, that a key relevant public was the organized sphere of Kosovar nationalism.

---

[34] I have explored this 'alliance' in detail elsewhere. See, eg ' "But the Alternative is Despair": European Nationalism and the Modernist Renewal of International Law', 106 Harv L Rev (1993) 1792.

Conversely, as this example shows, the relevant public may only discover itself through finding itself addressed by an act of internationalist power. One might imagine that some of the Albanian judges may have shared a technocratic idea about the rule of law until finding themselves jolted by the reinstatement of Yugoslav law—or by finding themselves jolted by pressure from the KLA. Finally, internationalist actors themselves may only discover their full identity through this dynamic. Kouchner was undoubtedly more surprised than anyone to discover his identity as a Serb puppet (that is, in the eyes of the KLA) and to be obliged to reconstruct his identity as an ally (however provisional and asymmetrical) of Albanian nationalism.

Internationalist actors like Kouchner must, therefore, necessarily take the risk of appealing for legitimacy without a guarantee of success or even certainty about the addressees of their appeals. And with each new fragile configuration of conflicting elements, the cycle can always begin again, as new challenges unsettle the provisional equilibrium among the regime's elements. Legitimacy must be continually reachieved—and each new achievement will be a new configuration of those elements.

Finally, at the very hour of his success, Kouchner managed to evoke a different kind of legitimacy-trouble. For in reporting the result of this speech, *Le Monde* tells us that the *'great majority of judges declared themselves satisfied with the statements of the UN "proconsul"'*. Try as he might to ally himself with the Albanians, Kouchner could not shake off another doubling of his role as legitimate international authority: this time not by the image of him as a Yugoslav proxy, but as an imperial 'proconsul'. The term 'proconsul' may be one the Albanians would have used or it may reflect *Le Monde's* elite irony about internationalist idealism. But it suggests the impossibility of any definitive achievement of internationalist legitimacy. International humanitarian, Albanian ally, or imperial 'proconsul'? Kouchner's variable ability to govern Kosovo, the changing measure of his legitimacy, depended on his ability to recognize these doublings of legitimacy and on his ability to shift among their attendant roles.

The 'our law' allegory presents the construction of legitimacy out of the shifts between its conflicting identities and elements diachronically, in terms of a dynamic unfolding. The UNMIK-promulgated Constitution of Kosovo (2001),[35] by contrast, presents this kind of construction in the form of a synchronic legal structure. This Constitution follows in the great tradition of internationalist attempts to resolve nationalist conflict through complex legal experiments, a tradition whose illustrious precursors include the interwar regimes for Upper Silesia, Danzig, and the Saar, the Palestine Partition Resolution of 1947, and the Washington and Dayton Accords for Bosnia in the 1990s—composite regimes,

---

[35] 'Constitutional Framework for Provisional Self-Government', UNMIK/REG/2001/9 (15 May 2001), available at <http://www.unmikonline.org/constframework.htm>.

at once local and international, designed for the pacification of seemingly intract-able conflict.

Among the features shared by these experiments, I would like to designate two here. First, they create a legal space for themselves by bracketing the question of sovereignty, either by explicitly deferring the question to a later time (the Saar and Kosovo), superimposing a unified, experimental regime on top of sovereign div-isions (Upper Silesia, Palestine), or creating a novel a-sovereign entity (Danzig).[36] Secondly, they seek to achieve their goals of resolving nationalist conflict by juxtaposing, in a single legal regime, elements that seem to be incompatible, or at least that stand in tension with each other. The competing elements may include partition (between sovereigns or ethnic units) and unity (economic or political), minority rights and individual rights, universal suffrage and representation based on ethnic identity, local judiciary and on-site international or mixed courts.

The tension among the elements that compose such regimes arises from the implicit reference each makes to distinct notions of personal and collective iden-tity, as well as distinct ideas about political organization. At least since the end of World War I, such regimes have wagered their legitimacy on the notion that a high level of legal complexity is needed to match the level of the complex-ity of the local conflict. Legitimacy would be attained when such complex and heterogeneous constructions could prove their ability both to pacify nationalist conflict and to provide all nationalist factions with a sense that their deepest longings have been satisfied. The legitimacy of any particular such regime, their proponents have contended, would emerge out of a suitable configuration of the conflicting concepts and institutions in the international toolbox. Thus, para-doxically, the advocates of such regimes have believed that *only a configuration of conflicting legal elements can achieve legitimacy in such conflicts.* In my studies of the interwar period,[37] I have used the phrase 'Modernist faith' to describe this paradoxical set of beliefs—a faith, now over 83 years old, rightly perceived by challengers such as Bin Laden as a rival to their own faith. The structure of Modernist faith shows the importance of the two dimensions of legitimacy I have highlighted thus far: (1) a situational legitimacy of coherence, that is, recognition by relevant publics that regimes embodying particular configur-ations of the conflicting elements in the international toolbox constitute a good response to local exigencies; and (2) status legitimacy, that is, recognition by relevant publics of the good title to 'internationalism' of the authority construct-ing and administering such regimes.

Following in this tradition, the Kosovo Constitution rests on the suspension of the question of sovereignty. It combines a variety of heterogeneous elements,

---

[36] See '"But the Alternative is Despair"': European Nationalism and the Modernist Renewal of International Law', n 34 above, at 1874–97.

[37] Ibid. See also Nathaniel Berman, 'Modernism, Nationalism, and the Rhetoric of Reconstruction', in Michael Loriaux and Cecilia Lynch (eds), *Law and Moral Action in World Politics* (1999).

which implicitly refer to distinct, and potentially conflicting, ideas of identity. Such elements include individual human rights and a variety of institutional-izations of the rights of 'Communities', defined by ethnic, religious or linguis-tic identity.[38] Such 'Community' rights include very robust versions of the kinds of rights originally developed to protect 'minorities' in a variety of inter-national instruments since 1919. In relation to the long historical debate about whether minority rights should focus more on groups or individuals,[39] the Kosovo Constitution opts in several specific ways for group-centred provisions for the region's 'Communities'. For example, rather than simply providing for non-interference with group educational institutions, it mandates public fund-ing of 'Community' schools. More strikingly, the Constitution reserves seats for non-Albanians in the Assembly.[40] It also provides for a complicated procedure, related to provisions in the Bosnia accords, whereby members of a 'Community' in the Assembly may temporarily block legislation that they declare violates the 'vital interests of the Community'.[41] The Constitution declares membership in a Community to be a wholly voluntary matter and non-membership to bring no 'disadvantage'.[42] Yet, it is clear from these provisions that non-participation in Communities could 'disadvantage' a Kosovar in the distribution of economic and political power—just one example of how the individualist and 'Community' strands in the document stand in very concrete tension.

The Constitution's judicial framework also juxtaposes ethnic-based and inter-nationalist conceptions of a proper judiciary. The Constitution provides for both international and local judges.[43] The identity of the local judges should 'reflect the diversity of the people of Kosovo'.[44] The Constitution leaves latitude in the hands of the Special Representative of the Secretary General to determine the number of international judges and the criteria for their appointment.[45] The balance between the competing elements in these provisions leaves room for reconfiguration aimed at achieving legitimacy among the various relevant con-stituencies. Such reconfiguration has occurred a number of times, including the

---

[38] cf. Chapters 3 and 4 of the Kosovo 'Constitutional Framework', n 35 above.

[39] See, eg O Janowsky, *The Jews and Minority Rights, 1898–1919* (1933). For more recent examples of such divergent views on minority rights, compare the relatively individual-rights focused approach of the European Framework Convention on National Minorities, reprinted in 34 ILM 351 (1995), with the more group-focused approach of the prior Council of Europe's Parliamentary Assembly 'Recommendation 1201, On an Additional Protocol on the Rights of National Minorities to the European Convention on Human Rights', reprinted in 14 HRLJ 144 (1993).

[40] See 'Constitutional Framework,' n 35 above, Chapter 9.1.3.

[41] Ibid., Chapter 9.1.39.

[42] Ibid., Chapter 4.2.

[43] Ibid., Chapter 9.4.7.

[44] Ibid.

[45] Ibid. The criteria were adumbrated in provisions such as Regulation No. 2001/2 Amending UNMIK Regulation No 2000/6, 'On the Appointment and Removal from Office of International Judges and International Prosecutors,' 12 January 2001, available at <http://www.unmikonline.org/regulations/2001/reg02-01.html>.

incident with the Albanian judges described in detail above. In a very different vein, a November 2001 Yugoslav-UNMIK agreement[46] provided for increasing the number of international judges (especially for 'inter-ethnic' cases) and of ethnic Serb judges.

In the history of such local, yet international, regimes, the unity of the complex legal construction may have an on-site human or institutional embodiment, such as the Governing Commission of the Saar. In other regimes, such as Upper Silesia, the unity may simply be intended to emerge from the relation between the elements, often ultimately placed under the distant authority of the Councils of the League or of the UN. In either case, the unity of the regime as a whole may stand in tension with the constitutive parts. In Kosovo, supreme authority is vested in the Special Representative of the Secretary General, whose authority is not 'affect[ed] or diminish[ed]'[47] by the Constitutionally established institutions—which are nonetheless intended to be precisely those of '*self-government*'.

Despite this ultimate tension, the entire document, with all its heterogeneities, expresses the classic Modernist faith: the composite regime seeks to respond to 'the legitimate aspirations of the people of Kosovo to live in freedom, in peace, and in friendly relations with other people in the region'. The legitimacy of any particular regime of this sort depends on its ability to persuade others, both the conflicting local populations and the international community, of the validity of Modernist faith in its particular configuration of conflicting principles—and on its ability to emulate Kouchner in a flexible willingness to reconfigure them if necessary. This ability depends on the agility of the embodiment of international authority in the particular situation, as well as on the status legitimacy of internationalism in the world generally.

Nevertheless, as we saw in the 'our law' allegory, even at the hour of the success of such endeavours, the entire complex structure remains haunted by the spectre of those disconcerting words: protectorate and proconsul. The shrewd role shifts of Kouchner, the skilful balancing of the Constitution—all this hard-won legitimacy is unable to shake off its disconcerting double. In the next section of this paper, I turn to face this double more directly.

5. Coming to Terms with the Past: The Spectre of Fez

On 30 March 1912, the French Republic and the Moroccan Sultan concluded the Treaty of Fez, with the goal of 'establishing a well-regulated regime' in Morocco.[48]

---

[46] See 'Unmik—Fry Common Document', 5 November 2001, available at <http://www.mfa. gov.yu/Policy/Priorities/KIM/unmik_e.html>.

[47] 'Constitutional Framework', n 35 above, Chapter 12.

[48] 'Traité de Protectorat du 30 Mars 1912', Préamble, reprinted in Nationality Decrees Case, Permanent Court of International Justice, Series C, Annex 8, at 343 (1923).

The treaty provided for the military occupation of Morocco by France.[49] The 'new regime' envisioned by the treaty would include 'administrative, judicial, educational, economic, financial, and military reforms which the French Government shall judge useful to introduce on Moroccan territory'.[50] This regime would 'safeguard the religious situation, the traditional respect and prestige of the Sultan, and the exercise of the Muslim religion and religious institutions'.[51] France also agreed 'to provide constant support to his Cherifian Majesty against any danger which might threaten his person or his throne or which might compromise the tranquility of his State'.[52] Finally, the treaty provided that France would 'be represented before his Cherifian Majesty by a Resident General Commissioner, in whom shall be vested all the powers of the Republic in Morocco, and who shall safeguard the execution of the present agreement'.[53] In short: France established a protectorate over Morocco.

On 10 June 1999, the Security Council passed Resolution 1244 relating to Kosovo.[54] In the resolution, the Security Council 'b[ore] in mind the purposes and principles of the Charter of the United Nations, and the primary responsibility of the Security Council for the maintenance of international peace and security'.[55] It declared itself '[d]etermined to resolve the grave humanitarian situation in Kosovo, Federal Republic of Yugoslavia, and to provide for the safe and free return of all refugees and displaced persons to their homes'.[56] The resolution provided for an international military presence and civil administration in Kosovo.[57] The goals of this international presence in Kosovo would be overseeing and re-establishing basic governmental functions, humanitarian assistance, democratization, institution-building, and economic reconstruction. Finally, the resolution provided for the appointment of 'a Special Representative to control the implementation of the international civil presence, and further request[ed] the Secretary-General to instruct his Special Representative to coordinate closely with the international security presence'.[58] One could easily say that, in short, the resolution provided for the establishment of a protectorate over Kosovo. Indeed, the irony and quotation marks which attended the use of the word 'protectorate' in the first year of debate about UNMIK gradually disappeared as time went on.

What is the relationship between these two documents? We could list their similarities. These would include: (a) *the recitation of international ideals*—in Fez, that of a 'well-regulated regime'; in 1244, that of international peace and security; (b) *military occupation*—in Fez, by France; in 1244, by the international security presence; (c) *the bracketing of sovereignty*—in Fez, by maintaining the nominal sovereignty of the Moroccan Sultan; in 1244, that of Yugoslavia; (d) *far-reaching internal reforms undertaken by the Protector*—in Fez, administrative, educational,

---

49 Ibid., Art 2.   50 Ibid., Art 1.
51 Ibid.   52 Ibid., Art 3.
53 Ibid., Art 5.   54 UN SC Res. 1244, S/RES/1244 (1999).
55 Ibid., Préamble.   56 Ibid.
57 Ibid., paras 7–11.   58 Ibid., para 6.

economic; in 1244, administrative economic, political, civil; (e) *the explicit provisions for human rights*—in Fez, in the form of Muslim religious liberty; in 1244, in the form of broad human rights; (f) *ambiguity about the ultimate goal of the protectorate*—in Fez, between annexation by France and ultimate independence for a modernized Moroccan state; in 1244, between the restoration of Yugoslav sovereignty and ultimate independence for Kosovo; and (g) *the vesting of supreme power in a representative of the Protector*—in Fez, the French Resident General; in 1244, the Special Representative of the Secretary General.[59]

But we could also list their differences. Such differences would in part reside in the source of the legitimacy of the documents, in particular their relative position on the axes of sovereign consent and international community authority. On the one hand, the protectorate instrument is in the form of a treaty, a nominally consensual document, while the Security Council resolution is in the form of a mandatory resolution under Chapter VII. Yet it is important not to overstate the starkness of this contrast. While Resolution 1244 is in the form of a Chapter VII resolution, it also recites the consent by Yugoslavia to the principles contained in the G-8 document of May 1999 and the EU document of 2 June 1999.[60] Conversely, while the protectorate document is in the form of a treaty, it was the culmination of steady military and political encroachment by France.

Moreover, both documents seek to ground the legitimacy of their entire structure in a set of substantive international values. The French protectorate treaty recites the principles of what we would today call 'good governance' as the goal of the treaty; moreover, the French elsewhere described the 'lofty aims of the protectorate,... [as] above all a work of civilization,... a matter in which all [nations] have an equal interest'[61]—the functional historical equivalent to the more familiar recitation in 1244 of 'the purposes and principles of the Charter of the United Nations, and the primary responsibility of the Security Council for the maintenance of international peace and security'.

If we cannot read unequivocal differences between the two regimes in the text of their founding documents, we probably need to look elsewhere. That elsewhere would include the political intent and historical context in which the two regimes were established. We would need to compare the political and economic motivations for the French occupation of Morocco with those animating the NATO and UN occupation of Kosovo. We would need to compare the substantive merit of the respective claims of France and the Security Council to represent the international community. We would need to look at the broader geopolitical context, particularly the outside powers that France and NATO were trying to ward

---

[59] It should be noted that just as regimes such as UNMIK find themselves doubled by the comparison to protectorates, so protectorates found themselves doubled by comparisons to colonies.

[60] Resolution 1244, n 54 above, Préamble.

[61] 'Final Conclusions of the French Government', Nationality Decrees Case, PCIJ, Series C, No 2, at 242 (1923).

off from the two regions. And we might, in the inevitably messy results of such multiple inquiries, arrive at a persuasive judgment of relative legitimacy.

But this judgment would not reside in a clear characterization of UNMIK as purely law and the French Protectorate as purely politics—a judgment that could only be anachronistic. France justified its action on legal grounds that were relatively plausible in 1912, just as the UN justified its actions on legal grounds that were relatively plausible in 1999. This is not to say that their relative legal plausibility, even in their respective contexts, was equivalent. But neither could we confidently assert a priori, without detailed comparative analysis, that one regime would come out ahead.

Bracketing for a moment the formal legal issues, normative judgment of international regimes should depend on an evaluation of the conception of the affected population that animates them. In the interwar context, I have argued that international lawyers viewed the nationalism to which their legal innovations responded as a 'primitive' force to be celebrated on account of its energy, and to be domesticated on account of its dangerousness.[62] This international legal 'primitivism', I argued, embodied the same kind of fear and fascination exerted on many contemporaneous cultural innovators by fantasies of racial, cultural, geographical, and sexual 'Others'. Much of Modernist creativity, across a range of domains—including art, music, literature, and architecture, as well as law— emerged from attempts to link these 'primitives' with the most advanced technical innovations of the day.

The Modernists' 'primitivist' fantasies, of course, only had the most dubious relationship with reality—except, perhaps, when these fantasies were internalized or performed by the Modernists' 'Others'. Still, these fantasies were often an improvement on colonial conceptions of the 'native'—often, though not always. In any case, though this topic would require another paper, a comparative evaluation of regimes such as UNMIK would have to look carefully at the conception of the affected populations animating them—how they are imagined politically, economically, culturally, and sexually, and how that imagination may be embedded in the details of the legal regime.

6. Legitimation Effects: Four Hypotheses

I conclude with four hypotheses about the effect on legitimacy of the seemingly unavoidable evocation by regimes such as UNMIK of the spectres of protectorates and colonies: the *delegitimizing effects hypothesis,* the *legitimizing effects hypothesis,* the *cautionary effects hypothesis,* and the *strategic effects hypothesis.*

The *delegitimizing effects hypothesis* is that evocation of the colonial past has the effect of an unmasking. In this view, audacious experiments like UNMIK

---

[62] See, eg 'But the Alternative is Despair', n 34 above.

purport to implement the most advanced internationalist principles, but actually represent the continuation or resurrection of colonial power in contemporary form. The claim of such regimes to have thoroughly pressed power into the service of humanitarianism would simply be an ideological cover for the reverse process. This kind of effect on legitimacy would primarily concern the status of the international regime.

By contrast, the *legitimizing effects hypothesis* is that this evocation actually serves to bolster the claims of these legal regimes. In this view, it is precisely their ability to evoke the colonial past and *to demonstrate their difference from it* that gives these regimes their distinctive legitimacy. To the extent that similarities exist, the regimes' advocates could contend, they stem from structural exigencies arising from any administration of territory by the power of an outside authority. But, the advocates would contend, it is the humanitarian manner in which such power is exercised and the goals for which it is exercised that demonstrate the radical difference of such regimes from their colonial counterparts—a demonstration of difference whose persuasive 'edge' depends precisely on the structural similarities. The evocation of colonialism would pose a high-stakes challenge to the regime to persuasively establish this differentiation. The achievement of such a legitimizing effect would depend on the ability of the particular international regime to demonstrate that the coherence of its elements proves its status legitimacy as a whole—in other words, that its actual practices work in such a way as to demonstrate that the regime as a whole is really 'internationalist' and not 'colonialist'.

The *cautionary effects hypothesis* looks at the association with colonialism as a useful tool in the hands of friendly critics of these regimes—for example, sympathetic, but wary, human rights NGOs. The association with colonialism would be a readily available and widely comprehensible criticism that can be made every time the regime threatens to step over the legitimate bounds of its powers. Such critics would be deploying the critique of status legitimacy strategically, as a pressuring device to lobby for a reconfiguration of the coherence of the regime's elements.

The *strategic effects hypothesis* combines the first three. Like the *cautionary effects hypothesis,* it sees the association with colonialism as a useful tool. But this hypothesis would extend the range of players in whose hands the tool might be useful. There might be times, for example, when the affected population may wish to deploy the colonial association's delegitimizing effect not because they wish to terminate the regime, but rather, because they are engaged in a particular struggle over a particular issue. There might even be times when the international authority might wish to affirm the association with colonialism in a threatening manner, in order to command respect from a variety of bad actors in the region who may be impervious to gentler, more legitimate, arguments about the common good. (After all, if military force can sometimes be appropriate, psychological force might also be.) And so on.

From the perspective of the situational, political-historical approach to legitimacy taken in this paper, each of these uses of the evocation of the colonial past might be appropriate depending on the particularities of a given international regime and its relation to the local conflict upon which it is deployed. Some regimes might, in fact, be illegitimate exercises of power; others might be noble ventures; still others might need to be kept on their toes by a range of vigilant actors. The legitimacy of neither the status nor the coherence of prevailing forms of internationalism should ever be taken for granted. Legitimacy, especially of the purported composites of power and idealism that have marked the most robust internationalism of the past century, can only ever be—and should only ever be—a provisional achievement, an achievement arrived at through internationalism's wrestling with its doubles, be they ideological adversaries, heterogeneous elements in local conflicts, or the spectres of its own unsavoury past.

7

States of Exception: Regulating Targeted Killing in a 'Global Civil War'

Nehal Bhuta

[The 1949 Geneva Conventions'] foundations remain the conduct of war based on the state and consequently a bracketing of war, with its clear distinctions between war and peace, military and civilian, enemy and criminal, war between states and civil war. When these essential distinctions fade or are even challenged, they create the premises for a type of war that deliberately destroys these clear distinctions. Then, many cautiously stylized compromise norms appear only as the narrow bridge over an abyss, which conceals a profound modification of the concepts of war, enemy and partisan—a modification full of consequences...[1]

1. Introduction

In his lectures on the *Theory of the Partisan*,[2] Carl Schmitt observes that the figure of the partisan not only disturbed conventional military strategy, but confounded the legal categories of classical European international law. These laws established clear distinctions between war and peace, combatants and non-combatants, enemies (*justis hostis*) and common criminals, and the conditions of possibility for maintaining these conceptual distinctions derived from the prevalence of a certain model of conventional warfare.[3] The essence of the partisan, by contrast, was his irregularity, his spatial mobility and the intensity of his political

---

[1] Carl Schmitt, *The Theory of the Partisan—Intermediate Commentary on the Concept of the Political* (1963), translated and published in *Telos* (2005) pp 11–78, at 32.

[2] Ibid. 16, 23.

[3] As Nabulsi documents, the revival and reinforcement of these conceptual distinctions after the Congress of Vienna resulted from a concerted effort by states with large standing land armies to delegitimize the notion of a 'people's war' and to forcefully repress partisan warfare: Karma Nabulsi, *Traditions of War* (Oxford: Oxford University Press, 1999), Chapter 2–4; see also GIAD Draper, 'The Status of Combatants and the Question of Guerilla Warfare', in Michael Meyer and Hilaire McCoubrey (eds), *Reflections on Law and Armed Conflicts: Selected Works on the Laws of War by the late Colonel GIAD Draper* (The Hague: Kluwer, 1997) 210–11.

engagement. The efforts in the 1949 Geneva Conventions[4] to widen the circle of those comparable to regular fighters could not adequately accommodate the partisan, because to satisfy these requirements the partisan would have to give up his strongest weapons, secrecy and opacity: the partisan could not relinquish the space of irregularity and still remain a partisan.[5]

The transnational terrorist[6] is not a partisan in Schmitt's terms,[7] because he lacks the latter's telluric nature and territorial particularity.[8] But like the partisan of the nineteenth century and the anti-colonial guerilla of the twentieth, the transnational terrorist and his network have challenged the basic distinctions which structure the legitimation of violence in international law.[9] The partisan and the guerilla threatened to render arbitrary the division between war and not-war, combatant and civilian, because the violence they effected was temporally and territorially discontinuous.[10] The figure of the transnational terrorist after September 11 2001, has become a fantastic ideal-type of radical discontinuity, and thus represents a 'purer' challenge to the 'cautiously stylized compromise norms'[11] that facilitate and limit violence.[12] The result has been a contentious and as yet inconclusive debate over which legal regime is properly applied to states' use of force to repress terrorism.[13] In a new global landscape of conflict which combines 'elements of an

---

[4] Geneva Convention relative to the Treatment of Prisoners of War, 75 UNTS 135, entered into force 21 October 1950, Art 4A, recognizing belligerent status of resistance movements which meet the criteria set out in 4A(2).

[5] GIAD Draper, 'Wars of National Liberation and War Criminality' [1979] reprinted in Meyer and McCoubrey (eds), above n 3, 200, 210.

[6] It is trite to observe that the concepts of 'terrorist' and 'terrorism' lack any clear legal content, and have innumerable polemical applications. For the purposes of this analysis, I adopt Neuman's terse but functional definition of terrorism as the deliberate killing or wounding of civilians by private actors (other than national liberation movements) for the purpose of achieving ulterior political purposes: Gerald Neuman, 'Humanitarian Law and Counter-terrorist Force' 14 EJIL 283 (2003) 289.

[7] Although the partisan may commit terrorist acts.

[8] Jan-Werner Müller, *A Dangerous Mind: Carl Schmitt in Post-War European Thought* (New Haven: Yale University Press, 2003) 144–55.

[9] This statement is not entirely correct. Transnational political terrorism has existed as a phenomenon throughout the twentieth century, without producing a spatially and temporally indefinite 'war on terror'. The historical precondition for the *possibility* of a *world-wide theatre* of active hostilities which shift, chameleon-like, from interstate to intrastate conflicts, is the global reach of a single, militarily dominant state whose concept of strategic interest is so broad, that it is potentially under threat at all times and in all places. In other words, a 'global war on terror' as a jurisgenerative reality is inconceivable without a global hegemon pursuing full spectrum dominance. For a description of the emergence of this form of strategic thinking in the US over the 1990s see Andrew Bacevich, *American Empire: The Realities and Consequences of US Diplomacy* (Cambridge, MA: Harvard University Press 2002), Chapter 5.

[10] Nathaniel Berman, 'Privileging Combat? Contemporary Conflict and the Legal Construction of War' 43 Columbia Journal of Transnational Law 3 (2004), 23–38.

[11] Schmitt, above n 1, 32.

[12] Berman, above n 10, 23.

[13] See, eg Neuman, 'Humanitarian Law and Counter-terrorist Force' above n 6; Gerald Neuman, 'Counter-terrorist Operations and the Rule of Law' 15 EJIL 1019 (2005); Derek Jinks, 'September 11 and the Laws of War', 28 Yale Journal of International Law 1 (2003); Kevin Watkin, 'Controlling the Use of Force: A Role for Human Rights Norms in Contemporary Armed Conflict'

international armed conflict, a global guerilla war and an international criminal investigation,'[14] the *topos* of legal categories also becomes a battlefield between contending efforts to narrow or expand the scope of legitimate violence;[15] legal terms derive their concrete determinacy through polemical contestation, and the exigencies of the new landscape of conflict have been invoked to deny the applicability of *both* international humanitarian law[16] and international human rights law.[17] The question of which legal categories can and should be applied is, in effect, also a question of whether we are to facilitate or restrain the creation of 'premises for a type of war that deliberately destroys these clear distinctions'. In other words, if the figure of the transnational terrorist renders these classifications arbitrary, *who decides* where the new lines will be drawn?

This paper reviews the way that the 'global war on terror' destabilizes legal categories regulating the scope of legitimate violence in international human rights law and international humanitarian law, through the prism of the targeted killings of terrorist suspects who are outside the territory of the state using force. The intentional use of lethal force against a specific individual takes on different legal complexions, depending on whether it is viewed through the frame of reference of international humanitarian law (IHL) or international human rights (IHR). Each provides different regimes for authorizing and regulating the use of force, and explanations of the interrelationship between these two regimes have been dependent upon the distinction between peace and armed conflict. The standard delineation stylizes IHR as principally regulating relationships between a state and individuals within its territory under conditions of 'peace' (allowing for derogations in temporally limited states of exception),[18] while IHL regulates a specific

---

98 AJIL 1 (2004); Antonio Cassese, 'Terrorism is also Disrupting Some Crucial Legal Categories of International Law' 12 EJIL 993 (2002); Stein Tonneson, 'A Global Civil War?' 33 Security Dialogue 389 (2002); Anne-Marie Slaughter and William Burke White, 'An International Constitutional Moment' 43 Harvard Journal of International Law 1 (2002); Joan Fitzpatrick, 'Jurisdiction of Military Commissions and the Ambiguous War on Terrorism' 96 AJIL 345 (2002); Charles Dunlap, 'International Law and Terrorism: Some "Qs and As" for Operators', Army Lawyer 23 (2002); R Schondorf, 'Extra-State Armed Conflicts: Is There a Need for a New Legal Regime?', 37 New York University Journal of International Law and Politics 1 (2004); Adam Roberts, 'Counterterrorism, Armed Force and the Laws of War' 44 Survival 7 (2002); Fred Borch and Paul Wilson (eds), *International Law and the War on Terrorism* (Newport, RI: Naval War College, 2004).

[14] Dunlap, ibid.
[15] Berman refers to this as 'strategic instrumentalization'. This is somewhat tautological, as strategic rationality is by definition instrumental.
[16] See the now-infamous memos concerning the inappropriateness of applying the Geneva Conventions to 'enemy combatants' captured in the Global War on Terror: reprinted in M Danner, *Torture and Truth: America, Abu Ghraib and the War on Terror* (New York: New York Review of Books, 2004).
[17] See memos by Yoo, Bybee, and others contending that coercive interrogation is permissible and does not constitute torture under US law, reprinted in Danner, ibid.
[18] GIAD Draper 'Relationship between the Human Rights Regime and the Law of Armed Conflict' [1971] reprinted in Meyer and McCoubrey, above n 3, 130; Geza Herczegh, *Development of International Humanitarian Law* (Budapest: Akademiai Kiado, 1984); Fausto Pocar, 'Human Rights under the International Covenant on Civil and Political Rights and Armed Conflicts' in

kind of exceptional state (armed conflict) in which the subjects of rights and obligations are either combatants or civilians. But if the war/not-war and combatant/civilian binomials are rendered ambiguous in application, how do we understand the interaction of these two regimes, and what are the implications of applying one rather than another?

I explore this question by considering the proposition that IHL applies as *lex specialis* to IHR during armed conflict,[19] and asking how we might understand this. I argue that while the notion of *lex specialis* is theoretically appealing because of its apparent conceptual neatness, it provides no concrete guidance as to the determinate content of the rules governing the targeted killing of terrorist suspects, and that attempts at application in fact problematize the notion of a *lex specialis* relation between IHL and IHR. I contend that there are no clear conceptual-logical bases to decide which of these frameworks is properly applied to the targeted killing of terrorist suspects, and thus that transparent political and policy choices must be made.

2. Targeted Killing and the 'War on Terrorism'

The assassination[20] of individuals alleged to have planned, facilitated, or authorized terrorist acts is most commonly associated with the Israeli practice of 'targeted killings'. Israel has employed the tactic of assassination for over 30 years,[21] but admitted its use as a matter of policy soon after the beginning of the

---

LC Vohrah et al. (eds), *Man's Inhumanity to Man: Essays on International Law in Honour of Antonio Cassese* (The Hague: Kluwer, 2003) 729–40.

[19] *Threat or Use of Nuclear Weapons Advisory Opinion* [1996] ICJ Reps para 25; *Legal Consequences of the Construction of a Wall in the Occupied Palestinian Territory* (ICJ, 9 July 2004), 43 ILM 1009 (2004), para 105–6.

[20] Some, such as US Air Force lawyer Michael N Schmitt, seek to distinguish between assassination and targeted killing, on the grounds that the former entails some kind of perfidy or treachery: Michael Schmitt, 'State-Sponsored Assassination in International and Domestic Law' 17 Yale Journal of International Law 609 (1992). This distinction seems untenable as a matter of ordinary language, and also as a matter of practice: the use of undercover military death squads to kill individuals, such as Israel Defence Forces Duvadem or mostavarim units (gunmen posing as Arabs), may reasonably be called assassination. I use assassination and targeted killing interchangeably, as do many authors: Amnesty International, *Israel and the Occupied Territories: State Assassinations and Other Unlawful Killings* (2001); Amnesty International, *Israel and the Occupied Territories: Israel must end its policy of assassinations* (2003); Human Rights Inquiry Commission, *Report of the Human Rights Inquiry Commission Established Pursuant to Commission Resolution S-5/1 of 19 October 2000*, paras 53–64; B'Tselem, 'Position Paper: Israel's Assassination Policy: Extra-Judicial Executions' (2000); Michael Gross, 'Fighting by Other Means in the Mideast: A Critical Analysis of Israel's Assassination Policy' 51 Political Studies 350 (2003).

[21] For example, the killing of Abu Jihad in Tunisia, 1985, and the use of undercover death squads in the Occupied Palestinian Territories: see Human Rights Watch, *A License to Kill: Israeli Undercover Operations Against 'Wanted' and Masked Palestinians* (1993); B'Tselem, *Activity of Undercover Units in the Occupied Territories* (May 1992).

Al-Aqsa *Intifada*.[22] In July 2001, it expanded the policy to include the killing of 'known terrorists' even when not directly involved in potential attacks.[23] Prior to September 11 2001, the US publicly criticized Israel's use of targeted killings as amounting to 'extrajudicial execution',[24] but a commonly cited interpretation of the Presidential Executive Order 12,333 (prohibiting assassination) concluded that the Order would not prohibit the use of covert or overt military force against 'a terrorist or other organization whose actions pose a threat to the security of the United States'.[25] After September 11, senior US government officials expressed conditional approval for 'preemptive' attacks on suspected individual terrorists.[26]

On 4 November 2002, suspected al-Qaeda senior commander Qaed Sinan al-Harithi was killed in Yemen, along with five passengers, when the car in which he was travelling was struck by a Hellfire missile unleashed from a Predator drone.[27] In a response to a letter critical of the strike by the UN Special Rapporteur on extrajudicial, summary, or arbitrary executions, the US refused to confirm or deny that it was responsible for the assassination—which took place outside a zone of armed conflict—but asserted its right to use force against 'legitimate military targets' in an 'international armed conflict' against al-Qaeda.[28] Other instances of the targeted killing have not been confirmed,[29] but President

---

[22] Shaul Mofaz in Ha'aretz, 1 November 2001, stating that the use of targeted killing was governed by rules drawn up by the IDF's Military Advocate General; Working Paper, 1 August 2001, quoting Deputy Defence Minister; Army Radio report, 6 November 2003: 'the war against Hamas will now be pursued without quarter and no limit exists on killing its leaders, including Sheikh Ahmed Yassin'.

[23] 'Kitchen Cabinet Okays Expansion of Liquidation List', Ha'aretz, 4 July 2001. A study by human rights NGOs concluded that between 1 and 13 January 2003, Israel undertook 20 targeted killings, in which 33 targeted individuals and 29 bystanders were killed. Only in two cases was it claimed that the targeted individuals were involved in planning future attacks: private communication from OPT researcher.

[24] Martin Indyk, US Ambassador to Israel, *Chicago Tribune*, 7 May 2001. Urbina and Toensing note that the full diplomatic picture is more complex, with State Department condemnations of Israel's use of targeted killing as extrajudicial executions undermined by milder White House responses during both the Clinton and Bush administrations: Chris Toensing and Ian Urbina, 'Israel, the US and "Targeted Killings"', *Middle East Report*, 17 February 2003.

[25] W Hays Park, 'Memorandum of Law: Executive Order 12333 and Assassination' *Army Lawyer* 4 (1989).

[26] Toensing and Urbina, above n 24.

[27] A Dworkin, The Yemen Strike: The War on Terrorism Goes Global, *Crimes of War Project*, 14 November 2002.

[28] Letter dated 14 April 2003, from the US Permanent Mission to the UN office at Geneva, in response to a letter from Asma Jehangir to Secretary of State Colin Powell, on 15 November 2002. The letter also contended that the Special Rapporteur had no competence to consider violations of IHL, because her mandate was based on IHR instruments and IHL applied to the exclusion of IHR.

[29] An unconfirmed report of a targeted killing emerged in May 2005, which alleged that suspected al-Qaeda operative Haitham al-Yemeni was killed in north-western Pakistan by a missile launched from a Predator drone: Douglas Jehl, 'Remote Controlled Craft Part of US-Pakistan Drive Against Al-Qaeda, Ex-Officials Say', *New York Times*, 16 May 2005. The US government neither confirmed nor denied the strike, but former intelligence officials stated that the target

Bush hinted ominously in his 2003 State of the Union that al-Qaeda members who have not been captured have been 'otherwise dealt with'.[30] In the context of the US occupation of Iraq, US military commanders stated in October 2004 that alleged terrorist leaders were targeted during air strikes on residential buildings in the city of Falluja.[31]

No significant public policy debate has yet occurred within the US concerning the legality and legitimacy of using targeted killings against suspected terrorists,[32] but the issue was considered by the semi-official 'Long-Term Legal Strategy Project'. (LTLSP).[33] The LTLSP differentiates between the use of targeted killing within a 'zone of active combat', and the targeting of a particular individual outside such a zone.[34] A zone of active combat is defined as 'territory designated by the President...as constituting a theater of military operations' in connection with a declared war or other armed conflict between the US and 'a foreign state, organization or defined class of individuals'. A designated combat zone may also be a territory militarily occupied by the US, or a territory in which US military personnel are assisting with the suppression of an armed insurrection or uprising at the request of the government. The report contends that the use of targeted killing in such 'zones of designated combat' is adequately regulated by IHL, and thus no further elaboration of procedures is required.[35]

In all situations and locations *other* than active combat, the report recommends that targeted killing be used only where it is 'necessary to prevent a greater, reasonably imminent harm or in defense against a reasonably imminent threat to lives of the target of the planned terrorist attack'.[36] The authors argue that their

---

was 'an important facilitator who would be important to moving messages, moving supplies' who 'would be an important person to take out of the equation'.

[30]   State of the Union, 2003, available at <http://www.whitehouse.gov>.

[31]   T Shanker and E Schmitt, 'Terror Command in Falluja is Half Destroyed' *New York Times*, 13 October 2004. The multiple uses of targeted killings are revealed by the statements of US officials and military officers quoted in this article. The air strikes not only aim to kill alleged terrorist leaders, but to increase the perceived cost to the local population of not cooperating with the occupying power in defeating the insurgents: ' "If there are civilians dying in connection with these attacks, and with the destruction, the locals at some point have to make a decision", one Pentagon official said, "Do they want to harbor the insurgents and suffer the consequences that come with that, or do they want to get rid of the insurgents and have the benefits of not having them there?" ' A similar rationale is invoked in support of the efficacy of Israeli targeted killings: 'The liquidation of wanted persons is proving itself useful...This activity paralyzes and frightens entire villages and as a result, there are areas where people are afraid to carry out hostile actions.' Israeli official, cited in *Ha'aretz*, 8 January 2001.

[32]   President Bush appears to have authorized the attack on al-Harithi based on 'the same set of classified presidential findings, legal opinions and policy directives...that have set the rules for the administration's campaign to prevent terror'. David Johnston and David Sanger, 'Fatal Yemen Strike was Based on Rules Set Out by Bush' *New York Times*, 6 November 2002, A16.

[33]   Heymann and Kayyem, *Long Term Legal Strategy Project for Preserving Security and Democratic Freedoms in the War on Terrorism* (JFKSG/Harvard Law School, February 2005), funded by National Memorial Institute for the Prevention of Terrorism and the Office of Domestic Preparedness, Department of Homeland Security ('LTLSP').

[34]   Ibid. 59–61   [35]   Ibid. 65.

[36]   Ibid. 67.

criteria for non-combat zone targeted killing are intended to make it an option of last resort, mandated only if no other options (capture, arrest, or extradition) are reasonable and the threat of lethal attack is imminent.[37] Where these conditions are met, the conduct of the operation must also be consistent with the 'familiar rules applicable to military action under the laws of war' such that the action is 'proportionate to the objective to be obtained' and avoids harm to innocent persons 'to the extent reasonably possible'.[38]

Using targeted killing as a means of retribution for past attacks is rejected, as is its use against US citizens, on US territory, or in the territory of a state display-ing a willingness to try, extradite, or 'otherwise incapacitate' those suspected of planning terrorist attacks on US citizens or facilities.[39] The recommendations set out a procedure by which the President must authorize each instance of targeted killing outside a designated combat zone, setting out the evidence on which the conclusions of imminent danger and no reasonable alternative were reached, and why there was no prospect of trial or extradition in the territory where the suspect is located.[40] The findings need not be made public, but would be provided to appropriate Committees of the Congress.

The report's suggested approach to targeted killings is an important first con-tribution to public and institutional deliberation concerning a strategy which, as the report's authors recognize, is dangerously corrosive *precisely because* it appears less costly in lives and money than invading and occupying another territory.[41] However, the report's categorical distinction between 'designated combat zones' and all other situations, obscures rather than clarifies the legal complexity of the position of targeted killings in international law.[42] The contention that IHL unambiguously and unproblematically regulates the targeted killing of indi-viduals, irrespective of whether it is undertaken during an international armed conflict with another state, an armed conflict with a non-state actor, under con-ditions of belligerent occupation, or in an (internationalized) intrastate armed conflict, is unsustainable. In the sections that follow, I examine the potentially relevant IHL legal concepts and argue that they are at once too permissive (over-inclusive) and too restrictive (under-inclusive) to adequately regulate the use of targeted killings. At the same time, the LTLSP report fails to explicate the legal basis for its approach to targeted killings outside a 'designated combat zone', or whether a person is determined to pose an imminent threat to the US by reason of his *status* (group membership, declared hostile intent etc) or his *conduct* (actual

---

[37] Ibid. 68.   [38] Ibid. 60.

[39] Ibid. 60.   [40] Ibid. 61.

[41] Ibid. 66. In practice, only a handful of modern states could utilize targeted killing on a global scale.

[42] In passing, one might also query what criteria govern the process of 'designation': if several leadership figures of an 'organization or defined class of individuals' with which the US has previously declared itself to be at war are found in a certain territory, can the President designate the territory a zone of combat? Reference to purely domestic law criteria for the designation of a zone of combat threatens to allow bootstrapping, whereby the more permissive IHL regime is applied by fiat.

or reasonable capacity to inflict lethal harm and a plan to do so). While it seems to me that the framework recommended to govern targeted killings outside a designated combat zone is closer to a 'law enforcement' model,[43] it's application of IHL notions of 'military necessity' and 'proportionality' and its implicit equation of the threat posed by an individual with *who he is* rather than *what he is about to do*[44] introduces standards sharing much kinship with the law of armed conflict. Yet this framework is specifically intended to be applied to locations which are expressly not considered to be zones of armed conflict, so what justification is there for engaging a military calculus at crucial points? These reasons are not articulated by the LTLSP report, but might be inferred as constituting an acceptance that effective measures to repress transnational terrorism require the use of an IHL frame of reference even outside a territorially localized 'war' environment. The elision reveals the somewhat insidious logic of *ex factis oritur jus*: the application of a military model makes the 'war on terror' a 'war', and thus the law of war applies. The purpose of examining the potential application and implications of the IHL and IHR frameworks in this paper is to expose this elision and indicate the extent to which it implies a set of policy decisions—decisions which go to the heart of the issue about what kind of 'war' the war on terror will become and the function of law in legitimizing this development.

3. Overview of the Interaction between International Humanitarian Law and International Human Rights Law

Although IHL has its origins in the nineteenth century's codification of European land war customs and usages, the contemporary versions of IHL and IHR share the post-World War II period as their context of origin. Despite their parallel development, the question of their precise interrelation and interaction—as a matter of practical application—has only recently begun to be debated in earnest.[45] Academic commentators who have considered the question commonly

---

[43] As I discuss below, this model is associated with the application of the IHL regime to targeted killings.

[44] For example, the report's commentary to the recommendations formulates the 'imminent threat' and 'necessity' requirements in terms of whether 'the harm posed by the *continued life* of the target is greater than the harm' resulting from violating another state's sovereignty, killing without due process and possibly killing innocent civilians. The language seems to suggest that it is status of the targeted individual rather than any imminent conduct which is the touchstone for assessing the necessity of the operation. As such, the targeted individual is rendered functionally equivalent to a military target (combatant or installation) under IHL.

[45] See, eg the discussion in Karima Bennoune, 'Towards a Human Rights Approach to Armed Conflict' 11 University of California Davis Journal of International Law and Policy 171 (2004); Michael J Dennis, 'Application of Human Rights Treaties Extraterritorially in Times of Armed Conflict and Military Occupation' 99 AJIL 119 (2005). The debate has in part been prompted by the decisions of the ICJ in the *Nuclear Weapons* and *Wall* Advisory Opinions, but also as a

conceive of it in one of three ways, which I shall gloss as the 'cumulative', 'interpretive complementarity', and 'incompatibility' approaches. In this part, I shall review each of these interpretations of the interrelationship between IHL and IHR, and consider which of them is consistent with the International Court of Justice's (ICJ's) holding that IHL operates as *lex specialis* to IHR in circumstances of armed conflict. I suggest that the concept of *lex specialis* as used by the ICJ is ambiguous, and could in fact encompass more than one of the common ways of conceiving of the interaction of IHL and IHR. As such, it provides no clear conceptual basis for determining which framework properly applies to the strategy of targeted killing of terrorists.

A. Three Articulations of the Relationship between IHL and IHR

'Cumulative' or 'Integrationist' Approach

The 'cumulative' approach begins from the premise that both IHL and IHR have as a common telos the protection of individual rights and interests, such that IHL is to be regarded as a subset of a single international law of human rights.[46] One exponent of this position thus contends that 'humanitarian law is one branch of the law of human rights, and human rights afford the basis for humanitarian law'.[47] The implication of the cumulative approach is that IHR constitutes the overarching framework regulating the use of lethal force, whether in times of

result of two other developments: the decisions of the ad hoc International Criminal Tribunals have entailed a need to give specific content to norms of IHL, in order to render them capable of individualized application. This has in some cases been achieved by using IHR to supplement IHL norms, and in other cases by distinguishing between the content of a term in IHL and its content in IHR. See, eg the discussion of the meaning of 'torture' as a criminal offence by the ICTY Trial Chamber in *Prosecutor v Dragoljub Kunarac, Radomir Kovac and Zoran Vukovic* [2001] ICTY 2 (22 February 2001) at para 471, where the Trial Chamber finds that 'notions developed in the field of human rights can be transposed in international humanitarian law only if they take into consideration the specificities of the latter body of law.' By contrast, in *Prosecutor v Furundzija* [1998] ICTY 3 (10 December 1998), the Trial Chamber relied upon the IHR definition of torture to given content to the term as found in Common Article 3 of the Geneva Conventions: paras 131–64. The second institutional development is the increased willingness by regional human rights treaty bodies to consider the conduct of states' parties during armed conflicts in terms of the provisions of regional human rights treaties. This has led to a debate as to whether regional human rights institutions can and should apply IHL directly, and if not, how IHL norms might influence the interpretation and application of IHR. For IACt HR cases, see, eg Case of *Juan Carlos Abella* (Argentina), IACtHR, Case 11.137 (18 November 1997); *Las Palmeras* (Colombia), Preliminary Objections, IACtHR (Ser. C) No 67 (2000); *Bámaca Velásquez* (Guatemala), Judgment, Inter.-Am.Ct.H.R. (Ser. C) No 70 (25 November 2000). For ECtHR cases, see: *Isayeva, Yusupova and Bazayeva v Russia*, ECtHR, App. Nos 57947–49/00 (24 February 2005); *Isayeva v Russia*, ECtHR, App. No 57950/00 (24 February 2005); *McCann and Others v United Kingdom*, ECtHR, App. No 18984/91 (27 September 1995). See also the discussion in Theodor Meron, 'The Humanization of Humanitarian Law' 94 AJIL 239 (2000) 266–73.

[46] Herczegh refers to this as the 'integrationist' approach: above n 18, 60.

[47] AH Robertson, 'Humanitarian law and human rights' in Christophe Swinarski, *Studies and Essays on International Humanitarian Law and Red Cross Principles* (The Hague: Martinus Nijhoff, 1987) 793–802.

peace or armed conflict, and that in the event of an inconsistency between IHR and IHL, the rule which provides the 'highest standard of protection' should be applied.[48] Such a reading of the relationship between IHL and IHR focuses on the protective provisions of IHL while tending to de-emphasize (or criticize) IHL's simultaneous authorization of a high degree of discretion to use certain kinds of violence (such as the concept of 'military necessity'). Instead, it promotes an interpretation and application of IHL which seeks to 'lift it up to the greatest proximity to the normal acceptance and operation of human rights'.[49]

Interpretive Complementarity Approach

The 'interpretive complementarity' approach constitutes a 'middle ground' in debates about the relationship between IHR and IHL. It accepts that IHR and IHL are two distinct regimes with different origins and functions, in which neither is necessarily subsidiary to the other. At the same time, this approach countenances situations where both regimes may apply non-exclusively to the same set of circumstances,[50] in which IHR rules and principles are used to inform and 'humanize' IHL rules; or IHL rules are used to give content to IHR rules in certain exceptional states.[51] In either case, one body of law supplements the other although the direction of this 'supplementation' is not fixed.[52] Watkin exemplifies

---

[48] See the debate in ICRC and San Remo Institute, *International Humanitarian Law and Other Legal Regimes: Interplay in Situations of Violence*, November 2003 at 8. This also seems to be the implication of Bennoune's argument for a 'human rights approach' to armed conflict: Bennoune, above n 45. It is noteworthy that the argument for the 'highest standard of protection' approach was rejected by the majority of participants in the ICRC meeting. Heintze seems to endorse the 'cumulative' approach, although his treatment is ambiguous: Hans-Joachim Heintze, 'On the relationship between human rights law and international humanitarian law' 86 IRRC 789 (2004). In an early paper on the topic, GIAD Draper also advocated the integrationist position, but subsequently rejected it. See 'Relationship between the Human Rights Regime and the Law of Armed Conflict' [1971] reprinted in Meyer and McCoubrey, above n 5.

[49] Draper, 'Relationship between the Human Rights Regime and the Law of Armed Conflict' [1971] reprinted in Meyer and McCoubrey, above n 5, 131. It appears that the 'cumulative' approach is also implicit in the Human Rights Committee's General Comment on Nuclear Weapons and the Right to Life, in which the Committee finds that compliance with IHL would not necessarily mean that the right to life under the ICCPR had not been violated. See: Human Rights Committee, General Comment 14, Article 6 (Twenty-third session, 1984), Compilation of General Comments and General Recommendations Adopted by Human Rights Treaty Bodies, UN Doc. HRI\GEN\1\Rev.1 at 18 (1994), paras 2–4.

[50] See, eg General Comment 29 of the Human Rights Committee, States of Emergency (article 4), UN Doc. CCPR/C/21/Rev.1/Add.11 (2001), para 3; Theodor Schilling, 'Is the United States bound by the International Covenant on Civil and Political Rights in Relation to Occupied Territories?' Global Law Working Paper 08/04, NYU Law School, 20–21; JA Frowein, 'The Relationship between Human Rights Regimes and Regimes of Belligerent Occupation' 28 *Israeli Yearbook of International Law* 1, 8–9.

[51] See, eg IACom HR, *Report on Terrorism and Human Right*, OEA/Ser.L/V/II.116, Doc.5, Rev.1 corr., 22 October 2002, para 61 ('[O]ne must necessarily look to and apply definitional standards and relevant rules of international humanitarian law as sources of authoritative guidance in the assessment of the respect of the Inter-American instruments in combat situations.')

[52] This approach was favoured by the majority of participating experts in the ICRC meeting on *International Humanitarian Law and Other Legal Regimes: Interplay in Situations of Violence*, above n 48.

this position when he asserts that 'international humanitarian law constitutes an integral, but separate, part of the right to life framework'.[53]

An example of this approach may be the jurisprudence of the Inter-American Court of Human Rights (IACtHR) in the *Las Palmeras* and *Bamaca Velasquez* cases.[54] In both of these cases, the IACtHR rejected findings by the Inter-American Commission on Human Rights (IAComHR) that the IAComHR was entitled to directly apply IHL in order to determine whether state conduct violated the American Convention on Human Rights (ACHR) in the course of an armed conflict. The IACtHR held that its jurisdictional competence was limited to determining violations of rights contained in the ACHR and did not extend to the direct application of IHL norms.[55] Nevertheless, the Court concluded that it could use IHL norms as an aid to interpreting the content of human rights stipulated in the ACHR and implicitly accepted that the existence of an armed conflict did not prevent the application of non-derogable human rights treaty norms.[56] The European Court of Human Rights (ECtHR) has arguably taken interpretive complementarity in the opposite direction, by using IHR principles to supplement or substitute for IHL norms when evaluating states' parties conduct during internal armed conflicts.[57]

Incompatibility Approach

The third approach insists that there is a firm conceptual and practical distinction between the human rights regime and the IHL regime, deriving from each framework's different history and field of application. Draper, in his later writings, exemplifies this point of view when he contends that human rights law regulates relations between government and the governed, and is concerned primarily with situations in which these relations are peaceful (although allowing for limited states of exception). By contrast, IHL regulates *hostile relations* between states or combatant groups engaged in armed confrontation.[58] The notion of 'human

---

[53] Kevin Watkin, 'Controlling the Use of Force: A Role for Human Rights Norms in Contemporary Armed Conflict' 98 AJIL 1 (2004) 32.

[54] *Las Palmeras* (Colombia), Preliminary Objections, IACtHR (Ser. C) No 67 (2000); *Bámaca Velásquez* (Guatemala), Judgment, IACtHR (Ser. C) No 70 (25 November 2000).

[55] *Las Palmeras*, Preliminary Objections, ¶ 33.

[56] '[T]he relevant provisions of the Geneva Conventions may be taken into consideration as elements for the interpretation of the American Convention.' *Bámaca Velásquez*, Judgment, ¶ 209.

[57] See, eg *Ergi v Turkey*, ECtHR, App. No 23818/94 (28 July 1998); *Isayeva, Yusupova and Bazayeva v Russia*, ECtHR, App. Nos 57947–49/00 (24 February 2005); *Isayeva v Russia*, ECtHR, App. No 57950/00 (24 February 2005). cf. the discussion in William Abresch, 'A Human Rights Law Of Internal Armed Conflict: The European Court Of Human Rights In Chechnya' 16 EJIL (2005); Hans-Joachim Heintze, 'The European Court of Human Rights and the Implementation of Human Rights Standards During Armed Conflicts', 45 GYIL 60 (2002); Aisling Reidy, 'The Approach of the European Commission and Court of Human Rights to International Humanitarian Law', 80 IRRC 513 (1998).

[58] GIAD Draper, 'Humanitarian Law and Human Rights' [1979] in Meyer and McCoubrey, above n 3, 145–50; 'Human Rights and the Law of Armed Conflict: General Principles of Implementation' [1974] in Meyer and McCoubrey, above n 3, 141–4.

rights in armed conflict' is rejected as unhelpful, because it ignores the different value horizons that constrain IHL and IHR.[59] IHL does not set limits on
the purposes for which a sovereign may use force, but constrains the means and
methods for using force. The sovereign of IHL is the sovereign of international
relations—omnipotent unless self-limiting. By contrast, the sovereign of IHR
is the sovereign of liberal constitutionalism, deriving authority from its subjects' consent and limited by the legal entitlements of its subjects.[60] Similarly,
Herczegh comments that IHL applies 'in the "abnormal" case when individual
man is in relationship not with his own State but when, under the particularly
difficult conditions of armed conflict, he is in the power of another State—an
enemy State—or exposed at least to the influence of such a hostile State'.[61] The
incompatibility argument contends that IHL's preoccupation with 'relations of
hostility' means that it has developed specific rules appropriate to armed conflicts between states or other armed groups, striking a suitable balance between
considerations of humanity and military necessity.[62] The logic of this argument
implies that where an armed conflict exists, IHL should prevail over or apply to
the exclusion of any conflicting IHR rules.[63]

B. The Indeterminacy of *Lex Specialis*

The 'interpretive complementarity' approach appears to be the most common
iteration of the relationship between IHR and IHL.[64] In the International
Committee of the Red Cross (ICRC) meeting on *International Humanitarian
Law and Other Legal Regimes*,[65] the majority of expert participants rejected the
view that IHL and IHR cannot apply *ratione materiae* to the same legal fact or
act, and agreed that the existence of an armed conflict was not of itself sufficient
to exclude the application of IHR (at least in respect of non-derogable rights).[66]
At the same time, they rejected the contention that the object of both bodies of

---

[59] See Keith Suter, 'An Enquiry into the Meaning of the Phrase "Human Rights in Armed
Conflict"' *The Military Law and Law of War Review* (September 1976) 393; Keith Suter, *An
International Law of Guerilla Warfare: The Global Politics of Law-Making* (New York: St Martin's,
1984) 34–5.

[60] Asbjorn Eide, 'The Laws of War and Human Rights: Differences and Convergences' in
Swinarski, above n 47, 676–97. Similarly, Abi-Saab notes that IHL emerges from classical interna-
tional law's 'law of coexistence' while IHR exemplifies the post-World War II 'law of cooperation'.
Georges Abi-Saab, 'Whither the International Community?' 9 EJIL 248 (1998).

[61] Herczegh, above n 18, 63.

[62] As Abresch points out, this observation is true of international armed conflicts but not of the
IHL regime regulating non-international armed conflicts. In the latter case, the rules are sparse
and not widely endorsed by states. Abresch, above n 57.

[63] For an explicit argument to this effect see Wolff Heintschell von Heinnegg, 'Factors in War to
Peace Transitions' 27 Harvard Journal of Law and Public Policy 843 (2004) 868–9.

[64] See, eg Meron, 'The Humanization of Humanitarian Law', above n 46; Pocar, above n 18;
Frowein, above n 50.

[65] Above n 48.

[66] Ibid. 8.

law was to ensure the protection of the individual and that therefore the 'highest level of protection' should apply in the event of a contradiction between IHL and IHR. Instead, the participants supported the proposition that IHL could be used in the context of armed conflicts to 'specify the precise content of non-derogable human rights'.[67] Some also contended that IHR could be used to give determinate content to certain provisions of IHL, such as the reference to 'judicial guarantees recognized as indispensable by civilized peoples'.[68] The participants concluded that this approach (which I have glossed as 'interpretive complementarity') was the meaning of the holding of the ICJ in the *Nuclear Weapons* and *Legal Consequences of the Wall* advisory opinions that IHL functions as *lex specialis* to the interpretation of certain non-derogable rights under IHR.

In the *Nuclear Weapons* opinion, the court held that:[69]

The Court observes that the protection of the International Covenant on Civil and Political Rights [ICCPR] does not cease in times of war, except by operation of Article 4 of the [ICCPR] whereby certain provisions may be derogated from in a time of national emergency. Respect for the right to life is not, however, such a provision. In principle, the right not arbitrarily to be deprived of one's life applies also in hostilities. The test of what is an arbitrary deprivation of life, however, then falls to be determined by the applicable *lex specialis*, namely, the law applicable in armed conflict which is designed to regulate the conduct of hostilities. Thus whether a particular loss of life, through the use of a certain weapon in warfare, is to be considered an arbitrary deprivation of life contrary to Article 6 of the [ICCPR], can only be decided by reference to the law applicable in armed conflict and not deduced from the terms of the [ICCPR] itself.

In the *Legal Consequences of the Construction of a Wall in the Occupied Palestinian Territory* opinion, the ICJ repeated and approved the above passage from the *Nuclear Weapons* advisory opinion and added:[70]

More generally, the Court considers that the protection offered by human rights conventions does not cease in case of armed conflict, save through the effect of provisions for derogation of the kind to be found in Article 4 of the [ICCPR]. As regards the relationship between international humanitarian law and human rights law, there are thus three possible situations: some rights may be exclusively matters of international humanitarian law; others may be exclusively matters of human rights law; yet others may be matters of both these branches of international law. In order to answer the question put to it [concerning the legal consequences of Israel's Separation Wall], the Court will have to take into consideration both these branches of international law, namely human rights law and, as *lex specialis*, international humanitarian law.

The ICJ's dicta in these two cases does appear to equate the idea that IHL is *lex specialis* to IHR, with what I have stylized as the 'interpretive complementarity'

---

[67] Ibid. 9.
[68] Common Article 3(1)(d) to the Geneva Conventions.
[69] *Threat or Use of Nuclear Weapons Advisory Opinion*, above n 19, para 25.
[70] Ibid., para 106.

approach to the interrelationship between IHL and IHR. Pocar explicates the ICJ's reference to the non-derogable prohibition against arbitrary deprivation of life, found in Article 6 of the ICCPR, as an example of the way in which specific IHL norms could be used to give determinate content to IHR norms in the context of armed conflict. He suggests that it is the concept of 'arbitrariness' which is given specific content by the interpellation of IHL norms:

[T]here is no doubt that the notion of arbitrariness, although distinct from the notion of unlawfulness, is linked to the rules and principles applicable as a whole in the situation in which such behaviour takes place and has to be considered. In peacetime, the said principles and rules are those contained in the [ICCPR] itself; conduct that is inconsistent with the overall standard of protection guaranteed by such principles and rules would therefore be arbitrary, thus entailing a violation of the right concerned. In wartime, however, the legal context that expresses the principle that may make behaviour arbitrary changes and includes the rules of humanitarian law that govern the conduct of military operations, as well as the protection to be afforded to combatants and civilians respectively. Consequently, as far as the right to life is concerned, in wartime a person would be arbitrarily deprived of his right to life only if death is inflicted in violation of the principles and rules of humanitarian law. It goes without saying that such principles are different as regards fighters and civilians, who enjoy different standards of protection both as to the right to life and other aspects of their treatment.[71]

This gloss on the ICJ's ruling has some attractive features: it appears to overcome, in principle at least, the antagonism between the IHR and IHL regimes argued for by proponents of the 'incompatibility approach'. It also maintains (again, at the level of an abstract principle) a seamless continuity in applicable laws, eschewing the possibility that a legal void may arise in respect of factual circumstances which do not categorically fit into either IHR or IHL. But it is equally arguable that ICJ's approach creates the *appearance* of logical coherence and continuity of norms, while in fact resolving very little at the level of practical application. Does it really shed much additional light on the practical interaction of IHR and IHL to observe that the 'right to life' continues to apply in principle but is now subject to the IHL rules concerning lawful objects of attack, proportionality, and military necessity? Could not the same result also be derived from the 'incompatibility approach', without the rhetorical (and one might say, disingenuous) gesture in favour of the continued 'right to life'? The proponent of the 'incompatibility approach' could plausibly argue that to propose that the 'right to life' during an armed conflict should be interpreted subject to the IHL principles of distinction and proportionality is simply to apply the IHL rules to the exclusion of IHR. Through its basic distinctions between combatant and civilian, and between proportionate and disproportionate means of warfare, IHL accepts the imperative of minimizing avoidable and unreasonable loss of life; but to conclude from this that IHL can therefore be understood as articulating the content of the

---

[71] Pocar, above n 18, 734.

'right to life' in war seems tenuous, if not self-contradictory as a matter of ordinary language.[72] The ICJ's position (as expanded upon by Pocar) can be read as simply rephrasing, without necessarily clarifying, the basic distinction between peace and war that the 'incompatibility approach' insists on as the fundamental difference between IHR and IHL. Indeed, as will be argued below in section four, when the conflict at issue defies easy categorization as between 'peace' and 'armed conflict', or between 'normality' and 'the exceptional', the lack of clarification afforded by the ICJ's dicta is even more apparent.[73]

When scrutinized more carefully, recourse to the notion of *lex specialis* also resolves little. The ICJ does not define its usage of *lex specialis* in the *Nuclear Weapons* or the *Wall* opinions, and as Koskenniemi's background paper for the International Law Commission notes, the maxim *lex specialis derogat lex generali* is used in several different ways.[74] The proposition that law A is *lex specialis* to law B could mean (a) that law A is a *particular application* of the more general law B in a given set of circumstances (a maxim of interpretation), or; (b) that law A *conflicts* with law B, but A should be *applied as an exception* to B because A is more appropriate to the particular circumstances at hand (a maxim for resolving conflicts between rules),[75] or (c) A is a self-contained regime, which operates to the exclusion of the general law principle B.[76] Each of these usages of

---

[72] The contradiction is even more apparent if one considers the paucity of IHL rules governing non-international armed conflicts. For example, while the direct targeting of civilians is prohibited under these rules, the incidental infliction of excessive civilian casualties is not. Yet, it would be difficult to argue that a civilian who lost her or his life under such circumstances was not arbitrarily deprived of the right to life. On the thinness of IHL rules in internal armed conflicts, see Neuman, 'Humanitarian Law and Counter-terrorist Force', above n 6, 296–7, and Abresch, above n 57.

[73] See below, p 259.

[74] Martti Koskenniemi, Background Paper for the International Law Commission Study Group on Fragmentation, 'Topic (a): The Function and Scope of the *Lex Specialis* Rule and the Question of 'Self-Contained Regimes'.

[75] This is the usage invoked by a Panel of the Dispute Settlement Body of the World Trade Organization (WTO) in the case of *Turkey—Restrictions on Imports of Textile and Clothing Products*, WT/DS34/R (31 May 1999), ¶ 9.94, n 42:

'[T]echnically speaking, there is a conflict when two (or more) treaty instruments contain obligations which cannot be complied with simultaneously. ... Not every such divergence constitutes a conflict, however. ... Incompatibility of contents is an essential condition of conflict. ... The *lex specialis derogat legi generali* principle 'which [is] inseparably linked with the question of conflict' ... between two treaties or between two provisions (one arguably being more specific than the other), does not apply if the two treaties "... deal with the same subject from different points of view or [are] applicable in different circumstances, or one provision is more far-reaching than but not inconsistent with, those of the other." ' (references omitted).

[76] Ibid. 6–10. Koskenniemi defines a self-contained regime as a case where 'a set of primary rules relating to a particular subject-matter is connected with a special set of secondary rules that claims priority to the secondary rules provided by general law. ... A regime is a union of rules laying down particular rights, duties and powers and rules having to do with the administration of such rules, including in particular rules for reacting to breaches. When such a regime seeks precedence in regard to the general law, we have a "self-contained regime", a special case of *lex specialis*.' (at 9) For scepticism concerning the existence of 'self-contained regimes', see Anja Lindroos and Michael Mehling, 'Dispelling the Chimera of "Self-Contained Regimes"—International Law and the WTO,' 17 EJIL 857 (2005).

lex specialis is potentially compatible with one or more of the three approaches to the relationship between IHR and IHL outlined above. Usage (a) is consistent with the integrationist approach, if we regard IHL as a particular application of the general law of human rights; usage (a) is also compatible with the interpretive complementarity approach. Usage (b) could be used to describe the interpretive complementarity approach, but might also encompass the incompatibility approach. Usage (c) is consistent with the incompatibility approach. Thus, the ICJ's invocation of *lex specialis* does not, of itself, clarify the relationship between IHL and IHR in any concrete sense, and does not provide a basis to choose between the three approaches discussed above. Rather, it is suggested that the notion of *lex specialis* has been used to provide a doctrinal gloss—and so preserve an appearance of logical necessity—for what are essentially a series of policy choices inherent in negotiating the interrelationship between IHL and IHR in contexts of practical application.

It is far from obvious that the 'interpretive complementarity' approach is that which *necessarily* follows from an evaluation and comparison of the structural features and value systems of IHR and IHL. As Abi-Saab notes, IHL emerges as an instance of the 'law of coexistence' that characterized the classical era of international law.[77] The law of coexistence aimed to manage the disintegration of a legal community (the *republica Christiana*) into a pluralistic world of sovereign states, in which the mechanisms of order were limited to forms of self-regulation: the subjects of the legal system themselves would make the legal system work, by means of their actions and reactions. The rules of sovereignty and reciprocity characteristic of this era rationalized the state's position as last instance decision-maker.[78] Although IHL's emphasis on reciprocity has been attenuated in the post-1945 period,[79] it nevertheless retains a structural debt to the 'law of coexistence'. IHL regulates wartime relations between belligerent states, and between states and certain classes of persons (civilians and combatants).[80] The relationship embedded in IHL is resolutely one of hostility, and has three structural principles: the legitimation of force to achieve victory at minimum cost, the delegitimization of those kinds of violence deemed unnecessary for the purpose of war, and a vestigial chivalry that demands a measure of fairness.[81] The interaction of these principles produces the result that IHL protects certain interests which are common to IHR, but this does not mean that it confers rights directly on individuals. Rather, IHL creates legally binding standards of conduct that are observed by states, subject to a limited discretion to depart from these standards where

[77] Abi-Saab, above n 60, 250.

[78] Ibid. 252–4.

[79] See the discussion in Georges Abi-Saab, 'The Specificities of Humanitarian Law' in Swinarski, above n 47, 265–80.

[80] Rene Provost, *International Human Rights and Humanitarian Law* (Cambridge: Cambridge University Press, 2002) 7.

[81] See Draper, 'Human Rights and the Law of Armed Conflict: General Principles of Implementation' [1974] in Meyer and McCoubrey, above n 5, 141–4.

'military necessity' requires. IHL applies *conditionally* upon existence of certain conditions and membership of certain categories. IHL is a patchwork of variable protections granted to the individual in specific circumstances, provided they meet the criteria linked to conduct, nationality, and/or group membership.[82]

By contrast, IHR constitutes a bundle of legal entitlements attaching to the individual *qua* human being in most places and situations. IHR regulates relations between states and individuals within their jurisdiction[83] and principally under conditions of normal political associational life. IHR endeavours to foster a certain kind of orderly relationship between the state and an individual, oriented towards the protection, personal development and flourishing of individuals and their capabilities.[84]

At this level of generality, it becomes clearer that the argument for the relation of 'complementarity' between IHL and IHR derives not from an intrinsic complementarity in the normative logic of the two bodies of rules, but from a policy choice that seeks to narrow the gap and articulate a desirable *via media* between the two. The point of the above analysis is *not* to contend that this *via media* is undesirable or impossible. Rather, it is to underscore that such an approach should be recognized as a policy choice, and thus undertaken in a manner which consciously considers the relevant policy issues, the potentially conflicting imperatives of the two bodies of rules, and the problems which arise at the level of application. In section four, below, I examine the tensions that arise between the two frameworks in relation to the use of lethal force against suspected terrorists, and the problems raised by the application of either framework in its pure form. I argue that the *lex specialis* approach does not resolve these problems, but reproduces them, and thus a consciously constructivist or functionalist approach is preferable.

4. The Applicable Legal Regime for Targeted Killing: IHL, IHR or Both?

A. 'Global Civil War' and the Problems of Categorical Incoherence

The kinds of legal indeterminacy provoked by the terrorist attacks of September 11 are numerous and, by now, relatively well known.[85] They will not be rehearsed here, but I will focus on the controversies that bear on the subject of this analysis. The notion of a conflict between a state and a transnational terrorist network has severely problematized the basic distinction between 'peace' and 'war'. This, in

---

[82] Provost, above n 80, 41.

[83] The concept of jurisdiction is not synonymous with territory: see Schilling, above n 50.

[84] See, eg International Covenant on Economic, Social and Cultural Rights, Arts 6, 11, 13, 15; Convention on the Rights of the Child, Arts 6, 11.

[85] See generally references in n 13, above.

turn, confounds the criteria used to determine which legal framework appropriately regulates the use of lethal force against an individual, leading Neuman to observe that no received category of IHL fits the nature of the hostilities between the US and 'al-Qaeda'.[86] The scale of the destruction wrought by the September 11 attacks qualified them as 'armed attacks' for the purposes of the modern *jus ad bellum* of Article 51 of the United Nations Charter, triggering the US's inherent right of self-defence.[87] The US and its allies used military force against Afghanistan in order to uproot terrorist networks and paramilitary forces that exercised territorial control and maintained military training camps with the acquiescence of the de facto government of Afghanistan. Aside perhaps from some controversy as to whether the September 11 terrorist attacks constituted an 'armed attack',[88] and whether these attacks could be imputed to the de facto government of Afghanistan and so justify an invasion of that country, this component of the response to September 11 does not give rise to especially perplexing legal controversies: once the decision to attack Afghanistan was made, there existed an international armed conflict of the kind envisioned by IHL: a conflict between two or more states parties to the Geneva Conventions, in which combat took place on battlefields within the territory of one state party and between groups of organized military forces—regular armies on one hand, and paramilitary forces and militias under some kind of responsible command on the other.[89]

But the US response to the September 11 attacks went further. The US Congress authorized the President to use 'all necessary and appropriate force against those nations, *organizations or persons* he determines planned, authorized, committed or aided' (emphasis added)[90] the attacks, and the President characterized the attacks as an act of war.[91] The use of the language of 'war'[92] and the adoption of

---

[86] Neuman, 'Counter-terrorism Operations and the Rule of Law', above n 6, 1019.

[87] Michael Schmitt, 'Counter-terrorism and the Use of Force in International Law' in Borch and Wilson, above n 13, 26; Yoram Dinstein, *War, Aggression and Self-Defence* (Cambridge: Grotius Publications, 1988) 181–2 (noting the 'scale and effects' definition of an 'armed attack') and 222 (arguing that armed attacks by non-State actors are still armed attacks, even if only commenced from—and not with the assistance of—another State). In the *Wall* case, the ICJ held that the right to use military force in self-defence arises only where the armed attack is imputable to another state: above n 19, para 139. This conclusion was stated without elaboration, although it seems far from self-evident.

[88] See Giorgio Gaja, 'In What Sense Was There an "Armed Attack"?' EJIL Forum, October 2001; Alain Pellet, 'No, This is Not War' EJIL Forum, October 2001.

[89] Few fighters in the Taliban's militia forces or camp-based fighters claiming allegiance to al-Qaeda were likely to be entitled to the status of privileged combatants in accordance with Article 4A of the Third Geneva Convention, but their characterization as unprivileged combatants was not, of itself, controversial. The question of the legal entitlements of unprivileged combatants has become controversial as a result of the US government's decision to intern unprivileged combatants apprehended in Afghanistan indefinitely, and subject them to forms of coercive interrogation—thereby purporting to place these individuals outside *both* IHL and IHR.

[90] Authorization for Use of Military Force, PL No 107–40, 115 Stat. 224 (2001).

[91] Address of President George W Bush before a Joint Session of the Congress, 37 *Weekly Compilation of Presidential Documents* 1347 (20 September 2001).

[92] See Frederic Megret, 'War? Legal Semantics and the Move to Violence' 13 EJIL 361 (2002).

a military mode of response to the threat posed by al-Qaeda implied the existence of an armed conflict between the US and a transnational terrorist group, in which the US had a 'right of ongoing offensive action against an adversary's paramilitary operations and network'.[93] The idea of an armed conflict between a state and a disparate, de-territorialized armed group destabilizes IHL's basic categorical distinction between an international armed conflict and a non-international armed conflict. The International Criminal Tribunal for the Former Yugoslavia (ICTY) Appeals Chamber's definition of an armed conflict as the threshold for the applicability of IHL reflects the international/non-international binomial: 'an armed conflict exists when there is resort to armed force between states or protracted armed violence between governmental authorities and organized armed groups or between such groups within a state'.[94] This definition provides only for the possibility of the use of force *between* states, or protracted armed violence between a state and a non-state armed group (or between such groups) *within* a state. The existence of a third possibility, a perpetual state of armed conflict between a state and a non-state actor outside the territory of any one state or across multiple state territories, is ruled out by some commentators as outside the purview of the current IHL framework.[95] On this 'narrow' view, IHL becomes applicable to anti-terrorist actions in only two circumstances: (a) Where a state uses force against the territory of another state which shelters or acquiesces in armed attacks launched by terrorist groups on the first state. The use of force, which roughly conforms to Dinstein's 'Extra-territorial Law Enforcement' model and the US invasion of Afghanistan, gives rise to an international armed conflict in which terrorist groups meeting the definition of 'combatant' under IHL[96] may be lawful objects of attack, or; (b) Where the state in whose territory the terrorist group operates consents to or cooperates with the attacked state's conduct of operations against the terrorist group. If the terrorist group can be characterized as an organized armed group, and there results a 'protracted armed conflict' between the group and the host state, then the law of non-international armed conflict has application. However, if there is no protracted armed conflict between the terrorist group and the host state, IHL has no application. Thus, the kind of conflict presupposed by the IHL of non-international armed conflict is a territorially

---

[93] Ruth Wedgewood, 'Responding to Terrorism: The Strikes Against Bin Laden' 24 Yale Journal of International Law 559 (1999) 575.

[94] *Prosecutor v Tadic*, No IT-94-1-AR72 (Decision on the Defence Motion for Interlocutory Appeal on Jurisdiction) (2 October 1995) 35 ILM 32 (1996) para 70.

[95] Georges Abi-Saab, 'There is No Need to Reinvent the Law', Crimes of War Project, September 2001; Dieter Fleck (ed), *The Handbook of Humanitarian Law in Armed Conflicts* (Oxford: Oxford University Press, 1999) 42. If the ICJ's reading of Art 51 of the UN Charter is followed, a terrorist attack which is not imputable to a state does not give rise to a right to use military force against another state.

[96] The problems of applying this definition to certain kinds of terrorist activity are discussed below. See text accompanying n 106.

delimited 'civil war' or insurgency between a state and non-state armed group,[97] not a transnational conflict between a state and a delocalized terrorist network. The mere presence of a member of the transnational terrorist network in the territory of another state would not, on this reading of IHL, be sufficient to justify the application of IHL to all interactions between the attacked state and the terrorist. Instead, the 'peacetime' rules of criminal law enforcement, and associated IHR protections,[98] would apply.

Critics of the narrow view highlight this conclusion as an example of how a strict reading of IHL's threshold of application leads to a *reductio ad absurdum*, which does not adequately grapple with the nature of contemporary terrorist threats.[99] They contend that al-Qaeda[100] operates with the primary purpose of conducting military-scale attacks on the interests and citizens of the US and its close allies, and that the number of attacks by al-Qaeda over the last decade would meet the threshold for an 'armed conflict' if such attacks had been committed by a state or an armed group within a state.

The argument for the appropriateness of applying an IHL framework concentrates on the nature of the *relations of hostility* between al-Qaeda and victim states, and derives a functional analogy between these relations and the kind presupposed by IHL. As such, the argument is reasonably persuasive and—notwithstanding a serious concern about the potential for overreaching inherent in the analogy—it seems appropriate to recognize that there are aspects of the conflict between al-Qaeda and the US which resemble an armed conflict. The conflict plays out across international boundaries, while sharing many operational features with internal warfare such as counter-insurgency actions. Tønneson's characterization of the hostilities as a 'global civil war' is apt to capture the paradoxical qualities of a 'war on terrorism'.[101] But the problem of how to determine the beginning and end of the applicability of IHL remains, because the present

---

[97] For this reason, the non-state armed groups that are the protagonists in national liberation struggles or anti-government insurgencies—and which are habitually branded 'terrorists' by their opponents—do not give rise to the same degree of legal ambiguity as the notion of an armed conflict between a state and a transnational terrorist network. National liberation movements have been assimilated into 'international armed conflict' model by Additional Protocol I (AP I) to the Geneva Conventions or, in the case of non-parties to AP I, to the non-international armed conflict model. Hence, the conflict between the State of Israel and armed groups based in the Occupied Palestinian territories can be categorized as a non-international armed conflict: see Orna Ben-Naftali and Keren R Michaeli, 'We Must Not Make a Scarecrow of Law: A Legal Analysis of the Israeli Policy of Targeted Killings' 36 Cornell International Law Journal 233 (2003) 257.

[98] Discussed below. See text accompanying n 130.

[99] See, eg Michael Schmitt, 'Counter-terrorism and the Use of Force in International Law' in Borch and Wilson, above n 13.

[100] It is noted in passing that, in the context of debates about *jus ad bellum* and *jus in bello*, the stylization of al-Qaeda tends to over-emphasize its parallels with a paramilitary group under centralized command. In fact, its evolution as an international network is highly decentralized, as the emergence and operations of 'al-Qaeda in Mesopotamia' suggest. Thus, to allege that an individual is a 'member of al-Qaeda' tells us little about his role in potential terrorist attacks or his relation with al-Qaeda progenitors such as Osama Bin Laden or al-Zawahiri.

[101] Tonneson, above n 13.

criteria for demarcating the end of an armed conflict and a return to the 'normal' condition of peace—an armistice agreement or a peaceful settlement—have little relevance.[102] Hence, the difficulty inherent in linking the application of IHL to the nature of the threat, or to the quality of the hostility of relations, is that the *temporal* and *spatial* markers for limiting the 'exceptional' situation are lost and states' discretion to choose an expedient legal framework is expanded.[103] The danger is not simply that states will choose an IHL framework over an IHR framework, as under certain conditions such a choice might be justifiable. Rather, it is that the 'cautiously stylized norms', which try to constrain states' entitlement to pursue the kinds of lethal force permitted under the 'abnormal' circumstances of 'war', lose their determinacy and so facilitate a much greater degree of violence than intended.[104] The alternative of reading existing norms strictly so as to minimize the range of permissible violence risks being utopian, thereby reducing incentives for compliance with a system of legal rules that still relies primarily on states' self-regulation. Koskenniemi's dilemmatic of Apology and Utopia reasserts itself with a vengeance, as we face a choice between formal categorical coherence and the reality-shaping power of state conduct.

In the next section, I compare the regulation of 'targeted killing' in IHL and IHR, and highlight the different logics inherent in each. I argue that a comparison of these two frameworks throws into relief the tensions between the values that they protect, and problematizes the *ideé fixé* that IHL can be applied in a manner that is 'complementary' to IHR. I also argue that neither framework can be regarded as unproblematically appropriate to regulate the targeted killing of suspected terrorists and that the laws themselves provide no clear answers to the question of applicability.

---

[102] In *Tadic*, the Appeals Chamber of the ICTY held that 'International humanitarian law applies from the initiation of such armed conflicts and extends beyond the cessation of hostilities until a general conclusion of peace is reached; or, in the case of internal conflicts, a peace settlement is achieved. Until that moment, international humanitarian law continues to apply in the whole territory of the warring States or, in the case of internal conflicts, the whole territory under the control of a party, whether or not actual combat takes place there.' *Tadic*, above n 94, para 70.

[103] It is for this reason that Kretzmer's assertion that the nature of the conflict between the US and al-Qaeda *is sufficient* to apply IHL norms fails to fully grasp the nature of the problem: see David Kretzmer, 'Targeted Killing of Suspected Terrorists: Extra-Judicial Executions or Legitimate Means of Defence?' 16 EJIL, at 195.

[104] This concern was implicit in the ICRC's caution that: 'It is doubtful…whether the totality of violence taking place between states and transnational terrorist networks can be deemed to be armed conflict in the legal sense. Armed conflict of any type requires a certain intensity of violence and the existence of opposing parties. The existence of opposing parties means armed forces or armed groups with a certain level of organization and command structure. *The very logic underlying IHL requires identifiable parties in the above sense because this body of law establishes equality of rights and obligations among them under IHL…when they are at war…There can be no wars in which one side has all the rights and the other side has none.* Applying the logic of armed conflict to the totality of the violence taking place between states and transnational networks would mean that such networks or groups must be granted equality of rights and obligations with the states fighting them, a proposition that states do not seem ready to consider' (my emphasis). ICRC, International Humanitarian Law and the Challenges of Contemporary Armed Conflicts (September 2003) 18–19.

B. Targeted Killing in IHL and IHR—Military Model vs Law Enforcement

Targeted killing takes on a different legal complexion depending on which legal lens it is viewed through.[105] Broadly, the critical difference between the legality of targeted killing under the IHL and IHR frameworks is that, in the former, the entitlement to use lethal force against an individual revolves around the question of whether the person falls into a certain category of persons, namely 'combatants'. In the latter framework, the essential question is the imminence and the scale of the threat to others' lives posed by the actual or likely conduct of the targeted person. Connected with this basic difference are competing kinds of values which are taken into account in the calculus of a decision to use lethal force: the IHL framework balances an *entitlement* to kill combatants with considerations of avoiding excessive incidental non-combatant casualties, but also permits consideration of the overall objective of military victory—the incapacitation or subjugation of the enemy[106]—when determining whether an attack is legal.[107] By contrast, the IHR framework establishes a non-derogable right to life which applies without discrimination between classes of persons, and violation of which requires a very high threshold of justification. As will be seen below, even though the language of 'necessity' and 'proportionality' is common to both the IHL and IHR frameworks, the meaning of these terms is quite distinct in each.

The Military Model

The fundamental tenet of the laws of international armed conflict is the principle of distinction, under which all persons within the field of application of the laws fall into one of two classes: combatant or civilian. A combatant is either privileged or unprivileged; privileged combatants, who meet the criteria in Article 4A of the Third Geneva Convention and or Articles 43 and 44 of Additional Protocol I, are entitled to participate directly in armed combat, and have a unique status when captured.[108] They may not be prosecuted for participating in hostilities (provided they have not violated laws of armed conflict), giving them, in effect, a right to use lethal force in accordance with the laws of war. A person who is not a combatant is a civilian and no intermediate category exists.[109] Civilians

---

[105] Kretzmer, above n 103 at 171.

[106] 'Military necessity permits a belligerent, subject to the laws of war, to apply any amount and kind of force to compel the complete submission of the enemy with the least possible expenditure of time, life and money.' *The Hostages Case (United States v List and others)*, cited in UK Ministry of Defence, *The Manual of the Law of Armed Conflict* (Oxford: Oxford University Press, 2004) para 2.2.

[107] See, eg grave breaches provisions of Geneva Conventions: GC I, Art 50, GC II, Art 51, GC III, Art 130, GC IV, Art 147; AP I, Arts 52(2), 57(2)(a)(iii). Note that the provisions concerning proportionality are not contained in A P II, governing internal armed conflicts.

[108] GC III, Art 4A; AP I, Arts 43–4.

[109] In the case of the laws of non-international armed conflict, no definition of 'combatant' exists and hence, no category of privileged combatancy. There is only one category of persons with

are protected from being objects of attack and their proximity to a valid military objective may render an attack on that target illegal if civilian casualties would be excessive in relation to the military advantage gained.[110] Civilians lose their immunity from attack 'unless and for such time as they take a direct part in hostilities',[111] whereupon they become 'unprivileged' combatants. Like other combatants, unprivileged combatants may be lawfully attacked at any time and killed without warning or attempts at capture,[112] but if captured they may also be prosecuted for participating in combat.

Suspected or actual members of a transnational terrorist network such as al-Qaeda are very unlikely to satisfy the criteria for privileged combatant status under the Geneva Conventions or the First Additional Protocol. Members of such a terrorist network are not part of the armed forces of a state,[113] and do not operate under responsible command,[114] wear a distinctive insignia visible at a distance,[115] carry arms openly,[116] or conduct their operations in accordance with the laws and customs of war[117] (not least because they directly target civilians). They are also very unlikely to 'distinguish themselves' from the civilian population while they are engaged in an attack or in preparation for an attack, or even carry arms openly during a military engagement.[118] It follows that, if the laws of armed conflict are applied, a transnational terrorist is not a combatant but must be a civilian. The question then becomes, is he a civilian who has lost his immunity from direct attack by virtue of his direct participation in hostilities ('unprivileged' combatant)? It is at this point that it becomes apparent that the application of an IHL framework to using lethal force against suspected terrorists results simultaneously in a problem of under-inclusion and over-inclusion.

The problem of under-inclusion arises from the orthodox interpretation of 'direct participation in hostilities'. This interpretation holds that the phrase

special protections, namely civilians. Civilians who participate directly in hostilities lose their protection from being objects of attack, but do not gain any privileges.

[110] Kevin Watkin, 'Warriors Without Rights? Combatants, Unprivileged Belligerents, and the Struggle Over Legitimacy' 8 (Occasional Paper, Harvard Program on Humanitarian Policy and Conflict Research) (Winter 2005), available at <http://www.hpcr.org/pdfs/OccasionalPaper2.pdf>.

[111] AP I, Art 51(3); AP II, Art 13(3). The notion that civilians lose their immunity from attack if they directly participate in hostilities appears to have general acceptance as a principle of customary law: Jean Francois Quéguiner, 'Direct Participation in Hostilities Under International Law', Program on Humanitarian Policy and Conflict Research, November 2003; *The Manual of the Law of Armed Conflict*, para 4.2.

[112] Hays Park, above n 25, 5; ICRC, *Direct Participation in Hostilities under International Humanitarian Law*, Summary Report, September 2003, p 6.

[113] GC III, Art 4A(1).

[114] GC III, Art 4A(2)(a); AP I, Art 43(1). Art 43(1) of AP I specifies that the meaning of 'under responsible command' includes subjection of members to an 'internal disciplinary system which, *inter alia*, shall enforce compliance with the rules of international law applicable in armed conflict'.

[115] GC III, Art 4A(2)(b).   [116] GC III, Art 4A(2)(c).

[117] GC III, Art 4A(2)(d).   [118] AP I, Art 44 (3).

encompasses a 'direct causal relationship between the activity engaged in and the harm done to the enemy at the time and the place when the activity takes place'.[119] The behaviour of the civilian must constitute an immediate military threat and his or her actions must constitute an 'uninterrupted, indispensable' part of the hostile activity.[120] These actions may include operations preparatory to an attack (such as travel to and from the location of an attack) or logistical activities necessary for an attack. The consequence of direct participation in hostilities is that a civilian loses his immunity from attack *during the time of such participation*. He or she recovers immunity once participation ceases, and cannot be the object of attack. On this interpretation, a suspected terrorist may reap the benefit of the so-called 'revolving door' between civilian and unprivileged combatant status, in which he or she benefits from immunity as soon as she or he resumes civilian activities, even though there is a likelihood that she or he may again participate in the preparation or conduct of an attack. Participants in an expert meeting convened by the ICRC in 2004 discussed the difficulties in applying this definition in light of the composite nature of entities that engage in terrorist attacks, which combine political and military roles (often clandestinely) with civilian activities:

> It was reiterated that when a civilian who had previously engaged in DPH [direct participation in hostilities] was subsequently spotted in peaceful activity, for example in a supermarket, the civilian could not automatically be targeted but had to benefit from doubt as to his or her continued direct participation in hostilities. In response, another expert recalled that the civilian in question may return from the supermarket to plan further activities amounting to DPH, with the effect that this person should be regarded as engaged in DPH even when spotted in the supermarket.[121]

Putting aside the informational problems inherent in deciding that an individual was likely to continue to participate in hostilities, the example highlights the dilemma in including or excluding a person from civilian status based on the DPH criteria. Drawing the line too narrowly may mischaracterize the nature of the threat posed by a member of a terrorist network; but drawing the line expansively allows the individual to be killed even if there is an opportunity to capture him or her during 'civilian' activities. One version of an expansive reading of 'direct participation in hostilities' is to conclude that confirmed membership of a terrorist network implies direct participation in hostilities. This interpretation essentially analogizes a terrorist network with an organized armed group, such

---

[119] ICRC, Commentary to AP I, para 1679. In the Commentary to AP II, the words 'sufficient causal relationship' are used. In his background paper for the ICRC Expert meeting on 'Direct Participation in Hostilities', Bothe concludes that the meaning of 'direct participation in hostilities' is essentially the same in international and non-international armed conflicts: ICRC, *Second Expert Meeting: Direct Participation in Hostilities under International Law*, 25–6 October 2004, Summary Report, p 15.

[120] Commentary to AP I, para 1679.

[121] ICRC, *Second Expert Meeting: Direct Participation in Hostilities under International Law*, above n 119, 19.

that membership is sufficient to make someone a combatant, irrespective of what is the conduct he or she actually engages in. The category of combatant is predicated on an operational logic comparable to regular armies, and thus, once we conclude that a terrorist is a combatant, the logic of the military model is to stylize him or her as a lethal threat at all times. Such a conclusion may be justified in the case of the 'armed wing' of groups such as Hamas or Islamic Jihad, but in general terrorist and other non-state actors (such as guerillas) have decentralized structures that have mixed military and political functions, and which include sympathizers, supporters, and political cadres. The group membership notion makes all of these persons susceptible to being objects of attack, irrespective of whether they bear arms, participate in hostilities, or provide 'infrastructural' support for the group.

The strict binomial logic of civilian or combatant does not adequately capture the character of the terrorist or the terrorist network. The ambiguity which arises when the IHL framework has the consequence of either narrowing or (as seems more likely in response to a serious threat) significantly expanding the scope for lethal force. This dynamic is replicated when we consider the other principles of the IHL framework. As noted above, the entitlement to kill a combatant is subject to the rules of proportionality and military necessity. The general principle of proportionality (specified in greater detail in Additional Protocol I) is that the losses (including incidental civilian casualties) from a military action should not be excessive in relation to the expected military advantage.[122] Military necessity permits the use of any amount and kind of force (within the laws of war) required to compel the submission of the enemy. But if the enemy is a diffused, delocalized network of individuals, what concrete content does either of these principles have? What does it mean to 'win' an 'armed conflict' with such an enemy? As military strategist Stephen Biddle comments:[123]

Terrorism, after all, is a tactic, not an enemy. Taken literally, a 'war on terrorism' is closer to a 'war on strategic bombing' or a 'war on amphibious assault' than it is to orthodox war aims or wartime grand strategies; one normally makes war on an enemy, not a method...

...Terrorism per se thus cannot be the enemy. But it is far from clear exactly who the enemy is. The administration has made some effort to delimit the problem by adding the phrase 'of global reach.' This is little help, however. In a globalized world, any terrorist with an airline ticket or an internet service provider has 'global reach'.

If an individual is determined to be a (political or military?) leader of a terrorist network, is the concrete military advantage obtained by killing him the disabling of the terrorist network? This seems implausible, as most terrorist networks operate on an autonomous cell structure precisely in order to survive the incapacitation of leadership figures. But even if such a result were possible, does

---

[122] *The Manual of the Law of Armed Conflict*, above n 106, para 2.6.
[123] Stephen Biddle, *American Grand Strategy After 9/11: An Assessment* (US Army War College, April 2005) 6.

this mean that the 'concrete military advantage' obtained by killing the individual is high and therefore justifies a higher degree of civilian casualties? There appears to be nothing intrinsic to the principle of proportionality in a military model which rules out this kind of conclusion. Similarly, how is the notion of the 'submission of the enemy' evaluated if the 'enemy' is a tactic? The limiting and restraining effect of these concepts in IHL is predicated on the existence of a certain set of *concrete situations*, to which IHL norms have been painstakingly adapted and formulated. If essential features of the situation change or are absent, the concreteness of the norms and their determinacy of application are eroded, and the strategic logic of military force may well promote an expansion of the kinds of violence sought to be legitimated under existing rules. An interesting example is provided by Michael Schmitt's early article on assassination.[124] He notes that a targeted killing conducted under the justification of anticipatory self-defence must be shown to be a response to an 'imminent' attack. But terrorists are hard to locate and identify, and locating a terrorist gives states a limited window of opportunity to act, irrespective of whether an actual attack is imminent. What is imminent is that an important strategic target may slip from view:

Unless international law requires the potential victim to simply suffer the attack, the proper standard for evaluating an anticipatory operation must be whether or not it occurred during the *last possible window of opportunity*. Hence, the appropriate question relates more to the correct timing of the preemptive strike then to the imminence of the attack that animates it…

…In this scenario, the timing of the preemptive action relative to the expected attack is irrelevant, since the various terrorist acts may be regarded as a *continuous operation*. This characterization is analogous to the battle/war distinction. Once the war has commenced, the initiation of each battle is not evaluated separately… The same reasoning applies to terrorism.[125]

While Michael Schmitt's reasoning may not be entirely persuasive, it is far from improbable within a military frame of reference. The military logic of a 'global civil war' threatens to make the notion of a 'battlefield' largely indeterminate. It also potentially expands the forms of violence legitimated under the colour of the 'laws of war'. As such, we may wish to question the desirability of applying the IHL framework in light of the implications of the military model. We might also question whether it is meaningful to assert that IHL can be applied in a manner which is 'complementary' to human rights law.

The Law Enforcement Model

The law enforcement model emerges from the IHR framework. Its starting point is a non-derogable right to life of all persons within the territory or subject to

---

[124] Schmitt, above n 20, 647–8.
[125] Ibid. 648–9.

the jurisdiction[126] of a state. Violations of the right to life can be excused only in exceptional circumstances and with a high burden of justification. There is a strong presumption in favour of the capture and trial of a person or persons who pose a threat of deadly violence. The use of lethal force by law enforcement officials is limited to situations of 'absolute' or 'strict' necessity in order to protect against an imminent threat of serious injury or death to themselves or others, and to use only such force as is proportionate to the risk of harm.[127]

In the law enforcement model, there are no combatants or civilians. There are only rights-bearers with a right not to be arbitrarily deprived of life, a right to be presumed innocent until proven guilty, and a right to be tried fairly if suspected of a criminal offence. The entitlement to kill an individual is never categorical, and is always a matter of degree in which the balance is between the extent and imminence of the threat and the availability of non-lethal options which preserve the rights of the individual while containing the threat.[128] The individual who poses a threat is not an enemy to be defeated but a criminal to be punished by society.

It has been commonly observed that the law enforcement model is inadequate to the nature of hostilities which characterize an armed conflict. The IACom HR notes that the human rights norms provided for in its constitutive documents are insufficiently specific to regulate the uses of force in an armed conflict,[129] while Watkin suggests that the attempt to apply human rights standards to a situation of armed conflict may have the perverse consequence of diluting the content of these norms and thus diminishing the level of protection that they afford in peacetime.[130] These concerns are persuasive if the situation under consideration is a conventional armed conflict between organized armed forces, as IHL is indeed formulated with regard to such circumstances. But the more unconventional and asymmetrical the conflict becomes, the less specificity is provided by IHL, and

---

[126] As Schilling has shown, the argument for the extraterritorial application of human rights treaties is strong where a state exercises territorial control outside its territory, such as in cases of military occupation. Territory under effective control comes under the 'jurisdiction' of a state party to a human rights treaty. See Schilling, above n 50. This approach has been endorsed by the ECt HR in *Loizidou v Turkey (Preliminary Objections)*, 23 March 1995, Series A no 310, para 62 and *Ilascu and Others v Moldova and Russia*, no 48787/99, 8 July 2004, paras 3–5. The extraterritorial application of the ICCPR has been endorsed by the ICJ in the *Wall* advisory opinion, above n 19, paras 108–11. For an argument against the extraterritorial application of the ICCPR (having regard to the *travaux* and pointing out that states have hitherto not invoked the derogation provisions when engaged in a military occupation, implying that they do not consider the ICCPR to apply to occupied territory) see Dennis, above n 45.

[127] See, eg IACom HR, above n 51, para 87; United Nations Basic Principles on the Use of Force and Firearms by Law Enforcement Officials, 7 September 1990, Arts 9–10; European Convention on Human Rights, Art 2.2. See also the discussion in Kretzmer, above n103, 176–85; Watkin, above n 53, 18.

[128] See, eg the discussion by the ECtHR in *McCann and Others v United Kingdom*, ECtHR, App No 18984/91 (27 September 1995).

[129] IACom HR, above n 51, para 61.

[130] Watkin, 'Controlling the Use of Force: A Role for Human Rights Norms in Contemporary Armed Conflict', above n 53, 22.

the more the line between 'law enforcement' and 'war' is blurred. A similar blur-ring of roles arises in the context of a military occupation, where effective control is a legal precondition for the existence of a state of occupation, and the occupying power plays a role which combines police activity, law enforcement and military operations within the occupied territory.[131] As argued above, the notion of a 'war against terrorism' is perhaps at the extreme end of the spectrum of asymmetrical conflicts—more so, even, then poorly-regulated internal armed conflicts. Hence, the assertion that, compared to IHL, the IHR framework is inherently unsuited to the nature of the threat posed by transnational terrorism is an overstatement.

At the same time, the application of IHR norms does appear to presume a high degree of 'normality' inasmuch as it is predicated on the reasonableness of identifying and monitoring the movements of a suspect, a real prospect for the collection of evidence and the apprehension of the accused, and the availabil-ity of judicial institutions to which the suspect may be subjected. The concepts of 'absolute necessity' and 'reasonable alternative' to the use of lethal force, and assessments about the imminence of risk, are central to the calculus of the law enforcement model, but their determinate meaning in circumstances where the suspected terrorist is outside the territorial control of the threatened state is quite unclear. As Kretzmer asks:[132]

What if the state has strong evidence that the suspected terrorist is continuing to plan terrorist attacks against people in its territory? That if it does not either apprehend or target him, there is a very strong probability that he will carry out or organize further attacks?...Could this not be regarded as a situation in which it was absolutely necessary to use lethal force? To put it another way: if the requirement of imminent danger rests on the availability of non-lethal, due process law-enforcement measures when the danger is not imminent, does the imminency requirement lose part of its force when such measures are unavailable?

As with the case of IHL norms when applied to transnational terrorists, it seems to me that the norms regulating the use of lethal force in the IHR framework lose their capacity to give a satisfactory answer to the question of under what circumstances a transnational terrorist may be lawfully killed. On the one hand, the norms, if strictly applied, will be under-inclusive in so far as there is a mis-match between the 'normal' meanings of 'imminence' and 'necessity', and the kind of risk posed by an active transnational terrorist network. On the other hand, expanding these concepts only seems to heighten the ambiguity and trans-mute them into highly discretionary notions that are not amenable to transparent and consistent application (unless subjected to some form of scrutiny and review).

---

[131] See Marco Sassoli, 'Legislation And Maintenance Of Public Order And Civil Life By Occupying Powers', 16 EJIL 694, at 698 (2005). For this reason, the LTLSP's assimilation of bel-ligerent occupation to armed conflicts generally is inappropriate, if considered in terms of which rules should govern targeted killing.
[132] Kretzmer, above n 103, 180.

Just as the IHL framework is based on a certain model of war, the IHR framework presupposes a particular kind of 'normal' situation in which law enforcement takes place.

5. Conclusion: Revisiting *Lex Specialis* through a Functionalist Approach

The foregoing analysis has compared the IHL and IHR regimes in terms of their rules for the use of lethal force against suspected transnational terrorists. Two key points emerge from this comparison. First, it has been suggested that neither framework can adequately grapple with the challenges posed by the figure of the transnational terrorist, and each suffers from problems of under-inclusion and over-inclusion in terms of delimiting the circumstances in which deadly force can be used. Secondly, that the IHL and IHR frameworks encode quite distinct normative logics and value hierarchies in respect of the decision to kill an individual, such that the proposition that 'international humanitarian law constitutes an integral, but separate, part of the right to life framework'[133] seems unsustainable. The IHL framework is not a particularization or elaboration of the content of the right to life for suspected terrorists but in fact imports a wholly different calculus. The notion of 'proportionality' in IHL lies between the goals of concrete military advantage and minimizing incidental loss of life, while in the law enforcement framework it connotes the relation between the harm sought to be prevented and the harm inflicted. Similarly, the 'necessity' of IHL is concerned with the speedy subjugation of the enemy, while the 'absolute necessity' of IHR concerns the strong preference against lethal force in favour of capture and trial.

Neuman observes that the military model entailed by the IHL framework is dominated by a strategic logic concerned to preserve flexibility and surprise, and so may prioritize secrecy and unpredictability as rational tactics.[134] In military operations, information is not evidence but intelligence and it is evaluated for operational purposes, not by an adjudicator.[135] The military model does not take as a core value the promotion of the rule of law, transparency, predictability or equal treatment. These are values with which the law enforcement model is concerned. The logic of the military model is to regard terrorists as combatants, whose death or incapacitation is a concrete military objective of hastening victory.

The argument that the 'interpretive complementarity' approach to the interaction of IHL and IHR is unhelpful in the case of targeted killings, is not an argument against attempts at synthesis between the two frameworks. It is an

---

[133] Watkin, above n 53.
[134] Neuman, 'Counter-terrorist Force and the Rule of Law', above n 6, 1020.
[135] Colin Warbrick, 'The European Response to Terrorism in an Age of Human Rights' 15 EJIL 989 (2004), 991.

argument which insists that no intrinsic legal-conceptual logic will resolve the need for policy and political choices about the kind of 'war' that the 'war on terror' will become. The problem of targeted killing of suspected terrorists is something of a 'vanishing point' for the interaction of the two regimes, and highlighting the indeterminacies of IHL and IHR law is an attempt to prompt a consciously constructivist approach which seeks to balance conflicting values.

I would suggest that the strategic logic of the military model is corrosive and, if unchecked, may continuously erode the place given to the values which are encoded in the law enforcement model.[136] The logic of 'the exception' tends to expand and intrude upon the 'normal', and for this reason a synthetic framework for 'targeted killing' ought to prioritize the values of transparency, due process and significant limitations on a categorical right to kill, which are at the heart of the IHR framework. There is evidence that some scholars have already begun to take such an approach, arguing that the appropriate legal framework governing the combating of transnational terrorism is one which takes human rights norms and adjusts them to give adequate weight to the nature of the conflict,[137] or in which the concepts of 'necessity' and 'proportionality' found in each model are synthesized to reach a workable compromise of differing values.[138] For example, Kretzmer[139] suggests a balancing of three factors: (1) the danger to life posed by the continued activities of the terrorists; (2) the chance of the danger to human life being realized if the activities of the suspected terrorist are not halted immediately; and (3) the danger that civilians will be killed or wounded in the attack on the suspected terrorist. In my view, this proportionality test is weighted heavily towards the 'military model' conception of proportionality, and against the law enforcement model. Another difficulty is that we have no basis to scrutinize the information upon which a threat assessment is made, why a particular individual is considered so dangerous that he must be killed, or what the realistic prospects of capture (including through the cooperation of third states) may be. Kretzmer is very much aware of the problems of applying the framework IHL, but seems

---

[136] An example of this corrosive tendency is given by Gross, in his description of the evolution of the targeted killing policy in Israel: 'Lacking the symmetry and international structure of a struggle between sovereign states, Israel initially viewed its adversaries as criminals. In this context, law enforcement officials recruited informers and collaborators to apprehend suspected terrorists. When the conflict turned violent, however, these same informers and collaborators facilitated assassinations. But assassinations were directed not toward attaining a singular strategic goal by removing a pivotal military figure, but toward mixed objectives that included retribution and harassment along with the legitimate aims of interdiction. Far from isolated cases of non-treacherous, strategic assassination, targeted killings became widespread, nurtured extensive networks of collaborators and imposed hardship on the civilian population.' Gross, above n 20, 361. The situations in the Occupied Palestinian Territories, and in Iraq, suggest that in the context of an occupation that is meeting a violent resistance which employs terrorist methods, targeted killing easily becomes a technique not of pre-emptive self-defence, but counter-insurgency and counter-terror, aimed at decapitating an insurgency's leadership.

[137] See Warbrick, above n 135, 991.

[138] See Kretzmer, above n103, 201–204.

[139] Ibid. 203.

less alive to the dangers of allowing the domination of the strategic logic inherent in the military model.

The promise of a functionalist approach is that it tries to grapple directly with the ways in which transnational terrorism blur the line between war and peace and between the exception and the normal. The risk, however, is that by creating an intermediate set of norms, one establishes an 'exception to the exception' which contains few rules for its own self-limitation, and which relies heavily on the self-judgment of states for the characterization of a given threat—functionalism tends to follow the logic of *ex factis jus oritur* to a degree which may be dangerous if the current notion of a spatially and temporally unlimited 'war on terror' is maintained. The only antidote may be a continuous vigilance and demand for accountability in the interpretation and application of these 'exceptional' rules, in a way that constantly scrutinizes their appropriateness and tests them against an accurate understanding of the nature of the threat.

8

The Schizophrenias of R2P

*José E Alvarez**

This chapter focuses on the current state of debates over humanitarian intervention, by examining a concept that is all the rage in UN circles, namely the 'responsibility to protect' (or 'R2P' for those in the know). In my brief analysis I want to warn against turning R2P from political rhetoric to legal norm. An alternative, more positive title for my analysis would be 'two cheers for humanitarian intervention'.

The responsibility to protect this concept was borne out of frustration with the international community's repeated failures to intervene in cases of on-going mass atrocity, in particular in Rwanda and Kosovo. The concept sought to deflect attention from the controverted 'right' of some states to intervene, to the duties of all states to protect their own citizens from avoidable catastrophes, and for third parties to come to the rescue. The idea was born and given its most detailed treatment in the 2001 Report of the International Commission on Intervention and State Sovereignty, sponsored by the Canadian government.[1] As that Commission conceived it, the virtue of R2P was that it would entice states to engage in humanitarian relief by shifting the emphasis from the politically unattractive right of state interveners, to the less threatening idea of 'responsibility'. R2P put the focus on the peoples at grave risk of harm rather than on the rights of states. It also stressed that responsibility was shared—as between the primary duty of states to protect their own populations and the secondary duty of the wider community.

R2P avoided the delimited connotations of 'intervention' to emphasize duties to prevent, to react, and to rebuild. As the Commission defined the term, R2P applied when there was 'serious and irreparable harm occurring to human beings, or imminently likely to occur' involving the large-scale loss of life, actual or apprehended, with genocidal intent or not, produced by either deliberate state action

---

* This paper originated as a panel presentation at the 2007 Hague Joint Conference on Contemporary Issues of International Law: Criminal Jurisdiction 100 Years After the 1907 Hague Peace Conference, The Hague, the Netherlands, 30 June 2007. The permission of the American Society of International Law to reprint the paper is gratefully acknowledged.
[1] Report of the International Commission on Intervention and State Sovereignty, *The Responsibility to Protect* (December 2001).

or state neglect, inability to act, or in a failed state situation.[2] R2P triggered the residual responsibility of the broader community (1) when a particular state was either unwilling or unable to fulfill its primary R2P; (2) when a particular state was itself the perpetrator of the crimes or atrocities; or (3) when 'people living outside a particular state are directly threatened by actions taking place there'.[3] On the crucial question of who is authorized to take military action in response, the Commission indicated that the Security Council was the first port of call but it did not categorically exclude the possibility that R2P could ultimately be exercised by the General Assembly, regional organizations, or even coalitions of the willing. But the Commission stipulated that legitimate interventions would require 'just cause', right intention, last resort, proportionality of means, and reasonable prospects of success.

The Commission's concept soon became part of ambitious proposals for UN reform in the December 2004 Report by the High-level Panel on Threats, Challenges and Change.[4] It was then embraced by the UN Secretary General's March 2005 Report 'In Larger Freedom'.[5] It was subsequently adopted by the General Assembly in Resolution 60/1, the 2005 World Summit Outcome and has since been cited by the Security Council in Resolution 1674 (of April 2006) where the Council 'reaffirmed' states' 'responsibility to protect populations from genocide, war crimes, ethnic cleansing, and crimes against humanity'.[6] Each of these iterations of R2P put a somewhat different spin on it. The High-level Panel Report did not envisage anyone other than the Security Council exercising the collective's right, but the Outcome document, reflecting the sensitivities of the US in particular, suggests that there is no systematic mandatory duty on the Council to act in all cases and leaves it open for states to intervene in humanitarian catastrophes where they have a legitimate basis to act in self-defence.[7] For its part, the Secretary General's Report removed the concept from the section on use of force and put it in a wider context: the freedom to live in dignity.[8]

The Canadian diplomats and intellectuals and others behind this concept, such as former Australian Foreign Minister Gareth Evans, can be very proud. Few 'norm entrepreneurs' have been able to see one of their ideas, created out of whole cloth, be 'reaffirmed'—as if it was a long-standing principle—by no less a body than the Security Council within a span of five years. R2P was widely

---

[2] Ibid., at XII.

[3] Ibid., at 2.31.

[4] Report of the High-level Panel on Threats, Challenges and Change, A More Secure World: Our Shared Responsibility, 2 December 2004, paras 201–203 (making reference to an 'emerging norm of collective international responsibility to protect').

[5] Kofi Annan, *In Larger Freedom, Towards Development, Security and Human Rights for All,* 21 March 2005, para 135.

[6] GA Res. 60/1 (2005 World Summit Outcome), 24 October 2005, paras 138–9. For an account of this history, see Carsten Stahn, 'Responsibility to Protect: Political Rhetoric or Emerging Legal Norm?', 101 AJIL 99 (2007).

[7] See Stahn, ibid. at 106–10.

[8] Ibid. at 107.

considered the only 'unequivocal success' of the World Summit of September 2005, where it was endorsed by both John Bolton, then US Ambassador to the UN, and the Non-Aligned Movement.⁹

Instinct should warn us there must be something wrong as well as right with an idea that can be endorsed by such strange bedfellows, and there is. R2P's normative 'legs' result from its not always consistent, various iterations as well as from the lack of clarity as to whether it is a legal or merely political concept. It means too many things to too many different people.¹⁰

If we examine how R2P has now been cited and by whom, it is clear that many invocations, whether in good faith or not, are at a considerable distance from what I suspect was the original Canadian core concept: creating an exemption (as in some countries' tort law) from liability for the good Samaritan who acts to save lives. We now find that R2P has been cited:

(1) By scholars and others as entailing a duty to protect national artifacts, a duty that the US allegedly violated by failing to protect the Iraqi National Museum after its Operation Iraqi Freedom;¹¹

(2) By policymakers (such as UK Foreign Secretary Jack Straw or President Bush) and scholars (such as Fernando Tesón) to justify the 2003 invasion of Iraq—either as part of a duty to protect people from tyrannical rule or to punish a regime for prior mass atrocities;¹²

(3) By policymakers (such as US Attorney General Alberto Gonzalez) and scholars who suggest that states have a duty to protect their peoples from terrorist acts and that this includes a duty to implement the dozen or so counter-terrorism, multilateral treaties that now exist as well as the Security Council's various counter-terrorist injunctions under Chapter VII;¹³

(4) By policymakers (such as the authors of the US' National Security Strategy) and scholars (such as Anne-Marie Slaughter and Lee Feinstein) who contend

⁹ See Thomas G Weiss, 'R2P After 9/11 and the World Summit', 24 Wisc. Int'l L. J. 741, at 745 (2006).

¹⁰ Differences exist even among those who understand R2P as responding only to human rights crises. See, eg, Vaclav Havel, Kjell Magne Bondevik, and Elie Wiesel, 'Turn North Korea Into a Human Rights Issue', *New York Times*, 30 October 2006, at A25 (arguing that R2P applies to North Korea given that regime's widespread human rights abuses).

¹¹ See generally, Wayne Sandholtz, 'The Iraqi National Museum and International Law: A duty to Protect', 44 Colum. J. Transnational L. 185 (2005). Although this article relies exclusively on international humanitarian law, its rhetoric is strikingly similar to that used by advocates of the responsibility to protect.

¹² See, eg Jack Straw, 'We are in Iraq to Bring about Democracy', Speech by Foreign Secretary Jack Straw, Labour Party Conference, Brighton, 28 September 2005, available at <http://globalpolicy.org/empire/humanint/2005/0928strawspeech.htm>; President's Remarks to the National Endowment for Democracy, 41 Weekly Comp. Pres. Doc. 1502 (6 October 2005); Fernando R Teson, 'Ending Tyranny in Iraq', 19 Ethics & Int'l Aff. 1 (2005).

¹³ See, eg Presentation by Kimberley N Trapp, 'Can There be International Responsibility For Failing to Prevent Terrorism?', at Canadian Council on International Law Annual Meeting, October 2006.

that there is a duty to prevent states and non-state actors, including through the use of force, from acquiring weapons of mass destruction (WMDs);[14]

(5) By other 'liberal' scholars (such as Allan Buchanan and Robert Keohane) who argue for the 'cosmopolitan' use of military force to promote democracies and the rule of law.[15]

(6) By Canadian liberals who assert that Canada failed in its duty to protect its citizens from the excesses of the US's war on terror when it did not protect Canadian nationals who were allegedly transferred by the US government into the hands of those who would torture them.[16]

Many defenders of R2P are horrified by these suggestions. They contend that all of these are erroneous or opportunistic applications of R2P by its 'false friends.' In a recent article, Gareth Evans argues, for example, that R2P properly understood could never justify Operation *Iraqi Freedom* because its use is restricted to on-going threats to human life, not a regime's past atrocities or its current disrespect for democracy. As he and Ken Roth of Human Rights Watch (properly) point out, 'better late than never' has never been a justification for humanitarian intervention and it should not be for R2P.[17]

But I want to suggest that these expansive citations of R2P are built into its very soul. We should not blame a few bad apples for R2P's current all-purpose misuse—any more than the US can continue to suggest that a few 'bad apples' were responsible for the human rights horrors committed by US agents in its war on terror. I will focus on just four core concepts of R2P, most of which were built into the original Commission conception of the term, to suggest some of the risks R2P poses if treated seriously as a legal concept.

1. The Redefinition of Sovereignty

The essence of R2P is that sovereignty implies responsibility. As Gareth Evans himself has suggested, the point of R2P was to change how we talk about sovereignty. The driving force was to reorient the interpretation of the UN Charter's concept of sacrosanct domestic jurisdiction and territorial integrity to reflect 'contemporary' values of human rights and human security. While the creators of R2P may not like what Slaughter does with this idea, when she argues, as she has in the

[14] National Security Council, The National Security Strategy of the United States of America (September 2002), available at http://www.whitehouse.gov/nsc/nss.pdf; Lee Feinstein and Anne-Marie Slaughter, 'A Duty to Prevent', Foreign Affairs, January 2004.

[15] Allen Buchanan and Robert O Keohane, 'The Preventive Use of Force: a Cosmopolitan Institutional Proposal', Ethics & Int'l Aff. April 2004, at 1.

[16] See generally, Craig Forcese, 'The Capacity to Protect: Diplomatic Protection of Dual Nationals in the "War on Terror",' 17 EJIL 369 (2006).

[17] Gareth Evans, 'From Humanitarian Intervention to the Responsibility to Protect', 24 Wis. Int'l L. J. 703, at 717 (citing Roth) (2006).

pages of the American Journal of International Law in 2005, that UN members now retain only 'conditional sovereignty'—and that they retain their ordinary rights under the Charter only so long as they fulfill their minimum human rights obligations and their international legal obligations toward fellow states—she is being faithful to their core concept.[18] When Richard Haas, then director of policy planning at the US State Department, reduces R2P to the bumper sticker 'abuse it and lose it'[19]—R2P supporters may object to his lack of nuance, but they can hardly claim his bumper sticker violates the core idea that, as Slaughter puts it, statehood has only an 'instrumental' rather than an 'intrinsic' value.[20]

R2P reflects a pre-9/11 (but post-Cold War) view of sovereignty. It treats sovereignty as more hindrance than protection; the UN Charter (and the Security Council) less as sovereignty's guarantor than the guarantor of the rights of individuals. Now, I do not deny that under the UN Charter or the Friendly Relations Declaration a state's rights may be infringed if it violates the self-defence rights of others, fails to respect the self-determination of its (or other) peoples, or engages in certain crimes (from genocide to apartheid), but at a time when the largest military and economic power seems all too ready to deploy the 'preventive' use of force anywhere and everywhere, when the Security Council itself seems all too ready to impose legal obligations on all sovereigns with respect to counter terrorism and WMDs, and when the US at least appears to see the greatest threat to its own nationals and to others as stemming from the acts of non-state terrorists, old-fashioned notions of un-impeachable sovereignty and non-intervention against overweening power retain their traditional appeal. Holding the line on expanding the categories of actions (or inactions) upon which sovereignty is ostensibly 'conditioned' and being particularly clear on when the interference with sovereignty includes resorting to the unilateral use of force, appears, to me at least, to be a singularly important project.

None of this means that it is not worth re-examining more specific questions such as, for example, what states owe one another under the Genocide Convention, particularly in light of the International Court of Justice's (ICJ's) recent clarification of that treaty. One look at Darfur and the world's inaction tells us as much. Perhaps it is time, in light of the ICJ's Bosnia decision, for a protocol to the Genocide Convention indicating much more clearly what its signatories have a right to do in the face of on-going genocide in another signatory state. But that question is far more targeted in nature than a principle like R2P, which by its nature is grounded in a more 'flexible' or permeable view of the legal rights of sovereigns (including their rights to territorial integrity). Now is not the

---

[18] Anne-Marie Slaughter, 'Security, Solidarity, and Sovereignty: The Grand Themes of UN Reform', 99 AJIL 619, at 628 (2005).

[19] Quoted in Weiss, above n 9, at 744, fn 19.

[20] Slaughter, above n 18. See also David Frum and Richard Perle, *An End to Evil: How to Win the War on Terror*, at 102 (2003)('National sovereignty is an obligation as well as an entitlement. A government that will not perform the role of government forfeits the rights of a government').

time for such a fundamental reinterpretation of the UN Charter or other fundamental norms of international law.

2. The Expansion of What it Means to 'Protect'

Notice, too, how readily the core concept of R2P leads down the slippery slope to the Bush Administration's controversial notions of the pre-emptive use of force. The Canadian Commission's original use of R2P emphasized the need to act to prevent imminent threats to the lives of others. It stressed the need for, first, the state where atrocities are likely, and thereafter third parties to act in response not only to on-going harms but to 'direct threats'. It envisioned action, including the use of force where necessary, when the target state was unwilling, unable, or incapable of action, including where states have 'failed'. Unlike later iterations of R2P, which attempted to confine its militaristic deployment to the Security Council, the Commission left open the possibility that others could resort to R2P should the Council fail to act. This was consistent, after all, with the fundamental reorientation of the international system suggested by the very concept of R2P, since it elevated the lives of people over those of abstractions, namely governments or states. While the Canadian Commission imposed conditions on the use of force that is justified under R2P, only some of these inherently vague conditions (such as 'proportionality' and perhaps 'last resort' if seen as a version of necessity) are terms of art under international law. I find it difficult to believe that the same international community that has so far failed to agree on a comprehensive definition of what 'terrorism' is will be any more able to define such elastic (and politically loaded) terms as 'just cause', 'right intention' or 'reasonable prospects of success'. That such conditions are not necessarily at odds with the US' National Security Strategy and its invocation of a doctrine of pre-emptive force suggests why the Canadian government's reliance on such conditions does not provide me with much reassurance.

More disturbing still is the fact that the Canadian Commission's allusion to 'just cause' harkens back to the pre-Charter 'just war' doctrine—just as the US doctrine of pre-emptive force does.[21] At the heart of both R2P and the ostensible doctrine of pre-emptive force is the bizarre (but, history tells us, sadly irresistible) idea that waging war, including 'preventive' war, is sometimes necessary to protect the 'dignity, justice, worth and safety' of individuals.[22] R2P is based on the proposition that while going to war is a mistake, it may be, as Gareth Evans himself argues, an 'even bigger mistake' not to go to war 'to protect fellow human beings from catastrophe when we should'.[23]

---

[21] See, eg Evans, above n 17, at 710.
[22] Report of the High-level Panel, above n 4, at 22, para 30.
[23] Evans, above n 17, at 722.

3. The Expansion of Security

Nor should it surprise anyone that R2P should now be used to justify counter-terrorist action. Although the Security Council has suggested that R2P was limited to action directed against the commission of recognized international crimes, R2P was originally conceived to enable reactions against 'serious and irreparable harm ... involving the large-scale loss of life', however this occurs, including as a result of a state's failure to act. The Canadian Commission wrote of the need to engage R2P when 'people living outside a particular state are directly threatened by actions taking place there'. Those who focused on the need to avert large scale loss of life can hardly complain if the hegemon argues that such threats emerge as much from terrorists' actions, including in Afghanistan or Iraq. A concept born from the need to protect people at grave risk seems readily adaptable to the considerable (and just as real) risks posed by terrorists armed with WMDs.

Witness the surface plausibility of the words of Anne-Marie Slaughter:

... the drafters of the Charter would have identified only scourges such as poverty and disease as threats to the extent that they directly threatened territorial integrity or political independence of individual states in a system of states. Today we understand that to the extent that poverty and disease contribute to state collapse, that collapse can threaten not only that state's neighbors but also states halfway across the world by providing a haven for terrorists and other criminals. So to that extent we can directly link state security and human security.[24] But for those of us who have long been critical of the concept of a 'failed' or 'collapsed' state and the uses to which that determination (and indeed the very definition of 'sovereignty') has been put over the course of history,[25] linking a state's right to enjoy its existing security to a highly malleable determination of whether that state respects 'human security' is not a positive or necessarily 'progressive' development of the law.

4. The Invocation of Legal Responsibility

R2P poses less serious but other troubling problems if taken seriously as legal principle. For international lawyers who worship at the shrine of the Articles of State Responsibility, all international legal persons are legally liable when they either take wrongful action or fail to act when action is demanded by international

---

[24] Richard Haas has also been quoted as follows: 'Sovereignty entails obligations. One is not to massacre your own people. Another is not to support terrorism in any way. If a government fails to meet these obligations, then it forfeits some of the normal advantages of sovereignty, including the right to be left alone inside your own territory. Other governments, including the United States, gain the right to intervene.' Quoted in Nicolas Lehmann, 'The Next World Order', *The New Yorker*, 1 April 2002, at 45.

[25] See generally, Antony Anghie, 'Finding the Peripheries: Sovereignty and Colonialism in Nineteenth-Century International Law', 40 Harv. Int'l L.J. 1 (1999).

law. If there is such a thing as a responsibility to protect, the legal mind naturally assumes that a failure to exercise such responsibility is an internationally wrongful act entailing the usual panoply of potential remedies, including the legal liability of the wrongful actor and the potential for countermeasures against that actor by others. Not surprisingly, R2P has now helped to inspire the experts on the International Law Commission (ILC) engaged in drafting provisions that would impose legal responsibility on those international organizations—such as the UN—or even regional organizations who fail to act in the face of international atrocity. The ILC's current draft articles of responsibility of international organizations (along with its proposed commentaries by its special rapporteur) suggest, for example, that the UN should have been legally liable for failing to act in the face of the Rwandan genocide.[26] However laudable this effort, such a duty is absurdly premature and not likely to be affirmed by state practice.

There are innumerable, obvious difficulties when we try to affirm R2P as a legal proposition in this fashion. We are not sure what is meant by finding the 'UN' legally responsible in such a case: do we mean the organization as a whole, such that all dues paying members owe Rwanda compensation for the organization's failure to protect? Or do we mean only members of the Security Council? Or only the P-5 whose votes were absolutely essential to the outcome? Or those states able but unwilling to contribute armed members to protect Rwandans? Or the Secretary General who failed to act quickly? Further, should we care whether those who created institutions such as the UN intended to impose such liability on their organization? Does the proposition that the UN committed a wrongful abdication of its responsibility to protect mean that others (including members) are entitled to impose countermeasures on it by, for example, failing to pay their UN dues? Does it matter if the UN's internal rules—such as the requirement that Council action draw the votes of nine members including the affirmative votes of the P-5—anticipate selective interventions by the Council? Or is it viable to suggest, as the ILC's current draft articles of International Organizations (IO) responsibility provide, that an organization's internal rules (like those of a state) provide no excuse from the duty to protect? But surely there is a distinction here between the internal rules of a state and the internal rules of the UN. The latter, such as its voting rules, are, unlike the laws of states, both 'internal' and rules of international law.[27]

Further, if we treat R2P seriously as imposing 'legal responsibility' on the UN, how does that idea comport with the legal responsibility of states? International lawyers would appear to be caught in a dilemma. On the one hand, we are

---

[26] See, eg Third Report on Responsibility of International Organizations, A/CN.4/553, para 10 (13 May 2005).

[27] For a more extensive critique of the ILC's effort to develop rules of IO responsibility, see José E Alvarez, 'International Organizations: Accountability or Responsibility?', keynote address before the Canadian Council of International Law, available at <http://www.asil.org/aboutasil/president.html>.

reluctant to say that states should be absolved from their responsibilities merely when they act in unison. States should not be enabled to abuse the law by acting collectively, like so many teenagers on a rampage. On the other hand, failing to uphold the accountability of states' international organizations fails to respect the distinct legal personhood of those organizations—much less the reality that in cases such as the genocide in Rwanda, the organization—and distinct actors within it such as the Secretary General—were capable of and failed to take certain autonomous action within their institutional competence. We are, I would submit, far from resolving such difficult doctrinal matters as a matter of real world practice, and the concept of R2P cannot plausibly short-circuit the difficult political negotiations that would be necessary to overcome such difficulties.

5. Two Cheers for Humanitarian Intervention

All of this leads me to suggest that for all its uncertainties, the concept of humanitarian intervention retains admirable qualities. My own preference would be for international lawyers to continue to work on elaborating the contours of that principle, which at least has been venerated by usage, rather than turning to the far more slippery (and dangerous) concept of R2P. Unlike R2P, the emphasis on 'humanitarian' suggests that anything justified by this doctrine requires attention to on-going 'humanitarian' needs. This would include on-going grave international crimes and perhaps crises stemming from natural disasters, but 'humanitarian' concerns probably do not embrace past crimes, undemocratic regimes, or threatened terrorist acts. In addition, the reference to 'intervention' emphasizes its opposite: the ordinary rule of non-intervention.

Humanitarian intervention, as advocates of R2P have rightly pointed out, does little to threaten the traditional rights of sovereigns. It does not suggest that by merely ratifying the UN Charter states sign away their sovereignty—subject to the vote of nine members of the Council or, worse still, whenever a ragtag 'coalition of the willing' decides to act preventively because they believe another has violated the Charter (or the R2P). Humanitarian intervention, however ambiguous its scope, was never conceived as anything but an add-on to the existing rules of international law, including the rules of self-defence. Unlike R2P, humanitarian intervention did not aspire to fundamentally reorient a state-centric system of rules away from its state-centricity.

Finally, humanitarian intervention, when legitimately invoked as a legal excuse by an intervening state, prevents a charge of unlawful action against the intervener. When invoked by lawyers, it seeks to protect the intervener from liability. It works like national rules precluding liability for good Samaritans. Unlike R2P it does not try to go farther: to require good Samaritans to act lest they be held legally 'responsible'. To the extent R2P tries to achieve that, this is likely to prove to be a step too far internationally (if not nationally).

Those of us who grew up in Samantha Power's twentieth century,[28] where states repeatedly failed to act in the face of genocide, hated all of these limits on humanitarian intervention. But in the midst of the twenty-first century's 'war on terror', many of us are coming to appreciate them.

The Canadian Commission that first elaborated R2P completed its work on 10 September 2001. Their members woke up to a changed world within the next 24 hours. The rest of us are learning that their idea, however politically attractive and motivated by the best of intentions, may have become a victim and not merely a product of its time.

[28] Samantha Power, *A Problem From Hell* (2002).

Index